Interlinkages and the effectiveness of multilateral environmental agreements

Interlinkages and the effectiveness of multilateral environmental agreements

W. Bradnee Chambers

**United Nations
University Press**

TOKYO · NEW YORK · PARIS

United Nations University Press
United Nations University, 53-70, Jingumae 5-chome,
Shibuya-ku, Tokyo 150-8925, Japan
Tel: +81-3-3499-2811   Fax: +81-3-3406-7345
E-mail: sales@hq.unu.edu   general enquiries: press@hq.unu.edu
http://www.unu.edu

United Nations University Office at the United Nations, New York
2 United Nations Plaza, Room DC2-2062, New York, NY 10017, USA
Tel: +1-212-963-6387   Fax: +1-212-371-9454
E-mail: unuona@ony.unu.edu

United Nations University Press is the publishing division of the United Nations University.

Cover design by Sese-Paul Design

Printed in Hong Kong

ISBN 978-92-808-1149-0

Library of Congress Cataloging-in-Publication Data

Chambers, W. Bradnee.
Interlinkages and the effectiveness of multilateral environmental agreements /
W. Bradnee Chambers.
    p.   cm.
  Includes bibliographical references and index.
  ISBN 978-9280811490 (pbk.)
  1. Environmental law, International. 2. Environmental pollution—Prevention.
3. Agricultural biotechnology—Law and legislation. 4. Genetic resources
conservation. I. Title.
K3585.C43   2008
344.04′6—dc22   2007036998

Contents

Figures

Major treaties

Vienna Convention on the Law of Treaties, opened for signature 23 May 1969, 1155 UNTS, 331 (entered into force 27 January 1980).

Ramsar Convention on Wetlands of International Importance Especially as Waterfowl Habitat, 2 Feb. 1971, TIAS 11084, 996 UNTS, 245. (chapter 5).

Washington Convention on International Trade in Endangered Species of Wild Fauna and Flora, 3 March 1973, 27 UST 1087, 993 UNTS, 243. (chapter 5).

Vienna Convention on the Law of Treaties between States and International Organizations or between International Organizations, done and opened for signature at Vienna on 21 March 1986. Not yet in force. UN Doc. A/CONF.129/15, *reprinted in* 25 ILM, 543.

Convention on Biological Diversity, negotiated under the auspices of UNEP, was opened for signature on 5 June 1992 and entered into force on 29 December 1993, 31 ILM, 818 (1992).

United Nations Framework Convention on Climate Change, 9 May 1992, 31 ILM, 849 (1992).

Agreement on Trade-Related Aspects of Intellectual Property Rights, Marrakech Agreement Establishing the World Trade Organization, Annex 1C, Legal Instruments–Results of the Uruguay Round, 31, ILM, 81 (1994).

International Treaty on Plant Genetic Resources for Food and Agriculture, negotiated under the Food and Agriculture Organization's Commission for Genetic Resources for Food and Agriculture [hereinafter CPGRFA] was adopted on 30 November 2001, entered into force on 29 June 2004.

Rotterdam Convention on the Prior Informed Consent Procedure for Certain Hazardous Chemicals and Pesticides in International Trade, opened for signature on 11 September 1998, UNEP/CHEMICALS/98/17.

Cartagena Protocol on Biosafety to the Convention on Biological Diversity, 2000, 39 ILM, 1027 (2000).

Agreement on the Conservation of African–Eurasian Waterbirds (AEWA), signed 16 June 1995 in The Hague, http://www.unep-aewa.org/about/introduction.htm.

Cases

International Court of Justice

Legality of the Use by a State of Nuclear Weapons in Armed Conflict, ICJ Reports (1996).

Libyan Arab Jamahiriya v. United Kingdom concerning Questions of Interpretation and Application of the 1971 Montreal Convention Arising from the Aerial Incident at Lockerbie (Request for the Indication of Provisional Measures), ICJ Reports (1992).

Libyan Arab Jamahiriya v. United States of America, ICJ Reports (1992).

Aegean Sea Continental Shelf Case, ICJ Reports (1978).

Case Concerning the Gabčíkovo-Nagymaros Project (Hungary/Slovakia), ICJ Reports (1997).

European Court of Human Rights

Neumann Case, ECHR 1974 A No. 17 (1974).

GATT reports

Dolphin-Tuna, GATT Panel, BISD 29S/9 (1992).

WTO panels and appellate body reports

United States – Gasoline, Appellate Body Report, WT/DS2/AB/R (1996).

Brazil Measures Affecting Desiccated Coconut, Report of Panel, WT/DS22/AB/R (1997).

WTO Bananas Case (European Communities – Regime for the Importation, Sale and Distribution of Bananas), WT/DS27 (1997).

US – Shrimp, Appellate Body Report, WT/DS58/AB/R (1998).

EC Measures Concerning Meat and Meat Products (Hormones), WT/DS26/AB/R, para. 123 (16 Jan. 1998).

Australia – Measures Affecting the Importation of Salmon, Report of the Panel, WT/DS18; modified by Report of the Appellate Body, AB-1998-5, 20 (1998).

Japan – Measures Affecting Agricultural Products, Report of the Panel, WT/DS76 (1999).

Chile – Measures Affecting Transit and Importation of Swordfish, WT/DS193 (suspended 23 Mar. 2001).

US – Section 110(5) Copyright Act Panel Report on US – Section 110(5) Copyright Act, WT/DS160 (2000).

US – Hot Rolled Steel, Appellate Body Report, WT/DS184/AB/R (01-3642) (2001).

Foreword

It has been over ten years since a group of young scholars from the United Nations University Institute of Advanced Studies (UNU-IAS) came back from assisting the Secretariat of the Framework Convention Climate Change Conference of the Parties in Kyoto, Japan, where the now famous Kyoto Protocol was negotiated and signed. After recovering from the all-night negotiating sessions that were necessary to finalize the Kyoto deal, they convened a debriefing at the UNU-IAS to discuss what they had observed during the two-week process. What immediately became apparent from the discussion was that the Kyoto Protocol was not simply an environmental agreement on reducing GHG emissions, but rather a complex and intertwined agreement that held implications for many other multilateral environmental agreements on issues such as biodiversity, chemicals, land degradation and wetlands. It also has deep implications for international agreements outside the environment such as with international trade, development, human health and many other sectors.

These observations led the scholars to form a small group at the UNU-IAS in order to develop a research study to better understand the implications of international agreements like the Kyoto Protocol with other agreements. This was the beginnings of the UNU Initiative on Interlinkages that began in 1998 and which has continued until today to contribute thinking on how to strengthen international law and science through more coherent approaches internationally. Having published many reports and held numerous international meetings, workshops and symposia on the topic, this book by W. Bradnee Chambers is the latest contribution to the Interlinkages Initiative from the UNU-IAS.

Dr Chamber's book is an important contribution for the work on forging a stronger, more coherent and effective international system for environmental institutions and agreements. As the UN Reform Process moves forward and the UN member states deliberate on fulfilling the recommendations made by the Millennium Assembly and the "Delivering as One" report, they will need to be well-informed and aware of the tangible benefits that more coherence can bring. *Interlinkages and the Effectiveness of MEAs* makes this case clear and provides the substantive foundations of why a more coherent international environmental governance system will lead to stronger and more effective MEAs.

A. H. Zakri
Director, UNU-IAS

Acknowledgements

I would like to thank Professor Alan Boyle for his advice and keen eye for seeing the most critical issues for the future of public international law. He is truly a gifted teacher and an outstanding academic. His work continues to guide a whole generation of lawyers, policy-makers and young academics pursuing the better understanding of international environmental law all around the world. I would also like to thank the UNU-IAS staff and Professor A. H. Zakri for their support to sustainable development law and governance issues and the emerging concept of interlinkages. I would like to thank my mother Joan Chambers for her encouragement and confidence in me and I would particularly like to thank Jenny who gave me a chance for the education that she always dreamed of and deserved to pursue.

Abbreviations

ABS	Access and Benefit-Sharing
ACC	Administrative Committee on Coordination
AEWA	Agreement on the Conservation of African–Eurasian Waterbirds
AJIL	American Journal of International Law
APEC	Asia Pacific Economic Cooperation
ASEAN	Association of Southeast Asian Nations
BG	Bonn Guidelines
BISD	Basic Instruments and Selected Documents
Brit. Y.B. Int'l L.	British Year Book of International Law
Brooklyn J. Int'l L.	Brooklyn Journal of International Law
Case W. Res. J. Int'l L.	Case Western Reserve Journal of International Law
CBD	Convention on Biological Diversity
CEB	Chief Executive Board
CFR	Code of Federal Regulations
CGRFA	Commission on Genetic Resources for Food and Agriculture
CISG	Convention on the International Sales of Goods
CITES	Convention on International Trade in Endangered Species of Wild Fauna and Flora
CMS	Convention on Migratory Species
CODEX	Codex Alimentarius (The Food Code)
Col. J. Int'l Envtl. L.	Colorado Journal of International Environmental Law
Colum. J. Envtl. L.	Columbia Journal of Environmental Law

COP/MOP	Conference/Meeting of the Parties
CSD	Commission on Sustainable Development
CTE	Committee on Trade and Environment
DDA	Doha Development Agenda
ECOSOC	United Nations Economic and Social Commission
EMG	Environmental Management Group
Eur. J. Int'l L.	European Journal of International Law
FAO	Food and Agriculture Organization
GA	General Assembly
GATT	General Agreement of Tariffs and Trade
GC	United Nations Environment Programme Governing Council
GEF	Global Environment Facility
Geo. Int'l Envtl. L. Rev.	Georgetown International Environmental Law Review
Geo. L. J.	Georgetown Law Journal
Geo. Wash. Int'l L. Rev.	George Washington International Law Review
Glob. Envtl. Pol.	Global Environmental Politics
GMEF	Global Ministerial Environment Forum
Harv. Int'l L. J.	Harvard International Law Journal
HLCM	High Level Committee on Management
HLCP	High Level Committee on Programmes
IAEA	International Atomic Energy Agency
ICJ Rep.	International Court of Justice Reports
IEG	International Environmental Governance
ILC	International Law Commission
ILM	International Legal Materials
ILO	International Labour Organization
IMF	International Monetary Fund
Int'l L. & Comp. L.Q.	International Law and Comparative Law Quarterly
Int'l Law Comm'n Report	International Common Law Report
Int'l Org.	International Organizations
Int'l Pol. Sci. Rev.	International Political Science Review
IPCC	Intergovernmental Panel on Climate Change
IPIC	Treaty on Intellectual Property in Respect of Integrated Circuits
IPR	Intellectual Property Rights
ISO	International Standards Organization
ITLOS	International Tribunal for the Law of the Sea
ITPGRFA	International Treaty on Plant Genetic Resources for Food and Agriculture
J. Dev. Econ.	Journal of Development Economics
J. Int'l Econ. L.	Journal of International Economic Law
JLG	Joint Liaison Group
JPOI	Johannesburg Plan of Implementation
Law Libr. J.	Law Library Journal

MA	Millennium Ecosystem Assessment
Marq. Intell. Prop. L. Rev	Marquette Intellectual Property Law Review
MEA	Multilateral Environmental Agreement
Mercosur	Southern Common Market
MFN	Most Favoured Nations Status
Mich. J. Int'l L.	Michigan Journal of International Law
Minn. J. Global Trade	Minnesota Journal of Global Trade
MOU	Memorandum of Understanding
MS	Multilateral System
NAFTA	North American Free Trade Agreement
NILR	Netherlands International Law Review
NT	National Treatment
NW. J. Int'l L. & Bus.	Northwestern Journal of International Law and Business
N.Y.U. J. Int'l L. & Pol.	New York University Journal of International Law and Politics
ODA	Official Development Assistance
Ramsar	Ramsar Convention on Wetlands
RECIEL	Review of European Community and International Environmental Law
SADC	Southern African Development Community
SBI	Subsidiary Body on Implementation
SBSTA	Subsidiary Body of Scientific and Technological Advice
SBSTTA	Subsidiary Body of Scientific, Technical and Technological Advice
SMG	Senior Management Group
SPS	Sanitary and Phytosanitary Agreement
Syracuse J. Int'l L. & Com.	Syracuse Journal of International Law and Commerce
TBT	Technical Barriers to Trade Agreement
Tex. L. Rev.	Texas Law Review
TNC	Trade Negotiating Committee
TRIPS	Trade-Related Intellectual Property Rights Agreement
Tul. J. Int'l & Comp. L.	Tulane Journal of International and Comparative Law
UNCCD	United Nations Convention to Combat Desertification
UNCED	United Nations Conference on Environment and Development
UNCHE	United Nations Conference on the Human Environment
UNEP	United Nations Environment Programme
UNESCO	United Nations Educational, Scientific and Cultural Organization

UNFCCC	United Nations Framework Convention on Climate Change
UNFCCD	United Nations Framework Convention to Combat Desertification
UNGA	United Nations General Assembly
UNHCR	United Nations High Commission for Refugees
UK	United Kingdom
UNCLOS	United Nations Convention on the Law of the Sea
UNU	United Nations University
UNU-IAS	United Nations University Institute of Advanced Studies
US	United States of America
UNSC	United Nations Security Council
UNSG	United Nations Secretary-General
UNTS	United Nations Treaty Series
U. Pa. J. Int'l Econ. L.	University of Pennsylvania Journal of International Economic Law
U. Rich. L. Rev.	University of Richmond Law Review
Va J. Int'l L.	Virginia Journal of International Law
Vand. J. Transnat'l L.	Vanderbilt Journal of Transnational Law
VCLT	Vienna Convention on the Law of Treaties
VCLTIO	Vienna Convention on the Law of Treaties between States and International Organizations or between International Organizations
WCO	World Customs Organization
WHC	World Heritage Convention
WHO	World Health Organization
WIPO	World Intellectual Property Organization
WMO	World Meteorological Organization
WSSD	World Summit on Sustainable Development
WTO	World Trade Organization
Yale J. Int'l L.	Yale Journal of International Law
Y.B. Int'l E. L.	Year Book International Environmental Law
Y.B. Int'l L. Comm'n	Year Book of International Common Law

Part I

Introduction and overview

1

Introduction and overview

A major challenge to policy-makers is to develop a more integrated approach, identifying the natural synergies between different aspects of our environment and exploring the potential for more effective policy coordination.
                    Kofi Annan, United Nations Secretary-General, 1992–2006[1]

The 1997 UN reforms breathed new life into an issue that academics and experts have been debating since Stockholm – this was the idea of how best to create a coherent and well-coordinated international governance structure for the protection of the environment. At the 1972 Stockholm Conference it was a critical issue that eventually led to the creation of the United Nations Environment Programme (UNEP), not as a fully fledged organization but as a programme that would act as a catalyst to bring all the other organizations to work together on environmental issues. At the Rio Earth Summit, once again the creation of this governance structure became an important issue and the result was the Commission on Sustainable Development (CSD), yet another creation seeking to bridge existing work but this time on the new concept of sustainable development.

By 1997, the failure of Rio+5[2] showed the ugly side of the lack of cooperation on issues of environment and sustainable development. As the

---

1. Speech by the Secretary-General on the occasion of the 1999 UNU Conference on Synergies and Coordination among Multilateral Environmental Agreements, on file with the author.
2. Rio+5 refers to the Fifth Anniversary of the United Nations Conference on Environment and Development held in Rio de Janeiro, Brazil, 1992.

Interlinkages and the effectiveness of multilateral environmental agreements,
W. Bradnee Chambers, United Nations University Press, 2008, ISBN 978-92-808-1149-0

president of the General Assembly at the time, Ismail Razali of Malaysia, said, the results were "sobering"; the failure reflected a new low point for the environmental sustainable development movement. More importantly, it was a wake-up call and showed that in order to continue the momentum of the past decades, especially in the field of treaty-making, international policy-making would require more innovative approaches and politically and economically[3] sound policies to recapture the attention and the commitment of the policy-makers.[4] The concept of interlinkages was one that ideally met these needs.

The debates that ensued over coherence and integration (interlinkages) were reminiscent of the political debates that had taken place at Stockholm and at Rio on coordination, but they were to be more sophisticated because they built upon the existing system of environmental treaties and environmental institutions. Unlike past attempts to have an integrated governance system for the environment, this time the debates did not call for a new organization to replace all existing ones; rather they advocated a simple notion of better cooperation between existing Multilateral Environmental Agreements (MEAs) and international organizations and institutions, calling for these bodies to resolve their conflicts, end their turf wars and create synergies in their work.[5]

In many ways the concept of interlinkages was not a new one. The roots of interlinkages can essentially be found in the practical elements of policy-making and treaty negotiations. Academics later tried to conceptualize this behaviour by developing theories and models to explain what was happening in practice. In the policy arena interlinkages theories emerged firstly from early international trade, navigation and commercial agreements. Steve Charnovitz has traced the linkage between such agreements and other issues such as religion, slavery, emigration, narcotics and labour issues from as early as the mid-1800s industrial revolution period.[6] In contemporary terms, linkages models and theories have continued in the area of global trade liberalization, investment and financing and their

---

3. At UNCED developed countries agreed to give 0.7% of their GNP to ODA. However, this declined dramatically in the years following Rio in 16 out of 21 members of the OECD's Development Assistance Committee (DAC), which led to an overall decrease in combined aid from 0.34% of GNP in 1992 to 0.27% in 1995 and 0.25% at present. See OECD online statistics at www.oecd.org/dac/stats/dac (accessed 30 August 2006).

4. See W. Bradnee Chambers (2002), "Why the Summit Must Fail to Succeed", Special to *The Daily Yomiuri*, 21 August.

5. On turf wars and cooperation problems among MEAs see Kristin Rosendal and Steinar Andresen (2004), *UNEP's Role in Enhancing Problem-Solving Capacity in Multilateral Environmental Agreements: Co-ordination and Assistance in the Biodiversity Conservation Cluster*, FNI Report Oct. 2003. Lysaker, Norway: Fridtjof Nansen Institute, p. 29.

6. Steve Charnovitz (1998), *Symposium: Linkages as a Phenomenon: An Interdisciplinary Approach: Linking Topics in Treaties*, 19 U. Pa. J. Int'l Econ. L. 330.

impacts on social issues such as human rights, labour and intellectual property.

The most heated debates in this context have concerned trade and environment linkages. In the late 1980s and throughout the 1990s, there was increased pressure towards globalization and economic interdependence. At the regional level this produced trading blocs, which emerged in the Americas, blocs such as the North American Free Trade Agreement (NAFTA) and Mercosur (Southern Cone Market), which created concerns about pollution and lapses in environmental standards. At the same time in global forums, such as the Bretton Woods institutions and the World Trade Organization (WTO), NGOs (non-governmental organizations) raised questions of balancing economic development and environmental safety and developing countries suspected green policies from the North as being potential protectionist measures.

It was not until the 1990s that we see interlinkages developing as a concept between environmental treaties. This occurred for several reasons, both conceptually and from a policy-making point of view. The 1987 Brundtland Report had established the connection between environmental issues and socio-economic concerns and reversed the conceptual trend of approaching "environment" and "development" issues separately. The Report noted: "We can see and study the Earth as an organism whose health depends on the health of all its parts. We have the power to reconcile human affairs with natural laws and to thrive in the process. In this our cultural and spiritual heritages can reinforce our economic interests and survival imperatives."[7] The report laid the foundations for an integrated approach under the broader principle of sustainable development. This approach became the basic concept underlying environmental issues as the largest gathering of countries and heads of state endorsed the concept at the United Nations Conference on Environment and Development, and developed in 1992 a global action plan for the twenty-first century: Agenda 21.[8]

From the legal standpoint the increasing number of treaties and suggestions of how to improve their effectiveness led to concern in several contexts. Compliance theory, spurred by Louis Henkin's hypothesis that "almost all nations observe almost all principles of international law and almost all of their obligations almost all of the time" became a major focus in the 1980s and linked the concepts of compliance and effectiveness together. The UNCED Preparatory Committee in 1991 defined criteria for evaluating the effectiveness of existing environmental agree-

---

7. The World Commission on Environment and Development (1987). *Our Common Future*, Oxford: Oxford University Press.
8. Agenda 21 could be seen as one of the first approaches using interlinkages as it tries to bridge many environmental issues and multiple sectors based on the concept of sustainable development.

ments.[9] In 1993, Martti Koskenniemi also talked of the need for international law to concentrate more on making existing treaties more effective and on designing better treaties.[10] In 1995, in an article reflecting on several years of environmental treaty-making and the emergence of issues for the future of public international environmental law, Edith Brown Weiss introduced the concept of "treaty congestion"; a concept that soon became a catchword in international legal discourse[11] as well as in the policy-making world. Brown Weiss argued that success in negotiating a large number of new MEAs has led to "treaty congestion" that has had a number of side effects. These side effects included "operational inefficiency" (the time and resources required by a country to participate in numerous policy forums), inconsistencies and overlap between treaty coverage, and a general overload at the national level in implementing international agreements.[12]

This concept slowly became defined in policy literature as a concern for treaty conflicts and the reason why environmental treaties, though strongly connected with natural ecosystems, had few connections as legal instruments. At the time, there was also a growing realization that international legal mechanisms have not been adequate. For instance, the authors of the Vienna Convention on the Law of Treaties could never have imagined the explosion in the number of treaties that would take place in the few decades since its adoption. Many would agree that it is therefore unable to deal with the complexity and uncertainty that exist over the legal relationships between successive treaties.[13]

During this period, environmental scientists began to see the need to address more concretely the complexities and the interconnectivity of issues such as climate change, biodiversity loss, soil degradation and water issues. As the negotiations on climate change intensified, the enormity of its scope and how it had the potential to be a major direct driver of environmental change soon became apparent. In 1997, the first group of prac-

---

9. See Peter Sand, ed. (1992) *The Effectiveness of International Environmental Agreements*, Cambridge: Grotius.

10. Martti Koskenniemi (1993) *Breach of Treaty or Non-Compliance? Reflections on the Enforcement of the Montreal Protocol*, 3 Y.B. Int'l Envtl. L. 123. Also see David G. Victor (1996) *The Early Operation and Effectiveness of the Montreal Protocol's Non-Compliance Procedure*, ER-96-2, Laxenburg, Austria: International Institute for Applied Systems Analysis, May.

11. Gunter Handl observed that "treaty congestion" had "become [a] buzz word ... in international environmental legal discourse". See Gunter Handl (1997) *Compliance Control Mechanisms and International Environmental Obligations*, 5 Tul. J. Int'l & Comp. L. 29, 29–30.

12. Edith Brown Weiss (1995) *International Environmental Law: Contemporary Issues and the Emergence of a New World Order*, 81 Geo. L. J. 675, 697–702, 698.

13. See Bethany Lukitsch Hicks (1999) *Treaty Congestion in International Environmental Law: The Need for Greater Coordination*, 32 U. Rich. L. Rev. 1643, 1659.

titioners and science experts convened a small workshop in Israel on the synergies between the so-called Rio Agreements (UNFCCC, CBD, UNCCD and Forestry Principles).[14] The following year, one of the scientists, Robert Watson, who believed in the importance of the interlinkages issue very early on, led a collaboration of other scientists under a joint project of the World Bank, UNEP and NASA. The project looked at the primary scientific connections between some of the key environmental and development issues.[15] The ground-breaking report concluded that the scale of human demands had now grown so large that human beings are degrading the ecosystems upon which their health and livelihood depend at an unprecedented rate with a potential for surprises and non-linearities. They argued, however, that sustainable development can be realized by adopting an appropriate mix of technologies, policies and practices that explicitly recognize the linkages among environmental systems and human needs. The report stressed that environmental issues can be addressed in an integrated manner through many of the same technologies and policy instruments that are used to contend with the issues separately, but in different combinations and through improved institutions.

These initiatives and concepts culminated in the first international conference on the concept of "interlinkages"[16] convened by the United Nations University and UNEP in 1999. The conference involved most of the key international actors that were significant in moving the interlinkages concept forward, including the MEA secretariats, UN and international organizations and respected experts and NGOs. Up until this point, these diverse groups saw the interlinkages concept as a threat to their own coherent programmes and had fervently defended their turf. This conference was the first time they were assembled in one place. For smaller conventions, such as Ramsar, the concept provided the opportunity to reinforce its own importance and link to more recent MEAs that had significant implications for their own mandates. For larger MEAs, like the Climate Change Convention, the connection with issues other than their own was seen as an unwanted distraction, particularly when the FCCC parties were in the midst of negotiating the Kyoto Protocol – a process

14. See UNDP (1997) *Synergies: National Implementation of Rio Agreements*, UNDP Report (on the expert meeting organized by the Sustainable Energy and Environment Division and held in Israel March 1997, New York: UNDP.
15. R. T. Watson, J. A. Dixon, S. P. Hamburg, A. C. Janetos and R. H. Moss (1998) *Protecting Our Planet Securing Our Future: Linkages Among Global Environmental Issues and Human Needs*, Nairobi: UNEP.
16. The UNU Meeting defined interlinkages as "a key to developing a more integrated approach, is the identification of the inherent *synergies* that exist between different aspects of the environment, and an exploration of the potential for more effective *coordination* between multilateral environmental agreements." See UNU (1999) "Interlinkages: Synergies and Coordination between Multilateral Agreements", Tokyo: UNU.

with its own complexities. This attitude was reflected in their decision not to participate in the interlinkages discussion.

The 1999 Interlinkages Conference marked the beginning of a series of activities in the field of policy-making that attempted to rationalize and manage the complexities of multilateral environmental agreements. The historical record of these activities occurred mainly in the context of UN reforms under Secretary-General Kofi Annan, the preparations for the World Summit on Sustainable Development and the UNEP's International Environmental Governance process. Through the academic experts who attended, and others researching in the area, the conference sparked further development of the idea of interlinkages into a concept and theory that would try to promote and explain the interaction of regimes and international accords.

From that time, the concept has firmly taken hold internationally and it has become the topic of continual discussion within policy-making forums such as the General Assembly,[17] the UNEP Governing Council[18] and many decisions of COP/MOPs. In 2005, the World Summit continued to reaffirm the desire of governments to create better interlinkages between environmental activities:

> Recognising the need for more efficient environmental activities in the UN system, with enhanced coordination, improved policy advice and guidance, strengthened scientific knowledge, assessment and cooperation, better treaty compliance, while respecting the legal autonomy of the treaties, as well as better integration of environmental activities in the broader sustainable development framework at the operational level, including through capacity-building, we agree to explore the possibility of a more coherent institutional framework to address this need, including a more integrated structure, building on existing institutions, and internationally agreed instruments, as well as the treaty bodies and the specialised agencies.[19]

This outcome, together with the UN Reform process, has led to ongoing analysis of coherence within the UN System. One aspect of this coherence relates to the environment regime and includes the promotion of synergies among MEAs and the mainstreaming of their goals within broader poverty-reduction strategies and plans.

Similarly, the letter dated 1 February 2006 from the Permanent Representative of France to the United Nations addressed to the President of the General Assembly (GA A/60/668) mentions:

---

17. UN General Assembly Resolutions 52/445, A/53/463, 53/242, 53/190, 53/186, 54/216, 54/217, 54/221, 54/222, 54/223, 55/201, 55/198, 56/199, 56/197, 56/196, 57/270, 57/260, 57/259, 57/257, 57/253, 58/243, 58/242, 58/240, 58/218, 58/212, 58/209, 59/236, 59/235, 59/234, 59/227, 59/226, 60/1 2005, 60/189, 60/193, 60/202.
18. See UNEP Documents 17/25, 18/9, 19/9c, 20/18B, 21/21, 21/23, *Decision VII/I of the Seventh Session of the Governing Council*, UNEP/GCSS.VII/6.
19. Declaration of the 2005 World Summit, para. 169.

Problems of coherence and efficiency linked to the increasing number of multilateral environmental agreements (MEAs) and environmental forums: although the development of this architecture has made positive advances possible, international environmental governance is characterized by fragmentation. It is often a source of inconsistency, inefficiency, additional cost and imperfect allocation of human and financial resources. It weakens the capacity of international environmental governance to contribute to sustainable development.

Given this background, it is evident from both legal scholarship and policy-making that there is interest in using the interlinkages approach. However, what is not well known is that, contrary to the research that is under way on natural and environmental sciences concerning interlinkages,[20] there is a serious lack of understanding of interlinkages in social science research and law, and an absence of any conceptual frameworks by which to focus policy and scholarship on the topic. Since Brown-Weiss's paper coining the term of "treaty congestion", there has been relatively little written on the topic in the field of law and few legal studies have been applied to the other side of the coin, which is treaty cooperation and which this book views as "interlinkages".[21]

20. Several scientific studies have looked at the natural environmental drivers of interlinkages. See for example Habiba Gitay, A. Suárez, R. T. Watson and D. J. Dokken, eds (2002) "Technical Paper V on Climate Change and Biodiversity", *Intergovernmental Panel on Climate Change*, available from http://www.ipcc.ch/pub/tpbiodiv.pdf; Convention on Biological Diversity (2002) *Ad Hoc Technical Expert Group on Biological Diversity and Climate Change*, UNEP/CBD/AHTEG-BDCC/2/2, available from http://www.cbd.int/doc/meetings/cc/tegcc-02/official/tegcc-02-02-en.pdf; OECD (2002) *DAC Guidelines Integrating the Rio Conventions into Development Cooperation*, available from http://www.oecd.org/dataoecd/49/2/1960098.pdf; ICSU's Sustainability Science Initiative, at http://sustainabilityscience.org; GEF Scientific and Technical Advisory Panel (2004) *Assessment of Inter-linkages between Biodiversity, Climate Change, Land Degradation and International Water – A report focusing on the needs of the GEF*, Washington, DC: Global Environment Facility.

21. The exception to this is Rüdiger Wolfrum and Nele Matz (2003) *Conflicts in International Environmental Law* (Berlin: Springer), which does discuss how environmental treaties cope with possible conflicts and approaches to coordination but most works have focused on treaty conflicts rather than treaty cooperation. For these works see Charles Rousseau (1932) *De la Compatibilité des Normes Juridiques Contradictoires dans l'ordre International*, 39 Revue Générale de Droit International Public 133, 150–151; C. Wilfred Jenks (1953) *The Conflict of Law-Making Treaties*, 30 Brit. Y.B. Int'l L. 401, 426; Bethany Lukitsch Hicks, op cit.; Jonathan I. Charney (1999) *The Impact on the International Legal System of the Growth of International Courts and Tribunals*, 31 N.Y.U. J. Int'l L. & Pol. 697; Benedict Kingsbury (1999) *Foreword: Is the Proliferation of International Courts and Tribunals a Systemic Problem?* 31 N.Y.U. J. Int'l L. & Pol. 679; Wolfram Karl (2000) "Conflicts between Treaties", in Rudolf Bernhardt ed., *Encyclopedia of Public International Law*, 935, 936; Int'l Law Comm'n (2002) *Report of the Study Group on Fragmentation of International Law*, U.N. GAOR, 54th Sess., U.N. A/CN.4/L.628 at 2; Gilbert Guillaume (1995) *The Future of International Judicial Institutions*, 44 Int'l L. & Comp. L.Q. 848; Christopher Borgen (2005) *Resolving Treaty Conflicts*, 37 Geo. Wash. Int'l L. Rev. 573.

The end result of this absence of reliable studies from these disciplines is that this will likely hinder progress towards improving environmental legal instruments and public international law through coordination and synergy. Without first understanding how treaty performance can be improved through treaty-to-treaty cooperation it is unlikely that treaty bodies and contracting parties will be motivated to work more cooperatively together. Moreover, without knowing what types of interventions work more than others or how interlinkages can improve treaty effectiveness it is difficult to direct policy interventions at the right target.

This book therefore raises two questions:

(1) *Can interlinkages improve the effectiveness of multilateral environmental agreements?*

(2) *Can interlinkages improve the effectiveness of MEAs outside the branch of international environmental law and outside the sector of the environment but still under the umbrella of sustainable development?*

To answer these questions, and in doing so contribute to the better understanding of the greater corpus of international law and the understanding of a subject rarely written about in the field of law in general, this book will create, in chapters 4 and 5, a conceptual framework showing how environmental treaties work together and how this cooperation can improve their effectiveness. In chapters 6 and 7 the book will test this framework on two types of case studies: one within the traditional ambit of environmental treaties and the other across treaties that are considered to be cross-sectoral and connected by the principle of sustainable development. The case studies will use the same subject matter as genetic resources[22] so that their results are comparable across treaties. According to these parameters, the first case study in chapter 6 will examine the interlinkages between the 1992 Convention on Biological Diversity[23] and the International Treaty for Plant Genetic Resources for Food and Agriculture[24] while the second case study in chapter 7 will examine the relationship of CBD and ITPGRFA to the Trade-Related

---

22. Plant genetic resources are any materials of plant that contain functional units of heredity and are of actual or potential use (see Convention on Biological Diversity, Article 2).

23. The Convention on Biological Diversity [hereinafter CBD], negotiated under the auspices of UNEP, was opened for signature on 5 June 1992 and came into force on 29 December 1993. 31 ILM, 818 (1992).

24. The International Treaty on Plant Genetic Resources for Food and Agriculture [hereinafter ITPGRFA], negotiated under the Food and Agriculture Organization's Commission for Genetic Resources for Food and Agriculture [hereinafter CGRFA], was adopted on 30 November 2001 and came into force on 29 June 2004. Available online at http://www.fao.org/ag/cgrfa/IU.htm.

Intellectual Properties Agreement,[25] a treaty outside the sector of the environment and outside the branch of international environmental law. Thus, the second case study will examine treaties that are interrelated but exist under different sectors of sustainable development.

The first two chapters of the book support the principal and secondary theses and serve as a background. Chapter 2 shows the legal history on interlinkages and examines the *travaux préparatories* on coordination and synergy efforts from Stockholm to Johannesburg (1972–2002). Chapter 3 looks at existing legal mechanisms under international law, such as the Vienna Convention on the Law of Treaties, and examines the new concept of "autonomous institutional arrangements" as well as examining more thoroughly aspects such as memorandums of understanding (MOUs) between treaties and other legal institutional arrangements. Chapter 8 is the concluding chapter where I will extrapolate from the analysis how interlinkages can be a means to improve effectiveness for international environmental and sustainable development treaties and what this implies for future law-making. The concluding chapter will also draw implications for the future of public international law and treaty management.

25. Agreement on Trade-Related Aspects of Intellectual Property Rights, Marrakech Agreement Establishing the World Trade Organization [hereinafter WTO Agreement], Annex 1C, *Legal Instruments–Results of the Uruguay Round*, Vol. 31, 33 ILM 81, (1994) [hereinafter TRIPS Agreement].

Part II

Historical overview of the international process to improve coordination and create synergies between intergovernmental sustainable development institutions

2

From Stockholm to Johannesburg via Malmö: A historical overview of international coordination of environment-sustainable development institutions[1]

Introduction

In the preparations and the negotiations of the 1972 United Nations Conference on the Human Environment (UNCHE) in Stockholm the question of coordination was highly controversial. Developed countries were reluctant to create more costly organizations, and existing UN agencies that were already working on environmental issues were fearful of being rendered subservient to or redundant by a new "superagency". A similar push for institutional coordination was evident at the UN Conference on Environment and Development (UNCED), which took place in Rio de Janeiro 20 years later. Yet by this time, governments had started to lose their confidence in UNEP's ability to play a strong and effective coordinating role in environmental governance – ironically a role it was created to pursue.

By the end of the 1980s, UNEP's political position was in decline. Developed countries had been alienated by Director-General Mostafa Tolba's strong support of the interests of developing countries. Tolba's successor was equally unappealing to developing countries, who believed that UNEP was overemphasizing its efforts on the "green northern

1. A version of this chapter was published in W. Bradnee Chambers and Jessica Green, *Reforming International Environmental Governance* (Tokyo: United Nations University Press, 2005). It was titled *From Environmental to Sustainable Development Governance: Thirty Years of Coordination within the United Nations*, 13–19.

Interlinkages and the effectiveness of multilateral environmental agreements,
W. Bradnee Chambers, United Nations University Press, 2008, ISBN 978-92-808-1149-0

agenda" (i.e., biodiversity, climate change) instead of "brown-on-the-ground" (i.e., air pollution and clean drinking water), which were of greater concern to them. The resulting loss of confidence culminated at Rio, where developing nations looked elsewhere for coordination and follow-up to Agenda 21 and two new treaties on climate change and desertification. As a result, a new institutional personality was created, the Commission on Sustainable Development (CSD), under the UN Department of Economic and Social Affairs.

Kofi Annan's appointment as Secretary-General of the United Nations in 1996 marked a distinct shift in UN leadership. Secretary-General Annan came from within the organization and, as a UN functionary with a 20-year career, he thoroughly understood the workings of the UN and its administration. Most importantly, Annan understood the reality of competition between UN organizations and had specific ideas about how the UN could be improved.

With this experience behind him, Annan launched a major reform initiative set out in his 1997 *Renewing the United Nations Report.*[2] The report spurred new interest in creating greater effectiveness and efficiency and in addressing criticism that the organization was overly bureaucratic and wasteful. This eventually set in motion a process within the UN and special agencies, non-governmental organizations and academia to re-evaluate the international institutions associated with environment and sustainable development. This reform has continued and was evident in the 2002 World Summit on Sustainable Development process and its follow-up.

The purpose of this chapter is to recount the processes and initiatives over the course of the past three decades of environmental and, subsequently, sustainable development policy-making. Efforts focused on creating effective institutions for environmental protection and sustainable development through stronger coordination and interlinkages between UN organizations, which has helped lay the foundation for understanding the current framework for environmental governance.

The first section of this chapter traces the early initiatives to create institutional coordination mechanisms, which mainly arose out of the preparation for and deliberations at the 1972 Stockholm Conference. These deliberations revolved around the creation of UNEP and the role it would play vis-à-vis other UN agencies. The chapter then goes on to deal with the Rio Earth Summit and emergence of the concept of sustainable development, which effectively added a new layer of coordination to the environmental organization rubric by introducing the necessity for

---

2. See UNGA (1997) *Report of the Secretary-General: Renewing the UN, A Programme for Reform*, A/51/950.

environmental policy-making to take better account of societal and economic sectors. The section looks in detail at the creation of the CSD as
well as other inter-agency coordination mechanisms, and how these function in relation to existing environmental and sustainable development
governance structures.

Section three then looks at the UNEP International Environmental
Governance process launched by the UNEP Governing Council in
Malmö, Sweden in 2000. The section traces some of the problems that
have curtailed opportunities for strengthening environmental governance.
It reviews some of the proposals offered, and the series of meetings that
led up to the third preparatory meeting of the World Summit on Sustainable Development. The final section looks at the WSSD itself and examines in detail the outcome as contained in the Johannesburg Plan of Implementation (JPOI).

The results of this historical analysis suggest that the global summits at
Stockholm, Rio and Johannesburg represent missed opportunities for reform. International environmental governance, and now sustainable development governance, could have benefited greatly from strong reform
efforts at these three critical meetings. The chapter concludes that coordination has now become extremely complex, and any assessments of the
institutional arrangements for environment and sustainable development
issues must be seen in the context of inter-sector cooperation, between
social, economic and environmental organizations (e.g., WTO, UNEP,
ILO), and intra-sector cooperation, between independent environment
organizations (e.g., UNEP, CSD, FAO), and must be distinguished according to the nature of the coordination or potential interlinkage
sought. For the most binding of the environment-sustainable development institutions, the multilateral environmental agreements – the subject of this thesis – the implications are equally clear that they require
greater cooperation both among themselves and with multilateral agreements outside the branch of international environmental law such as the
economic and social branches of international law.

The early days of Stockholm

In 1968, the Economic and Social Commission (ECOSOC) reported to
the General Assembly their concern about mounting environmental degradation.[3] This move by the Commission represented the culmination
of a growing movement internationally from NGOs, conservationists
and ornithologists that had raised alarm over the worsening state of the

3. See ECOSOC, Resolution 1346 (XLV), (30 July 1968).

environment. The UN had no mandate on the environment but because its impact cut across numerous issues, such as health, culture and development, several UN organizations were already at work in the field. Economic and social issues were also viewed as a prerequisite to peace and security, the UN's mainstay, and thus were intrinsically linked to the environment.[4] With growing interest and activity in environmental protection, the next important question focused on the institutional structure and management within the UN. Would there be a new superagency? Or would an existing agency be given additional responsibility in this new area and, if so, which one? Or would the agencies that were already working on environmental issues simply receive an additional mandate and the Administrative Coordinating Committee (the standing committee of heads of UN organizations) be mandated to coordinate yet another issue within the UN family?

At the start of the Stockholm Conference, opinions were deeply divided on exactly what would be the necessary institutional arrangements for the environment. At the very initial stages of planning for the conference, the architect behind Stockholm, Secretary-General U Thant, proposed the idea of an environmental "superagency", but this view quickly became entangled in New York politics (this frequently happens in the UN headquarters), institutional turf wars, financial concerns and sovereignty questions. There was thus a general aversion to the creation of a new UN organization.

Given these constraints, any attempts to launch a new environmental organization would have to be accompanied by assurances that the potential organization was not going to be an organization at all, but rather a non-intrusive entity to complement existing organizations. Such an organization would have to have a minimal administration, and would not compete legally or financially with existing organizations. This, in fact, is precisely what happened.

Two major information notes had a great deal of influence on the deliberations of the Stockholm Conference about a new environmental organization. Both quashed any idea of creating of a free-standing independent organization for the environment. The first was document A/CONF.48/12 prepared by the Administrative Coordination Committee (ACC). The ACC comprised heads of different UN and Specialized Agencies, and its informational document emphasized that any approach taken in Stockholm should be complementary and should give existing

4. See for example, the 1975 Helsinki Final Act, 14 ILM, 1292, which states that "their efforts to develop cooperation in the fields of trade, industry, science and technology, the environment and other areas of economic activity contribute to the reinforcement of peace and security in Europe and in the world as a whole ...".

organizations "additional support, fresh impetus and a common outlook and direction".[5] The document outlined the argument that traditionally UN organizations have taken a vertical approach to international
problem-solving, organizing themselves according to sectoral patterns in
national governments. While the ACC argued that this sectoral approach
"remains adequate to deal with a number of these problems", document
A/CONF.48/12 clearly argued for a more horizontal approach given what
they saw as the intersectoral, diffused and interdisciplinary nature of
environmental problems.[6] The document elaborated in detail the actions
already taken or planned by other UN organizations for the environment. Based on these existing efforts and the ACC's current coordinating
role at the time, it subtly argued that the "United Nations system has
institutions, experience and machinery which can be adapted to new
tasks and needs".[7] In other words, according to the ACC, the UN did
not need any organization for the environment or a new mechanism for
coordination.[8]

The document reflected many of the political undercurrents at the
time. Organizations such as the International Atomic Energy Agency
were reluctant to lose successful environment-related programmes on
radiation monitoring and were clearly prepared to defend their turf.[9]
The ACC document also played equally into the hands of both developing and developed countries, but for very different reasons. Developed
countries such as the UK did not want to pay for yet another international organization and wanted the "absolute minimum" for new institutions.[10] Developing countries also objected to a large new environmental
organization on the grounds that regulations on environment could be a
new form of colonialism or at the very least a restriction to their economic development.

But the ACC position represented only half the politics that were at
play in New York at the time; the efforts of Maurice Strong represented
the other half. Not to pre-empt the outcome of Stockholm, and in the
face of growing support for an approach of working within the existing

5. UNGA (1973) *The United Nations System and the Human Environment*, A/CONF.48/
   12, 4.
6. Ibid., 5.
7. Ibid., 73.
8. Peter B. Stone (1973) *Did We Save the Earth at Stockholm?: The People and Politics in
   the Conference on the Human Environment*, Earth Island.
9. This was demonstrated by an account by Peter Stone in his book on the Stockholm Conference of a telegram sent to the US, Swedish and other delegations but leaked to ECO
   that was intended to weaken any potential organization arising from the conference. See
   ibid. at 56.
10. Op. cit. Stone, 33.

UN system, Maurice Strong, who had been appointed the Secretary-General of the Stockholm Conference, decided that he would hire an outside writing team to take responsibility for the preparation of Stockholm's basic information documents. This was a strategic move as their work would serve as a counterbalance to the ACC's interests, demonstrated in the partisan document A/CONF.48/12.

Strong, an entrepreneur and self-made man, had already been responsible for the creation of the Canadian International Development Agency and International Development Research Centre, two innovative and forward-looking national organizations within the complicated political structure of the Canadian Government. As an iconoclast he had his conference secretariat prepare a second document that made subtle but more powerful arguments for at least some form of new institutional mechanism for the environment. Document A/CONF.48/11, which was submitted with the ACC document for consideration by the preparatory committee, argued that there still existed many gaps in environmental governance, and thus new approaches and institutional arrangements were needed.[11] Though the Strong document acknowledges that existing organizations were already addressing environmental issues and that coordination was needed, these gaps could not be resolved within the current institutional frameworks.

The document was the culmination of a number of meetings and consultations that Strong had held with governments and international organizations.[12] It laid out nine criteria that were said to represent the

11. UNGA, *International Organizational Implications of Action Proposals*, A/CONF.48/11, at para. 5.
12. Also see A. O. Adede who cites the plethora of meetings convened on this issue including meetings at the International Organization and the Human Environment, co-sponsored by the Institute on Man and Science and the Aspen Institute for Humanistic Studies, held at Rensselaerville, New York, 21–23 May 1971; The Crisis of the Human Environment and International Action, sponsored by the International Studies Program, University of Toronto, held at Toronto, Canada, 25–27 May 1971; Sixth Conference on the United Nations of the Next Decade, sponsored by the Stanley Foundation, held at Sinaia, Romania, 20–26 June 1971; First International Environmental Workshop, co-sponsored by the International Institute for Environmental Affairs and the Aspen Institute for Humanistic Studies, held at Aspen, Colorado, 20 June–6 August 1971; Panel of Experts on International Organizational Implications, convened by the Secretary-General of the United Nations Conference on the Human Environment, held at Geneva, Switzerland, 8–9 July 1971; International Legal and Institutional Responses to the Problems of the Global Environment, co-sponsored by the Carnegie Endowment for International Peace and the American Society of International Law, held at Harriman, New York, 25 September–1 October 1971; and the UN System and the Human Environment, sponsored by the Institute for the Study of International Organizations, University of Sussex, held at Brighton, England, 1–4 November 1971. See A. O. Adede, *In Renewing International Environmental Governance: Issues for Consideration by African Countries*, ACTS, at http://www.acts.or.ke/Renewing.pdf (last visited 1 June 2004).

consensus reached through these meetings. In summary, these criteria affirmed that:

- Any potential organization should be based on agreed need;
- No unnecessary new institutional machinery should be created;
- A network approach instead of a superagency should be used;
- Any organization should be flexible and evolutionary;
- The highest priority should be given to coordination;
- The organization should not have operational function so as to avoid competition;
- It should have a regional outlook;
- The UN should be the principal body to host any new organization and the organization should be designed in a way to strengthen the overall UN system.[13]

Whether these criteria represented a true assessment of the institutional arrangements needed to address emerging environmental concerns or a savvy compromise by a Secretary-General of the conference with a knack for consensus building remains unknown. Though the report was more realistic than the ACC proposal, it still failed to understand the difficult nature of coordination within the UN, and the need to empower institutions with the political clout required to get independently mandated organizations to cooperate.

The Strong document recommended two potential setups within the UN for the new organization on environment. The first was to create a subsidiary body of the ECOSOC under Article 68 of the UN Charter.[14] This made sense given that the environmental issues fell closer to the mandate and substantive content of the Council's deliberations. However, at the time, questions about ECOSOC were being raised, especially given that it represented nearly half the UN membership, and that it could only make recommendations to the General Assembly.[15] There was also concern that if the new organization was under ECOSOC, it might not be able to attract ministers and senior officials on a regular basis and therefore would not be capable of recommending credible decisions to the Assembly.[16]

The second choice, which was eventually accepted, was to create a subsidiary body of the General Assembly under Article 22 of the Charter. This arrangement would allow the organization to inform the Assembly "to tackle problems posed by the interconnections of development with the need to safeguard the environment and to provide policy guidance

13. Op. cit. A/CONF.48/11, para. 7.
14. Ibid., para. 57.
15. R. Gardner (1972) "The Role of the UN in Environmental Problems", 26 *International Organization*, 237 and 248.
16. Ibid.

thereon".[17] It was also thought that, as a subsidiary body of the General Assembly, the new body would enjoy higher visibility and status, and thus more political credibility than under the ECOSOC.

Nowhere, however, was the proposal to create a highly specialized agency under Article 59 of the UN Charter. Perhaps this was too much to ask given the political environment at the time, and so Strong believed it was a non-starter. Yet, the absence of this choice, or some other organizational arrangement politically stronger than the two put forth, was a fundamental mistake. This decision has put the UNEP and environmental issues on a path that has made them subservient to other interests. The disadvantaged position within the larger international governance system has made it difficult to balance equally with the other two pillars of sustainable development.

Document A/CONF.48/11 accurately sketches the terrain of needs for a future organization with regard to monitoring, reporting and information requirements, but in considering the central role of coordination it misses the true nature. At the time, most environmental activities were conducted by well-established and well-financed special agencies such as the Food and Agriculture Organization, the International Atomic Energy Agency, the Inter-Governmental Maritime Consultative Organization, the World Health Organization and the World Meteorological Organization. Other activities were under way in financial institutions, such as the World Bank or the GATT, yet these organizations had other interests (such as economic development), which were counterpoised with environmental concerns.[18] As semi-autonomous or fully autonomous organizations, coordinating efforts were difficult at best. When heads of these agencies sat together under the umbrella of the ACC, each came with their own political agendas and, more importantly, their own governance system, to which they would be held accountable. Each agency has its own intergovernmental council and thus could not be compelled to undertake any activities not approved by its council.

These competing institutional arrangements and priorities explain part of the shortcomings of the Stockholm conference. One of the main outcomes with respect to institutional reform was to call for the creation of

17. Supra., A/CONF.48/11, para. 60.
18. Really the only UN-based agencies having principal environmental activities were the Department of Economic and Social Affairs, which had activities on transport, housing, population and planning, and UNESCO, which had a number of activities on atmospheric pollution, land and conservation of marine environment, water and selected pollutants. For an overview of UN-related activities in 1970 see Appendix 1 of B. Johnson (1972) "The United Nations Institutional Response to Stockholm: A Case Study in the International Politics of Institutional Change", 25 *International Organization*, 289.

an Environment Coordination Board under the framework of the ACC. Yet, this body lacked the power to coordinate environmental issues and promote new agendas in a meaningful way. The institutional machinery was awkward and burdensome, and UNEP had no operational features to implement new environmental concerns on its own. UNEP was to make recommendations to the General Assembly, which would in turn recommend actions at the country level or by other parts of the UN family.[19]

Another major shortcoming of Stockholm was a misdiagnosis of the problem: What was needed in 1970 was not coordination but consolidation. A new organization needed to be on the same footing as the other specialized agencies, and it needed the ability to implement programmes instead of just reviewing policy. Though environmental programmes were already under way in several agencies, gaps remained on issues not taken up by any organization. And the way in which they evolved under the mandate of different agencies was ad hoc. Consolidation under a new organization could have addressed these two problems.

In 1970, these concerns were well known among analysts. In fact, there was discussion of some very innovative proposals for institutional arrangements. For example, an environmental council was proposed in 1972; it would have the same status as the ECOSOC and thus have clear legal authority over specialized agencies.[20] Another, which is still raised as an option today, was to re-orient the Trusteeship Councils towards protecting the global commons. But both of these proposals would have required (and would still require) an amendment to the UN Charter under Article 108, which raised fears that opening up the Charter to amendments could spark debates over other, more sensitive, areas.[21]

One of the most innovative ideas put forth was that of giving UNDP the environment portfolio. This idea was based on the United Nations Fund for Population Activities, which had begun a new fund to implement population programmes. Since the fund was executed by the UNDP through its country offices, it was argued that "placing environmental responsibilities within UNDP might help to ensure that environmental considerations are included in projects from their inceptions".[22]

---

19. For example through the Environment Coordinating Board (ECB), which was abolished later in 1977, see supra.
20. Supra, Johnson, 272. Also see UN Charter Article 63 which allows the ECOSOC to coordinate the activities of the Specialized Agencies through consultation and recommendations.
21. Supra, Johnson, 273.
22. Supra, Johnson, 274.

Turning the environment portfolio over to UNDP would have also given the UN the reach it needed to execute a variety of projects at the national level.

However, in the 1970s, many believed that the debate on institutional arrangements was premature. Instead of trying to decide the outcome of a new organization for the environment without full understanding of the future directions of environmental governance, it was better to create a strategic unit using the existing UN machinery and with minimal investment. This feeling was reflected in the consensus cultivated by Strong: "Any action envisaged should allow for the preliminary state of knowledge and understanding of environmental problems and should be flexible and evolutionary." Or, as Richard Gardner said, "any new organization established to deal with environmental problems should be capable of growth and adaptation.... Governments may be willing to make commitments for tomorrow that they may not be willing to undertake today."[23] In many ways, this was a savings clause for the future and left the possibility open to "upgrade" UNEP in the future, as circumstances warranted. However, the principle came without mechanisms to implement it, and it would be 20 years until governments had another chance to think about implementation and creating the appropriate institutional arrangements. By that time, however, the principles of sustainable development would also have to be considered in tandem with environmental governance.

Rio and institutional coordination deliberations

Just as the representatives to Stockholm[24] wrestled with the seemingly competing issues of environment and trade, so did the policy-makers at Rio. In the 20 years between the two summits, the trade/environment debate did not wane but rather intensified. This growing tension warranted further exploration of institutional remedies; thus, it became apparent that any future world conference would have to treat environment and development issues simultaneously, and that coordination rather than reconciliation of these two issues would be the challenge.

Yet, just as in Stockholm, politics trumped policy at UNCED, and the institutional outcomes would prove to be sub-optimal. The Rio Earth

23. Supra, Gardner, 245 .
24. UNGA (1971) *Report of the Deliberation of the Second Committee on Natural Resource Management and Development, Chapter X,* A/CONF.48/14/Rev.1 at paras. 170–259. Also see preparatory meeting reports such as *Environment and Development,* Founex, Switzerland, (4–12 June).

Summit did produce some outcomes to enhance coordination with other sectors beyond environment; its decisions created greater coordination problems within it.

Between the areas of development and environment, there were several outcomes of the Rio Summit that went to the heart of coordination. At the conceptual level, the appropriation of the concept of sustainable development, as put forth by the Brundtland Commission Report, was an attempt to reconcile these two areas, which had previously been considered separately.[25] If sustainable development formed the basis for the deliberations of the institutional arrangements, Agenda 21 became the blueprint of how this goal should be achieved.[26] Chapter 38 of Agenda 21 sets out various layers of coordination. First, it calls on all relevant agencies of the UN system to "adopt concrete programmes for the implementation of Agenda 21" and publish regular reports and reviews of these activities.[27] It also set up three new bodies: a high-level inter-agency coordination mechanism under the ACC, a high-level advisory body to provide guidance to the Secretary-General, and a high-level commission under the ECOSOC to follow up on the implementation of Agenda 21. The most significant of these was the last.

The Commission on Sustainable Development (CSD) was established as a result of the Rio Summit as a body to monitor the implementation of Agenda 21 and to promote the integration of the three pillars of sustainable development. It was formally established by ECOSOC Decision 1993/207.[28] The Commission meets annually, reporting to the ECOSOC and, through it, to the Second Committee of the General Assembly. The CSD also has a role in coordinating the Rio follow-up within the UN system, through the now defunct Inter-Agency Committee on Sustainable Development (IACSD),[29] which was a subsidiary body of the

25. For a definition of sustainable development see Brundtland Commission (1987) *Our Common Future*, Oxford: Oxford University Press. See also UN General Assembly, *Report of the Brundtland Commission*, A/42/427.
26. See A/CONF.48/11.
27. See A/CONF.151/26 (Vol. III) at para. 38.8 and para. 38.4 respectively.
28. ECOSOC (1993) *Establishment of the Commission on Sustainable Development*, E/1993/207 (12 February), available at http://www.un.org/documents/ecosoc/res/1993/eres1993-207.htm.
29. *Infra*, Chapter 3. The IACSD was a subsidiary body of the UN Administrative Coordinating Committee (ACC), which in turn acted as a kind of "cabinet" for the Secretary-General. The IACSD was chaired by the Under-Secretary-General in charge of the Commission on Sustainable Development and was made up of senior-level officials from nine core members of the ACC–FAO, IAEA, ILO, UNDP, UNEP, UNESCO, WHO, World Bank and WMO. Officials from other UN bodies, intergovernmental agencies and representatives from major groups are able to attend by invitation.

Administrative Committee on Coordination (ACC) and which was later renamed the Chief Executive Board for Coordination (CEB).[30]

Though the CSD was created to follow up on Agenda 21, in fact it displaced and overlapped with UNEP. UNEP was already playing a major role in sectoral issues outlined in Agenda 21, such as oceans and seas, freshwater, land management, forests, biodiversity, chemicals, hazardous waste and air pollution. UNEP was either acting as a catalytic organization, by identifying emerging issues and threats, or it was working with other agencies to address these issues.

The cross-sectoral issues taken up in Agenda 21 also caused difficulties in coordinating work between UNEP and the CSD. The CSD was in addition responsible for considering cross-sectoral issues such as education, the role of major groups and financial resources.[31] Yet it is widely agreed that the CSD was not effective at addressing these cross-sectoral issues. Much of the work that the CSD did became more environmental rather than development-oriented, and its successes are more focused on environmental policies, such as the Forestry Principles, or work on energy and freshwater. Issue areas such as education, technology transfer, capacity-building or strengthening coordination with the Bretton Woods Institutions and the WTO, where clearly CSD should have played a role, have garnered little success in the 10 years since Rio. It has been credited with putting new issues on the international agenda, such as energy, tourism and transport, but according to some analysts this work on emerging issues clearly fell under UNEP's mandate.[32]

What was needed, but never came to pass, was a clearer division of labour between UNEP and the CSD. UNEP was already well placed in a number of sectoral issues, and could have continued its work in these areas, with Agenda 21 and the renewed commitment by Rio to strengthen its mandate. The CSD, by contrast, was better suited to work on integrated policies and substance between the issues as well as clearly identified cross-sectoral issues such as the nexus of the three pillars of sustainable development, education, the role of major groups and financial matters.[33] The creation of the CSD brought about an often unneces-

30. The role the CEB is discussed in greater detail in Chapter 3.

31. For an overview of criticisms of CSD from 1994 to 1996 and from 1997 to 2001 see Felix Dodds, Rosalie Gardiner et al. (2002) "Paper #9 Post Johannesburg: The Future of the UNU Commission on Sustainable Development", *Stakeholder Forum*, Vol. 5.

32. Pamela Chasek (1997) *The United Nations Commission on Sustainable Development: The First Five Years*, Paper for "The United Nations University Conference on the Global Environment in the 21st Century: From Common Challenges to Shared Responsibilities", Tokyo.

33. For a discussion of the issues surrounding sustainable development governance see Marie-Claire Cordonier Segger (2004) "Governing and Reconciling Economic, Social and Environmental Regimes", in Marie-Claire Cordonier Segger and C. G. Weeramantry, *Sustainable Justice*, Leiden, the Netherlands: Martinus Nijhoff.

sary layer of bureaucracy, which was detrimental to the division of labour between CSD and UNEP and caused larger coordination problems over environmental governance. As mentioned earlier, there is considerable overlap between the CSD and UNEP as well as with other intergovernmental bodies. Thus, the CSD has little to offer that has not been presented, discussed or decided elsewhere. Critics have also argued that the CSD can create a "decoy effect" by considering sectoral issues that have been dealt with in more specialist fora for many years, thereby drawing attention from, or potentially conflicting with, other international decisions. The recent reform of the CSD, following the decision of the World Summit on Sustainable Development to "place more emphasis on actions that enable implementation at all levels", is part of the attempt to address some of these criticisms.[34] The first meeting of the reformed structure and focus of the CSD took place in April–May 2004, where the emphasis was on exchange of information rather than negotiating a formal decision. While it is too early to know what the effects of these reforms will be, they have certainly served to structure the CSD's work around particular sectoral issues on a two-year biennial basis.

The CSD is true to the outcomes of Rio in the sense that it views sustainable development as a cross-cutting concept – much like the environment was regarded when UNEP was created. Though the CSD was to provide the coordination to implement Agenda 21, it did not strengthen UNEP or enhance its implementation capability. Thus, environmental governance was re-christened as sustainable development, yet as with the creation of UNEP, the corresponding institutional infrastructure was again lacking. Nowhere is this more evident than in contrasting the multilateral institutional apparatus for economic development, social development and environmental protection. Economic institutions such as the WTO, World Bank, IMF, UNIDO and UNCTAD are numerous, well developed and, in the case of the WTO, even have a compliance mechanism. Institutions for social development, such as the ILO, WHO, FAO and the Human Rights Commission, are similarly strong. By comparison, the corresponding environmental institutions are quite weak.

UN reform and the Malmö process: UNEP's comeback?

The loss of confidence in UNEP in the late 1980s and early 1990s was replaced by a renewed confidence placed in UNEP's potential by Kofi Annan shortly after he became the Secretary-General in 1996. Annan put the question of improving coordination and effectiveness of

34. UNGA, *Plan of Implementation of the World Summit on Sustainable Development*, A/CONF.199/20, para. 146.

international environmental institutions on the international political agenda with the release of his 1997 programme for reform titled "Renewing the United Nations". In the report, Annan makes strong statements concerning the performance of environmental institutions and the "need for a more integrated systematic approach to policies and programmes".[35] The Secretary-General prepared the report in response to the growing criticism that the UN had become a wasteful, self-serving organization where there was a lot of talk but very little action. The sentiments were shared by a number of countries, including the US, which refused to pay its arrears to the UN of over one billion dollars until the UN initiated reforms. Conscious of the pressures to improve the UN's efficiency, Annan knew that the most important task when he took office would have to be the creation of a comprehensive reform strategy – which would necessarily involve addressing environmental and sustainable development issues. For UNEP, this was a chance to reassert its importance in the international community, and with the insight of Maurice Strong behind the scenes, it began a process that has led to a strengthening of UNEP's institutional foundations to this day.

On 14 July 1997, only four months after taking office, Annan transmitted a letter to the President of the General Assembly, officially submitting the report to the General Assembly and outlining the motivation behind it. In the letter Annan states that the objective of the report was to achieve "nothing less than to transform the leadership and management structure of the Organization, enabling it to act with greater unity of purpose, coherence of efforts, and agility in responding to the many challenges it faces".[36] The Report was not only aimed at the internal management and administration of the UN system but also "intended to renew the confidence of Member States in the relevance and effectiveness of the Organization and revitalize the spirit and commitment of its staff".[37]

This renewal included UNEP. As has been noted earlier, the creation of the CSD and the emergence of the concept of sustainable development shifted policy conversations away from traditional environmental issues towards the notion of balancing environment with economic and social priorities. The Commission on Sustainable Development gave the perception of competing with UNEP and left UNEP searching to define

35. UNGA (1997) *Report of the Secretary-General: Renewing the UN, A Programme for Reform*, A/51/950 (14 July).

36. UNSG (1997) *Letter of Transmittal to President of General Assembly*, (14 July 1997) contained in *Report of the Secretary-General: Renewing the UN, A Programme for Reform*, A/51/950 (14 July).

37. Ibid.

itself in its role in implementing Agenda 21. As the UN Office of Internal Oversight Services, the auditors of UN activities, observed: "The basic issue facing UNEP concerns its role following the United Nations Conference on Environment and Development. It is not clear to staff or to stakeholders what that role should be."[38]

Until this point, UNEP was mandated to act as coordinator and focal point for environmental action within the UN system. Though sustainable development was not entirely within the scope of the environmental sector, it served to anchor environmental discussions leading up to the Rio Summit. Three major treaties emerged from Rio, the Convention on Biological Diversity, the Climate Change Convention[39] and the Desertification Convention.[40] All had been had initiated by UNEP, but the Climate Change Convention and Desertification Convention were both put under the UN Secretariat instead of UNEP. Annan's predecessor, Boutros Ghali had sent a strong signal of non-confidence when he created the new internal coordination structure for the UN system on sustainable development without a major role for UNEP. In a report to the General Assembly following Rio, Boutros-Ghali recommended the creation of a new department for implementing Agenda 21. The Department of Policy Coordination and Sustainable Development would be headed by an Under-Secretary-General to whom UNEP would report via the newly established Commission on Sustainable Development. In addition to this, two further layers of structure were also created, a high-level Advisory Board made up of 15 to 25 eminent persons from around the world to advise the Secretary-General of the follow-up to UNCED. The Board did not include the Executive Director of UNEP. Boutros-Ghali had also created a new Inter-Agency Committee on Sustainable Development that placed coordination of environmental issues outside the leadership of UNEP.[41] This last move in effect took the role of inter-agency coordination out of UNEP's hands and put into New York's.

Following the adoption of General Assembly Resolution 2997 that created UNEP, the General Assembly (GA) also created an internal mechanism by which UNEP could coordinate the rest of the UN on envi-

38. Daniel J. Shepard (1998) "Linkages between Environment Development and UN Reform", 3 *Linkages Journal*, 1–2.
39. United Nations Framework Convention on Climate Change, entered into force on 21 March 1994, 31 ILM 849 (1992) [hereinafter UNFCCC or Climate Change Convention].
40. United Nations Convention to Combat Desertification in Those Countries Experiencing Serious Drought and/or Desertification, Particularly in Africa, entered into force December 1994, UN Doc. A/AC.241/15/Rev.7, reprinted in 33 ILM 1328 (1994) [hereinafter Desertification Convention].
41. UNGA (1993) *Institutional Arrangements To Follow Up the United Nations Conference on Environment and Development*, A/CONF.47/191 (29 January).

ronmental issues. The Environment Coordinating Board (ECB) was set up under the auspices of the UN Administrative Committee on Coordination (ACC). But within only five years of its creation, the Board had "failed to live up to expectations and was abolished" by GA through Resolution 32/197 of 10 December 1977. These tasks then reverted back to the ACC. UNEP then attempted to produce a "system-wide medium-term environment programme" through lower-level meetings of Designated Officials for Environment Matters (DOEM). This system worked fairly well and became the backbone for organizing the inputs into Rio. This mechanism was later replaced in 1995 by the Inter-Agency Environment Coordination Group (IAECG).[42]

Though the IAECG functioned up until 1999, it was perceived by many as ineffective and unable to establish the authority and vision for coordination.[43] But the primary problem was that it was overshadowed by the Inter-Agency Committee on Sustainable Development (IACSD). According to Chapter 38 of Agenda 21, the IACSD was created to assist the ACC in identifying issues to follow up on UNCED.[44] It was crafted in the likeness of the DOEM, so it used a system of focal points between agencies, so-called task managers with one manager per chapter of Agenda 21. The taskforce, however, would be composed of executive heads from each relevant agency. Given the fact that Agenda 21 was a comprehensive plan covering almost every environmental issue, including cross-cutting issues and emerging issues identified at Rio, it left little room for the UNEP and the Inter-Agency Environment Coordination Group to work.

Annan's report marked the first step towards changing all this and renewing the confidence that had shaken UNEP. Written by Maurice Strong, the chairman of the Stockholm and the Rio Conferences, and the first Executive Director of UNEP, the report paid explicit attention to ensuring that UNEP was recognized as the "environmental voice" of the United Nations and the "environmental agency of the world commu-

---

42. IAECG has since been replaced with yet another attempt of coordination under a mechanism called the Environment Management Groups, see infra, chapter 3.
43. UNEP (1999) *Inter-Agency Coordination Group and System-wide Strategy in the Field of the Environment*, UNEP/GC.20/7.
44. The IACSD was a subsidiary body of the UN Administrative Coordinating Committee (ACC), a committee considered to be the "cabinet" for the Secretary-General. The IACSD was chaired by the Under-Secretary of the Department of Economic and Social Affairs and was made up of senior-level officials from nine core members of the ACC – FAO, IAEA, ILO, UNDP, UNEP, UNESCO, WHO, World Bank and WMO. Officials from other UN bodies, intergovernmental agencies and representatives from Major Groups are able to attend by invitation. The ACC and the IACSD was replaced after the review of ACC in October 2001 established the UN System Chief Executives Board (CEB).

nity".[45] The report calls for UNEP to be given the status, strength and access to resources it requires to function effectively. This support was also in accordance with the Nairobi Declaration that same year made by the UNEP Governing Council, in which it affirmed the continued relevance of UNEP, and the importance of its mandate.[46] The report briefly touches on the past rivalry between the new Rio institutions and UNEP when it states that the IACSD should not "preclude or inhibit" UNEP's role as both the IACSD and UNEP report to the General Assembly through the Economic and Social Council.[47]

Later that year the General Assembly undertook a five-year review of the outcome of the Earth Summit and adopted the Programme for the Further Implementation of Agenda 21. The Programme underscored that, given the increasing number of decision-making bodies concerned with various aspects of sustainable development, including international conventions, there is an ever greater need for better policy coordination at the intergovernmental level as well as for continued and more concerted efforts to enhance collaboration among the secretariats of those decision-making bodies.[48] At the five-year review of Agenda 21 governments stated that, "the conference of the parties to conventions signed at the United Nations Conference on Environment and Development or as a result of it, as well as other conventions related to sustainable development, should cooperate in exploring ways and means of collaborating in their work to advance the effective implementation of the conventions to continue to pursue sustainable development objectives".[49]

As part of renewing the United Nations Programme of Reform, the Secretary-General, in consultation with the Executive Director of UNEP and of UN Habitat, would make certain recommendations for strengthening and restructuring the organization to the 53rd Session of the General Assembly. To initiate the process the Secretary-General decided to create a Task Force on Environment and Human Settlements. That would work under the following terms of reference:

- To review existing structures and arrangements through which environment and environment-related activities are carried out within the United Nations, with particular reference to departments, funds and programmes that report

---

45. See UNSG (1997) *Report of the Secretary-General: Renewing the UN, A Programme for Reform*, A/51/950 para. 176.
46. See UNEP (1997) *Nairobi Declaration on the Role and Mandate of UNEP*, UNEP/GC19/1/1997 [hereinafter Nairobi Declaration].
47. See UN (1997) *Report of the Secretary-General: Renewing the UN, A Programme for Reform*, A/51/950 para. 175.
48. UNGA (1997) *Rio+5 General Assembly Special Session*, A/S-19/29 (27 June).
49. See ibid.

to the Secretary-General but also taking into account the relevant programmes and activities of the specialized agencies;

- In this respect, to focus particularly on the distinctive functions of policy, development of norms and standards, programme development and implementation, and financing, as well as relationships among those functions;
- To evaluate the efficacy and effectiveness of existing structures and arrangements, and make recommendations for such changes and improvements as will optimize the work and effectiveness of United Nations environmental work at the global level and of UNEP as the leading environmental organization or "authority", as well as the role of UNEP as the principal source of environmental input into the work of the Commission on Sustainable Development;
- To prepare proposals for consideration by the Secretary-General and subsequent submission to the General Assembly on reforming and strengthening United Nations activities in the area of environment and human settlements.[50]

This task force concluded that substantial overlaps and unrecognized linkages characterize current UN activities and gaps and that these flaws were "basic and pervasive".[51]

The task force made a number of important recommendations to the Secretary-General that the General Assembly later adopted.[52] Of particular significance was Recommendation One to establish an Environmental Management Group (EMG) and abolish the ineffective Inter-Agency Environmental Group (IAEG) and Recommendation Thirteen that suggests the establishment of "an annual ministerial-level, global forum in which ministers can gather to review and revise the environmental agenda of the United Nations in the context of sustainable development".[53] The rationale behind these recommendations was simple. The IAEG had been in place since 1995 as a successor to the DOEM and had two formal meetings, but according to the task force the need for coordination tended towards substance and not administration. It foresaw a stronger role based on an "issue management" approach, whereby once the inter-agency cooperation identified a problem it could have the capability to mobilize the right agencies and resources to tackle the problem.

50. See UN (1998) *The Report of the United Nations Task Force on Environment and Human Settlements to the Secretary-General*, annexed in the *Report of the Secretary-General: United Nations Reform – Measures and Proposals – Environment and Human Settlements*, A/53/463 (6 October).
51. Supra, *Report of the United Nations Task Force on Environment and Human Settlement* (1998).
52. See chapter 3.
53. The UN General Assembly supported this recommendation through a resolution passed on 10 August 1999.

In this regard, there was a need to create collaboration members but also to link with other organizations and financial institutions outside the UN system. The IAEG was too rigid for this purpose; it was not operationalized towards actions but rather review and information sharing.[54]

The proposal to create a high-level minister's forum, which later became the Global Ministers Environment Forum (GMEF), was directed at re-establishing the importance of UNEP and attracting ministers back to UNEP decision-making. The task force also considered the possibility of universalizing participation in the Governing Council – beyond the current 58 members. In order to do this without undermining the existing credibility of the Council established over 30 years ago, it was recommended that the ministerial meeting should have universal membership and convene every year but that in alternate years it would be in the form of the UNEP Governing Council. This proposal, however, eventually became controversial, and though the Final Report adopted by GMEF on the IEG process recommends universal membership,[55] the JPOI deferred the decision to the 57th Session of the General Assembly. The GA in turn decided the issue was a complex one and required further examination by the UNEP Governing Council, and other relevant bodies of the United Nations system, and that it would revisit the issue at its 60th session.[56]

However, the task force set in motion a major review of UNEP's role and how to strengthen environmental governance. At the first meeting of the GMEF, which took place in Sweden from 29 to 31 May, over 100 ministers adopted the Malmö Declaration that requests the WSSD to:

review the requirements for a greatly strengthened institutional structure for international environmental governance based on an assessment of future needs for an institutional architecture that has the capacity to effectively address wide-ranging environmental threats in a globalizing world. UNEP's role in this regard should be strengthened and its financial base broadened and made more predictable.[57]

---

54. Supra, *The Report of the United Nations Task Force on Environment and Human Settlements* (1998).
55. UNEP Governing Council, "International Environmental Governance", Appendix SS.VII/1, 2001, para. 11 (a).
56. UNGA (2003) *Report of the Governing Council of the United Nations Environment Programme on Its Seventh Special Session*, A/RES/57/251 (21 February), Agenda Item 87, para. 4.
57. Malmö Ministerial Declaration, Adopted by the Global Ministerial Environment Forum – Sixth Special Session of the Governing Council of the United Nations Environment Programme, Fifth Plenary Meeting, Malmö, Sweden (31 May 2000).

This clause of the Declaration was operationalized by the UNEP Governing Council Decision 21/21 on international environmental governance, which called for an open-ended intergovernmental group of ministers or their representatives on international environmental governance "to undertake a comprehensive policy-oriented assessment of existing institutional weaknesses as well as future needs and options for strengthened international environmental governance".[58]

With this mandate, the IEG group set to work on coming up with a number of recommendations for the GMEF to be fed into the WSSD. In total, six sessions took place from April 2001 until the final meeting was held in Cartagena in February 2002. The level of documentation was impressive and the group considered many possible reforms, including the upgrading of UNEP to a specialized agency, the clustering of MEAs and a means of stabilizing UNEP's financial base. From early on in the process, however, ministers and representatives agreed that the "process of strengthening international environmental governance should be evolutionary in nature" and based on an incremental approach.[59]

The final recommendations represent this cautious approach to institutional change. Clearly, countries placed a great deal of confidence in the newly established GMEF as a means to improve coherence. The basic premise behind the forum is to attract decision-makers at a high enough level so that they may have a significant impact on policy guidance and coordination with other UN entities. The balance of the CSD with the GMEF has been an issue; some analysts are concerned that the "work of the Environment Forum does not become undermined and/or paralysed by the unconstructive political dynamics which have impaired the work of the CSD, and which have dominated many recent international environmental negotiations".[60] This concern in the context of how the GMEF reports its work concerning sustainable development to the CSD in New York is an important one, especially since the CSD has been criticized for renegotiating existing commitments and could have the potential to water down the GMEF's high-level inputs.

The greatest potential for progress in coordinating environmental governance in the late 1990s was at the level of multilateral environmental agreements (MEAs). It is also the area where the results from the IEG process were far too cautious. Several years before the IEG process there

---

58. UNEP (2001) *International Environmental Governance*, Decision 21/21.
59. UNGA (2002) *International Environmental Governance: Note by Secretary-General*, A/CONF.199/PC/3, at para. 5.
60. Johannah Bernstein (2001) "Paper # 2 Analysis of UNEP Executive Director's Report on International Environmental Governance (UNEP/IGM/1/2)", *Stakeholder Forum*, Vol. 4 (May).

had been a great deal of research conducted on MEA coordination,[61] and some MEA secretariats had responded strongly to strengthening their synergies and interlinkages. The documents prepared by the UNEP secretariat clearly demonstrated the potential for collaboration in the areas of technology transfer, finance, scientific assessment, indicators, education, awareness-raising and capacity-building.[62] Despite the evidence and richness of the inputs, the recommendations by the working group merely called for a soft approach such as the "initiation of pilot projects",[63] the promotion of collaboration and more coordination in the periodicity and scheduling of meetings for MEAs. The problem that the working group faced was the question of how far they could go in suggesting reforms given the fact that most MEAs had autonomous decision-making authority. The recommendations do, however, call for UNEP to provide periodic reviews of the effectiveness of MEAs.[64] Hopefully, future UNEP Governing Council meetings can follow up on this mandate and provide a system for evaluation which includes assessing the degree of collaboration between MEAs. This type of analysis is crucial for decision-makers for strengthening individual MEAs as well as realizing a more systematic legal framework between MEAs in the future. As we will see in Chapters 7 and 8, even though some MEAs such as the International Treaty on Plant Genetic Resources for Food and Agriculture and the Convention on Biological Diversity are collaborating effectively despite the lack of clear and well-mandated systems for inter-MEA collaboration, other MEAs and their relationship with treaties outside the realm of the environment are badly in need of a more coherent governance structure for interlinkages.[65]

61. See for example *United Nations University Interlinkages Initiative*, at http://www.unu.edu/inter-linkages/; Daniel C. Esty and Maria H. Ivanova (2002) "Revitalizing International Environmental Governance: A Function-Driven Approach", in Daniel C. Esty and Maria H. Ivanova (eds) *Global Environmental Governance: Options and Opportunities*, pp. 181, 193–194, at http://www.yale.edu/environment/publications; Joy Hyvarinen and Duncan Brack (2004) *Global Environmental Institutions: Arguments for Reform*, Royal Institute of International Affairs.
62. See for example UNEP (2001) *Implementing the Clustering Strategy for Multilateral Environmental Agreements*, UNEP/IGM/4/4 (16 November).
63. UNGA (2003) *Report of the Governing Council of the United Nations Environment Programme on Its Seventh Special Session*, A/RES/57/251 (21 February), para. 27.
64. Ibid., para. 28. This has occurred informally to a certain degree, for example UNEP Division of Environmental Law and Conventions (DELC) sponsored two High-Level Meetings on *Envisioning the Next Steps for MEA Compliance and Enforcement* (Colombo and Geneva, 2006). This was known as the Colombo Process; see MEA Enforcement and Compliance Meeting Bulletin Vol. 121, No. 2 Monday, 5 June 2006, at http://www.iisd.ca/ymb/unepmea2/ymbvol121num2e.html.
65. See infra chapter 7 and chapter 8.

On 25 March 2002, the Executive Director of UNEP, on behalf of the Secretary-General, transmitted the recommendations of the IEG Working Group and the Governing Council to the third preparatory meeting of the CSD, which was acting as the preparatory committee for the World Summit on Sustainable Development (WSSD).[66]

The Johannesburg plan of implementation

Preparation for the Johannesburg Summit began in 2000 with meetings (prepcoms) carried out by the UN regional economic and social commissions and a preliminary international prepcom in New York that laid out the objectives and process of the Summit.[67] Institutional issues were first categorized under the title of "Sustainable Development Governance" but were later changed to "Institutional Framework for Sustainable Development" and taken up by Working Group IV.[68] Since UNEP's Governing Council had planned to conclude its discussions on international environmental governance later in 2002, it was decided that the working group would not deliberate until Prepcom III – after UNEP's discussions had concluded.[69]

Until this point in time, there was widespread expectation that the WSSD would produce significant institutional reforms. The in-depth assessment by UNEP and the ministerial-level contributions to the IEG process, coupled with the considerable criticism of overlap between UNEP and CSD and the calls for an international organization for environment and sustainable development, led many to be optimistic. In addition, it was well known that many European countries such as France and Germany were pushing quietly for UNEP to be upgraded to a specialized agency.

66. UNGA (2003) *Report of the Governing Council of the United Nations Environment Programme on Its Seventh Special Session*, A/RES/57/251.
67. See UNGA (2001) *Ten-Year Review of Progress Achieved in the Implementation of the Outcome of the United Nations Conference on Environment and Development*, A/RES/ 55/199 (2001). Also see ECOSOC (2001) *Secretary-General Report on the Progress in Preparatory Activities at the Local, National, Subregional, Regional and International Levels, as Well as By Major Groups*, E/CN.17/2001/PC/23.
68. UNGA (2002) *Report of the Commission on Sustainable Development Acting as the Preparatory Committee for the World Summit on Sustainable Development Third Session*, A/CONF.199/PC/14.
69. UNGA (2002) *Report of the Commission on Sustainable Development Acting as the Preparatory Committee for the World Summit on Sustainable Development Second Session*, A/CONF.199/PC/2.

Despite the forces in place pushing for institutional reform, pressure from development agencies and from countries not wishing to allow the UN to gain control over bodies like the WTO had considerable impact in blocking progress towards reform. The first volley against changes to the status quo came from Nitin Desai, Secretary-General of the Summit and head of CSD in his opening speech to Prepcom III. His job was to advise the governments on the priority areas and the organization of work for the meeting but his comments went much further. In introducing the agenda item on sustainable development governance, Desai stated frankly that the CSD had been the "centrepiece" for sustainable development governance for the last decade. He further asserted that it was largely an "innovative organization" that had made significant achievements such as attracting non-environment ministers to its deliberations, engaging "a high-level interest from capitals", attracting many stakeholders through its dialogues, and developing a "strong inter-agency process [to] guid[e] it". He conceded that the CSD had weaknesses, such as not generating "sufficient pressure for effective implementation", but stated the partnership initiative launched by the Johannesburg preparatory committee would likely address this shortcoming. He also mentioned the need to connect better to the regional level, which he believed that CSD could achieve through working with regional organizations to create stronger regional processes.[70]

These observations, though perhaps accurate, presumed that the CSD should continue its role of coordinating sustainable development governance. Nowhere in the discussion was there an independent review of the institutional effectiveness of the CSD, nor a formal information paper for governments on how it might be strengthened. This was an obvious omission given that the CSD was created as a result of the previous summit 10 years earlier and that governments were about to be asked again to deliberate on institutional questions concerning sustainable development governance. It is unclear if this lack of independent analysis was an intentional omission or rather the result of international organizations trying to protect themselves during a time of scrutiny and potential criticism. Thirty years earlier, at Stockholm, Maurice Strong avoided any conflict of interest by using an independent secretariat. Perhaps this is an approach to reconsider for future summits.

The discussion paper put out by the co-chairs of Working Group IV placed the existing organizations (CSD, ECOSOC and GA) at the heart

---

70. Opening Remarks, Mr Nitin Desai, Secretary-General for World Summit on Sustainable Development, Third Preparatory Committee for the World Summit on Sustainable Development, 25 March 2002.

of the framework for sustainable development governance and any deliberations the working group would make.[71] This arrangement stuck and remained the general structure of the final section within the Johannesburg Plan of Implementation (JPOI).[72] The paper raised three main dimensions of coordination, which were based on the Secretary-General's report on implementing Agenda 21, prior discussions at the second Prepcom and informal discussions that were held in New York. The first related to potential new roles for the CSD, ECOSOC and GA in strengthening sustainable development governance,[73] the second to the coordination of regional institutions, and the third and by far the most controversial concerned how to "provide for effective policy formulation, coordination, implementation and review" as well as "coherence and consistency"[74] between the economic, environmental and social sectors.

Though these aims raise the right kinds of questions, the outcome of the JPOI is disappointing. It offers very few changes from the status quo and certainly nothing imaginative for a future vision of effective institutional arrangements.[75] Earlier drafts of the JPOI had sought to address the coordination between the pillars; in particular the Bali draft proposes the creation of a new "inter-agency coordination body on sustainable development to ensure effective coordination between international agencies in the follow-up to the Johannesburg Summit outcomes and which would include the principal UN agencies dealing with sustainable development, the international financial institutions and the WTO and which would report to the CSD".[76] Paragraph 10 also calls for a strategic partnership "formed at the highest level, between agencies and organizations of the UN system, international financial institutions and the WTO". The references to the coordination of the WTO, however, became a sticking point in the negotiations. The final language of the JPOI is intentionally ambiguous and leaves unresolved the questions of the re-

---

71. See paras. 11, 12 and 18, "Sustainable Development Governance at the International, Regional and National Levels: Discussion Paper Prepared by the Vice-Chairs Mr Ositadinma Anaedu and Mr Lars-Goran Engfeldt for Consideration at Third Session of the Preparatory Committee for WSSD", Prepcom III, 25 March 2002 [hereinafter Prepcom Discussion Paper].
72. Johannesburg Plan of Implementation [hereinafter JPOI] UNGA (2002) *Report of the World Summit on Sustainable Development*, A/CONF.199/20, see paras 137–170.
73. "Prepcom Discussion Paper", para. 1.
74. "Prepcom Discussion Paper", para. 3.
75. Nicolas A. Robinson (2002) "Befogged Vision: International Environmental Governance a Decade After Rio", 27 *William and Mary Environmental Law and Policy Review*, 339.
76. "Prepcom Discussion Paper", para. 14.

lationship of the WTO to the follow-up to Agenda 21 and achieving the goal of sustainable development.[77]

The objectives for strengthening governance laid out in the JPOI include "strengthening coherence, coordination and monitoring", "increasing effectiveness and efficiency through limiting overlap and duplication of activities of international organizations" and integrating "the economic, social and environmental dimensions of sustainable development in a balanced manner".[78] These are all important priorities but the plan proposes no new concrete actions. The JPOI places the future of the sustainable development governance in the hands of the existing institutional framework. At the top of the hierarchy in the JPOI plan is the General Assembly, which should be the overarching key element for achieving sustainable development and providing the political direction to implement Agenda 21. It is already placed to perform these tasks.[79]

The ECOSOC will continue to be the key coordination mechanism of the UN system but it should strengthen its oversight for integrating the three pillars of sustainable development, "make full use of its high-level coordination" abilities, promote greater coordination, provide closer links to the follow-up of WSSD to the Monterrey Process, and explore ways to "develop arrangements for meeting with the Bretton Woods Institutions and WTO".[80] In no way does the JPOI explains how ECOSOC should go about achieving these goals. As early as 1970, ECOSOC had been criticized for its lack of coordination in the field of environment.[81] In 1992, Chapter 38 of Agenda 21 already clearly designated ECOSOC to "undertake the task of directing system-wide coordination and integration of environmental and developmental aspects of United Nations policies and programmes" as well as "system-wide activities to integrate environment and development, making full use of its high-level and coordination segments".[82] Given its inability to fulfil this function over the last 30 years, and since it has not been provided any further power to

77. See coordination provisions referring to the WTO in the JPOI in paragraphs 84(d), 91 and 91(c).
78. UNGA (2002) *Report of WSSD and Plan of Action, Reissued Text*, A/CON.99/20, para. 137, available at http://www.johannesburgsummit.org/html/documents/summit_docs/131302_wssd_report.
79. Ibid.
80. See *Report of WSSD and Plan of Action, Reissued Text*, para. 144.
81. See the Stanley Foundation (1971) "Sixth Conference of the United Nations of the Next Decade", *Stanley Foundation*, Sinaia, Romania, 20–26 June, p. 20.
82. "Agenda 21, UN Conference on Environment and Development", A/CONF.151/26/Rev.1 (1992), Chapter 38, para. 10. Also see infra, Chapter 3.

operationalize these provisions, there is no reason to believe that the ECOSOC will ever realize the goals outlined in these short paragraphs.[83]

The JPOI does, however, place most of its emphasis for achieving the above objectives on what it phrases an "enhanced" CSD.[84] According to the JPOI, the CSD should continue to play its role as a "high-level commission for sustainable development within the United Nations system and serve as a forum for consideration of issues related to integration of the three dimensions of sustainable development".[85] However, an enhanced CSD should amend its approach to include "reviewing and monitoring progress in the implementation of Agenda 21", which is already part of its mandate, as well as "fostering coherence of implementation, initiatives and partnerships", which will be a new role given to the partnership initiative coming out of WSSD.[86] In addition, the JPOI states that the CSD should place more emphasis on action and implementation with "governments, international organizations and relevant stakeholders" and in terms of coordination it will *inter alia*:

- focus on the cross-sectoral aspects of specific sectoral issues and provide a forum for better integration of policies, including through interaction among Ministers dealing with the various dimensions and sectors of sustainable development through the high-level segments;
- focus on actions related to implementation of Agenda 21, limiting negotiations in the sessions of the Commission to every two years;
- limit the number of themes addressed in each session;
- take into account significant legal developments in the field of sustainable development, with due regard to the role of relevant intergovernmental bodies in promoting the implementation of Agenda 21 relating to international legal instruments and mechanisms.[87]

At the eleventh session of the CSD, the details of implementing these new components were negotiated. The result was the creation of a new two-year work cycle, which will include an "implementation" session and a "policy" session. Delegates will only negotiate in the second year of the cycle. After a long and divided debate, a 15-year programme was agreed upon. The initial session (the first meeting of which took place in April 2004) focuses on water, sanitation and human settlements (2004–2005); followed by energy, industrial development, air pollution

83. Infra, chapter 3.
84. JPOI, at 67.
85. JPOI, at 68.
86. Ibid.
87. Tom Bigg (2003) "The World Summit on Sustainable Development", *International Institute of Environment and Development*, Vol. 15.

and climate change (2006–2007). An overall appraisal of Agenda 21 will be undertaken in 2016–2017.[88] It was agreed that cross-cutting issues should be considered in every work cycle using most of the JPOI-agreed sections of poverty, unsustainable consumption and production patterns, protecting and managing the natural resource base and so on. The Type II Partnerships would be followed up with a voluntary reporting system and a learning/partnership fair that will serve to build awareness and disseminate these activities.[89]

With these reforms in place the future effectiveness of CSD clearly depends on its ability to add value to the international institutional arrangements for sustainable development by dealing with the substance that links the environment to economic and social development. If it can make these connections and produce results, then the confidence that the countries placed in it at the Johannesburg summit will not be lost.

Conclusion

The historical analysis presented here suggests that coordination and institutional needs for environment and sustainable development issues have changed according to the three periods demarcated by the Stockholm, Rio and Johannesburg Summits. Despite the shortcomings of the current institutional framework for sustainable development, and the missed opportunities at each of the summits, these changes indicate that states have recognized political and environmental changes and have tried – with some measure of success – to adapt to them. Today the institutional landscape has become so complex that it is no longer sufficient to think of addressing coordination and institutional arrangements through a singular approach, such as creating a World Environment Organization. However, to heed the cautionary words of the Stockholm, Rio and Johannesburg Summits and avoid major reforms in favour of an incremental approach has also produced far too few results.

Future improvements to sustainable development governance must focus on a number of institutions and varying levels of coordination. First and foremost, institutions within the environmental sector must be strengthened. The environment pillar of sustainable development is clearly the weakest. Despite the rhetoric and the Band-Aid solutions, there is still too much overlap between the CSD and UNEP. CSD must clearly forget the sectoral elements that it has clung to the last 10 years and focus on cross-cutting issues such as poverty, trade, health,

88. Ibid., 15.
89. Ibid.

education, finance and capacity-building. If strengthened, UNEP would be adequately equipped to bring to the CSD's intergovernmental forum the sectoral elements just as the economic institutions (WTO, Bretton Woods) and social institutions (World Health Organization, International Labour Organization) would respectively bring their own sectoral interests. Thus, the CSD could be the forum on sustainable development that was originally intended.

Within the environment sector, UNEP also has many opportunities to strengthen cooperation between MEAs. Though not originally mandated to be the legal umbrella for MEAs, UNEP has evolved into this role and in fact has performed it very well.[90] It must now progress to the next stage and, like GATT, think of creating a closer network for the MEAs to regularize cooperation, strengthen dispute settlement and codify principles. The modest suggestion made by the JPOI concerning clustering could be strengthened and lead to an overarching institutional structure if the political will existed.[91]

Intersectoral coordination for sustainable development governance is by far the greatest institutional challenge. There has been a consistent reluctance on the part of certain developed countries to bring organizations outside the UN, like the WTO, into the sustainable development fold. It is obvious that ECOSOC cannot rise to this task. Its ineffectiveness was notorious long before Stockholm, yet because it is a principal organ of the UN, there is a strong reluctance to amend the UN Charter, and so this piece of the institutional framework remains a problem. It is equally obvious from the Rio and Johannesburg summits that the most powerful countries will never allow the Bretton Woods Institutions and the WTO to be controlled by the UN. Some middle-ground solution must be found, such as a new mechanism where countries would be willing to discuss coordination. For the reason that intersectoral coordination of the dimensions of sustainable development is so important the case presented in Chapter 7 will explore this element in the context of treaties between the sector of environment and that of economics.

Finally, the implementation of intersectoral projects present real coordination challenges. Environment and sustainable development issues

---

90. See Adede, *Renewing International Environmental Governance*. An example of UNEP contribution to strengthening cooperation among MEAs has been its work in the chemicals area. See *UNEP Guide to Cooperation on the Basel, Rotterdam and Stockholm Conventions*, and the recent Open-ended Working Group of the Basel Convention on Synergies Among the Chemical Conventions at UNEP/CHW/OEWG//INF/18 (2006).

91. See chapter 3 for a discussion of some institutional reforms and the possibility of using principles such as clustering and organizational models based on the International Maritime Organization, International Labour Organization or the World Trade Organization.

have both been relegated to makeshift, ad hoc institutional arrangements because of their cross-cutting, multidisciplinary nature. As such, neither UNEP nor CSD have implementation arms at the national level. Rather, they must rely on institutions that are working on issues that have an environment-sustainable development dimension to carry out projects and activities.

To have a truly effective sustainable development regime, UNEP, the CSD and other institutions must be endowed with genuine implementation capacity, as well as compatibility at the national level and regional levels. This can only be achieved through deeper reforms than those that have been experienced to date in global summits. The remainder of this book looks at how legal instruments (a major pillar of the overall institutional framework for environment and sustainable development) might be improved through greater interlinkages and synergies.

The next chapter will narrow the focus of coordination to look more closely at MEAs themselves in the context of coordination. Whereas the present chapter has taken a historical look at coordination from a broad point of view, Chapter 3 will look more closely at what current legal and institutional mechanisms are in place to create interlinkages between MEAs, including the law of treaties and possible organizational reforms.

Part III

The legal milieu of interlinkages under international law

3

Legal mechanisms and coordination systems for promoting and managing interlinkages between multilateral environmental agreements

Introduction

In chapter 2 we took a historical look at the processes and initiatives over the course of the last three decades of environmental and sustainable development law and policy-making. I characterized this process as evolutionary in many ways – a process that developed out of a need for environmental protection and a balance between economic and social development. The process laid the foundations for the current system of environmental governance, which is now diffuse and, at times, reactive to the mounting environmental concerns. However, at the same time the processes and the systems themselves could be viewed as practical and aimed at strategically evading the need for heavy institutional barriers and for creating new fully fledged international organizations. To other observers the system could be viewed as progressive and, in spite of its complexities, it has become a model that pushes towards the outer reaches of organizational design, emerging as international and institutional law. No matter how it is viewed, diffuse or innovative, as a system it is sometimes opaque and difficult to navigate and understand. I will argue that this is particularly the case when attempting to understand the international legal personality of multilateral environmental agreements (MEAs), their relationship with their umbrella organizations and their legal relationship with one another. Consequently, it is the structure and institutional organization itself that has been a major factor in leading to

Interlinkages and the effectiveness of multilateral environmental agreements,
W. Bradnee Chambers, United Nations University Press, 2008, ISBN 978-92-808-1149-0

ineffectiveness and missed opportunities to create a coherent body of international environmental law.

MEAs cooperate in several ways and are governed by several modes of informal and formal rules. The Vienna Convention on the Law of Treaties (VCLT) regulates treaty compatibility to avoid conflicts of succeeding treaties. Internally within the world of environmental organizations, the UN system plays a major role attempting to coordinate and promote cooperation between MEAs and their corresponding institutional set ups. Externally, MEAs cooperate and coordinate their activities by entering into formal agreements with other MEAs and international organizations. The ability to enter into such agreements depends largely on their legal personality and the powers that have been bestowed on the MEA secretariats and bodies by their member states. There have been increasing arguments in the international legal literature that MEAs may, as international organizations, possess legal standing and personality through the doctrine of "implied powers".

The analysis of this chapter will show that the modes of cooperation between MEAs are tenuous and lack a strong model to guide cooperation and coordination with greater certainty. Given the fragmentation and diffusion within the international environmental treaty system, increasingly convincing arguments have been made as to how MEAs could be strengthened through improved institutional structures. This chapter offers some of these models and discusses which ones might make more sense than others.

The purpose of this chapter in the context of this book is to serve as a legal background to how MEAs operate, since this is not a well-known area of international law, and to demonstrate where the gaps are in the current governance structure. These will be addressed with reference to two case studies in Chapters 6 and 7 together with the question of how the potential interlinkages can be realized and also the existing ones enhanced.

The greater legal environment in which MEAs operate

When taken alone, in other words without considering their internal, supervisory organizations, treaties are governed by the 1969 Vienna Convention on the Law of Treaties.[1] This raises a preliminary question whether MEAs are considered treaties within the scope of the VCLT.

---

1. Vienna Convention on the Law of Treaties, opened for signature 23 May 1969, 1155 UNTS 331 (entered into force 27 January 1980) [hereinafter VCLT].

An MEA can be defined as a legally binding agreement between multiple states. MEAs generally involve a commitment to alter state behaviour in some way or form, for example, to reduce emissions or cease activities that degrade the environment. They could also agree to create programmes of actions or commit domestic or international funding to improve or promote actions for environmental betterment. Considering these characteristics, MEAs fit easily into the universally accepted definition of a treaty set out by the Vienna Convention on the Law of Treaties; a treaty is as an "international agreement concluded between States in written form and governed by international law, whether embodied in a single instrument or in two or more related instruments and whatever its particular designation".[2] MEAs also fit easily into what most domestic law considers as treaties. For example, the US Department of State has defined a treaty as "an undertaking between two states which legally binds the parties and an intent is clearly demonstrated by the parties to be governed by its terms".[3] "[It] may require a commitment of funds and a continuing or substantial cooperation in the conduct of a particular programme. The form is inconsequential if the agreement meets any of the other criteria set out in the administrative regulations of the Department of State."[4]

If MEAs are indeed considered as treaties this means that determining the interrelationship of MEAs requires the understanding of the elements of treaty succession under the VCLT, *lex specialis* and the interpretation of treaties in light of specific reference to other treaties.

Succession and Article 30

The VCLT provisions on the relationship of successive treaties were created in anticipation of the need to codify a system under public international law that could manage the development of new treaties that might overlap with older ones or replace treaty provisions that have been renegotiated, clarified or strengthened in succeeding treaties.[5] However, the Vienna Convention is of a general nature and cannot provide a panacea for the kind of problems which might arise at the juncture of competing areas of international law or due to the proliferation of treaties that has occurred over the last 30 years.[6]

2. Ibid.
3. See US Regulation, 22 CFR § 181.1 (1993).
4. Erwin C. Surrency (1993) *How the United States Perfects International Treaties*, 85 Law Libr. J., 343.
5. See for example Ian Sinclair (1984) *The Vienna Convention on the Law of Treaties*, 2nd ed., Manchester, UK: Manchester University Press.
6. Ibid., 98.

Article 30 is the specific provision of the Vienna Convention that directly refers to treaty compatibility. The article, however, stipulates rules only for treaties that have the same common subject matter. This raises the question of whether the principles therein can actually be applied to treaties that have clearly different purposes or that are of a cross-cutting nature, such as those concerning trade and environment respectively or treaties controlling different aspects of the environment. If this fundamental question is put aside for a moment, and an assumption is made that the treaties in question fall into the same subject matter since there are many areas that are inseparable from one another, then the provisions set out by Article 30 are directly pertinent and would have the following determinations.

First, if a treaty establishes a subordinate relationship to another treaty within its text, then the other treaty will take precedence. Second, if all the parties to an earlier treaty ratify a new treaty, the common provisions of the two treaties will have precedence over the other provisions but, according to *lex posterior derogat priori*, the uncommon provisions will remain in force. Third, for new treaties which do not include all the original parties, the rule is also commonsensical. The parties that have ratified the new treaty are bound by it over the former treaty, while the parties that did not ratify it remain bound by the original treaty. Thus, the provisions of Article 30 of the Vienna Convention could be considered as a basis for establishing rules or principles of compatibility or balance between competing treaties. However, the parties to the Vienna Convention still have much to consider in light of the difficult questions emerging from the conflicts which are now occurring at the interfaces of competing bodies of international law. These have been called "the hard cases", where either the time of consent to the treaty by the party is difficult to pinpoint or the nature of the conflict is unclear and not outrightly identifiable.[7]

One of the intents of Article 30 is to clarify the rights and responsibilities that accrue to nations that ratify successive treaties with related subject matter in order that parties with multiple memberships in international agreements may be capable of interpreting the interactive effect and implications of these agreements on the basis of a full knowledge of the issues involved in their overlaps, gaps, conflicts, contradictions and so on.

Unfortunately, in practice, this is far from the reality. National and international agendas for multilateral political negotiations have become overwhelmed with the number and the range of international treaties,

---

7. Joost Pauwelyn (2001) *Role of Public International Law in the WTO: How Far Can We Go?* 95 AJIL, 535.

agreements and unsettled disputes. Often, because of the complexity of the issues and the lugubrious nature of the international legislative process, treaties are negotiated by specialized ministries or by functional organizations in relative isolation. This, of course, leads to treaties whose normative assumptions, principles or provisions incidentally overlap those of other treaties, in either complementary or conflicting fashion. The conflicts between treaties and agreements may be small or large, simple or complex.

Article 30 seems merely rudimentary in light of the practical demands for a more comprehensive and sophisticated framework for the construction and interpretation of international law. Moreover, if the remarks of Ian Sinclair, one of the original negotiators and recorders of the *travail préparatoire* of Article 30, are correct and the *inter se* agreement is decided by date of adoption not that of its entry into force,[8] then the implications could be far-reaching. For example, many agreements on trade, such as the Technical Barrier to Trade Agreement[9] or the WTO Agreement itself, could be interpreted as having precedence over the 1992 United Nations Framework Convention on Climate Change,[10] but its subsequent 1997 Kyoto Protocol would prevail over these WTO agreements.

Some legal experts have disagreed that such a hard and fast rule is possible under the modern regime of treaty-making.[11] Joost Pauwelyn has argued for example that "it would be absurd and inconsistent with the genuine will of states to 'freeze' such rules into the mould of the time". He states that treaties are "continuously confirmed, implemented, adapted, and expanded, for example, by means of judicial decisions, interpretations, new norms, and the accession of new states".[12] Consequently, he argues that no successive treaties exist, only "continuing treaties", and that the only way to resolve conflicts between treaties is to examine the intention of the parties *ratione materiae* or *ratione personae*.[13]

Pawelyn's viewpoint is consistent with the presumption of conflict avoidance under international law. Parties to overlapping treaties would not have deliberately intended for them to exist in conflict and in the event of an unintended conflict it would seem logical that the countries that signed the treaties would in good faith seek to have such a conflict resolved in accordance with their intent. This rationale is clear, for

8. Supra, I. M. Sinclair, 68.
9. Technical Barrier to Trade Agreement, see supra WTO Agreement, Annex One.
10. Infra, Climate Change Convention.
11. Supra, Pauwelyn, 548.
12. Ibid., 545.
13. Ibid.

example, in *US – Section 110(5) Copyright Act*, where the WTO Panel emphasized the need, in the light of general principles of interpretation, to harmoniously interpret provisions of the TRIPS Agreement with that of the 1971 Berne Convention:

> In the area of copyright, the Berne Convention and the TRIPS Agreement form the overall framework for multilateral protection. Most WTO Members are also parties to the Berne Convention. We recall that it is a general principle of interpretation to adopt the meaning that reconciles the texts of different treaties and avoids a conflict between them. Accordingly, one should avoid interpreting the TRIPS Agreement to mean something different than the Berne Convention except where this is explicitly provided for. This principle is in conformity with the public international law presumption against conflicts, which has been applied by WTO panels and the Appellate Body in a number of cases. We believe that our interpretation of the legal status of the minor exceptions doctrine under the TRIPS Agreement is consistent with these general principles.[14]

Lex specialis

Lex specialis is one tool at the disposal of international lawyers that can assist them to determine the original intention of the parties to a treaty. *Lex specialis* is a long-standing and widely accepted principle; it holds that *generalia specialibus non derogant* (general things do not derogate from special things).[15] The maxim dictates that, in determining the relationship between two treaties that are directly related, the specific clause should prevail over the general clause.[16] As the International Law Commission's Study Group on Treaty Fragmentation has observed, the *lex specialis* rule is sensible as such rules "have greater clarity and definiteness and are thus often felt 'harder' or more 'binding' than general rules which may stay in the background and be applied only rarely".[17] A major difficulty in employing the *lex specialis* maxim is in determining

---

14. Panel Report on US – Section 110(5) Copyright Act, para. 6.70.
15. ILC (2006) A/CN.4/L.682 *Fragmentation of International Law Difficulties Arising from the Diversification and Expansion of International Law: International Law Commission Study Group on Fragmentation*, finalized by Martti Koskenniemi, at 36.
16. ICJ (1996) *Nuclear Weapons Case*, at 240. "The Court observes that the protection of the International Covenant of Civil and Political Rights does not cease in times of war. … Respect for the right to life is not, however, such a provision. In principle, the right not arbitrarily to be deprived of one's life applies also in hostilities. The test of what is an arbitrary deprivation of life, however, then falls to be determined by the applicable *lex specialis*, namely, the law applicable in armed conflict which is designed to regulate the conduct of hostilities."
17. Ibid.

when a rule is specific and when it is general. For every specific rule in international law also contributes broadly to the general corpus of international law at the same time.[18]

A test often employed to overcome this interpretational problem between *lex specialis* and *lex generalis* is the application of the law to the subject matter. Subject matter is generally held to refer to a specific right, jurisdictional territory, an exception to general international law, or a reference to the object governed by the law in question. In determining the subject matter the intention of the parties is paramount and requires a careful examination of the parties' intention concerning the subject matter.[19]

The same subject matter can be better understood from the perspective of self-contained regimes; these are special sets of rules agreed by states to govern an explicit subject matter. These rules clearly prescribe the area to which they apply and the rules are often clustered around custom-tailored institutions.[20] Examples of such regimes include diplomatic and international organizations law, international human rights law, international humanitarian law, and WTO rules and agreements.[21] Self-contained regimes, however, are not completely isolated from general international law and must still be interpreted with the background of general international law, particularly instances where the regimes are silent on a specific matter.[22] In *US – Hot Rolled Steel* the WTO Appellate Body determined, in interpreting Article 17.6(ii) of the Anti-Dumping Agreement, which states "the agreement shall be interpreted in accordance with customary rules of interpretation", to refer to the relevant rules of interpretation under the VCLT Article 32.[23] As the ILC has stated, general international law is particularly important for the interpretation of self-contained regimes where the rules of the regimes fail to function properly. For example, if a non-compliance mechanism in an MEA failed to bring a violator into compliance, in such instances international rules of state responsibility and other relevant rules for the settlement of disputes would come into operation.[24]

---

18. Ibid.
19. Tunisia v. Libya (1982) *The Continental Shelf*, 38 ICJ Reports, para. 24.
20. Op. cit. A/CN.4/L.682 *Fragmentation of International Law*, pp. 66–67.
21. Pemmaraju Sreenivasa Rao (2004) *Multiple International Judicial Forums: A Reflection of the Growing Strength of International Law or its Fragmentation?*, 25 Mich. J. Int'l L., 933.
22. Op. cit. A/CN.4/L.682 *Fragmentation of International Law*, paras. 159–185.
23. Appellate Body Report on *US – Hot Rolled Steel*, para. 57. See also Panel Report on *US – Steel Plate*, para. 7.7.
24. Martti Koskenniemi (2006) *Fragmentation of International Law Difficulties: International Law Commission Study Group on Fragmentation*, available at http://untreaty.un.org/ilc/sessions/55/fragmentation_outline.pdf, 10.

Savings clauses and other demarcation techniques

With the advent of treaty proliferation in recent years, negotiating parties have increasingly turned to what is referred to as "savings clauses" in international treaties, which attempt to provide general guidance for the application of *lex specialis* and other rules of international law. However, increasingly these clauses have led to more ambiguity as many recent treaties have attempted to reflect the political undercurrents between conflicting interests of groups influencing the treaty negotiations.[25] Take, for example, the savings clause in the Cartagena Protocol on Biosafety:

- *Recognizing* that trade and environment agreements should be mutually supportive with a view to achieving sustainable development;
- *Emphasizing* that this Protocol shall not be interpreted as implying a change in the rights and obligations of a Party under any existing international agreements;
- *Understanding* that the above recital is not intended to subordinate this Protocol to other International agreements.[26]

In the first sentence of this preambular provision it states that there should be no problems with other agreements such as those under the WTO and, in fact, that they are "mutually supportive" and that the Protocol does not change "the rights and obligations" under any other international agreement. But in the subsequent sentence the Protocol states, in what many see as a contrary statement, that the Protocol should not be subordinate to any other agreements. So which is correct, "supportive" or "subordinate"? Legal experts are divided on whether a conflict exists and the problem has spurred much academic literature and

---

25. First used in the 1976 Barcelona Convention for the Protection of the Mediterranean Sea against Pollution (1102 UNTS 27), Art. 3(2) states "nothing in this Convention shall prejudice the codification and development of the Law of the Sea by the United Nations Conference on the Law of the Sea". Also see early use in the preamble of the Rotterdam Convention on the Prior Informed Consent Procedure for Certain Hazardous Chemicals and Pesticides in International Trade, opened for signature on 11 September 1998, UNEP/CHEMICALS/98/17. It states: "Emphasizing that nothing in this Convention shall be interpreted as implying in any way a change in the rights and obligations of a Party under any existing international agreement applying to chemicals in international trade or to environmental protection, Understanding that the above recital is not intended to create a hierarchy between this Convention and other international agreements".
26. See Preamble of Cartagena Protocol on Biosafety to the Convention on Biological Diversity (2000) 39 ILM [hereinafter Biosafety Protocol], 1027.

debate.[27] Interpretive guidelines from each respective governing body could greatly alleviate the ambiguity and ensure a coordinated approach. However, the organizational dynamics do not lend themselves to this kind of coordination as there is no overarching authority between the WTO and the Cartagena Protocol and no political will to create guidelines that are not mutually recognized. As a result, the relationship remains unclear until a legal dispute arises that could settle the matter.

Some treaties, whose negotiators were perhaps more aware of the difficulties of determining the *generalia specialibus non derogant* principle in Article 30, have used express references to define their subject and specificity. The CBD, for example, under Article 22.1, states its subject area in relation to other instruments to be only related to threats to biological diversity:

> The provisions of this Convention shall not affect the rights and obligations of any Contracting Party deriving from any existing international agreement, except where the exercise of those rights and obligations would cause a serious damage or threat to biological diversity.

Still other treaties, acutely aware of the ability to modify or suspend existing agreements with *inter se* agreements under Article 41 and Article 58 of the VCLT, have made specific reference in the treaty that prohibits future derogation. Under Article 41 *inter se* agreements are permissible on the same subject matter if there is no express reference in the treaty prohibiting this, if the *inter se agreement* does not alter the object and purpose of the original agreement or if the *inter se agreement* does not affect the rights or obligations of third parties.[28] Article 58 provides similar provisions to Article 41 in regard to suspending the operation of treaties.[29] Treaties that expressly prohibit or limit the derogation of *inter se* agreements are what Pauwleyn describes as "integral" or "collective" agreements because the agreement creates benefits for all countries as a

---

27. See for example Duncan Brack, Robert Falkner and Judith Goll (2003) *The Next Trade War? GM Products, the Cartagena Protocol and the WTO*, Briefing Paper No. 8, London: Royal Institute of International Affairs; Grant E. Isaac (2004) *The SPS Agreement and Agri-food Trade Disputes: The Final Frontier*, Journal of International Law and Trade Policy, 43; Barbara Eggers & Ruth Mackenzie (2003) *The Cartagena Protocol on Biosafety*, 3 JIEL, 3; and Gilbert R. Winham (2003) *International Regime Conflict in Trade and Environment: The Biosafety Protocol and the WTO*, 2 World Trade Review, 131–155.
28. Article 41 VCLT.
29. Article 58 VCLT.

collective and derogating from the collective benefit would result in diminishing the benefits for the whole collective.[30]

As Professor Alan Boyle has observed, Article 331 of the UNCLOS represents a treaty where this technique is particularly evident.[31] Article 331.1 allows for *inter se* agreements as far as they are compatible with the Convention and "do not affect the enjoyment by other States Parties of their rights or the performance of their obligations under this Convention".[32] Article 331.2 allows parties to enter into *inter se agreements* that modify or suspend the operation of the Convention between them so long as the agreement does not alter the rights and obligations of other parties or performance of the Convention.[33] Article 331.5 restricts any *inter se* agreements that are expressly preserved or permitted by the Convention and prescribes any amendment or derogation from the common heritage of mankind principle set forth in Article 136.[34] Given the comprehensive nature of Article 331 it is quite clear the parties' intent was to create a collective treaty system that could prevail over any future treaty attempting to contract out of the collective arrangements prescribed in the UNCLOS.[35]

The most useful type of arrangement which makes for legal certainty and predictability is explicit cross-referencing and this has been employed in several MEAs and related treaties. As Jacob Werksman has observed, this type of arrangement is generally used to demarcate a particular jurisdiction or a substance or activity that is regulated by one MEA and could potentially interact with those regulated by another.[36] The best known case of this type of provision is between the UNFCCC and the Ozone Convention in which the UNFCCC distinguishes greenhouse gases, as used in the Convention, as not including ozone-depleting substances covered in the Ozone Convention.[37] Other treaties that make explicit cross-referencing to the subject matter thus establishing their jurisdiction with greater certainty include the Rotterdam Convention on the Prior Informed Consent Procedure for Certain Hazardous

30. Joost Pauwelyn (2003) *A Typology of Multilateral Treaty Obligations: Are WTO Obligations Bilateral or Collective in Nature?* 14 EJIL, 915.
31. Alan Boyle and Christine Chinkin (2007) *The Making of International Law*, Oxford: Oxford University Press, Section 4.5.
32. Article 311.1 UNCLOS.
33. Article 331.2 UNCLOS.
34. Article 331.5 and Article 331.6 UNCLOS.
35. Op cit. Boyle and Chinkin, *The Making of International Law*.
36. See Jacob Werksman (1999) *Formal Linkages and MEAs*, background paper prepared for the International Conference on Synergies and Coordination of MEAs, Tokyo, 3.
37. UNFCCC, Preamble; Art. 4.; (a)–(d); 4.2 (b); Kyoto Protocol, Art. 2.1(a)(ii).

Chemicals and Pesticides in International Trade. Under Article 3.2, it expressly carves out narcotics and psychotropic substances, radioactive materials, wastes and food, all of which have international treaties.[38] The 1989 Basel Convention on the Control of Transboundary Movements of Hazardous Wastes and their Disposal eliminates from its jurisdiction "wastes which, as a result of being radioactive, are subject to other international control systems, including international instruments".[39]

Another helpful practice is to use cross-referencing to construct treaties that build additions to existing treaties, or use existing treaties as substructures. In the end the treaties are linked in a kind of architecture that requires the treaties to be read and interpreted together. For example, agreements such as the Sanitary and Phytosanitary Agreement actually create a bridge with other agreements by recognizing standards in such agreements (e.g., Codex Alimentarius and the International Plant Convention). Instead of creating new rules, the TRIPS Agreement essentially brings a dispute settlement mechanism to the existing well-established intellectual property agreements such as the Berne and Paris Conventions and the existing international intellectual property regime.[40] The North American Free Trade Agreement has a similar recognition system for establishing which treaties it recognizes as explicit exceptions to NAFTA's rules.[41]

Evolutionary interpretation

The discussion of *lex specialis* brings us to another point that still requires much more study under international law and in many way shares the

38. Rotterdam Convention, Art. 3.2.
39. Basel Convention Article 1.3.
40. See chapter 7.
41. North American Free Trade Agreement 32 ILM (1993), 289 and 605. Article 104 lists five agreements that will have precedence over NAFTA in the event of a dispute. These are the Convention on International Trade in Endangered Species of Wild Fauna and Flora, done at Washington, 3 March 1973, as amended 22 June 1979; Montreal Protocol on Substances that Deplete the Ozone Layer, done at Montreal, 16 September 1987, as amended 29 June 1990; Basel Convention on the Control of Transboundary Movements of Hazardous Wastes and Their Disposal, done at Basel, 22 March 1989, on its entry into force for Canada, Mexico and the United States, or the Agreement between the Government of Canada and the Government of the United States of America Concerning the Transboundary Movement of Hazardous Waste, signed at Ottawa, 28 October 1986; the Agreement between the United States of America and the United Mexican States on Cooperation for the Protection and Improvement of the Environment in the Border Area, signed at La Paz, Baja California Sur, 14 August 1983.

platform from which this book attempts to speak (of positive connections between treaties); this is the concept known as evolutionary interpretation.[42] As noted by the ILC, *lex specialis* need not be only about conflicts between treaties but could also assist parties to interpret treaties in light of their positive relationship with other treaties and the whole body of international law.[43] Article 31.3(c) requires that the interpretation of a treaty should take into account any relevant treaty made by all parties, any subsequent practices relating to the interpretation of the treaty and relevant general international law.[44]

The most important aspect of evolutionary interpretation is to establish the intent of the parties while not reading beyond their intent.[45] In *India – Patents (US)*, the Appellate Body warns of not emphasizing "words that are not there" or of "concepts that were not intended":

> The duty of a treaty interpreter is to examine the words of the treaty to determine the intentions of the parties. This should be done in accordance with the principles of treaty interpretation set out in Article 31 of the *Vienna Convention*. But these principles of interpretation neither require nor condone the imputation into a treaty of words that are not there or the importation into a treaty of concepts that were not intended.... These rules must be respected and applied in interpreting the *TRIPS Agreement* or any other covered agreements.... Both panels and the Appellate Body must be guided by the rules of treaty interpretation set out in the *Vienna Convention*, and must not add to or diminish rights and obligations provided in the *WTO Agreement*.[46]

42. For an application of evolutionary interpretation in international law see WTO Shrimp-Turtle where "the generic term 'natural resources' in article XX (g) was decided not to be 'static' in its construct but is rather 'by definition evolutionary' and interpreted broadly in light of other instruments such as the 1992 Rio Declaration and Agenda 21, the Biodiversity Convention of 1992, and the United Nations Convention on the Law of the Sea".

43. The European Court of Human Rights in the Neumann Case interpreted *lex specialis* as creating an exception to general rules of international law instead of regarding *lex specialis* as a means of assisting interpretation. Neumann Case, ECHR 1974 A No. 17 (1974), para. 29.

44. Article 31.3 VCLT. In the *Aegean Sea Continental Shelf* case, the ICJ stated that a general definition is "intended to follow the evolution of the law and to correspond with the meaning attached to the expression by the law in force at any given time", *ICJ Reports 1978* p. 32. In the *Gabčikovo-Nagymaros* case the ICJ pointed out that "by inserting these evolving provisions in the Treaty, the parties recognized the potential necessity to adapt the Project. Consequently, the Treaty is not static, and is open to adapt to emerging norms of international law". *Case concerning the Gabčíkovo-Nagymaros Project (Hungary/Slovakia) ICJ Reports 1997*, pp. 76–80, paras. 132–147.

45. Op cit. Boyle and Chinkin, *The Making of International Law*.

46. Appellate Body Report on India – Patents, paras. 45–46.

Evolutionary interpretation presents a potential tool for the better understanding of treaties that may not always be comprehensive or clear in light of the need to reflect the political consensuses that multilateral treaty negotiations inevitably face. As some scholars have argued, Article 31.3 may only be a weak source for interpretation that can supplement interpretation, but I believe its potential scope as a foundation for creating greater cooperation of treaties could become increasingly more profound. The current environment that has become oriented towards greater treaty cooperation through strategies such as interlinkages could make Article 31.3 appear in an important new light. One reservation as to this possibility will be how narrowly Article 31.3 (b) will be construed by future courts and tribunals. The current governance setting for sustainable development and environment (e.g. World Summits, General Assembly, Governing Councils, G8, G22, COP/MOPs) has led to enormous amounts of commentary, revision and reaffirmation of commitments under MEAs. To what extent can this material be regarded as relevant in the context of Article 31.3 (b)? If these materials become more widely accepted as a supplementary means to interpretation (as in *WTO – Shrimp-Turtle*) it could open the door to much greater MEA cooperation.

This brief analysis of the Vienna Convention and customary treaty law leads to the conclusion, which is generally agreed on by other authors, that treaty rules and customary international law on compatibility remain residuary.[47] Clearly, in an ideal world, the best way to avoid incidental conflicts between treaties would be to adequately consider, at all times, inter-treaty relationships in advance of striking and signing new agreements. This, of course, has little relevance to the real-world situation. Nevertheless, it is equally clear that if and when potential incompatibilities are predicted or anticipated, such as those set out in the case studies of this thesis, it behoves all concerned to exercise a mutual effort in the direction of taking appropriate preventative measures. The objective of establishing the relative strength of respective treaties and their provisions vis-à-vis one another is clearly part of the task of building interlinkages, whether this is through explicit laws concerning successive treaties, *lex specialis*, evolutionary and general rules of interpretation or through building institutional mechanisms and coherent structures that can ensure compatibility and effective cooperation between MEAs.

47. See Bethany Lukitsch Hicks (1999) *Treaty Congestion in International Environmental Law: The Need for Greater Coordination*, 32 U. Rich. L. Rev. (January), 1643. Also see W. Bradnee Chambers (2001) "International Trade Law and Kyoto Protocol: Potential Incompatibilities", in W. Bradnee Chambers, ed., *Inter-linkages: The Kyoto Protocol and the International Trade and Investment Regime*, Tokyo: United Nations University Press, 87–115.

The next two sections of this chapter describe the latter notion of compatibility and interlinkages between MEAs. This goes beyond the hierarchy of the law of treaties and seeks out further legal scope for positive cooperation. The nature of the cooperation can be viewed on two levels: external interlinkages, which are interlinkages between MEAs, and internal interlinkages, which refer to the internal institutional environment between an MEA and the umbrella or parent organization (often the UN or its agencies).[48] We will analyse in turn each of these two levels.

External interlinkages: Legal personality and cooperation between MEAs

The flexibility of the MEA to use or even develop cooperation mechanisms will depend largely on the extent of its legal personality. As such, the degree of legal personality defines the greater exterior legal environment in which MEAs lie and how they can interrelate – not in terms of succession or potential conflict, as Article 30 of the Vienna Convention is focused, but the extent to which its bodies (Conference or Meetings of the Parties (COP/MOPs), subsidiary bodies and secretariat) can legally cooperate and coordinate its activities as international legal entities.

The only developed codification of laws that addresses the legal capacity of international organizations is the 1986 Vienna Convention on the Law of Treaties between States and International Organizations or between International Organizations (VCLTIO).[49] The specific legal provisions of the Convention govern matters relating to conclusion and entry into force of treaties, reservations, interpretation of the provisions of such agreements, impact on third parties, amendment and modification, invalidity, termination and suspension, deposit of treaties and dispute settlement procedures. Although this convention is not in force, it represents

48. See Robin Churchill and Geir Ulfstein (2000) *Autonomous Institutional Arrangements in Multilateral Environmental Agreements: A Little-Noticed Phenomenon in International Law*, 94 AJIL, 649. Churchill and Ulfstein discuss the powers of MEAs on the internal plane and external plane. This analysis is useful for distinguishing the two levels of MEA cooperation; however, the scope of the internal plane as used by Churchill and Ulfstein is narrower and is focused more on the internal procedures under the MEA such as compliance, budgetary and administrative matters. This analysis uses a broader understanding of the internal plane, which includes relations with the parent organization (however detached); nevertheless the parent organization does maintain certain coordination powers that are important to examine more closely in this chapter.

49. Done and opened for signature at Vienna on 21 March 1986. Not yet in force. UN A/CONF.129/15, reprinted in 25 ILM, 543. Though this treaty has not entered into force yet it still represents a substantial codification of customary treaty law and accepted practice in this area of international law.

the culmination of several years' work by the International Law Commission and is based on existing customary rules. For these reasons, its text is per se the best source for understanding general requirements of legal personality of international organizations.

According to the VCLTIO, an international organization may enter into agreements with other international organizations as long as the organization has been granted this authority through its respective rules.[50] Therefore, the first important point in this discussion of the external plane between MEAs is to establish whether MEAs, in addition to being defined as treaties under 1969 VCLT, could also be considered international organizations and hence possess the legal standing to enter into formal legal agreements with other MEAs as international organizations. Following this analysis, we will return to the further criterion set out in the 1986 VCLTIO, which is whether the MEA itself, and which body of the MEA, has been granted this authority to enter into such agreements. Lastly, the following section will examine if, in the absence of explicit treaty language, there is still legal scope for the MEAs to formally cooperate.[51]

Preliminary question: Are MEAs international organizations?

When defining the nature of the institutions that encase an MEA, referring to the organizational part rather than the treaty part of an MEA, there begins to be some confusion on the overall nature of their legal standing. In the past, the legal standing of a treaty was relatively straightforward because the most common arrangement by which an international treaty entered into an external agreement was through its parent organization. Increasingly, however, this type of arrangement has been changing for MEAs. Instead, they are now frequently regarded as having independent legal personality even when the MEA is linked to a supervisory organization such as the UN. This power of MEAs to have legal personality and thus enter into external agreements or legal arrangements stems from three sources: firstly, recent legal opinions; secondly, the rules vested in the MEA by the hosting organization or the treaty itself; and lastly, from the legal concept of "implied powers".

The case of the Climate Change Convention (UNFCCC),[52] concerning its legal standing, has become something of a leading example for

---

50. VCLTIO, Article 6, 1986.
51. For a definition of an international organization see H. G. Schermers and N. M. Blokker (1997) *International Institutional Law*, 3rd rev. ed., Hingham, Mass.: Kluwer Academic Publishers, 23.
52. United Nations Framework Convention on Climate Change, adopted 9 May 1992, 31 ILM (1992), 849 [hereinafter Climate Change Convention or UNFCCC].

demonstrating the legal status of modern MEAs in the context of the first criterion. Though the UNFCCC is formally institutionalized under the UN Secretariat, and specifically as a legal entity under the Economic and Social Commission, it has never been regarded as formally managed by the UN Secretariat, but rather has had quasi-independent status. This standing originates from legal opinions from the UN Office of Legal Affairs (UNOLA) and decisions taken by the UNFCCC COP which have gradually taken place over several stages and which have eventually established its quasi-independence. By examining the UNFCCC case, I wish to draw some conclusions as to the status of MEAs as international organizations.

The first stage that has led to the development of UNFCCC's quasi-independence occurred while it was preparing the inaugural Conference of the Parties (COP 1). At this time, the UNFCCC Secretariat sought the advice of the UNOLA on whether it was able to sign an agreement with the German Government in order to host COP 1 or whether the UN itself needed to sign this agreement on UNFCCC's behalf. The UNOLA replied by stating that the answer to this question lay clearly under UNFCCC Article 8.2 (f) which stated that the Secretariat had the power to "enter into such administrative and contractual arrangements as may be required for the effective discharge of its functions".[53] The nature of the legal relationship of the UN and the UNFCCC was later clarified by a decision taken by the COP which stated that "the Convention secretariat shall be institutionally linked to the United Nations, while not being fully integrated in the work programme and management structure of any particular department or programme".[54] This decision clearly affirmed that the intention of the UNFCCC parties was to maintain the Secretariat with a certain degree of independence and for it to play a role beyond providing just the administration and basic services of the parties.

The second stage in the development of the UNFCCC's legal status came in the course of establishing its permanent seat for the secretariat

---

53. UNFCCC (1996) *Arrangements for the Relocation of the Convention Secretariat to Bonn*, FCCC/SBI/1996/7 (23 February), para. 11. An earlier opinion also made a similar point. On 4 November 1993 the UNOLA stated in a letter to the UNFCCC Secretary that "once this Convention enters into force it will establish an international entity/organization with its own separate legal personality, statement of principles, organs and supportive structure in the form of a Secretariat"; see text of Memorandum in Peter H. Sand (1997) *The Role of International Organizations in the Evolution of Environmental Law*, Geneva: UNITAR; see also Jacob Werksman (1995) "Consolidating Governance of the Global Commons: Insights from the Global Environment Facility", 6 *Yearbook of International Environmental Law* 27, at 44, note 76.
54. FCCC/CP/1995/7/Add.1, decision 14, para. 2.

in Bonn. Here, the Executive Secretary was asked to clarify who could sign the Headquarters Agreement with the German Government. Could it be the UN or could the UNFCCC Secretariat sign the agreement itself? When the issue was put to the Convention's Subsidiary Body on Implementation, it recommended that the Executive Secretary should again seek the legal advice of the UNOLA. Upon consultation, the UNOLA responded by stating that the UNFCCC COP had a certain legal personality as an international organization because it had created other bodies such as the Subsidiary Body on Scientific and Technological Advice and the Subsidiary Body on Implementation and a Financial Mechanism, but that it was not a UN subsidiary body:

> The Convention Secretariat is one of the bodies foreseen in this instrument.
>
> Thus, in accordance with paragraph 2 of Article 7, the Conference of the Parties is "the supreme body of [the] Convention". Furthermore, the Convention established a subsidiary body for scientific and technological advice (Article 9), a subsidiary body for implementation (Article 10) and, finally, a financial mechanism (Article 11). Our analysis of both the legal nature and functions of these bodies indicates that they have certain distinctive elements attributable to international organizations. However, it is clear that none of these bodies is *de jure* a UN subsidiary organ.[55]

With regard to the Secretariat's power, the UNOLA opinion went on to say that in spite of the view that the UNFCCC COP may have certain distinctions as international organizations do have, "and notwithstanding the fact that the Convention Secretariat is 'institutionally linked to the United Nations', the legal regime enjoyed by the United Nations under applicable agreements cannot be automatically attached to the Convention Secretariat".[56] Furthermore, the UNOLA warned that ambiguity still existed over the exact nature of the legal personality given the distinctiveness of the UNFCCC bodies and recommended that the COP should clarify this ambiguity and explicitly take a decision on the nature and scope of the Secretariat's juridical personality and legal capacity. It cited the Multilateral Fund of the Ozone Convention as a model example of the type of decision that would be needed to empower the UNFCCC Secretariat and clarify its powers.[57]

In the face of the recommendation of the UNOLA, such a decision to date has never taken place. The UNFCCC COP and the German Government decided that the UNFCCC Secretariat was able to enter into a

55. Supra, FCCC/SBI/1996/7.
56. Ibid.
57. Ibid.

headquarters agreement which was *mutatis mutandis* the same as the existing UN agency agreement already in place for resident UN agencies in Germany. At the time, this was the United Nations Volunteers Programme (UNV). This decision was based on the recognition by the German Government that the "other intergovernmental entities, institutionally linked to the United Nations" could also enter into agreement with them. In effect, this meant that the German Government recognized the UNFCCC's Secretariat as an international organization with the necessary legal personality to enter into and sign agreements independently. However, the COP did not explicitly define the legal personality or the limits that the UNFCCC could have. This was probably because, in general, governments have been wary of ceding power to international organizations, which they believe erodes their sovereignty and independence. The UNFCCC case is an example of this concern; governments through the COP empowered the secretariat with sufficient legal personality to carry out what was necessary to establish the seat and function of the secretariat, but preferred to remain ambiguous when it came to ceding any further power that could thus establish precedence for the future.

This type of arrangement by the UNFCCC has become synonymous with many other MEAs, as has been seen in the context of negotiating other host government agreements with such conventions as the Multilateral Fund of the Montreal Protocol,[58] the United Nations Convention to Combat Desertification and the Convention on Migratory Species.[59] Churchill and Ulfstein have argued that the UNFCCC-type arrangement has become predominant in other MEAs and this phenomenon represents a new type of international institutional design, which they call "autonomous institutional arrangements" (AIAs).[60] These are institutions that are autonomous and possess such internal powers as the "establishment of subsidiary bodies and the adoption of rules of procedure and a budget; powers to develop substantive obligations through various forms of law-making and treaty interpretation; powers to supervise the implementation of and compliance with those obligations ... and powers on the external plane to enter into arrangements with states, international organizations and the institutions of other MEAs (some of which may be regarded as genuine treaty-making powers)".[61] Churchill and Ulfstein

---

58. Montreal Protocol (1994) *MOP Decision* VI/16, UNEP/OzL.Pro.6/7.
59. UNEP (2002) *Agreement between the Government of the Federal Republic of Germany, the United Nations and the Secretariat of the Convention on the Conservation of Migratory Species of Wild Animals concerning the Headquarters of the Convention Secretariat,* annexed to AEWA/MOP2.22 23 (September).
60. Op. cit. Churchill and Ulfstein.
61. Ibid., 658–659.

warn, however, that AIAs are not fully fledged international organizations and that their powers may vary according to the MEA.

Apart from the developments made under COPs and legal opinions coming from the UNOLA, the doctrine of "implied powers" would also seem to suggest that treaty secretariats could have a certain degree of autonomy in their own right to enter into agreements with other organizations and governments. This possibility would be particularly important in the case of an MEA that does not have explicit clauses referring to its powers.[62] The origins of the doctrine of implied powers comes from domestic law and was used in statutory interpretations of a legislative body's implicit competence in matters ancillary to their explicit or stated authority. It has been frequently used in the international context as a means for justifying unilateral action by UN member states and it has also been used within the UN by both the General Assembly and the Security Council to justify desired action in new areas not clearly defined by the UN Charter.[63] In the context of this discussion, the doctrine has been the focus of debate with regard to the powers of treaty secretariats.

In its Advisory Opinion *Legality of the Use by a State of Nuclear Weapons in Armed Conflict* the ICJ stated that:

> The powers conferred on international organizations are normally the subject of an express statement in their constituent instruments. Nevertheless, the necessities of international life may point to the need for organizations, in order to achieve their objectives, to possess subsidiary powers which are not expressly provided for in the basic instruments which govern their activities. It is generally accepted that international organizations can exercise such powers, known as "implied" powers.[64]

The ICJ opinion would seem to imply that the secretariats of MEAs, if indeed quasi-international organizations or autonomous institutional arrangements, could possess a certain degree of legal personality under this doctrine. However, these powers must also be taken in the context of their powers vis-à-vis the member states or, in the case of MEAs, the COPs. The context is twofold; the powers may be clearly defined in the MEA itself, such as a provision describing the powers of the secretariat

---

62. For some examples of MEAs that have specific reference to certain powers to enter into external relationships with other international organizations, MEAs or states, see Article 8.2 (f) of the UNFCCC; also see UNCCD Art. 22 (j); and also Basel Convention on the Disposal of Hazardous Waste Art. 16.1(d).
63. For discussion on this see C. F. Amerasinghe (1996) *Principles of the Institutional Law of International Organizations*, London: Cambridge University Press, 44–48.
64. ICJ (1996) *Legality of the Use by a State of Nuclear Weapons in Armed Conflict*, para. 25.

or, more often than not, a general provision that grants the secretariat the powers needed to carry out its function. This grey area of "what is necessary" has become a source of confusion and perhaps a reason why the UNOLA has advised secretariats such as the UNFCCC to provide a COP decision that can clarify the powers of the secretariats. There also continues to be debate among legal scholars of the scope of personality the secretariat's powers enjoy, but most would seem to agree that while the UN does have certain functional powers in terms of its staff and operations, this power is not such that it is supra-national. But then again, it is commonsensical that a secretariat would not engage in activities against the will of its member states. If it did, it would certainly not be serving the interests of its members.

In sum, this discussion would suggest that some MEA secretariats do have a certain legal personality on the external plane and, as Churchill and Ulfstein argue, this is based on explicit provisions in the MEA, the legal opinions on the MEA's judicial personality and the doctrine of implied powers. However, MEA powers coming from such judicial personality are limited in scope to functional powers in service of their members. Nevertheless, at a minimum, these powers would certainly include entering into agreements of collaboration with other MEAs where there is a clear overlap or interest. It would also give the secretariats the legal ability to develop relations with other MEAs and present the results of such collaboration for a decision to be made by their member states. It would also be logical that the member states, which are often the same member states as in the UN and also other MEAs, would want MEA secretariats to coordinate their activities in good faith.

How do MEAs cooperate externally?

Through external interlinkages there are various means by which MEAs can cooperate. This can be by way of memorandums of understanding (MOUs) or other forms of external agreements, or by softer legal means such as a joint liaison group or some other joint exchange system.[65] MOUs between MEAs are by far the most common form of cooperation. However, they have some interesting features distinct from typical MOUs seen under international law. First, the MOUs are generally signed at the secretariat level and, although these agreements are usually non-binding in language, they are regarded as international agreements

---

65. Op. cit. Werksman, 10.

under international law by the International Law Commission.[66] This is further evidence of the growing trend for MEA secretariats to have legal personality. The second interesting feature is that they are commonly operationalized through "joint work programmes" that are formally adopted by a decision of the COP or its subsidiary bodies.[67] These programmes have more of a binding effect as they are taken as mutual decisions by the respective COPs and are based on scientific inputs that elaborate in very specific areas of interaction. Most of the MEAs that share common functional goals or have strong ecological connections have negotiated joint work programmes in the last several years. As to their effectiveness, this remains to be seen as most programmes are too young to make any overall assessment. However, the ability to develop the MOU and the work programmes often comes from the secretariats. Thus the capacity of having the legal personality is an important incentive for initiating this cooperation.

Joint liaison groups are another common form of MEA interaction. In recent years, a number of these groups have formed under pressure from the UN General Assembly to reduce overlap and fragmentation.[68] The Joint Liaison Group (JLG) between the secretariats of the United Nations Framework Convention on Climate Change (UNFCCC) and the Convention on Biological Diversity (CBD) was formed in 2001. The secretariat of the United Nations Convention to Combat Desertification (UNCCD) was subsequently invited to participate in the JLG to enhance

66. The International Law Commission, in determining the nature of the MOU, has stated that they were undoubtedly considered international agreements. According to the Commission, it was not the title of the instrument that determined its binding power but rather the content of the agreement. Thus, for an MOU to be signed by an official of an MEA secretariat, the secretariat must possess adequate judicial personality. See *Report of the International Law Commission to the General Assembly*, 2 Y.B. Int'l L. Comm'n (1966), 188; or UN A/CN.4/SER.A/1966/Add.1 (1986). Also see Hans Blix and Jirna H. Emerson, eds (1973) *The Treaty Maker's Handbook*, Dobbs Ferry, N.Y.: Oceana, 7, (1973), 316; Anthony Aust (1986) *The Theory and Practice of Informal International Instruments*, 35 Int'l L & Comp. L.Q., 787.

67. For example see CBD (2000) Proposed Joint Work Plan 2000–2001 of the Convention on Biological Diversity and the Convention on Wetlands (Ramsar, Iran, 1971), UNEP/CBD/SBSTTA/5/INF/12 (14 January); Joint Work Plan 2003–2005 between The Bureau of the Convention on Wetlands (Ramsar, Iran, 1971) and the Secretariat of the Convention on the Conservation of Migratory Species of Wild Animals (CMS) and between The Bureau of the Convention on Wetlands (Ramsar, Iran, 1971) and the Secretariat of the Agreement on the Conservation of African-Eurasian Waterbirds (AEWA), available at http://www.ramsar.org/key_cms_aewa_jwp.htm; Joint Work Programme between the UNCCC and CBD, see ICCD/COP(6)/4 (27 June 2003).

68. See UNSG (1997) *Report of the Secretary-General: Renewing the UN, A Programme for Reform*, A/51/950 (14 July).

coordination between the three conventions.[69] This informal forum for the exchange of information comprises the executive secretaries of the respective secretariats, officers of the respective subsidiary bodies and other members of the convention secretariats.[70] The secretariat of the Ramsar Convention on Wetlands shares information and participates in the meetings of the JLG as appropriate.

The mandate of the JLG is:

(a) to enhance coordination between the three conventions, including the exchange of relevant information; and
(b) to explore options for further cooperation between the three conventions, including the possibility of a joint work plan and/or workshop.[71]

The rationale for collaboration among the conventions arises from the interlinkages between the issues that they address.[72]

Cooperation at the level of the secretariats is already well developed.[73] Many of the possible areas for collaboration among the secretariats, the

---

69. UNFCCC (2002) *Cooperation with Other Conventions: Progress Report on the Work of the Joint Liaison Group between the Secretariats of the UNFCCC, the United Nations Convention to Combat Desertification (UNCCD) and the Convention on Biological Diversity*, FCCC/SBSTA/2002/3 (5 April), para. 2.
70. UNFCCC, "Options for Enhanced Cooperation among the Three Rio Conventions", Paper prepared by the secretariats of the Convention on Biological Diversity, the United Nations Framework Convention to Combat Desertification, and the United Nations Framework Convention on Climate Change for the Joint Liaison Group, para. 6. This paper was presented to the Subsidiary Body for Scientific and Technological Advice (SBSTA) of the UNFCCC and the Conference of the Parties (COP) to the UNCCD as FCCC/SBSTA/2004/INF.19, to the Subsidiary Body on Scientific, Technical and Technological Advice (SBSTTA) of the CBD as UNEP/CBD/SBSTTA/10/INF.9 and to CBD's Ad Hoc Open-Ended Working Group on Review of Implementation of the Convention as UNEP/CBD/WG-RI/1/7/Add.1.
71. UNFCCC (2001) *Report of the Subsidiary Body for Scientific and Technological Advice on Its Fourteenth Session, Bonn, 24 to 27 July 2001*, FCCC/SBSTA/2001/2 (18 September), para. 42 (d).
72. As stated in the paper titled "Options for Enhanced Cooperation among the Three Rio Conventions" prepared by the JLG:

    Climate change can be an important driver of desertification and biodiversity loss. Ecosystem dynamics can impact the earth's carbon, energy and water cycles and therefore affect climate. Further, measures undertaken under one convention to address climate change (including mitigation and adaptation activities), to combat desertification and land degradation, or for the conservation and sustainable use of biodiversity, might have consequences for the objectives of the other conventions. Id., para. 3. Footnotes omitted.

73. Ibid., para. 26.

subsidiary bodies and their respective expert groups are already being carried out or explored.[74] For instance, as a result of JLG-facilitated cooperation, the CBD programme of work on technology transfer was developed using a structure similar to the UNFCCC framework for technology transfer.[75] The JLG has met five times, with the last meeting being held on 30 January 2004.

As the report of the fifth meeting of the JLG points out:

> synergy among the objectives of the three conventions in adaptation activities can be promoted through collaboration among national focal points at the national level, and through consistent guidance from the respective COPs. The latter can be facilitated – though not guaranteed – by the JLG.[76]

This holds true for much of the work of the JLG, which can only be directed or brought to the attention of the parties to the respective agreements. While it has identified options for enhanced cooperation among the Rio Conventions, it has not set priorities and awaits guidance from the parties to the different conventions on the way forward.[77] To date, the UNFCCC COP's response to the work of JLG has been of a fairly general nature, focusing on information exchange and encouragement to parties to enhance coordination under the three Rio Conventions at national level.[78] The CBD COP has, on the other hand, identified specific areas of cooperation with the UNFCCC and the UNCCD, while also encouraging enhanced coordination at a national level.[79] As a result of the JLG's activities, some pilot activities are expected to receive

---

74. Ibid., para. 25.
75. Ibid., para. 14.
76. UNFCCC (2004) *Report of the Fifth Meeting of the Joint Liaison Group*, FCCC/SBSTA/2004/INF.9 (15 June), para. 41(l).
77. The UNCCD COP, at its seventh session (COP 7), invited parties to review the JLG paper and invited parties to submit comments to the secretariat prior to COP 8 (Decision 12/COP.7, para. 1). At its twenty-fourth session, the UNFCCC SBSTA invited parties to submit their views on the paper by 16 February 2006. (Paragraph 106, *Report of the Subsidiary Body for Scientific and Technological Advice on its twenty-third session, held at Montreal from 28 November to 6 December 2005*, FCCC/SBSTA/2005/10, 1 March 2006). See also paragraph 14, *Report of the Subsidiary Body for Scientific and Technological Advice on Its Twenty-First Session, Held at Buenos Aires from 6 to 14 December 2004*, FCCC/SBSTA/2004/13 (2 March 2005).
78. UNFCCC (2004) *Report of the Conference of the Parties at Its Tenth Session, Held at Buenos Aires, from 6 to 18 December 2004 (Part One: Proceedings)*, FCCC/CP/2004/10. See also, Decision 13/CP.8, Cooperation with Other Conventions.
79. See CBD (2004) *Cooperation with Other Conventions and International Organizations and Initiatives*, Decision VII/26; and CBD (2002) *Cooperation with Other Organizations, Initiatives and Conventions*, Decision VI/20.

attention and areas of potential synergy have been identified under the UNCCD.[80]

The Biodiversity Liaison Group[81] was created at the initiation of the Convention on Biological Diversity's (CBD) COP request to the Executive Secretary to form a liaison group with the four other biodiversity-related conventions (decision VII/26, paragraph 2) and to examine options for a flexible framework between all relevant actors, such as a global partnership on biodiversity, in order to enhance implementation through improved cooperation (paragraph 3). The Executive Secretary of the CBD thus invited the heads of the Convention on Conservation of Migratory Species of Wild Animals (CMS), the Convention on International Trade in Endangered Species of Wild Fauna and Flora (CITES), the Ramsar Convention and the World Heritage Convention (WHC) to form a liaison group, in order to enhance coherence and cooperation in their implementation. This liaison group, consisting of the executive heads of the conventions and relevant staff, has met four times.

The group has prepared a paper on "options for enhanced cooperation among the five biodiversity-related conventions" (UNEP/CBD/WG-RI/1/7/Add.2) which has been considered by the CMS and Ramsar COPs and the General Assembly of the WHC. The conventions have also cooperated through the liaison group to prepare a joint statement on the importance of biodiversity for achieving the Millennium Development Goals and have issued joint statements at meetings of the governing bodies of Ramsar, CMS and the UNFCCC. In Bonn, on 4 October 2005, the liaison group discussed the development of future work plans and options for cooperation. The liaison group also keeps under review the invitation of other biodiversity-related organizations to participate in the group. Bilateral cooperation among the different biodiversity-related conventions is also taking place and evolving.

One of the most difficult problems faced by MEA coordination mechanisms, such as the Rio Convention Liaison Group and Biodiversity Liaison Group, is their lack of legal authority to create clear programmes that will achieve genuine cooperation between the MEAs. For example, the Conference of the Parties has rarely delegated authority or given these liaison systems the power to carry out clear areas of work or given them the financial means to do so. The result is that these cooperation

---

80. UNCCD (2005) *Review of Activities for the Promotion and Strengthening of Relationships with Other Relevant Conventions and Relevant International Organizations, Institutions and Agencies, in Accordance with Article 8 and Article 22, Paragraph 2(i) of the Convention (Note by the Secretariat)*, UNCCD/COP(7)/5 (5 August).

81. UNEP (2006) *Cooperation with Other Conventions, Organizations and Initiatives and Engagement of Stakeholders, Including Options for a Global Partnership (Note by the Executive Secretary)*, UNEP/CBD/COP/8/25 (21 January).

mechanisms lack focus and clear legal mandates, so their decision-making is marginalized and thus forced to rest on good faith, discussion and best endeavours to achieve their objectives. Nevertheless, they play an important role in developing joint programmes, exchanging information, and trying to reduce fragmentation and prevent conflicts.

Internal interlinkages: Cooperation in the UN and between MEAs and their parent organizations

External systems for cooperation between MEAs, such as those just described, have been fashioned as a "second choice" to a strong centralized system for governance and, consequently, yield "second choice results" for cooperation. Although these systems have improved cooperation since the mid-1990s, their limitation in terms of their legal scope and non-binding governance structures will always serve as a hindrance and they should be characterized as being cosmetic rather than representing deep binding systems that would bring about the cooperation needed for substantive change and real effectiveness between MEAs. Some of the potential deeper forms of cooperation will be discussed later but, before doing so, I would like to turn to some of the internal mechanisms that are in place for cooperation. The internal plane can be described as the means of cooperation between MEAs and their parent or supervisory organization. This section will concentrate on examples within the broad UN system as it administers the majority of MEAs.

The internal plane also has several barriers to cooperation, and although more often than not these are political by nature, there are several profuse legal and administrative characteristics that are at play. Many of the barriers are entrenched in resistance to internal coordination struggles between MEAs and their parent and supervisory organizations. For example, there are internal coordination problems between UNEP-administered conventions and non-UNEP-administered conventions such as the UNFCCC and UNFCCD. Some of this internal bickering (turf wars) is rooted in the 1992 Rio Summit's deliberate choice to place UNFCCC and UNFCCD outside the sphere of control of UNEP and to give them a certain degree of autonomy within the UN. Although, technically, all of these aforementioned MEAs remain in the UN family and are bound (albeit in a qualified manner) to its overall rules and general governance structure, they do not always answer to the call of coordination. UNEP, as the environmental arm within this governance structure has been given a legal mandate by the General Assembly and the UNEP Governing Council, through its Global Ministerial Environment Forum, to play a greater role in facilitating cooperation between all conventions.[82] In 1999, it even created a whole division for promoting implementation and synergies between MEAs,[83] but rarely does the UNFCCC or the UNCCD interpret the situation this way. On the surface, you will hardly ever see the internal squabbling but behind the scenes the problems are well-known. Simply put, the conventions outside of UNEP see UNEP as a potential master they do not wish to serve.

Another problem – as noted earlier – is that as MEAs become better defined and more mature they are playing ever more independent roles and acting more as international organizations. In the case of UNEP, which administers most of the MEAs, but from afar being based outside Nairobi, the MEA secretariats have had mounting demands from their parties to become more effective in delivering their services. This point is particularly salient when every year UNEP takes a mandatory 13 per cent of the MEA's core budgetary contributions as a flat rate administrative overhead for management while, increasingly, MEA secretariats are required to create their own administrational units as UNEP administrative services do not respond quickly enough from afar or cannot meet the specialized and local needs of the MEA secretariats. Thus, UNEP-administered MEA secretariats are asking themselves what value they are really getting for their 13 per cent.[84]

As outlined in chapter 1, and in the historical analysis of interlinkages in chapter 2, treaty congestion and increasing calls for UN reform have created mounting political pressure for UN treaty secretariats to cooperate more intensely.[85] Consistently, the Secretary-General's reform plans,

---

82. UNEP (2002) *International Environmental Governance*, Decision SS.VII/1, (15 February), para. 11.2 (iii).

83. See UNEP Division of Environmental Conventions [hereinafter DEC], available at http://www.unep.org/dec/about_dec.html.

84. See discussion of UNEP's 13 per cent overhead charges to the CITES Convention Funding, in CITES (1996) *Thirty-Seventh Meeting of the Standing Committee Rome (Italy)*, SC37 Summary Report, 14; for example, the representative of Central and South America and the Caribbean (Argentina) noted that the comments on the flexibility of UN rules had come from UNEP at the meeting of the working group. She said that there was a need to look at the application of heavy procedures in such small bodies as the CITES Secretariat. She said the working group agreed that it was unacceptable that UNEP should spend 13 per cent of the contributions of parties just as it likes, especially as the amount increases with each increase in the budget, and she requested that detailed information on the expenditure of the 13 per cent administrative charge should be circulated to the parties for analysis. For further discussion of the overhead see CITES (1998) *Fortieth Meeting of the Standing Committee, London (UK)*, SC40 Summary Report, 55; and CITES (2005) *Fifty-Third Meeting of the Standing Committee, Geneva, Switzerland*, SC53 Summary Record Rev. 1, 7.

85. UNGA (1998) *Report of the United Nations Task Force on Environment and Human Settlements*, A/53/463, annex, para. 30.

such as the 1997 "The United Nations", his 2006 High-Level Panel on UN System-wide Coherence in the Areas of Development, Humanitarian Affairs and Environment,[86] and outcomes from multilateral meetings such as the Johannesburg Plan of Implementation,[87] have all urged the MEAs to end their fragmentation and seek better cooperation under the UN. However, all politics aside, what are the real internal legalities of MEA cooperation and the ability of the parent or supervisory organizations to internally enforce cooperation upon MEAs?

From a legal point of view, MEAs hosted by the UN, or by one of its programmes or subsidiary bodies, are subject to UN rules of operation, procurement, contracts, maintenance of facilities, recruitment and staff rules, which are all governed by the UN Financial and Staff Regulations and Rules. All UN professional staff appointments take an oath of office to follow the UN principles and rules and to remain impartial with respect to the influence of any one government. The heads of the MEA's secretariats are appointed by the UN Secretary-General or, on his behalf, by the Executive Head of the subsidiary organization or programme and, as such, are accountable to both the Conference of the Parties and the Secretary-General as the Chief Administrative Officer of the Organization. Churchill and Ulfstein have suggested that there is a dual responsibility on the part of the professionals and the Executive Secretaries of the Conventions to serve both the COP and the UNSG as well as the UN itself, and this is a fair assessment of the division of powers.[88] In matters related to the MEA, the parties, through the COP or subsidiary bodies, can instruct the Secretariat officials to carry out these functions. However, in matters pertaining to administration or personnel the UN rules and regulations would apply. It is assumed that the instructions given to Secretariats by the MEA bodies would not violate the aforementioned UN Rules and Regulations and that the UN would not impose upon its officials instructions that would violate the commitments undertaken by parties in the MEA.[89] In the event of either case happening it would be grounds for the annulment of the institutional arrangements that the MEA and UN share.[90]

86. UNSG (2006) *Letter of Transmittal from President of the UN General Assembly to Permanent Representatives and Permanent Observers to the UN in New York of the Concept Paper Prepared for the High-Level Panel on UN System-wide Coherence in the Areas of Development, Humanitarian Affairs and Environment* (26 January).
87. UNGA (2002) *Plan of Implementation of the World Summit on Sustainable Development*, A/CONF.199/20 9.
88. Op. cit. Churchill and Ulfstein, 635.
89. Ibid.
90. Ibid.

However, the UN's internal ability to coordinate and influence activities in organizations under its umbrella may not be as straightforward as Churchill and Ulfstein have portrayed. Through its structure, the UN maintains other levels of influence and internal coordination which are legally mandated over UN-administered MEA secretariats. This is primarily through activities generated under the UN Economic and Social Commission (ECOSOC). Under Article 60 of the UN Charter, ECOSOC's principal role is coordination. It conducts this task by undertaking reports and studies, consultations, holding global conferences and making recommendations to the General Assembly.[91]

All the UN specialized agencies report to the ECOSOC, as well as programmes such as UNEP[92] and UN entities such as the UNFCCC and UNCCD.[93] In 1994, under UN reforms, the ECOSOC was also given the additional responsibility of oversight and policy coordination.[94] In practice, the ECOSOC carries out its coordination role through numerous avenues, but in the last several years, and in close consultation with the Secretary-General's reform process, it has created, or newly mandated, a number of smaller forums and mechanisms to assist with its coordination function. The most important of these, in terms of influence over MEAs, is the Chief Executive Board[95] and the Environmental Management Group.[96]

In 2000, the ECOSOC replaced the Administrative Committee on Coordination (ACC) with the Chief Executive Board and appointed the UN Secretary-General as its Chairman. The Board was formed to improve the flow of information and coordination between UN agencies and also

---

91. United Nations (1948) United Nations Charter, Article 60–66.
92. In the case of UNEP, it reports directly to the UN General Assembly, though the report is procedurally submitted through ECOSOC.
93. See, for general roles of coordination, H. Hazelzet (1998) *The Decision-Making Approach to International Organisations*, in B. Reinalda and B. Verbeek, eds, *Autonomous Policy Making By International Organisations*, New York: Routledge.
94. See UN Charter Article 63.2 which states that ECOSOC "may co-ordinate the activities of the specialised agencies through consultation with and recommendations to such agencies and through recommendations to the General Assembly and to the Members of the United Nations". On the role of ECOSOC see http://www.un.org/docs/ecosoc/ecosoc_background.html; accordingly, it "has the power to assist the preparations and organization of major international conferences in the economic and social and related fields and to facilitate a coordinated follow-up to these conferences. With its broad mandate the Council's purview extends to over 70 per cent of the human and financial resources of the entire UN system". Also see UN (2003) *The Role of the Economic and Social Council in the Integrated and Coordinated Implementation of the Outcomes of and Follow-Up to Major United Nations Conferences and Summits*, E/2003/67.
95. See Chief Executives Board (CEB), available at http://ceb.unsystem.org/.
96. See UNEMG, available at http://www.unemg.org/.

to deal with substantive issues facing the UN,[97] whereas the ACC had been designed more for management-related issues. The CEB is served by two high-level committees, the High Level Committee on Programmes (HLCP)[98] and the High Level Committee on Management.[99] The HLCP is more important in terms of issue coordination, as its main function is "to advise CEB on policy, programme and operational matters of system-wide importance and to foster inter-agency cooperation and coordination on these matters on behalf of CEB". The committee is made up of senior representatives of UN organizations, agencies and entities who are responsible for programme matters and are authorized to take decisions on behalf of their Executive Heads.[100]

There is also the inner cabinet of the UN Secretary-General, which is also supposed to play a role in coordination. This is called the Senior Management Group (SMG), "a committee of senior UN managers that serves as the Secretary-General's cabinet and the central policy planning body of the United Nations".[101] Its objective is to "ensure strategic coherence and direction in the work of the Organisation".[102] The cabinet was approved by the General Assembly in 1997 as part of the reform proposal submitted by Secretary-General Kofi Annan. The SMG has enabled the United Nations to refine its leadership and management by allowing senior managers to plan together, share information, pool efforts, coordinate activities, avoid duplication and work for common objectives.[103]

Both of these central planning groups include specialized agencies and international organizations but do not include the executive heads of any of the MEAs, including the UNFCCC or UNCCD, both of which are considered to be UN entities according to the UN Legal Affairs Office.[104] The Executive Director of UNEP, however, is a member of both the CEB and the SMG and it is assumed that he will then coordinate environmental activities including those of MEAs under the legal umbrella of UNEP and in his position as Executive Director. The main architecture for achieving this coordination is through his Chairmanship of a group called the Environment Management Group set up under the

---

97. Op. cit. CEB.
98. See HLCP, available at http://ceb.unsystem.org/hlcp/overview.htm.
99. See HLCM, available at http://ceb.unsystem.org/hlcm/default.htm.
100. Op. cit. CEB.
101. See SMG, available at http://www.un.org/News/ossg/sg/pages/seniorstaff.html.
102. Ibid.
103. Ibid.
104. Supra.

General Assembly and which does not include representation from the MEAs outside UNEP, including Ramsar, UNFCCC and UNCCD.[105]

The EMG was created as a result of a recommendation made by the Task Force on Environment and Human Settlements[106] and adopted by the UN General Assembly[107] to promote inter-agency coordination related to specific issues in the field of environment and human settlements. According to the EMG's terms of reference its objectives are to provide a flexible and coordinated UN response to emerging environmental issues, promote interlinkages, exchange information and compatibility of approaches and find common solutions to problems that add value to the existing United Nations system-wide inter-agency cooperation.[108] The group has representation at the senior decision-making level of "specialised agencies, programmes and organs of the United Nations system, including the secretariats of multilateral environmental agreements".[109] The manner in which the group operates is by identifying cross-cutting issues and then setting up a corresponding "issue-management group" made up of the members but led by the relevant agencies that would have a mandate to provide action on that issue.[110] The issues are then, theoretically, to be addressed within a designated time frame. The EMG is supposed to be connected back to the UN central coordination system through two mechanisms. Firstly, if the results of the group have bearing on the UN System the Chairman will report to the Chief Executives Board for Coordination and, secondly, in cases of issue management involving groups not chaired by UNEP, the Executive Director or UNEP may inform the UN Secretary-General of the group's report.[111]

Unfortunately, despite having a potential for greater cooperation and coordination on environmental activities, especially with MEAs, the EMG, from the beginning, has not been an effective mechanism. Firstly, it has suffered attendance problems; the Executive Director of UNEP (now former), although he has made efforts, has only attended 5 full ses-

---

105. On the role of EMG see Philippe Roch and Franz Xaver Perrez (2005) *International Environmental Governance: The Strive Towards a Comprehensive, Coherent, Effective and Efficient International Environmental Regime*, 16 Colo. J. Int'l Envtl. L. 1, 11–13.

106. See Secretary-General reports to GA on *Environment and Human Settlements*, A/53/463 (6 October 1998).

107. UNGA (1999) Res. 53/242, UN GAOR, 53rd Sess., Agenda Item 30, UN, A/Res/53/242, 6.

108. See *Terms of Reference of Environment Management Group* in UN Doc. *High-level Forum of the United Nations Environmental Management Group*, UNEMG/HLF/12 (2006), 3.

109. Ibid.

110. Ibid.

111. Ibid.

sions out of 10. The smaller MEAs such as Ramsar, CITES and CMS have consistently attended at the Executive Secretary level, but the other conventions have had a very poor record, particularly the UNFCCC. which has missed several meetings, and the Executive Secretary has only attended once. At other times, the meetings were held below senior level. Often, a representative listed as attending only stays for the relevant session and leaves. The lack of enthusiasm in the group can also be seen through its results. So far, in five years of existence, the group has not provided any real concrete results, and at one point the group failed to meet for two years between October 2001 and July 2003. Five ad hoc issue management groups have been created so far, none of which have borne any fruit.

One of the most serious problems of the EMG is its disconnection from the rest of the UN central coordination systems. The legal links are especially difficult to trace back to the ECOSOC and the General Assembly. In fact, reporting to these bodies does not take place in any formal way, particularly to the ECOSOC, which has the UN coordination function.

The EMG was originally envisaged to replace the Inter-Agency Committee on Sustainable Development. Shortly after the EMG began its work, this committee ceased to exist with the dismantling of its parent body, the Administrative Committee on Coordination, in October 2001. The EMG's terms of reference, however, were never clarified or updated to take this change into account and there is still no formal reporting system outside the UNEP Executive Director to raise the relevant issues with the UN Secretary-General. Technically, the EMG is supposed to report to the non-existent Inter-Agency Administrative Committee on Sustainable Development (IACSD). On several issues this has led to overlap and confusion; for example, members of the EMG have proposed new issues, such as on energy and on water, but have been reminded that HLCP has already undertaken coordination efforts in the area that would overlap with the EMG.[112]

The Chairman has made efforts to try to direct the EMG to make inputs into the CSD and the UNEP Global Ministerial Environment Forum. These initiatives have been welcomed by members of the group, but there is always concern that, without formal recognition, the inputs will go unrecognized.[113] At the ninth meeting, the EMG Chairman seemed more acutely aware of the EMG's standing being somewhat outside the whole UN coordination process and proposed a work programme in 2005 that would try to define its role via the HLCP, the UN

112. UNEP (2003) *Report of the Environmental Management Group*, Fourth meeting (July).
113. UNEP (2005) *Report of the Environmental Management Group* Tenth meeting (8 February), para. 26.

Development Group and other coordination systems.[114] In 2004, the UNEP Executive Director upon request from the UNEP Governing Council commissioned an independent evaluation of EMG. The study confirmed that EMG had an important role to play in coordinating key agencies but that there were "growing concerns about the ability of the EMG to fulfil its original mandate". Key concerns were over the slow pace of the EMG secretariat, the notion that EMG was "perceived as a support body for UNEP", the agenda having been over-focused on UNEP issues instead of balanced with issues from other agencies, and poor attendance with representation at a lower level than originally designed.[115] Without a clear role, no real incentives and a shortage of funds to carry out joint programming or clear modalities of how joint MEA initiatives could be undertaken, the EMG, which was supposed to reduce the fragmentation and overlap in the system, actually only added to it.[116]

This last point is also further reinforced by some of the responses that UNEP has made on its own to redress the lack of synergy and coordination in the environmental portfolio of the UN. In 1999, shortly after the "Renewing the United Nations" report,[117] the Executive Director of UNEP, Klaus Toepfer, created a new Division of Environmental Conventions (DEC) under UNEP to address the growing number and needs of environmental conventions and, more importantly, to try to build synergy between the MEAs. However, DEC's work with conventions outside UNEP's legal umbrella, such as with the UNFCC and the UNCCD, still remains especially difficult for UNEP. The DEC has offered its services to these conventions and invitations to participate in its efforts, but not wanting to be under the control of UNEP the convention secretariats are reluctant to have cooperation beyond what is superficial or politically necessary. Nevertheless, progress is being made with the hard work of the current DEC division that has now merged with the law arm of UNEP to become the DELC (Division of Environmental Law and Conventions).

But for now, as this discussion has shown, the MEA secretariats are isolated from the internal UN coordination mechanisms, since there are no financial or regulatory incentives. As a result, coordination has become very difficult to achieve on overarching issues from the UNSG of-

---

114. UNEP (2004) *Report of the Environmental Management Group*, Ninth meeting (8 November), para. 31.3.
115. UNEP (2004) *Evaluation and Oversight Study of EMG* (Restricted Doc. on file with the author).
116. On an assessment by the EMG, see Evaluation and Oversight Unit (2004) *A Study of the Environmental Management Group*, UNEP (30 December), on file with the author.
117. Report by the Secretary-General (1997).

fice, such as the Millennium Development Goals, Education for Sustainable Development or other cross-cutting issues. Ideally, since the MEA Executive Secretaries have a duty to inform their parties of relevant issues, including those coming from the UN Secretariat and the General Assembly, they would provide modalities concerning how the MEA can work towards the goals of these mandates while remaining within the mandate of their respective conventions. In practice this does not happen, and many secretariats take a very sectoral role and normally only pursue issues raised by their own parties when the political timing and environment make it safe to do so. For example, if you were to conduct a search for "EMG" in COP decisions using a keyword search engine you will find very little reference. Instead, the MEAs themselves have preferred to create and use their own external mechanisms for coordination, for example, the Rio Convention Liaison Group and the Biodiversity Liaison Group, as described above.

On the other hand, the UNEP Executive Director exerts much more influence over the MEAs that it itself administers. This is probably more due to "spill-over" from the influence of the UNEP administration's bearing on the daily operations of the MEAs under its care than any other factors. Also, the Executive Secretaries are appointed by the UN Secretary-General but in consultation with the UNEP Executive Director (ED) and sometimes the COP or its Bureau. This power of appointment has proved to provide a certain degree of influence over the secretariats and allows the ED to bring them into closer consultation. However, this is by no means a legally bound mechanism for coordination. If the Executive Secretary proves to be uncooperative in terms of hardly trying to cooperate with coordination efforts, the Executive Director has the recourse of making a poor performance evaluation and eventually calling into question a future renewal of the Executive Secretary's appointment.[118] In recent years, UNEP staff performance assessments have included criteria on the level of cooperation and collaboration with other UN bodies.[119] Similarly, the power of appointment plays an important role in the case of the MEAs under the legal umbrella of the FAO

118. On the dismissal of the CITES Secretary-General by the UNEP Executive Director in 1990, and the ensuing conflict with the Contracting Parties, see Peter H. Sand (1997) *Whither CITES? The Evolution of a Treaty Regime in the Borderland of Trade and Environment*, 8 Eur. J. Int'l L. 29, 36 note 45.

119. UNEP has conducted outside assessments of its management effectiveness by independent consultants. One of the recommendations made by this assessment was on strengthening inter-divisional knowledge flows and coordination: "Create incentives for collaboration by including collaboration as a key indicator both in PAS (the official performance appraisal system) and the Key Performance Indicators (KPIs) used to measure divisional performance." On file with the author.

and UNESCO, as well others such as the Law of the Sea and Forestry Principle Secretariat which are under specific departments of the UN Secretariat.

Strengthening interlinkages: Environmental governance reform

Periodically, serious consideration has been given to addressing some of the external and internal coordination problems, discussed in the previous two sections, through major structural reform and revamping. However, one of the key challenges for structure change is the identification of the most appropriate basis for approaching global environmental management. The global environment is a complex ecosystem composed of a multitude of smaller, interlinked ecosystems (e.g., air, soil, water) most of which we do not yet fully understand. Environmental problems are located at all levels within this nesting of ecosystems, and so too are their solutions. Taking this complexity into account, the most appropriate and effective basis for international environmental governance has yet to be fully identified, and it is this failure which underpins many of the weaknesses attributed to the current system.

The challenges posed by the physical complexity of the global environment are heightened by the expectation that the institutions of international environmental governance perform such a diversity of roles and functions. These often include, *inter alia*, scientific assessment, early warning, administrative management, coordination, compliance monitoring and dispute settlement, capacity-building and financing.

Furthermore, to move beyond the objectives of environmental management and protection towards the more comprehensive goal of sustainable development requires that the institutions of environmental governance should at least be compatible with, if not integrated into, other regimes within the global governance system. For sustainable development to be realized the institutions of international environmental governance must be compatible, for example, with the institutions of international economic governance including the World Bank, the International Monetary Fund and the World Trade Organization.

It is also crucial that the institutions of international environmental governance are innovative and capable of adapting to their continually changing operating environments. For example, these institutions must be capable of responding speedily to advances in the fields of science and technology. This does not only involve a capacity to assimilate new information about the environment itself but also a capacity to utilize new information and new technologies in innovative ways in the management of the global environment. Similarly, in order to maintain relevance, these institutions must be responsive to the economic, social and political concerns and influences that shape the interests of key actors and stakeholders. Without the active support of these actors and stakeholders the large-scale implementation of environmentally focused actions and regulations would be even more difficult to achieve.

The recognition of the inherent weakness of the international environmental governance structure has prompted arguments for a more integrated, binding, coordinated and synergistic system. The degree of structural change recommended has ranged from the creation of a World Environment Organization (WEO) to many other types of structural reforms. This last section of chapter 3 will briefly give an overview of these proposals with a view to discussing those which look more promising for the case of interlinkages.

One of the earliest examples of environmental governance reform that has been suggested in various academic and policy forums involves revamping the UN Trusteeship Council, which had served as an international caretaker organ during the period of European decolonization. This recommendation was originally made by a number of senior people who had long been involved with environmental governance issues, such as Maurice Strong and the Commission on Global Governance in its report "Our Global Neighbourhood".[120] The recommendation proposed that the now idle Trusteeship Council should be reformed into an organ that could take care of areas that do not fall under any national jurisdiction, such as the global commons. Alternatively, specific areas could be designated as environmental trusts to be looked after by the Trusteeship Council. Proponents of this idea have argued that a reformed Trusteeship Council could serve as a direct link between the UN and civil society with regard to environmental issues.[121] Opponents of the proposal suggest it would represent a step backwards for sustainable development in that it would only further separate environmental concerns from those relating to development.[122]

Another proposal, which has attracted much attention, is the creation of a World Environmental Court. This idea has gained renewed momentum because of the example set by recent efforts to put in place an

120. The question has now been further discussed by the UN General Assembly; see Resolution 60/1 of 16 September 2005, "Outcome of the World Summit: Winding Up the Trusteeship Council".

121. This proposal is supported in Commission on Global Governance (1995) *Our Global Neighbourhood*, Oxford: Oxford University Press; also op. cit. *Renewing the UN*, A/51/950 (14 July 1998), and also the *Tokyo 1999 Declaration of the Global Environmental Action* (1999), available at http://www.gea.co.jp.

122. Catherine Redgwell (2005) "Reforming the United Nations Trusteeship Council", in W. Bradnee Chambers and Jessica Green, eds, *Reforming International Environmental Governance*, Tokyo: UNU Press, 178–203.

International Criminal Court.[123] At a conceptual level, it is envisaged that this specialized environmental court would provide binding decisions in a more time-efficient way than the existing International Court of Justice. The added-value of an international environmental court, however, would be marginal compared to the existing courts and tribunals that do exist, for example, the Permanent Court of Arbitration, which also has optional rules for the arbitration of disputes relating to natural resources and/or the environment, the International Tribunal for the Law of the Sea, which has a chamber on marine environment[124] and the ICJ, which has universal jurisdiction and has heard many environmentally related cases.[125] On the other hand, if a World Environment Court were to be established based on compulsory jurisdiction this would be a completely different matter.[126] Here the added-value could be useful for unavoidable disputes that cannot be resolved through facilitation and monitoring and require adjudication but whereby a disputant is not willing to give up its jurisdiction to a third party.

The prospect of changing the mandate of the UN Security Council has also been raised by various academics and in different international forums. The Security Council has primarily dealt with traditional conceptions of international peace and security, although this has expanded since the end of the Cold War to include a number of humanitarian and human rights issues. Some have suggested that this expansion could be pushed even further to include the potential threat posed by certain epidemiological and environmental challenges.[127]

---

123. See Joost Pauwelyn (2005) "Judicial Mechanisms: Is There a Need for a World Environment Court", in W. Bradnee Chambers and Jessica Green, eds, *Reforming International Environmental Governance*, Tokyo: UNU Press, 150–177. The International Criminal Court was established in 1998; see Rome Statute of the ICC of 17 July 1998, 2187 UNTS 3 (entered into force 1 July 2002).

124. The Marine Environment Chamber was set up in 1997 pursuant to Article 15 para. 1 of the Statute of the ITLOS.

125. Before the ICJ even now is the Pulp Mills Case (Argentina v. Uruguay) which involves a dispute concerning the construction of a paper mill on the Uruguay River.

126. Currently only 67 States had accepted the ICJ's compulsory jurisdiction and about 300 treaties referred to the Court in relation to the settlement of disputes. See Press Release of General Assembly, "Court of United Nations Is Rapidly Expanding", available at http://www.un.org/News/Press/docs/2006/ga10523.doc.htm.

127. See Lorraine Elliot (2005) "Expanding the Mandate of the United Nations Security Council", in W. Bradnee Chambers and Jessica Green, eds, *Reforming International Environmental Governance*, Tokyo: UNU Press, 204–226. Also see for the role of the Security Council's UN Compensation Commission (UNCC) in the settlement of environmental claims from the 1991 Gulf War: Mojtaba Kazazi (2002) "Environmental Damage in the Practice of the UNCC", in Michael Bowman and Alan E. Boyle, eds, *Environmental Damage in International and Comparative Law: Problems of Definition and Valuation*, Oxford: Oxford University Press, 111–131.

Some structural reform proposals have also emerged in the context of devolution and subsidiarity, that is, tackling environmental problems closer to where they actually occur. The reasoning behind them is that most predominant ecosystems, river basins, seas/coastal marine systems, mountain ranges and other geographic landforms are regional by nature. These regional geographic systems tend to have impacts that are similar in scope and characteristics for each country within the region. Environmental pollution is also facilitated, or spread, by geographic mediums and conditions, creating common problems within given geographic regions.[128] From a problem-solving perspective, the scale of shared environmental problems, and the connections between them, makes a regional approach to interlinkages an effective prospect. The question then arises, however, as to whether any regional-level institutions currently exist that could deal effectively with commitments at the multilateral level. For instance, could regional institutions such as ASEAN, APEC, SADC or MERCOSUR, which developed out of trade cooperation, serve as effective regional mechanisms for environmental governance? Alternatively, would UN regional commissions be better able to handle such tasks[129] or, perhaps, do we need to consider the possibility of creating new special-purpose institutions?[130]

Clustering MEAs has also been one of the more practical suggestions that have come up in the context of discussion of environmental governance reform. Introduced by the late Konrad von Moltke, clustering can be defined as the strategic integration of conventions.[131] This would involve minor, non-structural reforms of the current international environmental governance system and include such actions as the co-location of

128. Lee Kimball (1999) *International Environmental Governance: A Regional Emphasis on Structured Linkages among Conventions and IGOs*, 2 Translex 1 (April). Also see IPCC (1997) *Summary for Policy makers – Regional Impacts of Climate Change: An Assessment of Vulnerability*, R. T. Watson, M. C. Zinyowera and R. H. Moss (eds), Cambridge: Cambridge University Press, also available at http://www.grida.no/climate/ipcc/regional/index.htm.

129. The UN Economic Commission for Europe (UNECE) for example has played the role of a regional forum for MEAs such as the *1979 Convention on Long-Range Transboundary Air Pollution* (1302 UNITS), 217; and the 1998 *Aarhus Convention on Access to Information, Public Participation in Decision Making and Access to Justice in Environmental Matters* (2161 UNITS), 447.

130. W. Bradnee Chambers (2002) "UN Reform at the Regional Level is Key," *Environmental Change & Security Project*, Princeton, N.J.: Princeton University, Woodrow Wilson International Center (August).

131. See Konrad von Moltke (2006) "On Clustering International Environmental Change", in Gerd Winter, ed., *Multilevel Governance of Global Environmental Change: Perspectives from Science, Sociology and Law*, Cambridge: Cambridge University Press, 409–429; also see Konrad von Moltke (2001) *The Organization of the Impossible*, 1 Glob. Envtl. Pol. 23.

secretariats, rationalized scheduling of conferences, and the coordination of decision-making. Clustering could be based upon issue (e.g., atmosphere, chemicals, biological diversity, fresh water resources and oceans),[132] function (e.g., compliance, dispute settlement, enforcement mechanisms, technology transfer, capacity-building, scientific assessment, administrative management, monitoring and reporting, finance or standards training for public servants and diplomats) or region (e.g., UN regional commissions, EU, NAFTA, Mercosur).[133] Some of the less common proposals for clustering are based upon the source of harm or the impact on the ecosystem.[134] Recently, a proposal for tiered clustering based on issue and then function has gained support. However, potential difficulties have already been associated with the uncommon MEA membership.[135]

One proposal that has continued to resurface lies in the realm of deep structural change and involves the creation of a world environmental organization. Although the idea of a new global-scale international environmental organization was once sidelined in the UNCED process, it regained currency several years ago in the academic literature.[136] Providing for a coherent system of international environmental governance could be achieved by centralizing the current system under one umbrella institution. Such an institution could be a World Environment Organization operating along the same lines as the World Trade Organization, International Maritime Organization or the International Labour Organization, in terms of their coordination and standard-setting functions.

Combining the above clustering approach and a compulsory dispute settlement system with the approach of a central organization such as a

132. As an example of the scientific linkages that could be the basis for clustering see: IPCC (2002) *Climate Change and Biodiversity*, H. Gitay, A. Suarez, R. T. Watson, and D. Dokken, eds; IPCC (2001) *Technical Paper V*, available at http://www.ipcc.ch/pub/tpbiodiv.pdf.
133. Sebastian Oberthur (2005) "Clustering of Multilateral Environmental Agreements: Potentials and Limitations", in W. Bradnee Chamber and Jessica Green, eds, *Reforming International Environmental Governance*, Tokyo: UNU Press, 40–65.
134. See UNEP (2001) *Implementing the Clustering Strategy for Multilateral Environmental Agreements*, UNEP/IGM/4/4 (16 November).
135. See UNEP (2001) *The Concept of Waste and Clustering: Waste Clustering*, UNEP/IGM/2/INF/2.
136. See G. Palmer (1992) *New Ways to Make International Environmental Law*, 86 AJIL, 259; D. Esty (1994) *Greening the GATT: Trade, Environment, and the Future*, Washington, D.C.: Institute for International Economics; F. Biermann and U. E. Simonis (1998) *A World Environment and Development Organization*, SEF Policy Paper 9, Bonn: Development and Peace Foundation; G. Ulfstein (1999) *The Proposed GEO and Its Relationship to Existing MEAs*, paper presented at the International Conference on Synergies and Coordination between Multilateral Environmental Agreements, UNU, 14–16 July. See also the statement that came out of the conference, "Strengthening Global Environmental Governance", New York, 4–5 June 1998.

World Environment Organization (WEO) could make a lot of sense. A WEO based on a centralization model would not necessarily require the disbanding of any existing environmental bodies; these bodies would simply fall under the WEO's oversight and direction.[137] This organization could have the authority to coordinate MEAs and other environment-related institutions on the basis of certain agreed principles such as those already well established under international law, such as the polluter pays principle, common but differentiated responsibility, the precautionary principle and prior informed consent. The first step could be to place agreements into clusters under the central organization; for example CITES, CMS, Ramsar and the CBD could be placed in one group related to biodiversity and ecosystems; the chemical conventions such as the Stockholm Convention on Persistent Organic Pollutants, the Basel Convention on the Control of Transboundary Movement of Hazardous Wastes and Their Disposal and the Rotterdam Convention on the Prior Informed Consent Procedure for Certain Hazardous Chemicals and Pesticides in International Trade could become a chemicals group; the UNFCCC, the Ozone Convention and LRTAP could represent yet a fourth group on atmosphere; UNCLOS, the regional seas conventions, OSPAR Convention and other ocean/sea- and marine-related conventions could be a fifth group; the last group could be on land degradation and encompass UNCCD, the International Forestry Principles and any other relevant conventions.

Similar to the WTO there could be a central governing council that took major decisions on amendments, protocols or multiple-year work plans. Each cluster could have a separate committee under the central governing council, much like the specialized committees under the WTO on agriculture, development, services and trade and environment. There could be a number of cross-cutting committees, one on development and environment, environment/trade/investment and environment/human rights. Alternatively, the cross-cutting committees could take a more progressive approach than the traditional sectoral and UN divisions and comprise committees based on the services that ecosystems provide, such as provisioning, regulating, supporting and cultural services.[138] Here human well-being would be at the centre of the cross-cuts instead of sectors that are processes-driven rather than objective-based. Having cross-cutting committees on ecosystem services would also create interlinkages between the main committees as these would address the connections between main committees both through their biophysical

---

137. See Lawrence David Levien (1972) *A Structural Model for a World Environmental Organization: The ILO Experience*, 40 Geo. Wash. Int'l L. Rev., 464.
138. See Millennium Ecosystem Conceptual Framework, 2004.

connections and through their combined interactions to provide services for the benefit of human beings.

The committees could meet on a regular basis with permanent representation instead of having major COP/MOPs and subsidiary meetings on a yearly basis. Permanent representation would be more cost-effective and allow more integration between the MEAs as the same representatives would regularly service the committees and experts from the respective capitals would only be needed on specialized topics. Such an arrangement would also more efficiently manage the cross-cutting issues that transcend almost all the MEAs, but which now under the current governance structure must rely on other forums such as WTO or the CSD for action. Every two to four years ministerial meetings could take place to review the implementation of the MEAs and look at ways at improving cooperation and strengthening commitments. Every 10 years there could be a world summit of heads of states that would start with regional and national preparation and would choose major themes of negotiations and then would use the WEO committees and council as a means for negotiations leading to a summit that that would make the final negotiations and agreements. These 10 year summits would act like the WTO trade rounds or the world summits such as UNCHE, UNCED and WSSD and would be targeted at reviewing the whole system and looking for deeper commitments. Unlike the WTO, the committees, general council and summits would be open to civil society and would abide by the liberal rules of participation that the MEAs and environmental community have developed in the 35 years since Stockholm. The summits could also take on cross-cutting themes with other ministerial processes such as WTO or on human rights – perhaps a ministerial forum within these areas.

Within such an organization, various functions of international environmental governance, such as scientific assessment, monitoring and reporting and capacity-building, could be streamlined and centralized. Currently, scientific assessments and monitoring are highly fragmented and there lacks clear intergovernmental consultations to establish the information and knowledge needs that the policy-makers require to address environmental challenges. Most of the MEAs have their own scientific mechanisms, such as the UNFCCC, which uses the Intergovernmental Panel on Climate Change, or ad hoc assessments that are periodically conducted, such as the Ozone Assessment, the Biodiversity Assessment or the Millennium Ecosystem Assessment that had mandates from the UNCCD, CBD, CMS and Ramsar Conventions. In addition, most of the MEAs have technical and advisory committees. UNEP and GEF also have separate science assessments such as the Global Environmental Outlook (GEO), which is conducted every four to five years for

UNEP, and the Scientific and Technical Advisory Panel (STAP), which provides ongoing advice to GEF on its focal areas. The knowledge, assessment, data and monitoring needs could be wholly integrated and draw on national and regional monitoring and observing systems that already exist but that are now scattered or loosely based on separate networks. A central WEO could integrate these various components and could be based on schemes such as that which the UNEP Governing Council is exploring through the creation of Environment Watch. This would be a coherent system that placed data, monitoring, indicators and assessments under one roof. It would also strengthen the science–policy interface and the needs of the committees, council or ministerials could request scientific information, and the scientific side of the organization would have the capacity and the integrated reach to be able to address the questions posed by these intergovernmental processes.

Regional MEAs could also be integrated much as the regional trade unions are set up now under the WTO. This would mean that they would be able to set regional standards or address regional environmental problems but could not derogate from the standards set within the WEO (and the MEAs under it); it would also mean that the regional arrangements would have to comply with the application on the aforementioned standard principles and disciplines set under the WEO.[139]

The WEO could also assist greatly in harmonizing all the administrative procedures and complications of the international institutional rules that are not well defined and which often act as barriers to cooperation or create uncertainty on whether MEAs' secretariats can cooperate. Under a centralized system such as a WEO, the need to be defining whether the MEA is semi-independent, has legal personality or has the scope to cooperate with other organizations would become irrelevant as the MEAs would operate under the same institutional framework.

The financial side of the WEO could come from integrating the GEF into it instead of placing it under the World Bank. The GEF could still operate independently but from a special council set up under the WEO that could oversee all the financing and best decide where projects were cross-cutting, either geographically or issues-based, and work and respond to country needs more directly.

At first, the integration could move towards a GATT-like system, which might be politically more feasible, but eventually it could move to stronger integration if it were to create a compulsory dispute settlement system with both the capacity to facilitate compliance in cases where non-compliance is due to a lack of technical know-how or provide strong

---

139. UNEP (2006) *UN Reform: Implications for the Environment Pillar*, Nairobi: UNEP-DEWA.

enforcement measures in cases of more serious breaches of treaty obligations.[140] Here the arguments for a centralized governance system have
been quite succinct. The lack of direct enforcement procedures or obligatory dispute settlement mechanisms within most MEAs has led to serious
questions that have been raised about treaty implementation at the national level. Several countries have been criticized with regard to their
efforts – at a practical level – to implement their binding obligations
under various MEAs. Proponents of greater integration in environmental
governance draw upon the WTO as an example of how such compliance
and dispute settlement issues could be addressed. The WTO has a comparatively effective and well-developed compliance and dispute settlement system. While over 20 agreements fall under the WTO umbrella,
they all operate within a common and obligatory dispute settlement
framework. This framework provides the opportunity to use economic
sanctions as counter measures or to nullify membership benefits in cases
of treaty non-compliance.

If a centralized model of international environmental governance were
to be adopted, and a WEO created, it is possible that this new organization would emanate from a reformed UNEP.[141] This is the proposal that
originally came from the French Government but has now also been officially adopted by the European Council of Ministers in June 2005.[142]
The EU's argument is that "an UNEO (United Nations Environment Organization) will be the equal of the other agencies and will benefit from
stable financing". The idea would be to upgrade UNEP to the status of a
specialized agency under Article 59 of the UN Charter. Though not part
of the EU proposal, if such a move were to take place, all MEAs could be
placed under the jurisdiction of the new agency, which would have a
more substantial coordination and decision-making role than currently
held by UNEP. This new agency could have access to the regular UN
budget, although it would have to compete with other agencies for its

---

140. See Gary Sampson (2005) "The World Environment Organization and Global Environmental Governance", in W. Bradnee Chamber and Jessica Green, eds, *Reforming
International Environmental Governance*, Tokyo: UNU Press, 124–149.

141. Supporters of the proposal to create an umbrella organization out of UNEP include
Germany and France. See Speech by Dr Helmut Kohl, Chancellor of the Federal
Republic of Germany, at the Special Session of the General Assembly of the United
Nations, New York, 23 June 1997, and Speech by Jacques Chirac, President of the Re-
public of France, to the World Conservation Union, Fontainebleau, France, 3 Novem-
ber 1998. For other views see supra Konrad von Moltke, *Multilevel Governance of
Global Environmental Change*.

142. Council of the European Union (2005) *Conclusion of Presidency from 18 to 19
June 2005*, (20 June), available at http://www.eu2005.lu/en/actualites/conseil/2005/06/
17conseur-concl/index.html.

share of funding. This proposal makes the most sense by far from a political and organizational point of view.[143]

Over the past number of years there have been many objections to the centralized model, most of which have been political arguments. The same dominating factor has led to the fragmented, overlapping environmental governance system that is in place now, a result of political bargaining, compromise and deal-making in a hopeless effort to attempt to satisfy and balance the diverse interests that the multilateral system embodies. Politics has guided the design of international environmental governance for far too long; there is a serious need to develop a system based on a coherent organizational rationale. This may indeed come sooner rather than later; as environmental problems worsen and natural resources become scarcer, effective environmental governance will become more of a necessity than a luxury and in the end may require the creation of stronger systems to deliver the optimal results.

Another political argument that is often made is that the MEAs and international organizations all have separate governing structures and it would be politically unfeasible to get their permission to create a superstructure over the top of these intergovernmental bodies. This argument carries some weight and it is true that this would be the major hurdle, but most MEAs can be amended and the membership is overlapping, which would offer the practicality of coordinating any integration from the national level. It may also be a chance for national governments to update their own legislation, which tends to suffer from the same redundancy, fragmentation or non-implementation. Greater national integration could be achieved through the creation of what is sometimes referred to as "umbrella legislation" or framework laws that implement multiple convention obligations through a single coordinated national law. There are also some precedents where post facto integration of international agreements has taken place. The most cited of course is the WTO, which subsumed all the GATT agreements under a single organization umbrella with a common dispute settlement system, but as Steve Charnovitz points out this example is not a good one as the GATT agreements were already integrated, which is not the case with the MEAs.[144] A better

---

143. There is a vast literature on the creation of a world environment organization. See for example: Frank Biermann (2000) *The Case for a World Environment Organization*, 42 Environment, 22, 23–24; Daniel C. Esty (1994) "The Case for a Global Environmental Organization", in P. B. Kenen, ed., *Managing the World Economy: Fifty Years after Bretton Woods*, Washington, D.C.: Institute for International Economics, 287, 287–307; Udo E. Simonis (2002) *Advancing the Debate on a World Environment Organization*, 22 The Environmentalist, 29; Steve Charnovitz (2002) 27 Colum. J. Envtl. L., 323.

144. Steve Charnovitz (2005) "A World Environment Organization", in W. Bradnee Chamber and Jessica Green, eds, *Reforming International Environmental Governance*, Tokyo: UNU Press, 99.

example is the World Intellectual Property Organization, which in 1967 brought together the major intellectual property treaties under it and now administers 21 different agreements.[145]

The second set of arguments against centralization have been of a bureaucratic nature, along the lines that a centralized system would be overly bureaucratic and its scope too large for a single organization and that this would ultimately lead to inevitable inefficiencies.[146] This argument has some foundation but at the same time it is useful to compare a centralized model such as the one proposed here to that of the current system which has become so complex it is difficult to even begin to understand it as a functional system (see fig. 3.1). It is also worth considering that the current system is financially burdensome. A recent study by the UN System Joint Inspection Unit has estimated that it requires US$5 billion annually to operate;[147] others have put this much higher at over US$10 billion annually.[148] In comparison, the figure for the WTO, which is the secretariat and dispute settlement body for nearly 30 agreements and operates on a central model similar to the one portrayed above, is roughly US$14 million per year.[149] I am not saying that all the MEAs bundled into a WEO could operate under a budget similar to the WTO, because the scope of environmental issues are much broader; however, there are gains that could be made by making the environmental governance system more efficient. Moreover, full integration may not be desirable, as Charnovitz has argued a calculus for the reorganization of MEAs towards a centralized model does not necessarily mean that all current institutions would have to fit under one umbrella of a WEO. Rather the rationale for integration could be based on weighing the costs of reorganization against the expected gains.[150]

While many of the proposals put forward may be attractive at first glance, those seeking to probe deeper into the feasibility and utility of each are confronted with a whole host of complexities and challenges

---

145. Ibid.
146. Calestous Juma (2000) "The Perils of Centralizing Global Environmental Governance", *Environmental Matters*, at 13, 15.
147. Draft of study on file with author.
148. A study done by the International Institute for Sustainable Development has estimated the costs of a number of the principal MEAs, and environment-related organizations as well as a few major non-governmental organizations and estimated that this would be around US$10 billion per year; see Adil Najam, Mihaela Papa and Nadaa Taiyab (2006) *Global Environmental Governance: A Reform Agenda*, Winnipeg: International Institute for Sustainable Development, Annex, available at http://www.iisd.org/pdf/2006/geg.pdf.
149. See WTO budget for 2006 at http://www.wto.org/english/thewto_e/secre_e/budget06_e.htm.
150. Supra, Charnovitz, *A World Environment Organization*, 100.

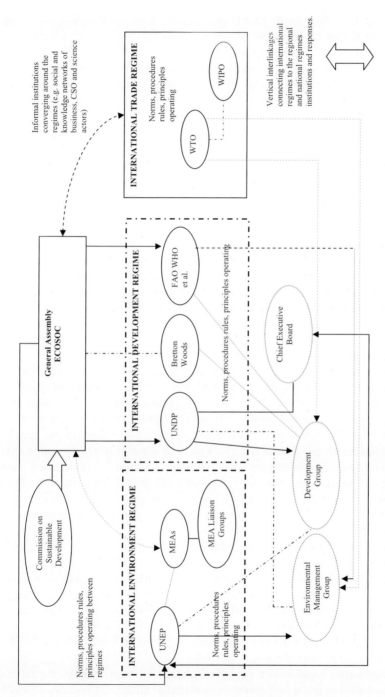

Figure 3.1 Portrait of the fragmentation of international environmental governance

that need to be assessed. This is particularly the case with regard to the proposed WEO. Many of the complexities are a consequence of the myriad of interrelated functional, political and legal aspects to the challenge of effective environmental governance. The question of whether any of these proposals offer a more effective system remains to be seen and would require strong comparative assessments between what is the current system and what a new structure could offer.

What this chapter has shown, is that, at a minimum, the current environmental governance system and legal milieu for promoting interlinkages amongst MEAs remains ineffective and badly requires fundamental redress and legal reform. As will be shown in the two case studies in chapters 6 and 7, improving the interlinkages between MEAs leads to greater effectiveness and mutual benefits for the cooperating treaties. Indeed, if interlinkages can be a positive force for effectiveness would it not be logical for reforms such as a WEO that promotes integration to be more actively sought? Perhaps the jury is still out, but this book will fill a gap and assist decision-makers to understand the value-added of MEA cooperation and help them to understand concretely the benefits of integration and how to use this in their calculus for reform.

Conclusion

The legal milieu for interlinkages of MEAs can be defined at three levels. The Vienna Convention on the Law of Treaties defines how successive MEAs, as international treaties, avoid conflict and relate to each other. These rules, though important, are not reflective of time and are residuary to the needs of modern MEAs, which, in a world of treaty congestion and pressure to cooperate, require rules more suited to cooperation than conflict or succession. The international rules that do exist occur at both the external and internal levels but in many ways are either too complex or badly defined and, as a result, are unhelpful for dealing with the current needs of MEA modern cooperation.

The legal milieu for external interlinkages depends largely on the judicial personality of the MEA in question. Today's MEAs are showing increasing independence from their parent or supervisory organizations, so much so that many are regarded as autonomous institutional arrangements with legal personality equated to fully fledged international organizations. The legal personality provides the scope for MEA secretariats and their bodies to formally cooperate with other MEAs under MOUs and to create liaison groups.

The internal legal milieu for interlinkages between MEAs is perhaps the least well defined and requires substantial structural redress. Coordination problems exist between parent/supervisory organizations and their quasi-independent MEAs. Legally, the MEA bodies and their officers are bound by the rules and regulations of the parent, as is demonstrated in the case of the UN, but for governance matters the MEA secretariats remain independent to take instructions from the COPs or their subsidiary bodies. Internal coordination can have another dimension, not always well understood or legally defined, as is the case in the UN system that administers the majority of the MEAs. Through the UN ECOSOC, the UN has created myriad internal mechanisms such as the CEB and the EMG that are supposed to guide cooperation and spur coordination but, to date, these mechanisms have not created the kind of effective cooperation that might be possible if a more structurally defined MEA governance system was in place. When looking at the overall legal milieu for MEAs to promote and manage interlinkages with other MEAs, the words of the late Konrad von Moltke ring loud. He reminds us that "at no time has the entire structure of international environmental management ever been reviewed with the goal of developing optimum architecture".[151] It might be high time that more studies take place to understand the benefits of greater MEA cooperation, such as this book provides. Subsequently, based on such studies, organizational models (such as the centralized WEO model described here) could be developed to better capture the positive benefits for MEAs derived from interlinkages.

151. Konrad von Moltke (2001) *Whither MEAs? The Role of International Environmental Management in the Trade and Environment Agenda*, Winnipeg: IISD (July), at 6, 14–22, 30–32.

Part IV

Theoretical foundations and basis for an analytical framework

4

Towards an improved understanding of effectiveness of international treaties[1]

Introduction

Given that the international community has negotiated countless treaties over the last several decades, one would imagine that it would have a clear conception of what constitutes effective international law. However, despite its frequent use, and the numerous studies that have dealt with the topic, there remains a poor understanding of effectiveness in international law. Just a few of the references to effectiveness in international law demonstrate the wide variety of definitions and understanding of the concept.

Effectiveness is a concept often referred to in international law literature:

- Effectiveness of different regulatory and enforcement techniques is largely determined by the nature of the problem.[2]
- The effectiveness of international law rests on the recognition it receives from the governments of the world.[3]

1. A version of this chapter was published in 14 *Georgetown International Environmental Law Review*, W. Bradnee Chambers (2004) "Towards an Improved Understanding of Legal Effectiveness of International Environmental Treaties", 501–532.
2. Patricia Birnie and Alan Boyle (2002) *International Law and the Environment*, 2nd ed., Oxford: Oxford University Press, 10.
3. Natsu Taylor Saito (1998) *Justice Held Hostage: U.S. Disregard for International Law in the World War II Internment of Japanese Peruvians – A Case Study*, 40 Boston College Law review, 275, 340.

Interlinkages and the effectiveness of multilateral environmental agreements,
W. Bradnee Chambers, United Nations University Press, 2008, ISBN 978-92-808-1149-0

- The validity and effectiveness of international law depends on the continuing consent and support of nation-states.[4]
- The effectiveness of international law largely depends on the flexibility of the international law-making processes, as well as its ability to combine new concepts and techniques.[5]
- ... the effectiveness of international law as its capacity to be implemented at the international and national levels. ... The effectiveness of international law ... is ultimately measured according to its enforcement at the local level.[6]

Perhaps international law is considered effective because it is a political exercise and, therefore, non-negotiable? Is effective international law one that achieves the objectives set out in the treaty? Or perhaps effectiveness can be defined philosophically, as those laws that achieve justice and fairness? Or does effectiveness conform to the positivists' notion that law is effective when it achieves sufficient compliance to be accepted by all? Whatever the perception, the reality is that laws are often crafted without any understanding of what is effective and what is not.

The traditional principle of effectiveness focused more on the form and power of treaties rather than their design or impact. As Hans Kelsen stated more than 70 years ago, the pure theory of law was "what and how the law is, not how it ought to be". The reality of the effectiveness of treaties is quite the contrary;[7] design and impact are critical to a treaty's effectiveness. Treaty-making on the environment is testimony to this fact: during a period that created an unprecedented number of treaties and international rules to protect the environment, we have also seen unprecedented environmental degradation.[8]

This chapter will draw from work from various disciplines to offer a more ample and multifaceted definition of effectiveness in international treaties. It will examine the various concepts of effectiveness from the standpoint of treaties, the main source of international law, and will focus on environmental law, although the insights will be useful for international public law at large. The chapter establishes that effectiveness can be defined in several ways. Whereas social sciences view effectiveness from the broader notion of the effect institutions have on societal behav-

---

4. Jianming Shen (2000) *National Sovereignty and Human Rights in a Positive Law Context*, 26 Brook. J. Int'l L., 417, 419.
5. Erik M. Limpitlaw (2001) *Is International Law Waterproof? The Impact of Technology on Oceans as Commons*, 29 Syracuse J. Int'l L. & Com. 185, 196.
6. Catherine Giraud-Kinley (1999) *The Effectiveness of International Law: Sustainable Development in the South Pacific Region*, 12 Geo. Int'l Envtl. L. Rev., 125, 170.
7. Hans Kelsen (1970) *Pure Theory of Law*, Berkeley: University of California Press, 1.
8. Shona Dodds et al. (2002) *International Sustainable Development Governance: The Question of Reform: Key Issues and Proposals*, UNU-IAS Report.

iour, the definition used in this chapter will be from the legal standpoint, which looks specifically at international treaties and their impact on solving the problem stated by their objective(s).

First, the chapter will examine works to date that have studied effectiveness – drawn largely from the field of international law. These works have looked to implementation and compliance as essential components of effectiveness. Next the chapter will chronicle additions to the effectiveness discussion made by the international relations literature. Specifically, this portion of the chapter will argue that international relations studies have provided a great deal of insight into how implementation is important to understanding the impact that institutions have on the behaviour of both state and non-state actors. While international relations studies have made strides in outlining the relationship between institutions and effectiveness, proving direct causal connections between the specific operations of an institution and the corresponding effect on behaviour is very difficult with the current quantitative and qualitative data that exists. This section of the chapter will suggest that studies so far on compliance have also led to important contributions to understanding how obligations that are specifically laid out in the treaties are met at the domestic and international levels but still do not give a full picture of treaty effectiveness. To equate compliance with effectiveness, however, would merely be a rule-based positivistic approach that would not necessarily show whether the objectives of the treaties are in fact being met.

Based on the analysis in Part II, the remainder of the chapter will argue that a legal definition of effectiveness should be expanded beyond the positivistic notion of compliance as it is commonly used in the literature. A new approach to effectiveness must incorporate the work of other disciplines and also embrace more recent understandings of international law that view it as a process rather than a set of rules. The process view of international law offers one explanation of why states obey international law without an enforcement regime: As an evolving process, international law can incorporate and then reflect domestic norms on the international level. In the third section, I will argue that an expanded definition of effectiveness must account for the robustness of a treaty and its ability to reflect domestic norms continually. With these norms incorporated, each party improves its ability to meet its stated objectives.

In addition to the robustness of a treaty, other criteria of effectiveness must also be considered. These include a comparison of the treaty's core objectives to its performance data, compliance of obligatory measures and the role and impact of a treaty's supporting programmes and procedure. The treaty's financing and international legal environment are also important factors that can affect its validity and effectiveness.

Models of effectiveness

The discussion of the term "effectiveness" in the modern context has grown primarily out of two larger debates over the last decade. The first is a long-standing debate about the importance of international law, and the second pertains to the growing consensus that certain environmental problems can only be dealt with through multilateral approaches.

Since Grotian times, international law has been grappling with the question of whether it really matters. Since international laws are, for the most part, self-executing rules rather than enforceable rules, the question of whether international law actually has any influence over the behaviour of states has persisted. Many studies have sought the answer to these questions by focusing on compliance. If states are in compliance with international laws, then international law is changing state behaviour and hence international law indeed matters and can be considered effective. In recent years, this debate has shifted its focus from whether states comply with what has motivated them to comply. Louis Henkin's hypothesis that "almost all nations observe almost all principles of international law and almost all of their obligations almost all of the time" has spurred a growing body of literature on compliance theory.[9]

The second debate to which the legal interest in effectiveness has been applied is that of global connectivity. For example, in the field of economic law, lawyers have started to pay much more attention to the effectiveness of international treaties. In a globalizing world, as the regulation of economies is becoming more diffused and lies outside the control of national regulations, governments see a stronger role for international regulation. The role of effectiveness is to strengthen international policy and to "attempt to recover the possibly lost or at least diminished grip of national law over business activities".[10] Similarly, environmental lawyers are observing a growing number of actors, NGOs representing global constituencies, multinational corporations with operations in multiple jurisdictions and, most importantly, environmental problems that transcend borders and that can only be tackled through global cooperation. For these types of issues effective international law is the only means of solving such problems.

For these reasons, international lawyers have increasingly become concerned with the concept of effectiveness. However, as with many other disciplines, international lawyers have narrowed the definition of effec-

9. See Louis Henkin (1979) *How Nations Behave*, 2d ed., New York: Columbia University Press.
10. Thomas Waelde, *Effectiveness: The Holy Grail of Modern International Lawyers*, The CEPMLP Internet Journal, available at http://www.dundee.ac.uk/cepmlp/journal/html/vol3/vol3-5.html.

tiveness to the theoretical standpoint of international law. Thus, to move towards a new, more expansive understanding of what an effective law really is, we must build from the various theoretical roots of law and other disciplines. This includes contributions from international relations that have implications for the effectiveness of international treaties. This chapter will examine these contributions, tracing the theoretical roots from various legal and international relations models, in an effort to provide a more comprehensive understanding of effectiveness.

Legal models

Rule-based positivist models

One of the most practical means of looking at effectiveness is through the lens of compliance, which focuses on the actual rules and obligations found in treaties themselves. This type of approach is derived from the positivist point of view. Traditional legal positivists concern themselves with the actual laws. They regard rules and regulations as artefacts with practical authority over a sufficient number of subjects to be generally efficacious in ordering their practical affairs.[11] From an empirical standpoint, laws are comparably easier to collect data on than more intangible variables such as norms or justice put forward by other legal scholarship in the effectiveness debate. So, it is not surprising to see that positivists are the first to take up the effectiveness question: Harold Jacobson and Edith Brown Weiss authored one of the pioneering studies on the subject.[12]

As rules-based positivists, their work focuses on implementation and compliance. Implementation refers to how international rules are transformed into domestic laws. Jacobson and Brown Weiss are quick to point out that, although some international rules may be self-executing, requiring no ratifying legislation, these rules require policy measures to ensure compliance – such as financial incentives, forms of legislation, directives,

---

11. Larry Alexander and Emily Sherwin (2001) *The Rule of Rules: Morality, Rules, and the Dilemmas of Law*, Durham, N.C.: Duke University Press, 188.
12. See generally Edith Brown Weiss and Harold K. Jacobson, eds (1998) *Engaging Countries: Strengthening Compliance with International Environmental Accords*, Tokyo: UNU Press. The *Jacobson-Brown Weiss Study* is in fact a collaboration between political scientists and legal academics and is often referred to as a multidisciplinary study. In many respects this is true, particularly since social science methods of data collection and analysis were used that legal academics tend not to use. However, the fact remains that the model itself is a more legal positivist one. Harold Jacobson was also a self-proclaimed "positivist political scientist". See Harold K. Jacobson (1998) *Afterword: Conceptual, Methodological and Substantive Issues Entwined in Studying Compliance*, 19 Mich. J. Int'l L., 569, 573.

procedures or sanctions.[13] According to Jacobson and Brown Weiss, the second concept of compliance "goes beyond implementation", in the sense that it looks not only at the substantive and procedural obligations that are found in the treaty but also at the treaty as a whole, from the preamble to the specific obligations, express specific intent or spirit that is also expected to be followed at the domestic level.[14]

Measuring compliance in some cases is elusive. In more straightforward legal obligations, such as submitting progress reports, assessing compliance can be relatively easy. But other laws may call for more complex methods of assessment, which are not as easily measured. The Jacobson–Brown Weiss study believes that effectiveness cannot be understood unless the first steps of understanding compliance and implementation are first taken.[15] The authors' analytical framework looks at factors surrounding implementation and compliance: the characteristics of the accord; the negotiating environment; the actors involved; and the depth of the accord, which includes its obligations (binding or hortatory), as well as its precision. The study also considers other factors that influence effectiveness, including the intrusiveness of the activity; mechanisms for implementation; treatment of non-parties; the existence of freeloaders; other countries' approaches to compliance; and the role of international organizations and the media.[16] Finally the study looks at the factors involving the country, "the social, cultural, political, and economic characteristics of the countries" and how they influence compliance and implementation of the accord.[17]

All of these variables impact a country's implementation of and compliance with international treaties. In turn, implementation and compliance have a direct bearing on a treaty's effectiveness. According to Jacobson and Brown Weiss, effectiveness is looking at the overall objective of the treaty and determining whether it has been successful at achieving its objectives. Therefore, compliance is similar to effectiveness but it is not exactly the same: Parties can be in compliance with treaty obligations, even though the treaty fails to meet its objective. For example, a treaty may unintentionally create incentives to switch to other technologies that may be equally as damaging to the environment but in a different way. To be effective, an international treaty must achieve its policy objective.

13. See Edith Brown Weiss and Harold K. Jacobson, eds (1998) *A Framework for Analysis*, in *Engaging Countries: Strengthening Compliance with International Environmental Accords*, 1, 2.
14. Ibid., 4.
15. Ibid., 5–6.
16. Ibid., 6–12.
17. Ibid., 7.

There have been very few other studies using the positivist perspective that have approached the scale and depth of the Jacobson-Brown Weiss study. UNEP has conducted some assessments of effectiveness based on specific criteria that was to a large extent rule-based data contained in the agreements. For instance, in 1991, just prior to the Rio Earth Summit, it led a survey on existing international legal agreements and instruments in the environmental field.[18] The survey based its evaluation on a set of criteria recommended by an open-ended working group of the UNCED Preparatory Committee made up of government representatives and diplomats, so in fact the criteria were based more on the consensus of the committee than on any explicit methodology.[19] Nevertheless the approach was from a positivist standpoint and included the following aspects, objectives and achievement of the instrument: participation (i.e., membership, reservations, involvement of developing countries); implementation (i.e., entry into force, compliance, performance review, dispute settlement); operations (secretariat, financial costs); and codification (i.e., coordination).

A number of international lawyers and legal experts then applied these criteria to the existing environmental legal instruments. The survey failed to make any definitive conclusions concerning the effectiveness of the individual instruments or generally about the effectiveness of environmental treaties. This was in part due to the difficulty in measuring the achievement of the instruments, as many of the objectives in the instruments were abstract or hortatory. Furthermore, many of the agreements did not have measurable data or quantitative targets, which made it difficult to evaluate the agreements' impact.[20] A similar type of assessment was done prior to the 2002 World Summit on Sustainable Development, but the scope was limited to only 10 major multilateral agreements and it changed its approach considerably from the more positivist approach earlier undertaken by the 1991 survey, using instead the process approach.[21]

The 1991 UNEP survey, along with the Jacobson–Brown Weiss study, shows the importance of compliance at different scales, the need for engagement of all actors including state and non-state actors, and the importance of external factors in determining effectiveness of the legal instrument. The studies described proven techniques in negotiating the accord, setting up the institutional architecture and targeting specific

18. Peter Sand, ed. (1992) *The Effectiveness of International Environmental Agreements*, Cambridge: Grotius [hereinafter Sand].
19. Ibid., 19.
20. Ibid., 11.
21. Kal Raustiala, *Reporting and Review Institutions in 10 Multilateral Environmental Agreements* [hereinafter *Review Institutions*], available at http://www.unep.org/geo/pdfs/ MEA PM 70 Part B FFF.pdf.

measures to countries to enhance effectiveness. At the same time, the studies illustrate the difficulty in comparing the objectives of the treaties to demonstrable outcomes because of either a lack of measurable targets or ambiguity in the objectives themselves. Finally, these studies only offer a partial picture of effectiveness – one that is limited by the positivist approach. Since positivism assumes that states will comply with existing rules, and does not ask why this is so, this perspective does little to explain compliance in situations where there are neither strong positive incentives nor enforcement techniques.

Social legal models

Social legal theory bases its explanation of effectiveness on social change and the congruence of law with societal norms. There are several models in this body of literature but most are based upon social constructs such as norms and values and how they interact with law.[22] Social legal theory has been particularly condemning of the positivist view that laws are merely created and imposed upon society to follow. Social legal theorists have criticized this account of law as pious, stating that "might makes right" does not ensure that humans will follow the law as they expect to be given "reasons for obeying and conforming to the law".[23] In the view of social legal theorists, positivism does not explain where law comes from and how better laws that are more easily followed could be created. Ontologically, social legal theories begin by explaining law from the opposite end of the spectrum to positivists. Whereas positivist theory takes the law as pre-existing, social legal theory sees law coming from the values and norms created and accepted by society, which are then codified into laws to be applied in the various contexts and applications of society. So, for social legal theorists, effective laws are those that are closely prescribed to fit societal norms and values. According to social legal theory, law is in a constant state of flux. It operates in an "established milieu", it "projects certain goals and purposes", and it creates steps (or laws) to achieve these.[24] The goal is to achieve a balance of these three components.

Relatively recent legal discourse on compliance and rationalizing state behaviour has taken up explanations that utilize norms and values drawn from the perspective of international relations. These norm-based theories in international relations are often categorized as constructivist

---

22. For a general explanation of social legal theories, see H. L. A. Hart (1961) *The Concept of Law*, Oxford: Oxford University Press; and Iredell Jenkins (1980) *Social Order and the Limits of Law: A Theoretical Essay*, Princeton, N.J.: Princeton University Press.
23. Supra, Jenkins, 180.
24. Ibid., 119.

or post-modernist theories. However, law is also rich in theory and able to explain these contributions from the standpoint of social legal analysis. One important work that has contributed to the discussion of effectiveness from the legal perspective is Abram and Antonia Chayes' work, *The New Sovereignty: Compliance with International Regulatory Agreements*.[25] The Chayes study triggered an ongoing debate as to whether a managerial approach to the compliance of international law, which employs monitoring and cooperative mechanisms, is more effective than models of enforcement. The Chayes study argues that states comply with international rules because they are the norm.[26] Through a process of negotiation, Chayes and Chayes argue, the norms of the countries are incorporated into treaties.[27] So, in the end, states comply with treaties because they reflect their interests and because compliance makes economic sense. Further, they assert that non-compliance is usually unintentional and can be attributed to poor management or lack of capacity by the country.[28] Based on this theory, the Chayes study argues that compliance systems in treaties should therefore be managerial, approaching non-compliance with the goal of assisting the country to meet its obligations.[29]

The Chayes' conclusions have been criticized by a number of authors, particularly George Downs and his co-authors, who argue that states comply with international treaties because the treaties really do not commit the country to major changes but merely to marginal changes from the business-as-usual trend.[30] Downs claims that the use of stronger enforcement models for compliance is necessary when there are deeper commitments for countries and therefore stronger incentives to defect from the treaty.[31] Downs' assumption also falls squarely within social legal analysis. Deep commitments may push international law beyond societal norms and values; therefore, non-compliance may be more likely to occur. Such analysis would suggest that as legal systems develop and mature they become more in tune with the norms and values of their societies. Thus, the laws are "carefully designed to preserve the existent

---

25. Abram Chayes and Antonia Handler Chayes (1995) *The New Sovereignty: Compliance with International Regulatory Agreements*, Cambridge, Mass.: Harvard University Press.
26. Ibid., 27. For explanation of the process of how norms are created at the international level and then brought back to the domestic level, see Harold Honju Koh (1998) *Bringing International Law Home*, 35 Houston Law Review, 623.
27. Ibid., 4.
28. Ibid., 14.
29. Ibid., 28.
30. See George W. Downs et al. (1996) *Is the Good News about Compliance Good News about Cooperation?* 50 Int'l Org., 379.
31. See ibid.

social structure and to further the values that it seeks".[32] This conclusion poses a problem when deep legal reform is required; it causes the law to be separated from the aspirations of society. During reform, law is required "to posit not merely a mediating order but new orders to establish new patterns of fact and value".[33] Like Downs' "deep" treaties, such changes in social behaviour will require stronger power in the law itself or, as Downs' argues, stronger punitive and enforcement measures so there is less incentive to defect.[34]

Thomas Franck's *Legitimacy in the International System* is another important work in the last ten years that also has implications for the understanding of effectiveness.[35] Like the Chayes study, Franck's work is driven by the question of why states comply with international law.[36] He argues that states comply with international law when they perceive it to be legitimate. He offers a number of attributes that give rise to the perceived legitimacy of international laws and hence promote compliance. As with the Chayes model, these attributes are derived from the norms and values of society. For Franck, a legitimate international law must have determinacy, symbolic validation, coherence and adherence.[37] Thus, the starting point for Franck's theory of legitimacy is that Henkin's observation – that states do for the most part follow international law – is valid. However, the reasons for this compliance are not obvious as international law does not exert the same authority as domestic law.

For Franck, the more legitimate a rule is, the more "compliance pull" it has.[38] Each of the four characteristics listed above contributes to the legitimacy of a law, as it is perceived by states. Determinacy refers to the textual clarity of rules; the clearer the rule is the more compliance pull it will have. Certain rules are clearer than others, for instance, rules such as "red means stop" and "green means go" are considered very clear or "binary" rules.[39] On the other hand, the complexity of many sets of rules can cloud their determinacy, and in international law this is more often the situation than the exception. In the cases of complexity, Franck develops a further component of determinacy, which he calls pro-

---

32. Supra, Jenkins, 120.
33. Ibid., 121.
34. Supra, Downs, 397–399.
35. Thomas M. Franck (1988) *Legitimacy in the International System*, 82 AJIL [hereinafter *Legitimacy in the International System*], 705.
36. Thomas M. Franck (1990) *The Power of Legitimacy Among Nations*, New York: Oxford University Press [hereinafter *Power of Legitimacy*].
37. Supra, Franck, *Power of Legitimacy*, 712.
38. Ibid., 705.
39. Ibid., 722.

cess determinacy.[40] This concept posits that complex rules can still give rise to legitimate international law if institutions are able to resolve ambiguity, interpretation and error. If, after an institutional interpretation, the law is considered legitimate and embodies the other measures of Franck's legitimacy theory (symbolic validation, coherence and adherence), then the rules have process determinacy.[41] The implication of this aspect of Franck's theory is clear: If the international system does not provide for legitimate institutions to resolve the ambiguities of increasingly complex rules, then compliance by countries will be lower.[42]

Symbolic validation refers to the association of the law with what Franck labels ritual and pedigree.[43] Ritual is the symbolic association the law may have based on observance of ceremony and formal ritual; for instance, he cites the example of presidential decrees, which are recognized by the president's oath of office. Pedigree refers to the association of the rule or law with a person or institution of high reputation or pedigree. Franck's example of diplomatic accreditation clarifies this concept.[44] Coherence refers to the interpretation of a rule according to some form of consistency, though Franck allows for inconsistency so long as it is based on some form of acceptable rationality.[45] Adherence, the last attribute, concerns the hierarchy of rules. At the top of the hierarchy is the rule of recognition, which grants each country its sovereignty. Beneath these rules are "secondary rules" that guide the making of other rules, such as constitutions, bills of rights etc. Under international rules, Franck argues that rules such as *pacta sunt servanda* would be of this constitutive nature. Accordingly, if an international law is in adherence with these secondary rules, then there is additional incentive for state compliance.[46]

The message that becomes clear from both the Franck and the Chayes studies is that states follow international rules because of certain socially constructed values that they bring to the international system. The Chayes translate these assumptions into the implications that a managerial system is more effective, while Franck leaves the reader to makes their own assumptions based on their understanding of the motivations for states behaving the way they do.

---

40. Ibid., 85.
41. Ibid.
42. Anthony S. Winer (1998) *The CISG Convention and Thomas Franck's Theory of Legitimacy*, 19 NW. J. Int'l L. & Bus. 1.
43. Supra, *Power of Legitimacy*, 94.
44. Ibid., 105.
45. Ibid., 136.
46. Ibid., 187.

Other legal models

Two other legal approaches relevant to the discussion of effectiveness are the economic legal model and the natural legal model. The former borrows concepts from another discipline, economics, but bears the basic framework of a legal approach to effectiveness. An economic legal model, however, adds the elements of efficiency and effectiveness to legally effective rules or policies of the treaty.[47] There have yet to be any studies that take the economic legal approach to analysing the effectiveness of treaties, although some studies, such as those conducted by UNEP in 1991, have considered effectiveness of the policy and efficiency in terms of coordination with other instruments as determinants of effectiveness.[48] Efficiency and coordination have also become the focus of discussion and rationalization of the numerous programmes on the environment and sustainable development within the UN and other specialized agencies. Cost-effectiveness is a logical basis for achieving effectiveness more generally, given that financing for sustainable development and the environment has declined by more than one-third in the last three decades. Cost is also a factor due to the ever-increasing number of treaties, which stretch the already shrinking funding even thinner.

Natural legal models of effectiveness are closely associated with social legal models, which I will refer to as normative, as they both view the role of norms as concepts central to international law. The difference between natural law and the normative models described above is that the normative view looks at treaties as a reflection of social values and norms, while the natural model posits that the norms in treaties should be based on universal principles such as natural laws, usually pertaining to the moral principles of justice, equity and fairness. There are few modern studies that have looked at these principles in the context of international law, much less from the perspective of effectiveness. However, another work published by Thomas M. Franck, titled *Fairness in International Law and Institutions*, written after his earlier book on legitimacy, does offer some ideas of how effectiveness would be considered from the natural law standpoint.[49] Franck's proposition is that fairness is one of the most critical tenets of international law and that the creation of fair rules should not be trusted to those who govern nations. Furthermore, he asserts that fair rules can only be drafted through an inclusive

---

47. For a description of economic legal models on effectiveness, see Oran R. Young and Marc A. Levy (1999) "The Effectiveness of International Environmental Regimes", in Oran R. Young, ed., *The Effectiveness of International Environmental Regimes*, Boston: MIT Press, 1, 4–5.
48. Supra, Sand, 27.
49. Thomas M. Franck (1995) *Fairness in International Law and Institutions*.

international discourse with "actors – multinational corporations, churches, service organizations, gender- and ethno-culturally specific groups, scientific networks and a myriad others – who are already part of this discourse".[50] Franck examines various regimes and institutions to see how fair they have been, including some primary environmental regimes. In the context of the environment, Franck assesses fairness by examining how these regimes have attempted to instil the notion of distributive justice into their formal rules and implementation.

Natural legal models raise an important issue related to effectiveness that is still not well developed: The degree to which rules conform to basic human values or natural law as a reflection of their perceived validity. The congruence between rules and human values also has implications for the extent to which the rules are obeyed and how variance can impact the effectiveness of the rule.

International relations models

For a long time, international relations theory was overshadowed by more orthodox theories such as realism and its various interpretations. These focused on power and the anarchic inter-state system and dismissed institutions as epiphenomenal. Over the last few decades, however, international relations theories have developed much more interest in the role and understanding of international institutions. In recent years institutional theorists have been especially instrumental in establishing that "norms, principles, rules and procedures" as a system – a regime in the parlance of institutionalist literature – do in fact play a significant role in modifying how states behave. Institutional theorists have also come to a better understanding of how these factors can be improved or fine-tuned so that they give rise to more effective regimes. Institutional theories have been particularly useful for bridging the two disciplines of international law and political science.[51] International lawyers have long assumed that, as products of international law, institutions are a major influence on state behaviour, despite the fact that they do not have the binding characteristics or the central authority of domestic law. More recently, in relatively newer areas of treaty-making such as the environment and human rights, key concepts that have come from institutional theorists, such as the roles of non-state actors, epistemic communities and insights into sources of effectiveness, have played a role in shaping better institutions.

---

50. Ibid., 484.
51. See Kal Raustiala and Anne-Marie Slaughter (2002) "International Law, International Relations and Compliance", in Walter Carlnaes et al., eds, *Handbook of International Relations*, London: Sage.

A great deal of work, however, remains to be done in order to gain better insights and more understanding of the role that institutions play in the effectiveness of international law and how we can use this knowledge to craft better ones. The early work on institutions was caught up in a pedantic discussion with realists on whether institutions mattered.[52] As the body of knowledge matured, institutional theories moved away from traditional issues of economy and security and into then-emerging areas such as the environment. Environmental issues emerged as a timely subject in international cooperation as the role of non-state actors grew and the diversity of institutions gave further opportunity for study. In today's context of international relations studies, institutionalists have become more comfortable with the significance of their theories and have begun to elaborate the actual functions and variables of their school of thought. The ultimate goal behind this research agenda is the creation of stronger, more effective institutions, and attention has therefore focused on the actual determinants and sources of institutional effectiveness.

While the core international relations theory still focuses on traditional realist notions such as the role of power and the state as the primary actor, institutionalism now focuses much more on the strategic relationship of the state with the international system. The general assumption is that the state will participate in the international system to maximize its own self-interests. Within the institutional school of thought there are several variances, some of which have dealt specifically with effectiveness. For instance neo-liberalism straddles some of the basic assumptions that institutionalist and constructivist theories have employed but commits to neither side.[53] Neo-liberals view compliance with international law as promoting the interests of actors at the national level. They do not embrace the state as unitary; rather, they see it as a myriad of actors that are interacting and together constitute how the state will relate to the international system. Neo-liberalists reject the normative view that this interaction forms norms; instead, they assert that the state will reflect the interests of the domestic actors in strategic ways that will maximize the benefits of domestic interest groups. At the inter-state level, neo-liberalists believe that compliance occurs because institutions that share the liberal democratic traditions will share a common understanding of the world and will therefore treat institutions in similar ways. Neo-liberalist theories

---

52. See, generally, Susan Strange (1983) "Cave! Hic Dragones: A Critique of Regime Analysis", in Stephen Krasner, ed., *International Regimes*, Ithaca, N.Y.: Cornell University Press, 337.

53. International relations also have a pre-eminent school of thought on cognitive or constructivist theories that use norms to explain how states behave; however, there are significant divergences between these theories and the social legal theory that is presented under the previous section.

underlie much of the work that has been done on effectiveness from the international relations perspective.

A study conducted by David Victor, Kal Raustiala and Eugene Skolnikoff on the implementation of international agreements is good example of the work that is coming from the liberal international relations perspective, which is sometimes referred to broadly as new institutionalism.[54] Their model views the positivist rule-based approach as somewhat limited in its scope. Though they agree on the importance of demonstrating the degree of compliance and isolating some of its determinants, this does not necessarily indicate whether an agreement is effective.[55] According to their model, in order to understand the concept of effectiveness, there must be clearer distinctions between effectiveness, compliance and implementation. For example, there may be high levels of compliance but this may not change the social behaviour at which the legal measure is aimed. In some instances, states may be in full compliance without even implementing the specific legal measure. In the case of the Kyoto Protocol, Russia agreed to a 5 per cent reduction in its greenhouse gas emissions by the end of 2015,[56] but, because of the decline in industrial output, Russia can comply relatively more easily with the Protocol compared to other countries. The contrary is also true: low levels of compliance can occur in tandem with high levels of effectiveness. Raustiala uses the example of speed limits. They are not always obeyed but nevertheless maintain orderly speeds on the highways. These examples demonstrate that effectiveness requires a closer examination of the "stringency of the legal standard and the baseline of the behaviour".[57]

According to Victor, Raustiala and Skolnikoff, implementation is directly linked to treaty effectiveness, for it is the key variable that determines whether changes will occur in the behaviour of the target group. Their study looks at several aspects of the implementation process both from the international and domestic levels. The authors examine

54. David Victor, Kal Raustiala and Eugene B. Skolnikoff, eds. (1998) *The Implementation and Effectiveness of International Environmental Commitments: Theory and Practice*, Boston: MIT Press [hereinafter *Implementation and Effectiveness*]. Other studies that have been conducted from the liberal international relations perspective include an earlier work, Peter Haas et al., eds (1995) *Institutions for Earth: Sources of Effective International Environmental Protection*, Boston: MIT Press. This work, which takes a regime theory approach, addresses effectiveness to a certain degree but is more largely concerned with observing the role that social institutions play in the governance of environmental issues rather how the effectiveness of a regime can be improved.

55. *Implementation and Effectiveness*, supra, 6–7.

56. Kyoto Protocol to UNFCCC, Conference of the Parties, 3rd Session, Annex B, UN Doc. FCCC/CP/1997/L.7/Add.1 (1997).

57. Kal Raustiala (2000) *Compliance and Effectiveness in International Regulatory Cooperation*, 32 Case W. Res. J. Int'l L., 387, 394.

implementation from the perspective of governments and civil society, to see how they use international institutions to review implementation and how they deal with implementation problems. The focus here is the "systems of implementation review" (SIR). These vary by agreement but most entail basic methods such as regular reporting and monitoring systems. More advanced agreements use in-depth reviews and even country inspections. The study by Victor and his co-authors compares how SIRs operate in different environmental agreements over time, how these systems contribute to effectiveness and how SIRs can influence the behaviour of actors involved in the implementation process.[58] The study uses a regime approach, in that it looks not only at the legal requirements set out in the agreements but also at the participation of actors and the system-wide operating environment of the accord – even in some cases where formal procedures do not exist.[59] The authors also point out the fact that there are other variables that can affect the effectiveness of the agreement. These may include the nature of the problem, configurations of power, institutions, nature of the commitment, linkages with other issues and objectives, exogenous factors and public concern.[60]

The second component of the study by Victor and his co-authors examines national implementation, with a specific focus on participation and societies in transition.[61] This approach comes from a neo-liberalist perspective. Victor and his co-authors argue that these two aspects are of particular importance. Participation, which is defined as the involvement of stakeholders, is assumed to be a necessity for effective implementation. Societies in transition are strategically placed geographically to western pollution concerns and, besides, they have not yet been adequately studied.[62] So far the study by Victor and his co-authors is the only one that has focused on the implementation model of environmental agreements as a means of assessing effectiveness. These authors have made an important contribution to better understanding some of the basic assumptions that have been made concerning the effectiveness of environmental agreements and the operational environment in which the accord is working.

As David Freestone states, the study makes some often "challenging" and "iconoclastic" conclusions.[63] From the neo-liberal point of view, the

58. *Implementation and Effectiveness*, supra, 16–20.
59. Ibid., 48.
60. Ibid., 8–15.
61. Ibid., 20–26.
62. Victor makes the point that many economies in transition countries have significant impact on the environment. Ibid., 3.
63. David Freestone (1999) *Book Review*, 93 AJIL, 749, 751 (reviewing *Implementation and Effectiveness*).

study supports many of its assumption about compliance and cooperation. For example, the editors conclude that, while most literature focuses
on the inability of developing states to pay for implementation, their
cases suggest that the "internal characteristics of non-liberal states are
not conducive for promoting environmental cooperation".[64] Such states
"constrain the process of cooperation within those regimes they do
join".[65] These states are also less inclined to allow scrutiny of their performance and less likely to agree to deeper commitments. The study reinforces its central claim that implementation is of critical importance to
effectiveness because it allows states to evaluate and compare their participation in the regime and use what the editors describe as escape
clauses to deepen commitments. The recognition that liberalization is
taking place is shown by the trend that non-liberal states are increasingly
opening their domestic systems to scrutiny by accepting systems of implementation review.[66] The study downplays the significance of compliance
as a measure of effectiveness but stresses its importance as a tool for
demonstrating to other members of the international community that it
has met its commitments, at least in the letter of the law, and is thus in
good standing in the community. The study also makes important conclusions concerning participation and effectiveness. The research team
expected to find that participation of groups would be an important
variable to effectiveness but instead they found the record rather
ambiguous.[67] Participation, particularly by NGOs, did make policies
more environmentally friendly, which supports many of the arguments
that NGOs make as a justification for widening their participation in
international environmental processes, but when coming to the implementation phase the study concludes that the impact may not be as significant.[68]

Another important study examining the effectiveness of global environmental institutions was published shortly after Victor's by a research
team led by Oran Young.[69] Young, one of the most progressive thinkers
on institutionalism and the environment, together with his team, focused

---

64. It is implied by the Victor et al. study that environmental cooperation is a source of
    effectiveness and thus seen as a source of effectiveness. *Implementation and Effective-
    ness*, supra, 3. Also see the concluding chapter of the study by Raustiala and Victor sug-
    gesting that liberalism "makes international environmental cooperation more effective"
    as "liberal states are more supportive of international institutions needed for effective
    international environmental governance" and there is a higher degree of regulation for
    externalities. Ibid., 609.
65. Ibid.
66. Ibid., 689–92.
67. Ibid., 664.
68. Ibid., 665.
69. Supra, Young and Levy, *Effectiveness of International Regimes*.

on the causal connections between international regimes and the behaviour of the actors where change was to be targeted (e.g. non-state actors such as shipping companies). Political effectiveness, according to Young, is primarily focused on problem-solving and changing the behaviour of targeted actors; he considers a legal definition to be concerned with compliance and an economic definition to be concerned with efficiency.[70] By focusing on its political aspects, and promoting changes in the behaviour of targeted actors, he distinguishes his definition of effectiveness from that of other scholarly works and adds a useful perspective to this discussion.

Young teamed up with Marc Levy to create a typology of the seven different types of regimes, which their team believes are representative of the role that regimes play in changing behaviour. They classify these types of regimes, or what they call behavioural mechanisms, according to two different explanations of state behaviour. Utilitarian explanations are synonymous with institutionalism, and normative explanations he equates with international law. By looking at behavioural changes from these two perspectives, Young and Levy depart from "conventional hypotheses that seek to identify necessary or sufficient conditions for regimes to have an effect" and instead choose models that are important theoretically and determine if these regimes actually have an effect on the behaviour of the targeted actors.[71]

From their analysis of three cases on fisheries in the Barents seas, acid rain in North America and oil pollution, Young and Levy conclude that each of the seven types of roles that regimes play, as they subscribe to, do indeed have an effect on target actors' behaviour. However, they also conclude that their focus on behavioural change is problematic in the assessment of regime effectiveness. They concede that isolating the individual or specific mechanisms of behavioural change is difficult because the "signals" coming from these mechanisms are weak and are mixed in with other mechanisms, which increases the complexity of linking individual factors to specific behaviour changes. While finding such links is not impossible, Young and Levy believe that such an exercise would require a sufficient number of cases over time. They also warn that, although there will be similarity, the specific mechanism and their implications for effectiveness will vary from regime to regime.

In sum, Young and Levy's conclusions confirm that institutions can be effective and do impact behaviours of targeted actors and offers different roles that regimes can play to achieve these ends, by promoting the self-interest of states and by changing norms through learning, defining roles or realigning domestic interests. However, their model of effectiveness

70. Ibid., 4–6.
71. Ibid., 21.

does not provide concrete means for policy-makers to negotiate and produce more effective treaties.[72]

Redefining legal approaches to effectiveness

Now that we have gone through the various models and approaches to understanding effectiveness, the question is how can we enhance our understanding of effectiveness to improve treaty-making? Our stocktaking has shown a variety of approaches to effectiveness, considering compliance, legitimacy, institutionalism, societal norms and behavioural changes in turn. However, these respective studies leave gaps in terms of translating the specific measures of treaties or institutional designs that lead to improved effectiveness.

The legal studies have stressed the role that compliance plays in effectiveness and have also been helpful in understanding why states obey international rules – a logical first step towards designing better laws to improve effectiveness. However, as has been pointed out by several commentators, compliance is only one part of effectiveness of international treaties. The studies coming from international relations or multidisciplinary research have demonstrated the types of domestic political systems that create the right political conditions for effectiveness and have shown the importance of information and review systems.

Nonetheless, it is clear that there are major gaps in our knowledge. This raises the basic question of whether approaches so far or the framing of the question "what is effectiveness?" have been too ambitious and have expected too much of the treaty itself. To answer this question further investigation must limit its scope to the parameters of what we know now in terms of treaties and their impact. Thus, in order to reach a better understanding of effectiveness, we must revisit how we measure and define it, while adding the valuable contributions of various models just reviewed.

Resolving measurement parameters

There are several problems in the current approach to measuring the effectiveness of international treaties. First, many of the international relations studies have not clarified the object of analysis. These evaluations,

72. For other international relations studies that have dealt with the question of effectiveness, see Edward L. Miles et al. (2002) *Environmental Regime Effectiveness: Confronting Theory with Evidence*, Cambridge, Mass.: MIT Press. Also see Durwood Zaelke et al. (2005) *Making Law Work: Environmental Compliance and Sustainable Development*, London: Cameron-May, which contains further studies on effectiveness from both the law and international relations fields.

whilst claiming to be gauging the effectiveness of a treaty, more broadly use the regime as the object of analysis. Regimes and treaties are different and this may unnecessarily complicate an analysis of the treaty alone, and may also subject the treaty to performance criteria beyond what it was intended to meet. Second, the effectiveness analyses so far have run into methodological problems of securing the right data in order to establish the causal connection between the treaty or the regime and change in the behaviour of the targeted actor. To date, the research has been based on intuitive perceptions, expert analysis or on case studies. In the absence of strong data and concrete empirical connections, an approach to effectiveness that looks into the treaty itself and then looks for change is a more realistic one. This section examines these problems in greater detail.

Legal definitions of effectiveness focus on the actual object of effectiveness, that is to say the provisions to which the treaty gives effect, the specific obligations and objectives of the treaty or, in the case of a regime perspective, the system-wide components of a regime system. Institutionalists have criticized the legal definition of effectiveness as too narrow. It fails to link directly the operation of the regime with the behavioural change of the targeted actor at the most fundamental level – such as that of the industrial polluter or the average citizen. In short, the legal definition of effectiveness looks only at the treaty, while an institutionalist's definition looks more broadly at the "principles, norms, rules, procedures and programmes" that comprise the regime.

The distinction between the legal instrument and the regime is a significant one. Though there has been a great deal of enthusiasm among the disciplines of international law and institutionalism because of the similarities between regimes and treaties, it is important to point out that they are not the same.[73] A regime may include a treaty but it is a broader concept that comprises other social institutions such as norms, principles, procedures and rules that are both explicit and implicit.[74] Treaties are explicit rules and, as has been pointed out by many authors, they are ad hoc, dealing with a specific interest.[75] Regimes encompass social institutions that generally cover behaviour that has developed over time.[76] For

---

73. See generally Kenneth W. Abbott (1989) *Modern International Relations Theory: A Prospectus for International Lawyers*, 14 Yale J. Int'l L., 335; Anne-Marie Slaughter Burley (1993) *International Law and International Relations Theory: A Dual Agenda*, 87 AJIL 205, 207–220; John K. Setear (1996) *An Iterative Perspective on Treaties: A Synthesis of International Relations Theory and International Law*, 37 Harv. Int'l L. J., 139; Robert Keohane (1997) *International Relations and International Law: The Optics*, 38 Harv. Int'l L. J., 487.
74. See Supra, Krasner, *International Regimes*, 2.
75. Ibid., 3.

example, the precautionary principle is a basic tenet of international environmental law that has developed since the 1980s in various agreements.[77] Treaties such as the Convention on Biological Diversity (CBD) or the Convention on Climate Change may recognize the precautionary principle generally but at the same time both instruments qualify how the precautionary principle is used in specific circumstances. For instance, the CBD recognizes precautionary principle under its preamble[78] but the Cartagena Protocol to the CBD operationalizes the principle in the procedural part of the agreement, stating that a lack of scientific certainty should not prevent a party from taking a decision to restrict and import.[79] Though the Cartagena Protocol stipulates that decisions to restrict an import should be based on a risk assessment, it does not set any thresholds for invoking the principle, simply showing that there is some sort of scientific uncertainty and a risk to the environment seems to be sufficient. The UN Framework Convention on Climate Change (UNFCCC), on the other hand, inserts the precautionary principle under its general principles section, which is intended to guide the implementation of the Convention rather than operationalize it under specific circumstances.[80] It states a similar concern to the Cartagena Protocol, that scientific uncertainty should not become a reason to postpone action, but it explicitly mentions that the risk to the environment must be "serious and irreversible" and when measures are indeed taken these should be cost-effective and take into account different "socio-economic contexts".[81] One could interpret this as imposing certain criteria on the use of the precautionary principle, which would seem to restrict it in some way; however, unlike the Cartagena Protocol, there is no necessity to provide a risk assessment to show the uncertainty and the risk at hand. So, in other ways, it is much easier to invoke.

In some instances the treaty may even conflict with the regime. Though the precautionary principle is used widely in national law (for example Article 15 of the Rio Declaration, and it has been used in numerous trea-

---

76. Ibid., 3–4.
77. James Cameron and Juli Abouchar (1996) "The Status of the Precautionary Principle in International Law", in David Freestone and Ellen Hey, eds, *The Precautionary Principle and International Law: The Challenge of Implementation*, The Hague: Kluwer Law International, 29.
78. Convention on Biological Diversity, 5 Jun. 1992, preamble, 1760 UNTS 79, 31 ILM 818.
79. Cartagena Protocol on Biosafety to the Convention on Biological Diversity, 29 Jan 2000, art 10.6, 11.8, 39 ILM 1027, 1031–1032.
80. See Art 12, UNFCCC; also see UNFCCC (1992) *UNGAOR Intergovernmental Negotiating Comm., 5th Sess., UN Doc. FCCC/1992*; UNFCCC 31 ILM 848, 853 (1992) (entered into force 21 March 1994), available at http://unfccc.int/resource/docs/convkp/conveng.pdf.
81. Ibid.

ties and international agreements) under the World Trade Organization, it is not considered customary law.[82] Generally speaking, the precautionary principle has also been interpreted in more restrictive ways under the international trade regime compared to the international environmental regime.[83] The distinction between a treaty and a regime is an important one for understanding the effectiveness of treaties and one that generally falls along disciplinary lines. Legal scholars focus on the treaty itself, while the institutional studies that have been conducted so far take a broader regime approach.

Using the regime as basis for explaining the role of social institutions may be a more inclusive and systematic approach to theorizing inter-state relations. However, when trying to distinguish the impact of a treaty, regime analysis clouds the focus and brings into play too many variables. Like any system, to understand how it works and the role each component plays, it is more rational to deconstruct it. The same applies to a regime – to understand the role of the treaty, it is necessary to use it as the object of analysis and see how it affects change as a constant variable. This type of variation analysis may still be years off though, as there is still an empirical problem: There seldom exists sufficient data to do behavioural analysis, at least in the present circumstances.[84] Such studies would require databases of numerous cases with similar characteristics in order to do any type of variation analysis. Alternatively, effectiveness studies evaluating behaviour would require in-depth interviews and surveys to isolate the reasons that led to behavioural change. This type of effectiveness analysis has so far run into methodological challenges and data problems on how to establish the causal connection between the regime and change in the behaviour of the targeted actor. That is not to say that efforts to address these challenges are not under way. There have been impressive efforts to look for "persuasive methods to demonstrate the causal links between regimes and their consequences";[85] recent data

---

82. See WTO (1998) *EC Measures Concerning Meat and Meat Products* (Hormones), WT/DS26/AB/R (16 January), para. 123. There has been international debate whether the precautionary principle is a principle or an approach. According to the US State Department, in 1992 at Rio, the US "reject suggestions by some European countries to promote a 'precautionary principle' over a 'precautionary approach'"; see Jeffery D. Kovar (1993) *A Short Guide to the Rio Declaration*, 4 Col. J. Int'l Envtl. L. 103, 134.

83. See, for example, the provisional requirements to timely review scientific evidence when using Article 5.7 under the Sanitary and Phytosanitary Convention, in *Japan – Measures Affecting Agricultural Products*, WT/DS76/AB/R, para. 8.58 (22 February 1999).

84. See Oran R. Young (1999) "Regime Effectiveness: Taking Stock", in Oran R. Young, ed., *The Effectiveness of International Environmental Regimes: Causal Connections and Behavioural Mechanisms*, Boston: MIT Press, 249, 257.

85. See Oran R. Young (2002) *Evaluating the Success of International Environmental Regimes: Where Are We Now?* 12 Global Envtl. Change, 73.

on regimes is improving and a number of databases exist, such as the "International Regime Database" at the Technical University of Darmstadt in Germany.[86] Moreover, there has been promising methodological work that has sought to create models based on counterfactual hypotheses[87] or on quantitative analysis that may lead to methods towards improving regime design,[88] but so far studies have failed to find a suitable generalization because most regimes have very specific arrangements.[89]

Given the current limitations of the institutionalist approaches a more realistic starting point to effectiveness evaluation is the criteria that each treaty sets for gauging its own performance.[90] This data is usually collected and reported as a compliance requirement of the treaty. The data may range from bio-geophysical data such as catch sizes, emissions or land-use data, to the level of implementation, including programmes, procedures, focal points or national frameworks. In some rare circumstances, the data may relate directly to changes in the behaviour of the actors but there are few treaties that collect this kind of information because individuals normally do not have legal personality under international law. Using the individual treaty performance data as a measurement of change is much more tenable. The data exists, and it is usually inclusive enough to measure change in the amelioration of the problem from the entry into force of the treaty. This approach also allows for effectiveness to be judged according to the unique circumstances of each treaty. Since each treaty varies in terms of its provisions, problems and impacts on behaviour, judging a treaty by one set of criteria or conducting tendency analysis to discover a common trend in behaviour may not be a useful exercise.

However, using treaty performance data as a measurement of effectiveness also falls victim to the same criticism of not adequately showing the causal connections between the operation of the treaty and the improvement of the problem. The oft-cited Montreal Protocol demonstrates this problem of proving causality. Did the phasing out of CFCs occur because of the advent of the Protocol or because the industry leader, Dupont, found an alternative technology? There is no way of knowing for

86. See Helmut Breitmeier, Oran Young and Michael Zürn (2006) *Analyzing International Environmental Regimes: From Case Study to Database*, Cambridge, Mass.: MIT Press.
87. Detlef F. Sprinz and Carsten Helm (1999) *The Effect of Global Environmental Regimes: A Measurement Concept*, 20 Int'l Pol. Sci. Rev., 359, 359–369.
88. Ronald Mitchell (2002) *A Quantitative Approach to Evaluating International Environmental Regimes*, 2 Glob. Envtl. Pol., 58, 58–83.
89. Supra, Young, *Evaluating the Success of International Environmental Regimes*, 77.
90. This approach borrows on the Victor et al. approach, infra part II, but instead of the regime it uses the treaty as the object of analysis and does not necessarily require that a formal review should be in place under the treaty; an assessment can be done with data collected and compared to the objectives of the treaty.

sure the answer without doing in-depth interviews with Dupont to determine why it invested research and development money into alternative technologies. Thus, evaluating changes in behaviour is difficult at best, no matter what data used in the assessment. Using qualitative data such as interviews is no more exact than using treaty performance data. Each approach has its strengths and weaknesses, depending on the context and provisions of the treaty. In the cases where there is sufficient extant data established as criteria for assessing treaty performance, using performance data may be a more a fruitful approach for evaluating effectiveness. However, choosing to judge the effectiveness of a treaty by any other measurement would be judging the treaty according to a standard that the parties did not set for the treaty and would be an unfair evaluation.

The institutionalists' assessment of effectiveness is faced with the complexity of attempting to link behavioural changes of a target actor to a specific component of a regime. Given that a legal analysis focuses on the legal instrument itself, by contrast a legal approach to effectiveness must try to isolate the specific impact of the treaty provisions by seeing how the treaties' specific performance criterion works to accomplish the objective of the treaty. Just as with the institutional perspective, the legal approach to effectiveness is confronted with a host of obstacles.

Treaty objectives give rise to the first of a number of problems in the context of the legal analysis of effectiveness. Treaties have become increasingly complex over the years and often serve multiple interests. As a result, the objectives of the treaty are often not straightforward or, what is most likely the case, there will be more than one stated objective. There has also been the question of whether the preamble of the treaty should be used as the objective.

Nowhere is the problem of multiple, vague or conflicting objectives clearer than the preamble of a treaty. It will normally have an overall objective that the parties are cooperating to achieve: liberalize trade, eliminate child labour, protect the climate for present or future generations and so on. Preambles, as we know, set the broader environment in which the treaty operates and can serve as context from which other parts of the treaty are to be interpreted. Preambles are often a mixed bag of interests because states may not be able to operationalize directly into the treaty body. Moreover, because many modern treaties no longer use reservation systems, preambles have become a place to express concerns. By including these concerns in the preamble, the state may view this as a means of retaining more flexibility when implementing the treaty at the domestic level. However, preambles are not necessarily given specific effect and should not be considered as part of the evaluation of the treaty's effectiveness.

Conversely, treaties normally have specific objectives that are stated at the outset. These are generally straightforward but sometimes the language may be overly elaborate or inexact, which may make the objectives difficult to interpret. There may be specific conditions to the objectives or more than one objective. For instance, the Convention on Biological Diversity's stated objectives are twofold: "conservation of biological diversity, the sustainable use of its components" and the "fair and equitable sharing of the benefits arising out of the utilization of genetic resources".[91] In the case of the Convention to Combat Desertification, the objectives are complex and present the parties with language that is difficult to interpret, calling for "integrated approaches consistent with Agenda 21", and "improved productivity of land".[92] Though difficult in some circumstances to decipher, the core objectives of a treaty represent the baseline for judging effectiveness. In the instances where these objectives may be vague, complex or potentially conflicting, it is the role of lawyers to use appropriate tools and techniques for interpretation. If techniques such as the ordinary meaning of the words, preambular context, and *travail préparatoire* do not lead to any obvious conclusion, which is quite possible given that records and proceedings on modern treaty-making are just as ambiguous as the treaty, then one practical way of determining the core objectives is to look to the specific obligations (e.g. obligatory rules, procedures) of the treaty itself. If the obligations operationalize a particular objective while excluding other objectives, then it is generally understood that this specific objective is the one that the parties are most intent to achieve. Therefore this objective should be the baseline for measuring the performance of the treaty.

Compliance still matters

Comparing treaty performance data to treaty objectives may in some instances be exactly what the compliance system is in fact doing. For example, in the Kyoto Protocol the performance data is collected and reviewed for accuracy. It is then compared to the emission targets set in Annex B of the Protocol to determine whether a country is in compliance with its designated target. From this comparison an overall picture can be seen of whether the treaty is achieving its objectives. However, this is not always the case; some treaties monitor a problem or issue but may not

---

91. Convention on Biological Diversity, 5 Jun. 1992, art. 1, 1760, UNTS 79, 31 ILM 818.
92. United Nations Convention to Combat Desertification in Those Countries Experiencing Serious Drought and/or Desertification, Particularly in Africa, 12 Sept. 1994, art. 2, A/Ac.241/27, available at http://www.unccd.int/convention/text/pdf/conv-eng.pdf.

compare the performance data to the achievement of the treaty's overall objective. For instance, Article 3.2 of the Ramsar Convention requires the Contracting Party to provide data on the change of the ecological character of any wetland in its territory,[93] but it does not compare this to the overall objectives of the treaty to determine if the conservation of wetlands is declining or improving.

This is why relying solely on the compliance system of a treaty as a means of judging effectiveness is sometimes not adequate and why approaching effectiveness from the broader angle of reviewing the performance data with the treaty's objectives is a better method of assessment. Compliance can have multiple meanings. As has been pointed out earlier, non-compliance by a party at one point in time does not necessarily mean the treaty is not achieving its objectives. As a UNEP report on effectiveness explains: "It is unclear how a one-time violation of the prohibition against commercial trade in CITES Appendix I (endangered) species should be evaluated in terms of an overall assessment of compliance with CITES."[94] Often compliance requirements are also procedural by nature, such as regular reporting and meetings. Compliance by providing such reports may not be directly crucial to whether a party meets the objectives of the treaty but these reports nevertheless play an extremely valuable role. So while compliance in one sense is not necessarily a measure of effectiveness, in another sense (in the procedural sense), compliance still remains important for providing the data and information so that an evaluation can be made on whether the treaty is meeting its objectives.

Once the objectives are measured against the treaty's performance data and if the results shows no improvement, or if the programmes and procedures have not been created at the domestic level, then this is the first indication that the treaty's approach is ineffective. One argument that has been put forward as a criticism of legal methods on effectiveness, usually in the context of compliance, but that also bears reference to the techniques described here, is that treaties can achieve their objectives, often attaining high compliance, but may still have little impact on behaviour.

This raises another fundamental distinction between institutional versus legal approaches. Though this is changing slowly, legal approaches are typically about crafting sound legal agreements, so to judge a treaty as ineffective because the parties did not negotiate deeper commitments

93. Convention on Wetlands of International Importance Especially for Waterfowl Habitat, 2 February 1971, Ramsar Iran, Art. 3.2, available at http://www.ramsar.org/ key_conv_e.htm.
94. *Review Institutions*, supra.

should not be the focus of a definition of effectiveness.[95] Such circumstances are more likely to be a case of political will or perhaps a lack of understanding of the severity or importance of the issue and are the concern of political scientists, not lawyers. This observation raises the question of whether institutional arguments concerning effectiveness have not overstated the expectations they hold for treaties. Many of the studies have claimed their work is designed to improve the effectiveness of international agreements but have looked to features that are much broader for solving what they perceive as an issue that requires stronger commitments between countries. In many ways, this may reflect the normative motivations behind these studies that analysts such as Waelde have observed.[96]

Robustness as a determinant of effectiveness[97]

This is not to say that international law does not account for politics but only deals with the letter of the law. This positivist view of international

95. In recent years lawyers have began to progressively re-examine "compliance" in the context of MEAs. For example, since 1990, the International Network for Environmental Compliance and Enforcement (INECE) have sponsored a number of *International Conferences on Environmental Compliance and Enforcement* (see http://www.inece.org). Several of these workshops have contributed to a growing literature on compliance, notably the 1999 UNEP-sponsored Geneva workshop, which produced *Enforcement of and Compliance with MEAs: The Experiences of CITES, Montreal Protocol and Basel Convention*, and the 2004 Heidelberg Workshop, which produced Ulrich Beyerlin et al., eds (2006) *Ensuring Compliance with Multilateral Environmental Agreements: A Dialogue between Practitioners and Academia*, Lieden, the Netherlands: Martinus Nijhoff. Also see Fourth Colloquium of the IUCN Academy of Environmental Law at Pace Law School, October 2006, at http://www.law.pace.edu/environment/2006-colloquium-papers-index.html.

96. Waelde argues that one of the reasons for what he calls the "quest for effectiveness" is "the wish to see international law on environment, human rights and other subjects as are bound to emerge as not just a diplomat's business as usual, but something on a higher moral ground with the possibility to change the world for the better." Supra, Waelde.

97. "Robustness" in the context of this book refers to a treaty's built-in mechanism that allows it to learn and adapt by incorporating new provisions that strengthen its internal ability to solve the problems it has been created to address. This concept draws on early work by Ernst Haas who sees an important component of improving organizations to be its ability to learn; see Ernst B. Haas (1990) *When Knowledge Is Power: Three Models of Change in International Organizations*, Berkeley: University of California Press. Thomas Gehring observed a similar characteristic of robustness in the Montreal Protocol, which he calls adaptive learning in dynamic regimes. See Thomas Gehring (1990) *International Environmental Regimes: Dynamic Sectoral Legal Systems*, 1 Y.B. Int'l E. L., 35, 49. See also Oran R. Young (1998) *The Effectiveness of International Environmental Regimes: A Mid-term Report*, 10 International Environmental Affairs, 267, 267–89.

law has been, for the most part, refuted in the last 15 years by legal academics. International law is now widely understood as a process rather than an impartial set of rules.[98] International law has shown that it changes and reflects the social values and norms of society. This process approach has also been reflected to large degree in the treaties themselves and is also an important measurement of a treaty's effectiveness. Modern treaties contain various mechanisms that allow them to evolve with societal norms and values. These include mechanisms such as framework and protocol approaches, learning systems such as education clauses, science and technology mechanisms that review progress in knowledge and advancement on the issue area. Modern environmental treaties also have strong systems for the engagement of civil society actors, which Honju Koh has argued are important mediums for transferring domestic norms and values to treaty-making as these actors play roles as "transnational norm entrepreneurs" and "governmental norm sponsors".[99]

So treaties should not be understood as artefacts that are either effective or ineffective in one time and space. Evidence of a treaty's effectiveness must also include its robustness to evolve, better reflect domestic norms and strengthen itself towards achieving its objectives. Take, for example, the UNFCCC, which has the objective of "the stabilization of greenhouse gas concentrations in the atmosphere at a level that would prevent dangerous anthropogenic interference with the climate system".[100] In the last 10 years, emissions have grown on average at 1 per cent a year; obviously, the Convention has not been effective in meeting its objectives. However, according to what we have said, that is, that a measure of a treaty's effectiveness should also include its robustness to evolve and meet the changing norms of society, it has been very effective.

Between 1992 and 2001, there was a tremendous growth in the interests and understanding of climate change. Events such as the record number of weather-related disasters in the United States and around the world were strongly associated with climatic disruptions due to anthropogenic causes.[101] These events and the scientific link to greenhouse gas

---

98. See Colin Warbrick (1991) *Introduction* to Philip Allott et al., *Theory and International Law: An Introduction*, London: British Institute of International and Comparative Law, xi. See also Rosalyn Higgins (1994) *Problems and Process: International Law and How we Use It*, New York: Oxford University Press.

99. Koh, supra, 645–647.

100. Art. 2 UNFCCC

101. Nat'l Oceanic & Atmospheric Administration (2003) "Billion Dollar US Weather Disasters 1900–2003" ("The U.S. has sustained 52 weather-related disasters over the past 22 years in which overall damages and costs reached or exceeded $1 billion; 43 of these disasters occurred during the 1988–2001 period with total damages/costs exceeding $185 billion. Seven occurred during 1998 alone."), available at http://www.ncdc.noaa.gov/oa/reports/billionz.html.

emissions increased the public perception and its support for the climate change issue. The UNFCCC has a review system and a scientific mechanism that ensured that this new knowledge made its way into the membership of the parties. The fact that the treaty was also a framework convention meant it could incorporate the change in societal norms and values that had emerged in the 1990s into the new Kyoto Protocol. The Protocol itself also has built-in systems that allow it to adapt as norms may change again in the future, such as the review system slated for 2005, and designated commitment periods that allow for changes in targets and reductions every decade or so.

A treaty's supporting provisions

Another aspect of effectiveness that must not be forgotten is a treaty's supporting provisions that are often non-binding or "best endeavours" but which nevertheless play a significant role in achieving the objective of the treaty. The definition of implementation used by most studies have focused on "the process of putting international commitments into practice: the passage of domestic legislation, promulgation of regulations, creation of institutions (both domestic and international), and enforcement of rules".[102] While ratification and the extent to which obligations have been attained are important, lawyers usually consider this as part of the compliance definition. However, important parts of treaties that are normally non-binding but require other non-legal techniques for achievement are capacity-building programmes, financial assistance clauses and technology transfer provisions, each of which is of critical importance for enabling parties to implement the agreement and achieve the objectives of the treaty. The problem here is that that data on these aspects of the treaty are often not provided, although some treaties request general information in their national reports. The study by Victor and his co-authors stressed the importance of these provisions and attempted to measure the impact of the treaty provisions from the standpoint of domestic implementation through looking at the engagement of actors and through the treaty itself from the standpoint of SIRs (systems of implementation review). Other ways of measuring, at least the degree of implementation, could also include the number of programmes in existence such as community projects, awareness-raising campaigns, workshops, availability of training materials or the level of financing provided to countries. Linking these supporting treaty provisions to actual behaviour again is a near impossible task without interviews or questionnaires that could link through social science methods the operation of the programme to specific changes in behaviour. However, measuring the

102. Supra, Kal Raustiala, *Review Institutions*, 5.

degree to which these provisions have actually materialized at the national level, or where called for by the treaty, remains an important part of the effectiveness equation, and is not covered by measuring compliance per se.

Financing

So far the analysis and the determinants of effectiveness that have been put forward in this chapter have primarily looked within the legal components of the treaties themselves. Even though financing is an area that is outside what would typically be considered in a legal analysis of treaty effectiveness, it remains an important lesson that has been learned from the "whole experience of the evolution of environmental law since the 1960's, brought home with particular force in the forum of the Rio Earth Summit".[103] Michael Bowman, in an analysis of the effectiveness of the Ramsar Convention after its twenty-first anniversary, sees finance as important for treaties for both supporting institutional implementation infrastructure and administration and for actually addressing the environmental problem itself.[104] Financing is also an important lure for developing countries to ratify a convention; otherwise these countries are acutely aware that they will not have the resources to meet the convention's obligations.[105]

In the Kyoto Protocol negotiations, financing loomed large in the final deliberations. Negotiating parties realized that averting climate change required shifts to greener technologies and that these technologies would be more expensive and inaccessible to developing countries. They also realized that the impacts of climate change would be mostly felt by the poorest developing nations such as small low-lying states. As a result, before contentious issues, such as emission targets or the market mechanisms for implementation that concerned the interests of developed countries, could be solved, it was first necessary to ensure there would be adequate financing in the Protocol, hence the establishment of three funds to support developing countries was first agreed upon and then the final deliberations turned to the issues surrounding the interests of the North.[106]

103. M. J. Bowman (1995) *Ramsar Convention Comes of Age*, 42 NILR 1, 39.
104. Ibid.
105. Ibid.
106. Author's observations during final deliberations of UNFCCC COP 6 and COP 6 bis. There was a special negotiating group on "Finance", sometimes called "Adverse Effects" or "Developing Countries" in negotiating circles; this group dealt with Technology Transfer, UNFCCC Articles 4.8 and 4.9, Protocol Articles 2.3 and 3.14, capacity-building and potential funds. The final funds that were created were the Special Climate Fund, the Least Developing Country Fund and the Kyoto Fund.

The Monterrey Consensus and the WSSD plan of Action also recon-firmed the importance of financing. The Monterrey Consensus stressed the broader connection of environment, social and economic development with depleting ODA levels, while the WSSD Plan of Action examined more closely what types of areas for the protection of the environment should become prioritized, such as promoting environmentally sound technologies and environmental education.[107] These documents marked a shift in the approach to financing that is worth noting. Whereas at Rio financing by developed countries was viewed as a prerequisite for de-veloping country participation, the outcomes of Johannesburg and Mon-terrey saw developed countries now very cautious about writing blank cheques and emphasized that financing for sustainable development was first contingent upon good governance and improved administrative and public sector efficiency so that the money would not be wasted through corruption or the like. Developed countries pushed the idea that other means of financing were also important, such as the promotion of inter-national trade, foreign direct investment and mobilizing domestic sources of financing.[108]

Whatever the approach, the reality is that cold hard cash does run to the heart of the implementation of a treaty and that the level of financ-ing, the efficiency of how the finance is used and the innovativeness of how it is obtained are all important factors in the effectiveness imple-menting an environmental treaty.[109]

Conclusion

This chapter has explored the various concepts of the effectiveness of in-ternational treaties as an attempt to try and determine what could be categorized as an effective international law from the viewpoint of trea-ties, the main source of international law. From the analysis of legal, social science and multidisciplinary conceptualizations of effectiveness certain elements can be extrapolated that contribute to an improved un-derstanding of effectiveness. In this respect, the chapter has established that the positivistic notion of effectiveness simply as an examination of what specific provisions of the treaty have been complied with is an overly narrow approach and does not take into account in the first

---

107. See *Final Outcome of the International Conference on Financing for Develop-ment*, UNA/CONF.198/3 (1 March 2002), available at http://www.un.org/esa/ffd/0302finalMonterreyConsensus.pdf; see also *Report of WSSD and Plan of Ac-tion, Re-issued Text* (4 September 2002), A. CON.99/20, available at http://www.johannesburgsummit.org/html/documents/summit_docs/131302_wssd_report_reissued.pdf.
108. Ibid.
109. Supra, Bowman, 39.

instance the incentives and motivations of why states behave and in the second instance positivists do not take into account modern studies of legal scholarship that view law as a process instead of a static body of neutral rules and obligations.

Studies that have come from the social sciences (which could be categorized mainly under the discipline of international relations, particularly from the new institutionalist school of thought), on the other hand, have taken such a broad approach to studying effectiveness, from the standpoint of regimes, that it is very difficult to focus in on the treaty itself. These approaches have also defined effectiveness in the context of how institutions created by the agreement have led to a behavioural change in actors. However, in the absence of large-scale databases to observe behavioural change over long periods of time, with a variety of typologies or without questionnaires and interviews with the actors themselves to determine if their behavioural change was linked to the treaty, it is very difficult to establish the causal connections between the operation of the treaty and the behavioural change. These types of studies are outside the normal methods of legal analysis but, if such causal links were ever fully established, lawyers could take this knowledge into account when crafting international treaties.

Based on the review of studies of effectiveness thus far and drawing on many of their insights, it is possible to provide a better understanding of effectiveness, particularly from the legal standpoint. Such a theory of effectiveness considers the various components of the treaty itself and argues that there are three critical elements to the measurement of effectiveness that we can be certain of establishing with the knowledge that we have right now. The first is a measurement of a treaty's effectiveness based on its performance data and compared with its objectives. A second determinant of effectiveness, which has not been widely argued in the literature thus far and reflects a great deal of the legal analysis of why states comply with international rules without the enforceability of strong sanctions, is the robustness of the treaty itself. Modern treaties have various built-in systems that allow their parties to review a treaty's status through scientific mechanisms or effectiveness review systems, or that enable parties to learn and become familiarized with the problem the treaty is addressing. Combined with these review and learning mechanisms are additional built-in systems that allow treaty renegotiation and take on deeper commitments to tackling the problems they have been created to address.

A theory of effectiveness must also pay attention to the supporting components of the treaty which may not be binding on the parties directly but implementing these provisions enhances and enables parties to achieve the goals of the treaty. These include financing, national programmes, technology transfer, capacity-building and even institutional parts of the treaty such as the treaty secretariat. Though measuring the implementation of these supporting components of the treaty from the viewpoint of behavioural change is again methodologically difficult, it is logical that these provisions do have an impact, and measuring the degree of implementation in terms of the number of programmes or the level of financing is also an important component of determining the effectiveness of a treaty. Though not a key legal requirement of treaty effectiveness, financing is nevertheless a crucial lesson that has been learned from treaty-making in the past.

In conclusion, many studies have criticized legal scholarship for having no concern at all for the effectiveness of treaties. When legal scholars do study effectiveness it is from the standpoint of compliance alone and they are not concerned with behaviour or the actors the treaty is trying to change. Taking change in behaviour as the starting point for defining and measuring treaty effectiveness, however, is perhaps an infeasible approach and views treaties as instruments that can affect change rather than instruments that reflect and codify change between states. Viewing treaties as part of the process of building collective societies and reflecting agreed international norms in addition to how they change behaviour will provide treaty-makers further insights into how to strengthen and craft better treaties. Creating new mechanisms, techniques and procedures that, instead of inducing behaviour, allow parties that are interested in a collective agreement to develop consensus, learn and become accustomed to a problem and also provide the systems to develop or innovate new and deeper commitments to address collective problem-solving should be the starting point of any effectiveness study. By understanding treaties in this way we should have a more modest expectation of what treaties can achieve. This is not to say treaties cannot achieve more but to do so would mean inducing social norms instead of reflecting them. This requires treaties to be equipped with strong coercive measures of enforcement, which is not likely to happen within an inter-state system based on sovereignty.

The following chapter will now take these measurements of treaty effectiveness and apply them to an analytical framework in the context of treaty cooperation. Chapters 6 and 7 will then examine two case studies to determine whether these factors of effectiveness are strengthened when MEAs and other international treaties related to sustainable development work together under the concept of interlinkages.

5

Interlinkages and legal effectiveness: Laying the foundations of an analytical framework

Introduction

In chapter 4 we examined the work to date on the effectiveness of international accords and regimes and laid the conceptual foundations for an improved understanding of what constitutes effectiveness. The definition views treaties as reflectors and codifiers of domestic policies and values and looks within treaties themselves or within legal environments such as treaty systems for answers to effectiveness. It takes account of the work that has been done from multidisciplinary and social science studies on effectiveness but at the same time views this work as nascent. This approach to effectiveness is oriented towards linking treaties with fundamental behavioural change, which must still either create new methodologies to prove the causal link or collect stronger data to make this connection. The ability of policy-makers to establish causal links between treaty measures and specific predictable outcomes will be an extremely useful tool for lawyers involved in the treaty-making process and policy-makers alike. However, until such time, effectiveness, at least from the legal point of view, must look within the legal parameters to devise ways of strengthening environmental treaties.

Realizing the limitations there are for inducing change in an inter-state system based on sovereignty, policy-makers have directed their attention to reforms and improvements of the existing governance systems. Within this context debates have intensified on the diffuse nature of the environment and sustainable development governance systems. Criticism stems

Interlinkages and the effectiveness of multilateral environmental agreements,
W. Bradnee Chambers, United Nations University Press, 2008, ISBN 978-92-808-1149-0

from the decentralized nature of these systems and a perception that fragmentation automatically leads to ineffectiveness and inefficiency. This perception has created major debates among environmental agencies and environmental policy-makers.[1]

The criticism of the current environmental governance system originates from the notion that the global environmental institutions developed unsystematically, based on issues that attracted political agendas at one time or another. In turn, this ad hoc development led to fragmentation and a lack of coordination which has reduced institutional performance to deal with environmental problems.[2] Many policy-makers assume that improving the interlinkages between institutions and promoting greater connectivity between ecosystems and societal actions will reduce overlap and conflicts, capitalize on inherent synergies, and generally create more effective environmental laws.

These assumptions have never been fully explored or rationalized; however, they have led to both academic and policy-oriented theories of how international treaties could be strengthened through greater interlinkages. The purpose of this chapter is to first review the various definitions of interlinkages and then, based on this discussion, introduce a definition that can be used for the purposes of this book and further studies of MEAs. The chapter will then review the literature and theories that have been put forward in the area of cooperating[3] treaties in order to understand how this literature fits with the theoretical and conceptual framework on effectiveness that I introduced in chapter 4. From this analysis I will establish a framework for this book that I will use to prove the principal query that interlinkages can improve the legal effectiveness of treaties through the various determinants discussed in chapter 2: (1) meeting treaty objectives, (2) compliance, (3) robustness, (4) supporting provisions of a treaty, and (5) finance. In the last section of this chapter I will discuss the selection of case studies and how this contributes to proving the central query of the book (that interlinkages can improve the effectiveness of MEAs) and the second query (that interlinkages can also improve the effectiveness between MEAs and other international treaties outside the branch of international environmental law).

1. Supra, chapter 1.
2. In 1997, for example, the UN Secretary-General in his programme for reform stated that there is a "need for a more integrated systematic approach to policies and programmes", *Report of the Secretary-General: Renewing the UN, A Programme for Reform*, Doc. A/51/950, 14 July 1997; also see UNGA (1997) *Rio+5 General Assembly Special Session* A/S-19/29 (27 June); UNGA (1998) *Report of the United Nations Task Force on Environment and Human Settlement*, A/53/463.
3. An important distinction should be made here with respect to the literature of conflicting treaties which is dealt with in chapter 3 and described in chapter 1.

Resolving some definitional and theoretical questions on interlinkages

Some definitional parameters for interlinkages

The concept of interlinkages has become synonymous with multiple meanings both within environment and also in the context of sustainable development:

> Scientific understanding of the nature of the links among environmental issues and their relationships to meeting human needs, to facilitate the balancing of competing needs and the identification of strategies that capture as many benefits as possible.[4]

> ... the cause-and-effect relationships that link many of the human activities (pressures of drivers of change), including climate change, land-use and land cover change and land and water degradation.[5]

> ... interdependencies between and amongst environmental change, human well-being and responses developed to minimise the impact of environmental change and improve human well-being. There is recognition of interlinkages but few response options to address them. Many of the response options are still developed in the context of one environmental change (e.g. climate change) and not across interdependent environmental issues.[6]

Early usage of the term "interlinkage" was made in the general context of connecting the three pillars of sustainable development, both the environmental, social and economic interactions and trade-offs with associated institutions. The term "interlinkages" has sometimes been confused with other terms, understandably so given the similarities and overlap with related definitions. For example, interlinkages and the "ecosystem approach" have frequently been confused. The "ecosystem approach" is a strategy that advocates use of "appropriate scientific methodologies focused on levels of biological organization, which encompass the essential structure, processes, functions and interactions among organisms and their environment".[7] For some, however, the ecosystem

4. Bob Watson et al. (1998) *Protecting Our Planet, Securing Our Future: Linkages Among Global Environmental Issues and Human Needs*, Washington, D.C.: UNEP.
5. Habiba Gitay, ed. (2004) *A Conceptual Design Tool for Exploiting the Interlinkages between Focal Areas of the GEF: Report of the Scientific and Technical Advisory Panel to the Global Environment Facility*, available at http://www.unep.org/stapgef/documents/Interlinkages%20Report.pdf.
6. UNEP (2006) *Draft Global Environmental Outlook 4*, Nairobi: UNEP, chapter 7.
7. CBD (2004) *The Ecosystem Approach*, Montreal: CBD, 1, available at http://www.biodiv.org/doc/publications/ea-text-en.pdf.

approach did not bring in the human dimension adequately and so inter-linkages was a preferred term that was sometimes used to explain the complex interactions between ecosystems and human society.[8]

Other terms have also been used in association with the ecosystem approach and are sometimes associated or confused with interlinkages; these include terms such as "ecosystem-based management, sustainable forest management, integrated river-basin management, integrated marine and coastal area management, and responsible fisheries approaches".[9] All of these approaches bring in the concept of multidimensionality by bridging ecology with management and examining the interactions of multiple biomes. Like the "ecosystem approach", "interlinkages" does not preclude these practices or approaches; interlinkages is rather a term that has a much broader policy-oriented emphasis. The usage of terms will also depend on the scientific discipline or environmental community. For example, hydrologists may use the terms "integrated river-basin management" or "coastal zone management" while ecologists working in the field of biodiversity may use the ecosystem approach. On the other hand, those thinking about all the various issues of the environment, particularly in the context of the various environmental conventions and institutions, may use the term "interlinkages".

More recently the environmental assessment community has further developed the concept of interlinkages to describe all the interactions of direct drivers of environmental change (i.e., climate change and biodiversity loss) with the interactions of the indirect drivers of environmental change (i.e., trade, consumption, population growth).[10] The Millennium Ecosystem Assessment brought in the further dimension to the interlinkages models of the concept of "human well-being".[11] The expense of the interlinkages has therefore been broadened to include all of these multiple dimensions. In this context, the term has been useful to describe all the interactions but, as it expands, it also becomes difficult to understand

8. This was a perception rather than a fact as most definitions of the ecosystem approach admittedly include the human dimension as part of the ecosystem or by linking humans with the biological capacity of the ecosystem. World Resources Institute, "Adopting an Ecosystem Approach", in *World Resources 2000–2001: People and Ecosystems: The Fraying Web of Life*, Washington, D.C.: United Nations Development Programme, 225–239, available at http://pubs.wri.org/.

9. See supra, *The Ecosystem Approach*, at 1.

10. The Millennium Ecosystem Assessment (hereinafter the MA) has been the most comprehensive global assessment of earth ecosystems undertaken to date. The MA made the connection between drivers of environmental change and of human well-being. For definitions of direct and indirect drivers see Millennium Ecosystem Assessment (2005) *Ecosystems and Human Well-being: Synthesis*, Washington, D.C.: Island.

11. Millennium Ecosystem Assessment (2003) *Ecosystems and Human Well-being: A Framework for Assessment*, Washington, D.C.: Island.

a starting point to conceptualize all the interactions and eventually isolate the impacts of the interactions and the active drivers of the change.
The risk of overusing the term "interlinkage" to mean everything could
also lead at one point to mean nothing. It is therefore important that
a concise definition is set and maintained, particularly in the context of
this thesis.

Interlinkages is a strategic approach to managing sustainable development that generally seeks to promote greater connectivity between ecosystems and societal actions. On a practical level, it promotes greater
cohesiveness among environmentally issue-based and development-
focused policies and institutions across and between international, regional and national scales. The interlinkages approach to sustainable
development comprises two fundamental elements: synergism and coordination. It is believed that a synergistic approach to managing institutions will lead to more effective and resource-efficient assessment,
negotiation, decision-making, planning, and implementation of policies
and measures. Similarly, improved coordination of institutions at the
international, regional and national levels will minimize inadvertent conflicts between policies and measures and between different international,
regional and national regimes.[12]

"Synergies" can be understood as the point of convergence between
environmental science and environmental politics. They arise when scien-
tifically identified environmental interlinkages are accommodated within
the policy-making process – when, for example, national, regional and
international policy-making responds to existing interlinkages with pre-
scriptions that articulate objectives in two or more environmental issue
areas.[13]

"Coordination" relates to the need to minimize inadvertent conflicts
between environmental policies and with other different but interrelated
regimes. In the development of multilateral environmental agreements,
it is crucial that coordination should prevent the adoption of inconsistent policies that, when implemented, may prove to be contradictory.
Avoidance of conflict is especially important given the close relations
and interlinkages between natural ecosystems. Special care must be
taken to ensure that the environmental outcomes that arise due to the
implementation of one agreement do not hinder the intended outcomes
in the implementation of another.[14]

This definition of interlinkages and its constituent concepts of synergism and coordination make several basic assumptions concerning the

12. This definition is based on the definition that the UN University has developed. See
    op. cit. *UNU Interlinkages Report* (1999).
13. Ibid.
14. Ibid.

current state of global environmental institutions. First, it assumes that these institutions entrusted to manage the environment have not reached their full and effective performance potential on account of their intrinsic design, that is to say they were not created systematically but developed organically as environmental problems emerged onto political agendas.

Secondly, the definition assumes that the current international legislative environment is not conducive to the development of coordinated, or synergistic, approaches to collective environmental problem-solving. The complexities of the issues involved, as well as the very nature of treaty-making, mean that international agreements are often negotiated in relative isolation. They are negotiated by specialized ministries or functional organizations, in forums that are completely detached from the negotiating arena of other international agreements. Further, the consensus-building process that is necessary for effective multilateralism is difficult enough without the additional burden of attempting to accommodate the interlinkages of various issues. Overall, this creates global environmental institutions that are ineffective because they attempt to deal with extremely complex, interrelated systems – ecosystems – in piecemeal ways.

Based on these assumptions, an interlinkages theory postulates that environmental institutions must reflect the complexity and interrelatedness of ecosystems in their management of the environment. A theory of interlinkages hypothesizes that modelling environmental regimes based on the relationship between the given environmental elements (i.e., soil, water, atmosphere, climate), problems in the ecosystem (areas of degradation, types of pollution, toxins, etc.) and the appropriate policy interventions would create greater gains of efficiency and effectiveness. Such gains are manifested in policies, treaty-making and in the organizations responsible for environmental management. For the purposes of this thesis, however, the interlinkages definition will be applied only to the interactions of treaties and public international law. It postulates that treaties that have overlapping subject areas and contradictory obligations or purposes can work to solve these conflicts through greater cooperation through what I call an "interlinkages approach".

Review of relevant theoretical literature on overlapping treaties and institutions

There has been a growing social science literature on the classification of the interlinkages between international regimes; however, this has not led to any agreement on a single accepted theory, taxonomy or definition. None of this work has taken place in the field of international law but has rather been done in international relations and by political scientists studying the effects of overlapping international regimes.[15] This has included to a large extent an examination, from the behavioural point of view, of studies of international treaties in the field of the environment where there has been a marked increase in overlapping treaties. These studies are commonly referred to in political science and international relations literature as institutional interplay, defined by Oran Young as the interactions between institutions that deal with a common issue or that have overlap. According to Young, the critical elements to consider in terms of interplay are the roles of the interacting institutions and which institution or organization has the capacity to implement the preferred policy choice. Young argues that there are two dimensions to interplay, horizontal and vertical. Vertical interplay basically refers to the interaction of institutions across scales, such as the nexus between global, regional and local institutions, while horizontal interlinkages refer to the linkages between institutions at the same scale and between institutions of a similar structure such as UNEP and the WTO.[16]

Much of the work in this field of interplay has been carried out in an attempt to develop taxonomies or classifications of interplay in order to isolate and study the behaviour of the regime. These classifications have ranged from narrow distinctions, which have produced very elaborate descriptions of the various types of interplay, to very broad classifications that create simpler categories. Most classifications have attempted to describe typologies that define the problem-solving roles that institutional interplay could ameliorate. In other words, if regimes were to be linked together, what impact could this have on state behaviour? For example, Olav Schram Stokke has surveyed the recent literature concerning regime effectiveness and has found that most studies agree that regimes can affect human and social behaviour through compellence, prominence or incentives.[17] From these parsimonious categories, he determines that institutional interplay can have an impact on effectiveness whether by utilitarian interplay, where "rules or programmes undertaken within one regime alter the costs or benefits of behavioural options in another regime"; by normative compellence, where "an international regime may confirm or contradict the norms upheld by another institution"; or by ideational interplay, "which involves processes of learning" and "draw-

---

15. A regime is defined as "sets of governing arrangements that include networks of rules, norms, and procedures that regularize behaviour and control its effects", Robert Keohane and Joseph Nye, in Stephen Krasner, ed. (1983) *International Regimes*, Ithaca, N.Y.: Cornell University Press.
16. See Oran Young (2002) *The Institutional Dimensions of Environmental Change: Fit, Interplay, and Scale*, Boston: MIT Press, 98–99.
17. Olav Schram Stokke (2001) *The Interplay of International Regimes: Putting Effectiveness Theory to Work*, FNI Report 14/2001, Oslo: Fridtjof Nansen Institute, 10.

ing political attention – domestically or at the international level – to problems that are addressed by the recipient regime".[18]

Similarly, Rosendal distinguishes the types of interplay between regimes as either relating to general norms or specific rules and whether these relationships are compatible or diverging.[19] Thomas Gehring and Sebastian Oberthür, through a project that examined the interplay between European Union institutions and international institutions, created a much more elaborate system of identification based on the complexity and the nature of the interrelationships of the regimes.[20] Gehring and Oberthür stress the importance of identifying the difference between a recipient regime and a target regime and whether the cross-relationship is intentional or unintentional, synergistic or conflictive.[21] Young classifies the linkages between regimes from a structural point of view, describing them as embedded, nested, clustered or overlapping.[22]

Young, in a forthcoming book on interplay theory and the case of the Cartagena Protocol, makes the additional distinctions between regimes that are intended and unintended and a further distinction of regimes where the interplay is either shallow or deep.[23] He argues that unintended

18. Ibid.
19. Kristin Rosendal (2001) *Impacts of Overlapping International Regimes: The Case of Biodiversity*, 7 Global Governance, 95–117.
20. Thomas Gehring and Sebastian Oberthür (2000) *Exploring Regime Interaction: A Framework Analysis*, Proceedings of the Final Conference on the Effectiveness of International Agreements and EU Legislation, Barcelona. This has now become a book; see Sebastian Oberthür and Thomas Gehring, eds (2006) *Institutional Interaction in Global Environmental Governance: Synergy and Conflict among International and EU Policies*, Cambridge, Mass.: MIT Press.
21. Gehring and Oberthür describe a very useful way of categorizing and understanding institutional interplay by distinguishing between the regime that is the source of the interplay (source regime) and the regime that receives the impact of the interplay (which they call the target regime or recipient regime), ibid. 3.
22. See Oran Young (1999) *Governance in World Affairs*, Ithaca, N.Y.: Cornell University Press, 165–172. Embedded treaties are highly focused or specialized groups of treaties (e.g., the 1973 Polar Bear Treaty); nested treaties involve a series of treaties that have loose or limited recognition with each other and usually these treaties have formal memorandums of understandings recognizing their collaboration and connections; clustered treaties are a group of treaties that have a common overarching legal umbrella and then a series of smaller specific agreements of which parties may or may not be be part (UNCLOS or WTO). However, the legal umbrella usually sets out some basic principles that every party must adhere to (e.g., National Treatment). I would add to this list regional-global treaty systems, which are treaty systems that are often a series of smaller regional treaties that fall under the jurisdiction of or are coordinated with a larger international convention; this could also include looser arrangements such as in the case of the regional trade agreement connections with the WTO.
23. Oran Young (forthcoming) "On Institutional Interplay: Deriving Insights from the WTO/Cartagena Protocol Case", in Oran Young, W. Bradnee Chambers and Joy Kim, eds, *Institutional Interplay: The Case of Biosafety and Trade*, Tokyo: UNU Press.

consequences of regimes arise as a result of technical issues in the creation of the regime, for example the overlap that exists between the ozone-depleting substances such as HFCs in the Montreal Protocol and that of greenhouse gases in the case of the Kyoto Protocol. These sorts of issues are both unintended and shallow and thus comparatively easier to resolve. Intended regimes are a result of a different set of actors creating a regime, in effect as a sort of defence to counterbalance a regime that threatens a subject or issue that is of concern to other parties. This often results in regimes that are apt to conflict and that have deep interplay that is more difficult to resolve.

These categorizations do in fact offer many insights into the nature of the relationship between international regimes; however, each has limitations for the purposes of this study. Rosendal's and Gering and Oberthür's categories are not inclusive of all the types of interactions that are possible. Young describes structural relationships which are helpful, such as the differences between horizontal and vertical interplay,[24] which in a general sense helps distinguish scale and the nature of the interaction. His recent work on trying to refocus the debate on interplay on the origin and the consequences of interplay rather than classifications (that are often mutually exclusive and therefore difficult to compare) will undoubtedly spur more studies in this area. Stokke has based his categories on the outcome of the interactions, which is more closely aligned with the concept of interlinkages as a means to improve the effectiveness of the regimes and institutions (i.e., MEAs). However, the preoccupation has been centred on classifying these types of interactions instead of understanding which type of interactions help and which do not.

All of these categories show that there are many ways to look at the relationships among treaties but a workable taxonomy must be based on benefits that would logically give rise to a potential interlinkage. No policy-maker will advocate creating interlinkages among treaties for the sake of it. There must already be some predisposition among treaties towards making the interlinkage a potentially beneficial endeavour; generally, such predispositions would take the form of a normative or functional connection, a common subject area, a shared issue or, in some cases, a conflict, as will see in chapters 6 and 7. It is these existing relationships among treaties that policy-makers are looking to further exploit as a means of improving the effectiveness of the treaty.

From this review of the literature on institutional interplay an important distinction between interplay theory and interlinkages becomes very clear and it is important to clarify this for the purposes of this thesis. The definition of interlinkages introduced in this chapter and as applied to

24. Ibid.

MEAs in this book is concerned with the coordination between MEAs as a means to minimize conflict and create synergies; it is less about the study of the interaction of treaties from the perspective of understanding the behavioural consequences on which interplay theories are largely focused. In contrast to the work that the international relations and political science disciplines have carried out on the concept of effectiveness that we saw in chapter 4, the work that these disciplines have generally done on interplay has been less valuable. I argue this point because the work has not led to any applied outcomes, particularly for international lawyers looking to see how the interactions can lead to better designed treaties.[25] To the international lawyer, therefore, the means of managing the interaction of successive treaties, particularly when they are overlapping or contradictory on a particular predisposition, is more important than the behavioural phenomena of the interaction itself.

Interlinkages from the legal perspective can therefore be viewed as a normative theory that postulates that treaties can improve their legal performance through greater inter-treaty cooperation. This is a theory that remains for the most part still unproven and why this book should make some progressive contributions to public international law and to the future management of treaties.

A framework for analysis: How do interlinkages strengthen the effectiveness of international law?

In chapter 4 I clearly showed what is meant by the term "effectiveness of international treaties". I reviewed the existing literature and, from this analysis, I developed parameters for measuring the effectiveness of international treaties. These include examining the objectives of the treaty and to what extent these have been met; compliance with the principal obligations of the treaty and whether parties to the treaty are meeting these requirements; the degree to which the supporting provisions of the treaty are implemented; whether the treaty is able to adapt, learn and change progressively with the development of international law; and lastly whether the treaty has adequate financing to meets its goals and requirements.

Each of these criteria is important to a treaty's effectiveness and can individually strengthen its performance. The remaining part of my framework is to argue that interlinkages between treaties can in fact lead to the strengthening of each of these individual criteria and this too must be considered as an important factor for treaty effectiveness.

25. Supra, chapter 2.

Once I have elaborated this argument in the following section it will complete my analytical framework. I will then apply the framework to two case studies in chapters 6 and 7. In these cases, I will argue that, in each instance, the interlinkage between the treaties has led to an improvement in performance (meeting the obligations, compliance, supporting provisions, robustness and finance of the treaties) and thus, taking these measurements into account, has improved the effectiveness of the treaties.

Meeting the objectives of the treaty

As established in the previous chapter, achieving a treaty's objectives is the most fundamental determinant of legal effectiveness, and interlinkages can play a strong role in achieving those objectives. Interlinkages can work towards achieving treaty objectives by strengthening the coherence and meaning of a treaty's principles and provisions through interpretation and re-interpretation, and by accomplishing goals that contribute to achieving a treaty's objective but which the recipient treaty is unable to accomplish alone.

Treaty fragmentation has been one of the strongest criticisms of the current international environmental governance system.[26] It has also contributed to the weakening of the principles of various treaties. Countless treaties and organizations dealing with related environmental issues are engaged in negotiating and applying international legal principles; this has meant that these principles are often interpreted in different ways and appear differently in various international treaties.[27] The precautionary principle, for example, was first employed as a "measure" in the 1984 Ministerial Declaration of the North Sea Conference[28] and in the preamble of the 1985 Ozone Convention and it was subsequently solidified in the Rio Declaration. It is generally accepted as a universal principle after its inclusion in the five international legal instruments arising from the UNCED.[29] There has, however, been an inconsistency in how the principle has been used in subsequent treaties.

---

26. See supra, chapter 1.
27. Edith Brown Weiss (1995) *International Environmental Law: Contemporary Issues and the Emergence of a New World Order*, 81 Geo. L. J. 675, 697–702, 700.
28. See clause D.3 and H.7 of the 1984 Ministerial Declaration of Protection of the North Sea, http://www.seas-at-risk.org/1mages/1984%20Bremen%20Declaration.pdf? PHPSESSID=9a9e58a56400b09659375ab8395d618a.
29. See James Cameron and Juli Abouchar (1996) "The Status of the Precautionary Principle in International Law", in David Freestone and Ellen Hey, eds, *The Precautionary Principle and International Law: The Challenge of Implementation*, London: Kluwer Law International, pp. 29–53.

The Cartagena Protocol on Biosafety is said to be the strongest interpretation of the precautionary principle to date. The protocol describes the principle in detail, operationalizing it in its procedures. It has provided a version of the principle with fewer conditions than appear in other treaties that invoke the precautionary principle. Thus, the Biosafety Protocol takes a *carte blanche* approach in that it does not provide for the threshold of establishing "threats of serious or irreversible damage" or based on "cost-effectiveness measures" that are found in Principle 15 of the Rio Declaration. It only states that lack of scientific uncertainty should not hinder a party to the Protocol from taking action. Clearly, the Protocol's version of the principle is a departure from its previous versions under international public law and its application to other treaties such as the UNFCCC or even the CBD where the threshold of possible irreparable damage was expressly provided.

These types of inconsistencies become even more problematic because there are very few examples of international courts adjudicating on environmental cases. So many environmental principles, such as the precautionary principle, have not been applied to practical cases, which can help the solidification and consistency of a principle's meaning under international law. An inconsistent application of a principle can create loopholes for it to be used in ways that are inconsistent with its intended meaning.[30]

The interpretation and application of the precautionary principle under the WTO involving sanitary and phytosanitary standards is another instance of differences in interpretation and application of the same principle. Under the WTO Dispute Settlement Body (DSB),[31] the precautionary principle was interpreted in ways that are even more divergent than any of the previous applications under public international law. The WTO DSB has laid down several conditions that are outside any of its original interpretations. According to the results of four disputes arising over sanitary and phytosanitary standards, evoking the precautionary principle requires explicit proof of lack of scientific information;[32] it must be invoked only based on information directly pertaining to the case in hand. It means therefore that relevant international studies and/or SPS measures applied by other countries for similar situations is not sufficient

---

30. An "inconsistent approach" means that the same principle is defined or operationalized differently in separate treaties.
31. See infra, chapter 7 on WTO Agreement, Annex 2.
32. WTO, *Australia – Measures Affecting the Importation of Salmon*, Report of the Panel, WT/DS18; modified by Report of the Appellate Body, AB-1998-5, 20 October 1998; also see Steve Charnovitz (2002) "Improving the Agreements on Sanitary and Phytosanitary Standards", in Gary Sampson and W. Bradnee Chambers, eds, *Trade Environment and the Millennium*, 2nd ed., Tokyo: UNU Press, pp. 207–234.

proof. Furthermore, the principle can only be applied provisionally, which means a country must continually seek to find the scientific data necessary to establish scientific certainty.[33]

Strict consistency may not always be desirable; certainly different contexts and applications require flexibility to apply the intent of the principle, but there is also the other side of the coin – that inconsistency permits avenues to escape the intent of the principle. In the absence of strong measures of codification or a judicial tradition under international environmental law, it can be said that striking a balance between consistency and flexibility is important to ensure and maintain common meanings and applications of the principle. Multiple interpretations can result in a dilution of the principle and loopholes for countries to misuse it for their own gains. Consistency also contributes towards universalism and custom, which are goals of international law-making.

If treaty negotiations and implementation were more systematic across treaties, interlinkages could play a constructive role, particularly in terms of agreed definitions, indicators and principles. Treaty parties could, for example, create mutually agreed interpretations of principles and promulgate them in decisions in their respective decision-making bodies. This kind of cooperation could lead to common application of definitions and principles and more legal certainty that can only serve to strengthen international law and the respective treaty objectives.[34]

A second way in which an interlinkages approach can serve the interests of treaty objectives is by using one treaty to solve or address a problem that may be outside the mandate of another treaty. A recent example of this is the issue of bush meat between the International Convention on Endangered Species (CITES) and the Convention on Biological Diversity (CBD). The CITES Secretariat, through its monitoring system, noticed that local people in West Africa were continuing to kill endangered animals that were on CITES endangered lists. The reason for killing the animals was for food and not for trade, which meant that the issue was outside the auspices of CITES, which is a trade treaty. Nevertheless, the goal of CITES is the protection of endangered species from overexploitation, and its parties believed that the CITES Secretariat should take action.[35] As a result, the CITES Secretariat asked the CBD Secretariat to raise the issue on the agenda of the CBD SBSTTA.[36] SBSTTA has

---

33. See WTO, *Japan – Measures Affecting Agricultural Products*, Report of the Panel, WT/DS76; modified by Report of the Appellate Body, AB-1998-8, 22 February 1999.

34. See Conclusion of book on the need for an Interlinkages Principle, infra, chapter 8.

35. See, for example, CITES Preamble.

36. See CITES paragraph 14 of decision V/4, which asked SBSTTA to look into the issue and Paragraph 19 of Decision VI/22 for further action.

now taken up the issue and has begun examining the problem in more detail.[37]

Meeting a treaty's supporting provisions

Joint programmes are one of the most useful ways for improving the implementation of treaty-supporting provisions. Often these provisions are generic at the outset and include common schemes to increase capacity-building, awareness and education, technology transfer, and scientific study and research.[38] These clauses also have in common the fact that they tend to be less regarded in terms of prioritization, with clauses and provisions that go directly to implementing the core objectives of the treaty. Treaties could benefit immensely by creating joint programmes that implement these cooperatively. For example, since many of the MEAs are naturally linked or linked through ecosystems, joint environmental education activities make sense; perhaps joint environmental education centres at the national level for MEAs could even be a plausible suggestion. UNEP has suggested that joint capacity-building programmes could be created at the national level and could concentrate on general assistance "including training, technical, legal and administrative assistance".[39] Through such cooperative arrangements, these provisions could gain more prominence and priority and generally wider support for implementation. The importance that these supporting provisions play in terms of effectiveness is often forgotten. In a survey done by the Global Environment Facility (GEF) on capacity development for sustainable development, countries overwhelmingly ranked elements such as education, awareness, training and technology transfer among the highest needs for implementing MEAs.[40] One reason that these provisions are often not prioritized is that they generally require high levels of financing, always in short supply in environmental agreements. Cooperative arrangements

---

37. On the impact of unsustainable harvesting of non-timber forest resources, including bush meat and living botanical resources, see UNEP (2001) *Forest Biological Diversity Consideration of Specific Threats to Forest Biological Diversity*, UNEP/CBD/SBSTTA/7/7.
38. Ibid.
39. UNEP/IGM/2/5 (4 July 2000), paras. 33–34: UNEP suggests that a coordinated approach to capacity-building might involve elements such as "country-driven multi-stakeholder programmes"; "broadening skills in subjects related to capacity development – from mediation to environmental economics"; "devising new indicators for capacity development and developing new tools for building capacities".
40. See Global Environment Facility (2000) *Capacity Development Initiative: Country Capacity Needs and Priorities*, available at http://www.gefweb.org/Site_Index/CDI/Synthesis_Report.doc, vii.

between MEAs can also create greater cost-effectiveness, a factor that will be explored in more depth below.

Another key element in the implementation of the supporting provisions is performance at the national level. Meeting the binding obligations of a treaty and the supporting programmes relies on a national implementation system, which includes focal points and the division of labour for international negotiations, monitoring, and execution of the treaty provision. It is a key factor, therefore, in the effectiveness of a treaty's supporting programmes, and also, as we will see later, in its compliance.

The state of existing national architecture for executing MEAs is generally ad hoc and disjointed. The national arrangements for implementing MEAs tend to develop as the legal regimes develop internationally; in other words, to a large extent they mirror each other. As the national MEAs ratifications add up, the domestic authorities divide up the work among its ministries and departments but little thought is given to systematic coherence or management. As a result, there are coordination and communication problems, conflicting institutional roles and, generally, a duplication of labour. The measures that have been taken to create better coordination have been more of a Band-Aid nature rather than dealing with the source of the problem, which is more deep-seated and structural.

A United Nations University report, for example, on national and regional implementation of MEAs describes the problems of both a horizontal and vertical nature.[41] At the same level of government (the horizontal implementation) some coordination architecture may exist – such as the national committees that bring together stakeholders to plan negotiations or implementation. However, the meetings of these committees are often held infrequently and the sessions are more for information sharing rather than for devising clear implementation strategies or frameworks for cooperation. Moreover, the national committee practice is not widespread; in the Economic and Social Council for Asia and the Pacific (ESCAP) region only about 50 per cent of the countries have such committees.[42] At the vertical level, the problem depends upon the division of power and the ownership of natural resources. When these jurisdictions

41. UNU (2002) *Interlinkages: National and Regional Approaches to MEAs*, UNU Policy Report, Tokyo: UNU, 5–13.
42. Caroline Van Toen (2001) *Delegate's Perceptions on Synergies and the Implementation of MEAs, Views of the ESCAP Region*, UN University Background Paper prepared for Informal Regional Consultations on Interlinkages: Synergies and Coordination between MEAs, Tokyo: UNU, 14.

are dispersed between local, provincial and federal governments the cleavages are greater in terms of cooperation and coordination.[43]

Scientific mechanisms are another very important aspect of a modern environmental treaty's supporting provisions. For environmental treaties, science is a key factor in establishing that a problem exists and improving the knowledge of how the problem is being addressed (improving or changing). The parties to the treaty then use this knowledge as feedback to create and adapt policy responses. Linking the scientific mechanisms or technological or scientific advisory bodies together makes sense for a couple of basic reasons. The first reason comes back to the natural and ecological link between MEAs; natural systems are co-dependent and part of the same ecological equation, so mechanisms or bodies that just look at one part of the equation are not getting the full picture.[44] The second reason is that some MEAs, like the UNCCD, do not have scientific mechanisms. Thus, it is useful for them to "piggyback" with those treaties that do have scientific mechanisms whose work may have implications for the recipient treaty.[45]

Robustness

The previous chapter argued that robustness can be one of the determinants of an effective treaty, and that the built-in mechanisms that allow a treaty to take on changes, learn and adapt are indeed critical for strengthening the treaty. This is particularly the case in today's modern setting of changing science and slow and incremental progress towards consensus building in multilateral fora. When adding the variable of interlinkages as a component to the measurement of effectiveness, it is interesting to note that the recipient treaty's levels of robustness can increase. Stokke has described two ways in which this can occur. Firstly, interlinkages can build support with governments and the public for the recipient treaty. Secondly, interlinkages can inspire recipient treaties to learn through best practice from other treaties.[46]

Stokke uses the example of marine pollution in the North-East Atlantic to illustrate the first point. In the mid-1980s, the European Community and the Oslo and Paris Commissions were primarily responsible for

---

43. Supra, *Interlinkages National and Regional.*
44. Supra, Watson et al., *Protecting Our Planet, Securing Our Future.*
45. See recent document from the UNEP Executive Director updating the UNEP Governing Council on the strengthening of the scientific capacity of UNEP and the creation of an environmental watch system, at UNEP (2005) *International Environmental Governance: Report of Executive Director*, UNEP/GCSS.IX/3, 4–5.
46. Supra, Stokke, 20.

controlling dumping and land-based pollution. Several states were discouraged by the lack of progress that these regimes were making and as a result organized the first inter-ministerial International North Sea Conference. The Conference, which brought together the work of the three entities that managed the North Sea, breathed new life back into these regimes, and provided a rejuvenated legal and scientific platform that led to stronger governmental support and implementation of the respective regimes in the North Sea.[47]

The second way in which interlinkages can contribute to treaty robustness is from treaty learning, or incorporating best practices or lessons learned from another treaty into its own decision-making and design. Stokke argues that "vague general principles" tend to be exchanged easily between regimes, while the "emulation of substantive or operational solutions" is more difficult but "more interesting when it facilitates matters of controversy in the recipient regime".[48] Stokke's views are consistent with a study the UNU, the Massachusetts Institute of Technology and UNEP conducted on possible lessons learned between the Ozone Convention and the Climate Change Convention.[49] A group of well-known experts concluded from an analysis of the Montreal Protocol that there were a number of important lessons such as "institutional effectiveness, national capacity, use of regional focal points and the importance of mechanisms that can incorporate scientific advances into decision-making" that would have been useful in the Kyoto Protocol negotiations. The group believed, however, that because there had not been a close connection between these two regimes, particularly after 1997 when negotiations began on the Kyoto Protocol, that these lessons were for the most part lost.[50]

This type of inter-treaty connection, however, can have negative connotations. States far too often use this kind of practice as a way of stalling progress towards deeper commitments in international negotiations.[51] This is sometimes referred to as recycling text and is a typical practice when states do not have new ideas or proposals to table in their deliberations. In the 2002 World Summit on Sustainable Development (WSSD)

47. Ibid., 20–21.
48. Supra, Stokke, 23.
49. UNU, UNEP and MIT (2001) *Interlinkages between the Ozone and the Climate Change Conventions*, UNU Policy Report, Tokyo: UNU.
50. Ibid. Supporting this argument are comments made by Ambassador Richard Benedict to the author. See also Laura Thoms (2003) *A Comparative Analysis of International Regimes on Ozone and Climate Change with Implications for Regime Design*, 41 Columbia Journal of Transnational Law 795.
51. Ibid., 21.

preparations, this practice was very pronounced. Since the WSSD preparations took place amidst several other ongoing multilateral processes that had bearing on it (WTO Doha Development Round, Monterrey Finance for Development Conference, Millennium Declaration and the UNEP International Environmental Governance process), the draft plan from the early part of the preparations reflected a great deal of text from these other processes. The practice was particularly rampant because many states argued that there was nothing new to say, particularly since WSSD took place too soon after Rio. Even the final WSSD Plan of Action contains a large amount of text contained from these conferences.[52]

Compliance and monitoring

Interlinkages can improve and support the compliance of MEAs in several ways. One of the most speculative ways is through streamlining procedural obligations.[53] With the advent of so many environmental treaties and the pressure to join even more continuing to mount, countries face tremendous burdens in meeting their reporting and information obligations. These provisions are found in almost all MEAs and the procedural burdens of them have not gone unnoticed by governments. There has been concern "that reporting has become an end in itself rather than a means to an end".[54] The idea behind the procedural streamlining is that much of the reporting shares basic commonalties but is collected and recollected by different domestic departments, ministries or national centres. Countries also collect a fair amount of data for their own national purposes. By creating systems that could centralize the collection and the data storage and then develop harmonized reporting formats, the procedural burden could be substantially alleviated. Given that non-compliance in MEAs occurs most frequently for parties not meeting their reporting obligations, harmonized reporting, information and data collections "could lead to greater compliance with reporting requirements, more effective monitoring, more accessible information, and better, more consistent, information".[55]

Other procedures that are linked to compliance could also be synchronized between MEAs. For example, Oberthür suggests that the Climate Change Convention could learn lessons from the Montreal Protocol's

---

52. See for example the sections concerning development goals, WTO, etc.
53. This remains speculative as there are no good cases where the procedural streamlining outcomes have been well documented.
54. UNU, supra, *UNU Interlinkages Report.*
55. Ibid.; also see supra, *WCMC Feasibility Study*, 11; and supra, *UNDP Synergies.*

efforts to gather and analyse data on the trade, production and consumption of target gases. In particular, cooperating through the World Customs Organization (WCO) in developing harmonized customs codes for the trade in relevant substances may help parties to track the substances necessary to estimate or double-check emissions data.[56] It has also been thought that adapted custom procedures with the Harmonized Custom and Coding System (HT) of the WCO could assist MEAs in combating illegal trade in banned substances or endangered species.[57]

In the previous chapter, I argued that many MEAs collect environmental data on the areas in which they are concerned but sometimes do not analyse the data to determine if the overall problem is being ameliorated.[58] More effective use of performance reviews for treaties and for national performance could help in this regard. Some examples where these reviews have been employed successfully are the WTO's *Trade Policy Review* and the Organisation for Economic Co-operation and Development's (OECD) country environmental reviews. Reviews that were conducted internationally across conventions could systematically give an indication of the level of treaty compliance and performance towards meeting the treaty's objectives.[59] Moreover, as we see in chapter 7, treaties dealing with the same subject matter sometimes collect data and information that is useful for monitoring the compliance of obligations in another treaty.[60]

Mainstreaming MEAs into national development strategies is also a very powerful way of improving compliance. It has often been argued that environmental issues take a back seat to economic and security issues. Planning at the national level, whether it is local, regional or federal, needs to understand and account for the trade-offs and the implications concerning the environment. Most countries, particularly those developing or least developing nations, have national develop-

---

56. Supra, *Oberthür Clustering*. For an application of this in the CITES context also see John Lanchbery (2006) "The Convention on International Trade in Endangered Species of Wild Fauna and Flora (CITES): Responding to Calls for Action from Other Nature Conservation Regimes", in Sebastian Oberthür and Thomas Gehring, eds, *Institutional Interaction in Global Environmental Governance: Synergy and Conflict among International and EU Policies*, Cambridge, Mass.: MIT Press, 157–180.

57. UNEP (2001) *Report of the Workshop on Codes, Contraband and Cooperation Working with Custom Authorities to Implement Environmental Treaties*, UNEP/(DEC)/WCO/GVA/3, (June).

58. Supra, chapter 2.

59. Supra, *UNU Interlinkages Report*, 29.

60. Infra, chapter 6.

ment strategies that describe in detail economic targets, emerging sectors, infrastructure development and many other areas. By contrast, there are a very limited number of national strategies that have incorporated environmental priorities but, even when this has occurred, the environment is dealt with as a separate sector not integrated into planning.[61]

In practice, outright conflicts between treaties tend to be perceived as occurring more frequently than is actually the case. Nevertheless, speculation has fuelled a debate that has led governments and other stakeholders to question the systematic connections between treaties. Concern has typically arisen over the possible conflicts and contradictions and whether this incongruity could allow a party to find legal loopholes to avoid their obligations, free-ride or put one treaty priority over another. Legally this should not occur, as the Vienna Convention on the Law of Treaties does account for treaty overlap.[62] This states that, if all parties are members, the most recently adopted treaty should take precedence. In 1967, the negotiators of the Vienna Convention, however, did not envisage the number of treaties or the similarities they might one day share. So the speculation of conflict has continued. Forum shopping, when a party is accused of breach of treaty and has the option of looking for a dispute settlement body that would be more sympathetic to its case, is one of the deepest concerns.

A recent case of forum shopping that demonstrates this concern was between the European Community and Chile. The dispute erupted over Chile's refusal to allow EU ships from landing swordfish catches in its ports. Chile cited its own fishing regulations, which are aimed at conservation of seriously depleted fishing stocks.[63] Chile also claimed that it was in compliance with UNCLOS and Article 32 (3) of the UN Agreement on the Conservation and Management of Straddling and Migratory Fish Stocks and a trilateral agreement between itself, Colombia and Ecuador, called the Galapagos Agreement. The EU claimed that not allowing its ships to land their catches in Chilean ports violated GATT Articles V. 1–3, which say that members must be allowed free transit of goods through its territory, and Article XI.1, which prohibits quantitative restrictions on imports. The case resulted in Chile taking the dispute to the ITLOS (International Tribunal for the Law of the Sea), while the

---

61. UNU (2002) *Report on Synergies and Coordination between MEAs: National and Regional Approaches*, Tokyo: UNU, 20.
62. Supra, chapter 3.
63. Article 165 of Chile's Fisheries Law (Ley General de Pesca y Acuicultura), as consolidated by the Supreme Decree 430 of 28 September 1991.

EU requested a panel under the WTO.[64] The dispute amply shows that, as the President of International Court of Justice has said, "the proliferation of international judicial bodies could jeopardize the unity of international law".[65]

An interlinkages approach[66] that calls for more explicit recognition of other treaties and more discussion of where the parties intend inter-treaty disputes to be solved, or which treaty has supremacy or jurisdiction in the advent of a dispute, could address problems of forum shopping. Such an approach could also address other perverse conflicts between treaty provisions. For example, Article 104 of the NAFTA explicitly recognizes the supremacy of four environmental agreements over NAFTA rules. Many proposals to the WTO have also considered the option of an environmental side agreement that allows for explicit MEA carve-outs. As we will see in chapter 7, this may also be a solution to creating greater cooperation between the TRIPS Agreement and the Convention on Biological Diversity and FAO International Treaty on Plant Genetic Resources for Food and Agriculture.[67]

The use of one dispute settlement to achieve compliance in another area is nothing new. In fact many environmentalists are attracted to more binding dispute settlement systems as environmental treaty systems are perceived as weak and non-binding. It is often contemplated in commentaries that linking treaties together into a stronger singular system could allow the use of sanctions for achieving compliance. The example often heard in the corridors of treaty negotiations is the use of trade sanctions and, though it would be a complete violation of international

---

64. WTO, *Chile – Measures Affecting Transit and Importation of Swordfish*, WTO Doc. WT/DS193 (suspended 23 March 2001) [hereinafter *Chile – Swordfish*]. Another good example of the potential proliferation of dispute settlement options is the MOX Case where the dispute could have been taken up under the OSPAR Convention or the EC Treaty and the Euratom Treaty but was resolved under the UNCLOS. See *Dispute Concerning the MOX Plant, International Movements of Radioactive Materials, and the Protection of the Marine Environment of the Irish Sea* (Ireland v. United Kingdom), 2001 ITLOS Case No. 10, Request for Provisional Measures and Statement of the Case (9 November 2001) [hereinafter the MOX Plant case], available at http://www.itlos. org/case_docuinents/2001/ document_en_191.pdf.

65. See Speech by Judge Gilbert Guillaume, President of the International Court of Justice, to the Sixth Committee of the General Assembly of the United Nations on 31 October 2001, available at http://www.lawschool.cornell.edu/library/cijwww/icjwww/ipresscom/ SPEECHES/iSpeechPresident_Guillaume_6thCommittee_2001.htm, visited 23 February 2003. Also see the *Bluefin Tuna Case* in which the International Tribunal for the Law of the Sea found that it had prima facie jurisdiction but the Arbitral Tribunal set up by Australia, Japan and New Zealand ultimately came to the opposite conclusion.

66. See supra, on the meaning of an "interlinkages approach".

67. See infra chapter 7.

trade rules to use such sanctions, some still see this as a viable benefit of a stronger interlinked treaty regime.[68]

Finance

Adequate financing, though not within the legal realm, is without question one of the key factors for an effective treaty. Interlinkages cannot magically produce more money but they can lead to cost-effectiveness and savings that can make financing go further. Many of the outcomes of interlinkages (in terms of effectiveness) could be summed up in the cost-effectiveness category. In fact, one of the most obvious outcomes that governments frequently cite for their support of the concept of inter-linkages is the reduction of waste and improved efficiency of international treaties. Although the above sections have spanned some areas that deal with efficiency, it is important to spell out this factor in greater detail.

Overlap is perhaps the most cited example of inefficiency concerning MEAs. At the international level, there are multiple actors and institutions dealing with environmental issues; much of the interlinkages work has been trying to overcome the territoriality between the institutions and to develop better cooperation that could lead to lower costs and redundancy. There have been a multitude of mechanisms aimed at accomplishing this; proposals range from the creation of a World Environmental Organization to dusting off the chambers of the Trusteeship Council to administer the global commons. Many of the proposals (some of which will be explored in greater detail later on) would in fact be much more cost-effective systems. Yet, the problem with increasing efficiency at the international level by consolidating institutions encounters some political obstacles. Governments have a vested interest in preserving extant international institutions. Governments may host organizations, or the officials of the organizations are nationals of the government, or the government has benefited from those organizations. Whatever the reason, getting rid of organizations is much more difficult than creating new ones. However, an interlinkages approach as a principle for reorganizing the work of international organizations could be a powerful imperative for seeking greater cost-efficiency. Several proposals have been made that could lead to cost savings. These have included co-location of

---

68. One example that is often referred to is a common dispute settlement body for environmental disputes; a so-called World Environmental Court has also be contemplated more recently given the risk of forum shopping and dispute settlement bodies adjudicating on environmental issues, such as the WTO. See supra *UNU Report on Sustainable Development Governance.*

secretariat seats, back-to-back international meetings (e.g., COP/MOPs) and reducing the length of meetings.[69]

Another way in which an interlinkages approach can contribute towards effective financing is through common financial arrangements that work to achieve common objectives in more than one treaty. These kinds of arrangements, which are becoming more and more common for GEF financing, are especially helpful for treaties that do not have financial mechanisms. For example, one of the weakest points of the Ramsar Convention is that it does not have adequate access to financing or to a financial mechanism.[70] Yet Ramsar has been particularly good at connecting with related MEAs that have better access to financing and it has instigated joint projects that have improved its levels of overall financing.[71] Particular opportunities exist through incremental schemes whereby the "financial mechanism of one MEA could, for example, fund the incremental cost of upgrading the project or activities funded by the financial mechanism of another MEA to ensure that the objectives of both regimes are met".[72] There has been some concern expressed by governments, however, that using financial mechanisms and resources for purposes other than what the parties intended could conflict with the mechanism's legal purpose and such arrangements might require amendments before this could be a viable option.[73]

At the national level states are more open to improving efficiency, mainly as they see it as a means of reducing costs. There are also much stronger gains of efficiency that can be achieved nationally. Most of the efficiency gains could be explained in terms of coordination of implementation described above, which not only can improve compliance but also reduce costs.

Criteria for case studies selection

I have chosen two case studies that are comparable because they deal with a subject matter that overlaps within the treaties; this is the subject

69. See generally; Jakob Lau Holst (1999) *Elements of a More Cost-efficient Global Governance of the Biodiversity Convention*, Paper to the UNU Interlinkages Conference (1999); supra, *Oberthür Clustering*.

70. See M. J. Bowman (1995) *Ramsar Convention Comes of Age*, 42 NILR.

71. See for example the *River Basin Initiative* that is designed to implement the CBD's *Programme on Inland Waters and Biological Diversity* under CBD Decision IV/4 and the Ramsar Resolution VII, *Guidelines for Integrating Wetland Conservation and Wise Use into River Basins*. A detailed report on *River Basin Initiative* is contained in information document UNEP/CBD/COP/6/INF/13.

72. Supra, *UNU Interlinkages Report*, 18.

73. See supra, *UNEP Clustering Strategy*, para. 35.

of plant genetic resources. The first case study belongs in what is frequently regarded as international environmental law and deals with the two primary environmental treaties on the topic of genetic resources, the Convention on Biological Diversity[74] and the United Nations Food and Agriculture Organization (FAO) International Treaty on Plant Genetic Resources for Food and Agriculture.[75] From the common subject area of genetic resources, I will compare these treaties by applying the framework just described. Through an examination of each of the criteria of effectiveness, I will systematically analyse how interlinkages between the treaties have affected the criteria and if this has led to improving the effectiveness of either one or both of the treaties.

The comparisons will show which interlinkages have occurred or which have the potential to occur. These comparisons will be based on some of the examples I have just described in the preceding section and will demonstrate how the interlinkage has led or could lead to improving the effectiveness of the treaty according to the definition and parameters of effectiveness I set out in chapter 4. In this respect, this case study will provide proof of the principal query of this book, namely that interlinkages can improve the effectiveness of multilateral environmental treaties.

The second study deals again with the same subject matter, as it would be inconceivable to deal with a different subject and expect to have results that are comparable. The case study deals with the same treaties as the first case (i.e., CBD and ITPGRFA) but compares them to a treaty outside what is commonly regarded as international environmental law. In the second case study, therefore, I will again use the CBD and ITPGRFA but I will compare them to a third treaty, the Trade Related Intellectual Property Rights Agreement [hereinafter TRIPS or the TRIPS Agreement] under the World Trade Organization (WTO). In this case study, if my principal query is correct it should confirm the results of the first case study – that cooperation between these treaties in the form of interlinkages should improve the effectiveness of one of the three or all of the three treaties that are overlapping. The second case study, however, will help understand an additional dimension to this study that I have set as a second query. There is a growing perception today of fragmentation; that public international law is increasingly being carved up into separate branches of law with separate processes and principles that are not always consistent with each other. Proponents of this view argue that international law exists as independent different branches of law

---

74. [Hereinafter the CBD]; for dates on the entry into force see supra, chapter 1.
75. [Hereinafter the ITPGRFA or the "International Treaty"]; for dates on the entry into force see supra, chapter 1.

instead of a consistent unified body of law.[76] As Joost Pauwelyn and others have argued this is a narrow approach to a view of international law and has dangerous consequences for its future as it will only result in increasing conflicts between what is perceived as independent bodies of law. In this regard, it is important to establish that cooperation based on concepts such as interlinkages can demonstrate that, in a common subject area where overlap and conflict occurs, a holistic approach to international law, meaning resolving the conflicts between the competing treaties rather than under separate branches of international law, will increase the overall effectiveness of the treaties in both branches.

If the cases are correct and they indeed demonstrate my principal hypothesis, then this should have implications for the study of public international law. Firstly, it should show that treaties that conflict can improve their effectiveness through cooperation in the form of what this book defines as interlinkages. Secondly, the cases will demonstrate that this cooperation is not only reserved for treaties under what is perceived as similar branches of international law, such as international environmental law, but that positive cooperation between conflicting treaties across branches of international law can also increase treaty effectiveness. Indeed, this is confirmation that a consistent unified body of international law is desirable and preferable to that of a divided, separate or sectoral approach to international law.

For concepts such as sustainable development, which is founded on the basis of a common international system, this is good news because it demonstrates that the three sectors under the separate pillars of sustainable development (economic, social and environmental sectors) and their respective corresponding international rules and treaties have the greater potential to work together and can achieve more through cooperation than working separately.[77]

---

76. See supra chapter 3, Joost Pauwelyn 95 AJIL, 538. Pauwelyn discusses the misperception of WTO practitioners who view WTO rules as not part of the greater corpus of public international law. I believe this perception is occurring in other treaty regimes with practitioners who have similar perceptions. This is mainly attributable to the current international legal system, which treats treaties as successive whereas they are in fact, as Pauwelyn states, "continuous".

77. A dimensional aspect that so far has not been adequately examined in the interlinkages literature is intersectoral connections, particularly in terms of treaties with only limited implications for the environment but which are not environmental treaties per se. This is why the second case study is so important. Environment has been said to be not about environment per se but about the trade-offs and relationships with other sectors such as the trade or finance sector. One of the basic problems with achieving sustainable development is that the connections between the three institutional pillars (social, economic and environmental) of sustainable development are inherently weak. Strengthening the linkages between the institutions in the economic sector (WTO, World Bank, IMF) and

Conclusion

This chapter has laid out the analytical framework of our thesis. It has taken the determinants of effectiveness that were established in chapter 4 – meeting a treaty's objectives, compliance, robustness, supporting provisions of a treaty and finance – and has discussed the ways that interlinkages can improve these factors. These arguments, however, remain hypotheses; they will be substantiated by further exploration through the two case studies presented in the next two chapters outlining this thesis.

In this chapter, I have reiterated the definition of interlinkages from chapter 1, which will be used for the remainder of the analysis of our thesis, and I have provided a review of the only existing literature that deals with theories of overlapping treaties of international law, in this case viewed as institutional interplay. These theories present interesting ways of categorizing taxonomies of interactions but, as Oran Young has argued, they do not offer a concrete method for comparison, mainly because the classifications are not sufficiently exclusive to create an adequate basis for comparison. Moreover, the preoccupation of these theories is the study of social behaviour rather than the consequences of the interaction, which will lead to little of value, for example in terms of improving the performance of international law. From this review of the literature an important distinction between interlinkages and institutional interplay is revealed, which will guide the understanding of this book in reference to these theories. Institutional interplay is a study of the phenomena of interaction of institutions (including treaties, one type of institution) while interlinkages is a normative theory that presumes that cooperation between treaties will improve their performance by strengthening their effectiveness. Lastly, this chapter has provided a rationale for the case studies in the next two chapters and answers the question why these cases were chosen and what proving the cases will mean for the future development of international law.

---

the social institutions (FAO, WHO, UNHCR, ILO, UN Human Rights Commission etc.), or those in the environmental sector (MEAs, UNEP, CSD) could improve the performance record on sustainable development. Thus this book could contribute understanding to the cleavages and the need for interlinkages across sectors, which may provide some insights into sustainable development.

Part V

Case study one: Understanding interlinkages as a factor of effectiveness within international environmental law

6

The interlinkages of plant genetic resources: The Convention on Biological Diversity and FAO International Treaty on Plant Genetic Resources for Food and Agriculture

Introduction

Plant genes may be small in size but they are not so small in value. Used as active ingredients in products ranging from biopharmaceuticals to cosmetics, trade in plant genetic resources represents a multibillion dollar global market. Urged on by advances in modern biotechnology, chemistry and genomics, many companies made sizeable investments in the 1980s and early 1990s in bioprospecting and research to transform these hunches into profits. More than a decade later, these companies are finding that the payoff may not have been as easy as expected, at least in the medium term. Companies like Abbott, Merck or SmithKline Beecham, who once believed they could find the next epic drug or germplasm by sifting through plant genes in the tropical jungles of the world, are scaling back their drug discovery programmes.[1]

But the woes in the market are not dampening the hopes of those countries with rich biodiversity. They remember, with much regret, the missed commercial opportunities of the past. These countries, mostly developing, are hoping that the human mind will never be able to copy what Mother Nature can do naturally. Therefore, they are looking to the future when that next big boom in demand and knowledge will bring the bioprospectors back to their countries, and, at that time, they plan to be

1. Andrew Pollack (1999) "Biological Products Raise Genetic Ownership Issues", *New York Times*, 26 November.

Interlinkages and the effectiveness of multilateral environmental agreements,
W. Bradnee Chambers, United Nations University Press, 2008, ISBN 978-92-808-1149-0

ready with a global regime in place and a domestic regulatory system that will allow ready access to their resources but which will also ensure they do not miss out on that next big Klondike rush.

At the same time these countries also remain wary of the fact that their economies continue to rely heavily on agriculture as their primary industry and this requires free and easy access to seeds to ensure its longevity. As more and more farmers turn to very specific cash crops and employ more biotechnology to heighten yields, food security weighs heavily on the minds of their countries' leaders. With these interests uppermost, efforts to regulate the access and use of genetic plant materials and improve food security are stepping up and have been fuelled on by the interests of such developing countries. Two of the main international treaties governing these areas are the Convention on Biological Diversity (CBD) and the International Treaty on Plant Genetic Resources for Food and Agriculture (ITPGRFA).

On 30 November 2001, parties to the Food and Agriculture Organization (FAO) finalized the International Treaty on Plant Genetic Resources for Food and Agriculture after seven years of intense negotiations. Less than a year later, on 19 April 2002, parties to the sixth session of the Conference of the Parties to the Convention on Biological Diversity decided to adopt the Bonn Guidelines on *Access to Genetic Resources and Fair and Equitable Sharing of the Benefits Arising Out of Their Utilization* (BG). These guidelines added substantially to the existing rules already set out under the 1993 Convention on Biological Diversity (CBD). Only months after their adoption, the 2002 Johannesburg World Summit on Sustainable Development (WSSD) yielded a controversial decision to relaunch negotiations on a global regime to regulate the access and use of genetic resources under the Convention on Biological Diversity. Together, both of these agreements and the subsequent international regime, which is now under negotiation, represent what is becoming a burgeoning body of international law on access to plant genetic materials and the sharing of the benefits (ABS) derived from them. However, this body of law has become progressively more complex[2] as it overlaps with the WTO TRIPS Agreement – an agreement essentially outside the scope of mainstream international environmental law.

---

2. Kal Raustiala and David Victor have labelled this regime overlap as "regime complex", an array of partially overlapping and non-hierarchical institutions governing a particular issue area. Regime complexes are marked by the existence of several legal agreements that are created and maintained in distinct fora with participation of different sets of actors. The rules in these elemental regimes functionally overlap, yet there is no agreement upon hierarchy for resolving conflicts between rules. See Kal Raustiala and David Victor (2004) "The Regime Complex of Plant Genetic Resources", *International Organization* 58, (Spring): 277–309.

The complexity and overlap, however, offer an ideal case study setting to examine how the interlinkages between these legal regimes cooperate and how that cooperation can lead to improved effectiveness of the treaties dealing with the overlapping issue. The approach taken for this case study on the relationship between the Convention on Biological Diversity and International Treaty on Plant Genetic Resources for Food and Agriculture, as well as for the next chapter's second case study, is to first examine the background of the legal regime through its legal history. Following this, there is a comparative study of the provisions of each of the regimes related to plant genetic resources (PGR). The last part of the chapter applies the framework set out in chapter 3 in order to understand how the interlinkages between the two treaties can lead to improving their effectiveness as defined in chapter 5.

Brief legal history of the two agreements

International Treaty on Plant Genetic Resources for Food and Agriculture[3]

Prior to its adoption by the ITPGRFA, the 1983 International Undertaking on Plant Genetic Resources was the first comprehensive agreement dealing with plant genetic resources for food and agriculture.[4] Based on the principle of the heritage of mankind of plant genetic resources, this non-binding agreement provided a framework for international cooperation in matters regarding access, use and conservation of plant genetic resources. Its objectives were to "ensure that plant genetic resources of economic and/or social interests, particularly for agriculture, will be explored, preserved, evaluated and made available for plant breeding and scientific purposes".[5]

The adoption of a non-legally binding instrument, rather than a legally binding convention, was due to the objective of achieving the broadest possible support. The unwillingness of some countries to commit themselves to a binding instrument that was incompatible with their own

---

3. For an authoritative commentary on ITPGRFA, see Gerald Moore and Witold Tymowski (2005) *Explanatory Guide to the International Treaty on Plant Genetic Resources for Food and Agriculture*, IUCN Environmental Policy and Law Paper No. 57, Gland, Switzerland: IUCN.

4. FAO (1983) *Twenty-Second Session of the FAO Conference*, Resolution 8/83, 23 November.

5. Article 1, International Undertaking on Plant Genetic Resources [hereinafter the Undertaking, available at http://www.fao.org/ag/cgrfa/IU.htm.

system of plant breeders' rights might have inhibited the adoption of a full convention[6]. The less formal alternative of a code of conduct could only reflect an international consensus on principles, whereas the International Undertaking could establish specific commitments.[7]

The original text of the Undertaking was the subject of a series of "agreed interpretations"[8] which aimed to find an equitable balance between the interests of developing and developed countries, and between the farmers (informal innovators) and the rights of breeders (formal innovators of commercial varieties and breeders' lines). This process helped attract a broader acceptance of the Undertaking over the years, through Resolutions 4/89,[9] 5/89[10] and 3/91[11] of the FAO Conference. These resolutions were incorporated into the text of the Undertaking as Annexes 1, 2 and 3. They addressed some of the concerns that have been voiced by a number of developed and developing countries and, at the same time, contributed to preparing the way for the revision of the Undertaking in relation to connected international legal instruments.[12]

6. See Commission on Plant Genetic Resources, Sixth Session, *Revision of the International Undertaking Stage Three: Legal and Institutional Options*, CPGR-6/95/9.

7. Kerry ten Kate and Carolina Lasen Diaz (1997) *The Undertaking Revisited: A Commentary on the Revision of the International Undertaking on Plant Genetic Resources for Food and Agriculture*, 6 RECEIL.

8. These "agreed interpretations" are the consequences of the reservations registered by the US, Canada, France, Germany, Japan, New Zealand, Switzerland and the UK to the Undertaking. These countries considered that the heritage-based approach of the Undertaking could undermine the rights of plant breeders and therefore they instigated the explicit recognition of "plant breeders' rights" by FAO Resolution 4/89. This recognition was, however, counterbalanced by the simultaneous recognition of "farmers' rights", which took into account the interests largely advocated by developing countries.

9. Resolution 4/89, adopted on 29 November 1989, states that "plant breeders' rights", as provided for under the International Union for the Protection of New Varieties of Plants (UPOV), are not incompatible with the Undertaking. Paragraph 3 to the Undertaking says that states will recognize the enormous contribution that farmers of all regions have made to the conservation and development of plant genetic resources, which constitute the basis of plant production throughout the world, and which form the basis for the concept of "farmers' rights".

10. Resolution 5/89, adopted on 29 November 1989 endorses the concept of "farmers' rights" and explains what is meant by the term.

11. Resolution 3/91, adopted on 25 November 1991, recognizes that the concept of mankind's heritage is subject to the sovereign rights of nations over their plant genetic resources, and sets out that "farmers' rights" should be implemented through an international fund for plant genetic resources.

12. See Ali Mekouar (2002) *A Global Instrument on Agrobiodiversity: The International Treaty on Plant Genetic Resources for Food and Agriculture*. FAO Legal Papers Online No. 24 (January), available at http://www.fao.org/Legal/prs-o/lpo24.pdf.

In 1992, Agenda 21 called for the strengthening of the FAO Global System on Plant Genetic Resources,[13] and its adjustment in line with the Convention on Biological Diversity (CBD).[14] In adopting the agreed text of the CBD in May 1992,[15] countries also adopted Resolution 3 of the Nairobi Final Act,[16] which recognized the need to seek solutions to outstanding matters related to plant genetic resources. It was requested that these issues be addressed within the FAO Forum.

Consequently, in 1993, the FAO Conference adopted Resolution 7/93 for "the adaptation of the International Undertaking on Plant Genetic Resources, in harmony with the Convention on Biological Diversity", and for "consideration of the issue of access on mutually agreed terms to plant genetic resources, including *ex situ* collections not addressed by the Convention".[17]

The negotiations set up for this purpose in the Commission on Genetic Resources for Food and Agriculture (CGRFA)[18] were often difficult and took over seven years to complete. The negotiations included three regular and six extraordinary sessions,[19] an informal expert meeting[20], six

13. For an explanation of the FAO Global System on Plant Genetic Resources see infra.
14. United Nations Conference on Environment and Development, Agenda 21, Chapter 14, Programme Area 14G: Conservation and sustainable use of plant genetic resources for food and sustainable agriculture (Rio de Janeiro, 14 June 1992).
15. Convention on Biological Diversity (Rio de Janeiro, 5 June 1992).
16. UNEP (1992) Resolution 3 of the Nairobi Final Act of the Conference for the Adoption of the Agreed Text of the Convention on Biological Diversity, convened by the Executive Director of UNEP pursuant to Decision 15/34 of the UNEP Governing Council (UNEP, Nairobi).
17. FAO, *Twenty-Seventh Session of the FAO Conference, Rome*, C93/REP (6–24 November 1993) paras. 105–108.
18. The FAO established the intergovernmental Commission on Plant Genetic Resources in 1983. Renamed the Commission on Genetic Resources for Food and Agriculture in 1995, the Commission currently comprises 153 countries and the European Community. The CGRFA coordinates, oversees and monitors the development of the Global System for the Conservation and Utilization of Plant Genetic Resources for Food and Agriculture, which is composed of the Commission itself and the International Undertaking on Plant Genetic Resources, the Global Plan of Action and International Fund for Plant Genetic Resources, the World Information and Early Warning System, Codes of Conduct and Guidelines for the Collection and Transfer of Germplasm, and the International Network of *In Situ* Conservation Areas and of Crop-Related Networks.
19. The regular sessions were: Sixth Regular Session, Rome 19–30 June 1995; Seventh Regular Session, Rome 15–23 May 1997; Eighth Regular Session, Rome 19–23 April 1999. The Extraordinary Sessions were: First Extraordinary Session, Rome 7–11 November 1994; Second Extraordinary Session, Rome 22–27 April 1996; Third Extraordinary Session, Rome 9–13 December 1996; Fourth Extraordinary Session, Rome 15–23 May 1997; Fifth Extraordinary Session, Rome 8–12 June 1998; Sixth Extraordinary Session, Rome 25–30 June 2001.
20. Montreux, 19–22 January 1999.

intersessional meetings of the Chairman's Contact Group,[21] and an Open-Ended Working Group on the International Undertaking established by the FAO Council.[22]

The difficulties encountered during the negotiations were due to the complexity of reconciling the access to the genetic resources of food crops with the sovereign rights of the countries, and of balancing the divergent interests of farmers, breeders, biotechnology companies and others.[23]

The first steps were particularly difficult and the negotiations became deadlocked at the Fifth Extraordinary Session (1998) because an agreement on the issues of access and benefit-sharing, farmers' rights and financial resources could not be reached. The US, Canada and Australia defended an abstract character of farmers' rights. These countries tried to prevent the elevation of the concept described in FAO Resolution 5/89 as not being specific enough to be a legal right. Developing countries such as Ethiopia, the Philippines and India, on the other hand, insisted that farmers' rights were concrete rights, already implemented in several countries. The group of African countries proposed a range of measures to guarantee that farming and local communities that provided genetic resources participated fully in the definition and disbursement of any national and international funding mechanism and agreement on bilateral sharing of benefits.[24] Europe approached the position of the developing countries, accepting the reference to farmers' rights and also the recognition of the "right of farmers".

The informal group of negotiators (1999) was finally able to agree on key elements of the treaty and settled on a guide for the subsequent negotiations.[25] Most of the work to finalize the treaty, in the following three years, was carried out by the Chair's Contact Group. During its Third

---

21. The Contact Group comprised 40 countries and the European Community. Its meetings were: First Intersessional Meeting, Rome 20–24 September 1999; Second Intersessional Meeting, Rome 3–7 April 2000; Third Intersessional Meeting, Tehran, 26–31 August 2000; Fourth Intersessional Meeting, Neuchâtel, 12–17 November 2000; Fifth Intersessional Meeting, Rome 5–10 February 2001; Sixth Intersessional Meeting, Spoleto 22–28 April 2001.

22. Rome, 30 October–1 November 2001.

23. See H. David Cooper (2002) *The International Treaty on Plant Genetic Resources for Food and Agriculture*, 11 RECIEL 1.

24. Africa Group proposal for the Revision of the International Undertaking on Plant Genetic Resources for Food and Agriculture (15 May 1997).

25. Commission on Genetic Resources for Food and Agriculture. Eighth Regular Session. Rome, 19–23 April 1999. *Report of the Chairman of the Commission on Genetic Resources for Food and Agriculture on the status of negotiations for the revision of the International Undertaking on Plant Genetic Resources, in harmony with the Convention on Biological Diversity*, CGRFA-8/99/13 (1999).

Session (2000), the Contact Group came to an arrangement on the provisions for commercial benefit-sharing,[26] following an earlier proposal of the International Seed Trade Federation/International Association of Plant Breeders.[27] The agreement was later revised following pressure from various countries.

The Sixth Session of the Contact Group (2001) put forward a list of crops covered by the Multilateral System (MS). The application of the Multilateral System only to a list of crops responded to the interests of certain countries that are rich in biodiversity by leaving the issue of potential for bilateral arrangements, under Article 15 of the CBD, to be applied to all other plant genetic resources not covered by the Multilateral System. With the same scope, it was agreed that material made available through the Multilateral System should be provided solely for uses related to food and agriculture.

Although these limits were respected, major concessions on the coverage of the Multilateral System were made during the Sixth Extraordinary Session of the full Commission (2001), increasing the prospect of most countries adhering to the new agreement. The working group established by the FAO Council prepared the final texts, despite remaining disagreement on intellectual property rights. Among the interim arrangements for the implementation of the treaty, the FAO Conference established that the Commission on Plant Genetic Resources would act as the Interim Committee for the International Treaty. Its general scope is to perform the necessary functions to prepare for the effective implementation of the International Treaty.

In its first meeting in October 2002, the Interim Committee adopted its Rules of Procedure and decided to establish an Open-Ended Expert Working Group to meet in the intersessional period. The Working Group's assignment is to address the Rules of Procedure and the Financial Rules of the Governing Body, and the Promotion of Compliance. The Interim Committee also adopted the Terms of Reference (scope of the work, composition and schedule) for the Expert Group on the Terms of the Standard Material Transfer Agreement.

Matters such as consultation with the international agricultural centres and other relevant institutions, cooperation with relevant international

---

26. Text established by the Contact Group during its Third Intersessional Meeting for Article 11, Multilateral System of Access and Benefit-Sharing; Article 13, Facilitated Access to Plant Genetic Resources for Food and Agriculture within the Multilateral System; Article 14, Benefit-Sharing in the Multilateral System; Article 16, Financial Resources; and a new Article on Supporting Components of the Multilateral System, to be inserted in Part IV of the International Undertaking, Teheran, Islamic Republic of Iran, 26–31 August 2000, CGRFA/CG-3/00/TXT (2000).
27. See H. David Cooper, supra.

bodies and the funding strategy for the implementation were postponed until the second meeting of the Interim Committee, which was held in 2004, and it was agreed to adopt these matters at the First Governing Body Meeting.[28] In June 2006, the Governing Body of the ITPGRFA met for the first time in Madrid, Spain, and agreed on most of these issues. At this time there were 104 instruments of ratification, acceptance, approval or accession that had been deposited with the Director-General of FAO.[29]

The Convention on Biological Diversity

The Convention on Biodiversity entered into force on 29 December 1993, 90 days after Mongolia made the thirtieth deposit of ratification.[30] The Convention was the culmination of efforts by the ecological community and civil society to press governments and the UN to have an overarching legal instrument to protect biodiversity using a preventive approach. It was believed that such a treaty could be built on the shoulders and experiences of past treaties such as the Washington Convention on International Trade in Endangered Species of Wild Fauna and Flora,[31] the Ramsar Convention on Wetlands of International Importance Especially as Waterfowl Habitat[32] and the UNESCO World Heritage Convention.[33] As a result of this agenda-setting pressure, UNEP began initiating a number of scientific expert consultations and meetings to establish the basis for such an instrument and undertook decisions within its Governing Council in 1987 to get the process under way.[34]

An Ad Hoc Working Group of Experts on Biodiversity was then set up under these decisions and, in 1990, an Ad Hoc Working Group of Legal and Technical Experts began the task of drafting the main elements of agreement. Later, this group would morph into what was called the Intergovernmental Negotiating Committee (INC) under UNEP Governing

---

28. FAO (2002) *First Meeting of the Commission on Genetic Resources for Food and Agriculture acting as Interim Committee for the International Treaty on Plant Genetic Resources for Food and Agriculture. Rome, 9–11 October 2002*, CGRFA-MIC-1/02/REP.

29. FAO (2006) *Report of the First Session of the Governing Body of the International Treaty on Plant Genetic Resources for Food and Agriculture*, IT/GB-1/06/, para. 8.

30. CBD Article 36.

31. *Washington Convention on International Trade in Endangered Species of Wild Fauna and Flora* [hereinafter CITES], 3 March 1973, 27 UST 1087, 993 UNTS, 243.

32. *Ramsar Convention on Wetlands of International Importance Especially as Waterfowl Habitat* [hereinafter Ramsar], 2 Feb. 1971, TIAS 11084, 996 UNTS, 245.

33. M. Robert Ward (1994) *Is a UN Convention the Most Appropriate Means to Pursue the Goal of Biological Diversity? Man or Beast: The Convention on Biological Diversity and the Emerging Law of Sustainable Development*, 28 Vand. J. Transnat'l L., 823, 827.

34. UNEP (1987) *Governing Council Decisions* 14/26 and 15/34.

Council Decision 16/42 and would be assigned the role of negotiating a full draft of a treaty without bracketed text. The plan was to have the treaty ready for signature for the upcoming United Nations Conference on Environment and Development planned for the autumn of 1992 and which would mark the twentieth anniversary of the historic Stockholm Conference on the Human Environment.

By 1991, a first draft was put to this committee for its deliberations. Between 1991 and 1992, the INC met seven times to negotiate the draft text,[35] but several sticking points became evident early on in the meetings including *ex situ* genetic resources, farmers' rights and funding and implications for other agreements. Despite the problems, the Fifth Session of INC was able to work out most of the major disagreements and it was able to provide a clean text. This text was adopted by the parties in Nairobi in late 1991 and it was sent to Rio de Janeiro, the host city of the UNCED, to be opened for signature from 5 June 1992 to 14 June 1992.

Following the Rio Conference, the UNEP Governing Council instated an interim committee called the Intergovernmental Committee on the Convention on Biodiversity (ICCB) to look after the treaty until it entered into force and to prepare it for the first Conference of the Parties. This interim committee ran into several problems in its preparatory process, which led to several delays and slowed the Convention's eventual adoption. The source of ICCB's delays revolved around its inability to agree on the rules of procedure and to finalize its working group reports concerning issues such as biosafety and finance. However, after several compromises and a contingency plan,[36] the first COP took place in Nassau, Bahamas, one year after the treaty had entered into force.

In spite of this shaky start the CBD has made steady progress over the last 10 years and has held eight sessions of the Conference of the Parties that have adopted 216 Decisions as of 2006.[37] These include major decisions on Marine Biodiversity, Forests, a Clearing House Mechanism and

---

35. Seven Sessions of the INC were held as follows: the third negotiating session/first session of INC, in Madrid from 24 June 1991 to 3 July 1991; the fourth negotiating session/second session of INC, in Nairobi from 23 September 1991 to 2 October 1991; the fifth negotiating session/third session of INC, in Geneva from 25 November 1991 to 4 December 1991; the sixth negotiating session/fourth session of INC, in Nairobi from 6 February 1992 to 9 February 1992; and the seventh negotiating session/fifth and final session of INC was held at the headquarters of UNEP in Nairobi from 11 May 1992 to 22 May 1992. See Paul Roberts (1992) *International Funding for the Conservation of Biological Diversity: Convention on Biological Diversity*, Boston University International Law Journal 10(2): 303–349.

36. The COP was only able to meet with provisional documents and draft reports which had not been adopted by the ICCB plenary, ibid.

37. Calculated from the CBD website at http://www.biodiv.org/convention/cops.asp.

two multi-year thematic Programmes of Work. It has also negotiated a binding protocol on biosafety which entered into force in 2002. However, despite these relative successes, its work on genetic resources has lagged behind compared to other areas and negotiations on this topic and did not really get under way until the Convention was already fairly mature. This was despite the fact that "the fair and equitable sharing of genetic resources" has always been one of the prima facie objectives of the Convention.

The processes that eventually began to address genetic resources and the fair equitable sharing of benefits thereof came about in 1993 at COP4. At this meeting in Bratislava, Slovakia, the parties decided to establish a regionally balanced panel of experts appointed by governments but composed of representatives from the private and public sectors, as well as representatives of indigenous and local communities. Its mandate was to "explore all options for access and benefit-sharing on mutually agreed terms including principles, guidelines, and codes of conduct of best practices for access and benefit-sharing arrangements".[38]

The Expert Group met once, in October 1999 in San José, Costa Rica, and discussed options for access and benefit-sharing on mutually agreed terms and reached broad conclusions on other areas such as prior informed consent, mutually agreed terms, information needs and capacity-building.[39] An extraordinary session of the COP in 2000 saw this process substantially strengthened when the parties further agreed to continue the Expert Group[40] while, at the same time, launching an Ad Hoc Open-Ended Working Group with the mandate to develop guidelines and other approaches for submission to the Conference of the Parties at its Sixth Session.

Both of these groups met sequentially in 2001 and their efforts culminated in the successful negotiation of a set of draft guidelines on access and benefit-sharing in Bonn, Germany, on 26 October. The following year on 19 April 2002, at the sixth session of the Conference of the Parties to Convention on Biological Diversity (COP 6), parties adopted the Bonn Guidelines on *Access to Genetic Resources and Fair and Equitable Sharing of the Benefits Arising out of their Utilization.*[41]

However, this was not the end of the story for the CBD and ABS. In a way, the success was short-lived as less than a year later, in September

38. CBD (1994) *Report of the Fourth Meeting of the Conference of the Parties to the Convention on Biological Diversity*, UNEP/CBD/COP/4/27/.
39. CBD, *Report of the First Meeting of the Expert Group on ABS*, UNEP/CBD/COP/5/8.
40. CBD, *Report of Second Meeting of the Expert Group on ABS*, UNEP/CBD/WG-ABS/1/2.
41. The Bonn Guidelines [hereinafter Bonn Guidelines or Guidelines] to the Convention on Biological Diversity (CBD) Conference of the Parties (COP), Decision VI/24 A (2002).

2002, a newly formed coalition of 15 of the most biologically diverse countries in the world tabled a dramatic proposal at the World Summit on Sustainable Development (WSSD) that called] for a process to effectively reopen the negotiations on the Guidelines and move towards a more legally binding "international regime" on access and benefit-sharing (ABS).[42] The coalition was formed, in part, out of frustration over the Convention on Biological Diversity's (CBD) languorous speed on issues they believed were important to these nations' development, and, in part, out of the need to protect and be rightly compensated for use of their natural genetic resources. The coalition argued that a legally binding international regime should in fact depart from where the Bonn Guidelines left off and work towards a binding instrument, perhaps a full protocol to the CBD.[43]

In many ways, the proposal for a protocol on ABS was surprising coming so soon after the conclusion of two years of direct negotiations on the Bonn Guidelines. The possibility of a legally binding agreement was considered at CBD COP 4 when it was decided to set up an Expert Group on ABS and discuss "all the options for access and benefit-sharing arrangements".[44] It was then further discussed at two meetings of the CBD's Panel of Experts on ABS, the CBD's Scientific Body on Technology and Technological Advice (SBTTA), and in the final deliberations at COP 6 where the Bonn Guidelines were formally adopted.[45] In these discussions, most countries agreed ABS was an issue more contingent on

42. World Summit on Sustainable Development Plan of Implementation states that parties should "Negotiate within the framework of the Convention on Biological Diversity, bearing in mind the Bonn Guidelines, an international regime to promote and safeguard the fair and equitable sharing of benefits arising out of the utilization of genetic resources"; see Johannesburg Plan of Implementation [hereinafter JPOI], *Report of the World Summit on Sustainable Development* (A/CONF.199/20, 4 September 2002), Resolution 2, Annex, para. 44(o).

43. Presentation made by Alberto Glender Rivas on behalf of the Secretariat of the Group of Like-Minded Megadiverse Countries at the *Critical Role of Biodiversity and Ecosystem Services in Achieving the UN Millennium Development Goals* (London, 2–4 March 2003), available at http://www.undp.org/equatorinitiative/secondary/biodiversity_agenda.htm. Also, for more information on the Like-Minded Megadiverse Countries, see the Cancun Declaration of Like-Minded Megadiverse Countries (Cancun, 18 February 2002), found at http://www.megadiverse.org/armado_ingles/PDF/three/three1.pdf.

44. See CBD, Decision IV/8 (1998).

45. The Expert Panel on ABS [hereinafter the Expert Panel] met in San José, Costa Rica (4–8 October 1999). It was then decided at COP 5 under CBD Decision V/267A (2000) to reconvene the expert panel with additional government nominees and a more focused mandate. The Panel then met again in Montreal 19–22 March 2001. The report from the expert meetings was forwarded to SBSTTA, which met in Bonn and agreed on draft guidelines to be put forward to COP 6 in the Hague in 2002.

national regulation than on international regulation. Thus, where an internationally harmonized regime could not accommodate the diversity of national approaches, countries agreed that a set of guidelines which set forth broad principles was the preferred choice of legal instrument.

As surprising as it was, the WSSD proposal for new negotiations was agreed on by the CBD COP 7 in 2004. The COP, which took place in Kuala Lumpur, Malaysia, agreed on the terms of reference for these new negotiations in Decision VII/19, including the process, nature, scope and elements for consideration in the elaboration of the potential "regime". In doing so it reactivated the Ad Hoc Working Group on ABS to scope out the nature and technicalities of the regime. In late January 2006, on the eve of COP 8, the Ad Hoc Working Group met in Granada, Spain, and though it had met three times previously, in essence, this fourth meeting marked the start of serious negotiations of the future international regime. The scope of the regime, as defined in the outcome of these negotiations and later endorsed by COP8,[46] covers both access to and sharing of benefits arising from genetic resources as well as traditional knowledge. The nature of the so-called "international regime" is so far open since, according to the negotiating mandate, it could be composed of one or more instruments legally binding and/or non-binding. The elements that have been agreed on for consideration for coverage in the regime include: how to facilitate access, ensuring and promoting benefit-sharing, recognition and protection of rights of indigenous and local communities, compliance, Prior Informed Consent (PIC), Mutually Agreed Terms (MAT)/Material Transfer Agreements, functioning of the regime, derivatives from genetic resources and poverty eradication. The Ad Hoc Group is expected to report its progress at the Ninth Conference of the Parties in March 2008 in Bonn, Germany.[47]

General overview of the CBD and ITPGRFA provisions relating to genetic resources

Both the CBD and the ITPGRFA have the similar goals of conservation and sustainable use of biodiversity but the approaches of the two instruments are very different. With the objective of food security, the ITPGRFA covers all genetic materials for food and agriculture but specifically puts in place a "Multilateral System" (MS) to facilitate access to 64 of the most essential crops and their varieties. Since the MS is a group-

46. See CBD (2006) *Report of the Conference of the Parties, Eighth Session*, UNEP/CBD/COP/8/31.
47. CBD (2006) *Decision VIII on Access and Benefit-Sharing*, in UNEP/CBD/COP/8/31, 129.

based system, where parties deal directly with the MS for access to genetic resources instead of each other, the system is said use a multilateral approach. The treaty is intended to be legally binding and covers a number of areas such as intellectual property rights, benefit-sharing from the commercialization of genetic resources, food agriculture, farmers' rights, a funding strategy, a common fund to conserve seeds in the south and the creation of a governing body to oversee the treaty's implementation and further development.

In contrast, the CBD uses a bilateral approach to protect genetic resources and to promote equitable access and benefit-sharing. Through its Bonn Guidelines, the CBD creates a non-binding framework that is not intended to substitute national legislation but to enhance it and provide guidance for its development. The CBD Guidelines use voluntary measures to facilitate the access to genetic resources and to ensure that the benefits of any commercialization or research and development from those resources are rightfully shared with their owners. The CBD's approach is to create a two-way system between the parties that will use the genetic resources and those that will provide them. Relationships with third parties must be based on the original bilateral agreement.

Although the CBD Guidelines are intended to be simple in structure, as stated in paragraph 7(b), and as evidenced by its bilateral nature, it is in fact quite elaborate. There are two main reasons for the level of detail. First, because the Guidelines are not binding, governments were more inclined to accept detailed elaborations. In a legally binding setting, governments normally try to avoid this as it often leaves open the chance for loopholes and wider interpretations. In the case of a voluntary setting, like that of the Guidelines, governments were more generous and accommodating to a wider spectrum of views. In essence, since the agreement was only meant as a guide, there was less incentive to refine the document. In some ways the Guidelines look like a shopping list of good intentions; thus it is unsurprising that the parties agreed upon its provisions relatively quickly compared to that of the ITPGRFA. Second, since the CBD and its Guidelines take a bilateral approach, there was a need to include a number of provisions such as prior informed consent, mutually agreed terms and details of how to create overall strategies at the national level. The ITPGRFA, by contrast, consolidates these systems at the multilateral level, reducing the need to have all the provisos contained in the CBD.

Both the CBD and the ITPGRFA are meant to be evolutionary and not the final word on their respective goals.[48] One might look upon the CBD and its Bonn Guidelines as similar to the International Undertaking circa 1983. Like the Undertaking, it is a first start of a voluntary nature

---

48. See CBD, *COP6 Decisions of the Convention on Biological Diversity*, Part A para. 6.

but with the advent of the WSSD and the COP7 there is a strong move towards strengthening the Guidelines into a binding international regime. Likewise, the ITPGRFA leaves open a number of controversial areas that will still need to be developed, such as the question of intellectual property rights on the genetic parts of the crops listed in the Multilateral System and the details of its funding and finance. The ITPGRFA will also have to deal with the thorny issue of how to treat genetic material contained within the Multilateral System but which remain in private collections.

Like the ITPGRFA, the CBD has its fair share of areas that are still not agreed upon from the Bonn Guidelines process and that are now becoming difficult issues under the international regime negotiations. The use of terms, how to deal with derivatives from genetic resources and measures for realizing the compliance to the Guidelines' prior informed consent provisions were sources of disagreement at COP8 and will likely be so until the final international regime is actually signed and deposited.

One reality that both agreements must face is the lack of support from the United States. The US has never ratified the CBD and thus stands outside its provisions, although it acts as a very influential observer in the negotiations. The US participated whole-heartedly in the development of the ITPGRFA but in the end abstained from its adoption. As will be seen later, its main concern was over Article 12 (d), which restricted the intellectual property rights on parts of the genetic resources contained in the Multilateral System. In effect, this clause would prohibit many patents from US companies in the field of life sciences. The US was also concerned when the so-called security clause was voted out. This clause would have allowed the US to sidestep the treaty and deny access to genetic materials from countries that the US deemed a threat to their security (e.g., Cuba).

Some observers felt that the US showed benevolence for the ITPGRFA by abstaining in the final voting and this indicated that they were still considering the possibility of joining the treaty in the future. However, in the wrap-up sessions of the negotiations, the US may have reversed any possibility of joining. In an intervention on the final report to the Thirty-First Session of the Conference of the UN FAO, the US requested the chair to correct the language in the report that stated that one country has expressed its difficulty in ratifying the treaty because of the absence of a security clause; it asked the chair to correct that sentence to say that the missing clause would "not make it difficult but would preclude them" from joining the treaty.[49]

49. See ETC, *ETC Translator*, vol. 3 (December 2001): 8.

If this is the case and the US is indeed out of the ITPGRFA, some observers have suggested that this might simplify its future negotiations, particularly on the provisions concerning intellectual property rights.[50] Certainly there is more scope for cooperation on this and other matters between the G77 and the Europeans than there would be with US involvement.

Benefit-sharing arrangements

Both the CBD and the ITPGRFA have comprehensive sections on benefit-sharing but they differ in terms of the scope, type and nature of the arrangements. While the ITPGRFA envisages benefit-sharing arrangements only in the context of the genetic resources listed in the Multilateral System, the Guidelines' scope includes "all genetic resources and associated traditional knowledge, innovations and practices covered by the CBD".[51] The scope of the CBD is therefore much broader since the CBD covers all biodiversity, both *in situ* and *ex situ*.

Both agreements have detailed sections that elaborate on the type and nature of the benefit-sharing arrangements. The ITPGRFA, for example, distinguishes between the exchange of information, access to transfer of technology and capacity-building. It also views the "facilitated access" to the genetic resources in the Multilateral System, particularly by farmers in developing countries, as being a fundamental benefit in and of itself.[52] The CBD, on the other hand, sees benefit-sharing on a more case-by-case basis. The Guidelines describe the timing of the benefits: near-term (upfront payments), medium-term (milestone payments) and long-term (royalties), and they make a distinction between beneficiaries, such as those that contributed to the resource management, and scientific and commercial processes (e.g., governmental, non-governmental, academic institutions, and indigenous and local communities). The CBD Guidelines also distinguish between monetary and non-monetary benefits as set out in its Appendix II. The scope of benefits is broad and covers a variety of different types ranging from licensing fees and joint ventures to capacity-building and simple recognition.[53]

The delivery mechanisms for the benefit-sharing are different in the two agreements. Article 15 of the CBD and the elaboration through its Guidelines foresees a flexible approach whereby the partners would agree on the arrangements suited to their particular circumstance. These

50. Ibid.
51. Ibid., para 9.
52. ITPGRFA, Article 13.1.
53. See Bonn Guidelines Appendix II (Monetary and Non-Monetary Benefits).

arrangements would then be legally recognized in the material transfer agreements or some type of contractual arrangements that set out "mutually agreed terms" on benefit-sharing.[54] In the case of the ITPGRFA, the benefits are to be more broadly shared with "farmers in all countries" and with the contracting state themselves. A special emphasis will be given to farmers in developing countries and countries in transition (EIT), particularly those that have made a unique contribution to the diversity of plant genetic resources or those that have special needs.[55] The benefits will be delivered by means of a common fund which will be administered by the ITPGRFA Governing Body.

The fund calls for those parties that use material accessed from the Multilateral System and who create commercial value from the material to pay an "equitable share" of the benefits to the fund. The ITPGRFA already suggests that there may be a need to exempt small farmers, in developing and EIT countries, from such payments. Exemptions are also contemplated for those who commercialize products from the MS genetic materials providing they make such a product "without restriction, to others for further research and breeding, in which case the recipient of who commercialises shall be encouraged to make such a payment".[56] One question that still remains open is whether the benefits from derivatives – offshoots that may have started with the genetic resources but have been synthesized into another form and then commercialized – would have to pay into the fund. Determining what is a derivative and what degree it relied on the original genetic material is extremely difficult. Some national ABS laws explicitly identify derivatives and require benefits to be paid from commercial use of them.[57] The CBD has also attempted to deal with the issue of derivatives but did not make any progress. In the end, the parties referred the issue back to the Ad Hoc Open-Ended Working Group to address in the negotiation of the international regime.[58]

Perhaps one of the most practical steps the CBD has created for access and benefit-sharing so far has been to promote the creation of focal points and competent authorities at the national level. Biotechnology companies have long complained of the bureaucratic red tape and lack of organization at the national level for granting access to genetic materials. They claim that this has been a major barrier for foreign investment

54. See Bonn Guidelines, para. 41 and para. 42 (g).
55. See ITPGRFA, Article 13.4.
56. ITPGRFA, Article 13.2 (d) (ii).
57. See Andean Community (1996) *Common Regime on Access to Genetic Resources*, Decision 391 Signed in Caracas, Venezuela (2 July).
58. Supra, CBD, *COP 8 Report*, 126.

in genetic resources and has increased the likelihood of biopiracy.[59] Now, under the CBD Guidelines, ABS focal points will be established and will be responsible for providing information on procedures for gaining prior informed consent and mutually agreed terms, and identification of the relevant stakeholders and competent national authorities through the CBD clearinghouse mechanism.[60] The competent national authorities will have the power to grant access to users themselves, or may choose to delegate authority to grant access to other entities as appropriate. National authorities will also advise on the negotiating process, requirements for PIC, national ABS arrangements and mechanisms for effective participation of stakeholders in the ABS process. The new system, if properly implemented, should address many of the biotech industry's concerns.

The CBD Guidelines also take a practical approach to the creation of an overall strategy for access and benefit-sharing. The strategy envisaged by the Guidelines proposes three basic components: (1) identify all the steps that a user must follow to gain access and make this process transparent; (2) set up a system for obtaining prior informed consent of the owners of the genetic resource; and (3) create a set of mutually agreed terms that are legally clear, that minimize costs and that ensure the interests of the providers are met, including the types of equitable benefit-sharing arrangements the country foresees.[61] The creation of a national ABS strategy could in fact provide a synergistic mechanism where the CBD and the ITPGRFA, and other related international legal instruments, could converge. However, this will have to await the final results of the negotiations of the CBD international regime.

Intellectual property rights

Both the CBD and the ITPGRFA have provisions relating to intellectual property rights. Most of these implications rest on the question of derivatives from genetic resources and whether these components are in fact patentable. As we saw earlier, this question was one of the main sticking points between the US and developing countries in the ITPGRFA negotiations. The US did not want to preclude the possibility of their companies isolating a gene, such as reagents, cell lines or DNA sequencing

59. See Swiss Survey submitted to the CBD COP 4 which found that a restrictive policy would have negative effects on industry and university use of genetic resources, at CBD, UNEP/CBD/COP4/Inf.16 (1998); also see Thomas Cottier (1998) *The Protection of Genetic Resources and Traditional Knowledge: Towards More Specific Rights and Obligations in World Trade Law*, J. Int'l Econ. L., 555, 556.
60. Bonn Guidelines, para. 13.
61. Ibid., para. 45.

or some microbe from the genetic material and then patenting it. They argued that Article 12.3 (d) states that recipients are only restricted to claiming intellectual property rights on the genetic resource "in the form" received. According to their interpretation, the isolation of, for example, a DNA structure or a gene in the genetic resource would constitute a form other than the one received, and would therefore be fair game for patenting. Developing countries, with the tacit support of the EU, argued that the clause explicitly mentions "parts and components" which would consequently prevent any claims to intellectual property rights on microbes or any other part of the genetic resource even if still undiscovered.

Though the deletion of 12.3 (d) was finally put to a vote, the US eventually lost, with 97 votes opposed, 10 votes in support and 3 abstentions. There is still room for influencing the interpretation of this controversial clause in future Governing Body meetings. However, given the anticipated composition of the Council and its politics, predicted outcomes become less certain. Since the Americans are rejecting the ITPGRFA itself, it is unlikely that they will have much of a voice in such Governing Body meetings. Therefore, the G77 and European interpretation will almost certainly remain, at least in the current political setting. According to Article 12.4, the Governing Body was also to adopt a standard material transfer agreement (MTA) that could have contained, *inter alia*, provisions on Article 12.3 (d) but, as will be elaborated under the next section, in June 2006 this was indeed adopted in Madrid, Spain, without further controversy.

In comparison to the ITPGRFA, the CBD Guidelines' provisions are soft and do not set any specific restrictions on the intellectual property rights (IPR) for genetic resources. Under the CBD itself, there are hortatory provisions referring to IPR but these only emphasize the need to respect IPRs generally and for IPRs not to infringe on the transfer of technology to developing countries.[62] The CBD Guidelines' provisions on

---

62. CBD Article 16 (5) "recognizing that patents and other intellectual property rights may have an influence on the implementation of this Convention, shall cooperate in this regard subject to national legislation and international law in order to ensure that such rights are supportive of and do not run counter to its objectives." An information paper by the CBD Secretariat has interpreted this Article to mean the "placement of paragraph 5 in Article 16 implies that if IPR have an impact on the Convention's objectives, this is most likely to occur in the context of technology transfer, rather than in the context of conservation and sustainable use. The paragraph's language is, however, quite broad, implying the potential for influence on any of the Convention's objectives or provisions. It also implies the possibility that Parties will need to take steps cooperatively to manage the influence of IPR to ensure that it is positive rather than negative". See CBD (1996) *Impact of Intellectual Property Rights on the Sustainable Use and Equitable Benefit-Sharing of Genetic Resources*, UNEP/CBD/COP/3/22 (22 September).

IPR are set out in a separate section in Decision VI/24 and call for a closer examination of the role of intellectual property rights in genetic resources, their access and scientific research.[63] This decision, however, has potential implications for IPR procedures to ensure the patentee's compliance with prior informed consent and benefit-sharing. The Guidelines invite parties to encourage the disclosure of country of origin and the use of any indigenous knowledge for the development of discoveries in the patent application. Such a method would be the most effective means of eliminating biopiracy, particularly if the patent were conditional upon such a disclosure and were applied to patents which provide the greatest protection such as in the US, the EU or Japan. These issues will be explored more fully in the following chapter.

Material Transfer Agreements (MTA) and Mutually Agreed Terms (MAT)

MTAs are critical to the exchange of genetic resources and the obligations in the CBD and ITPGRFA will be legally binding through these contracts. These agreements will govern the transfer of intangible material between parties. They set up the terms of the use of the materials as well as the rights of the user and the provider. MTAs and MATs will often cover the use and commercialization of derivatives, as discussed above.[64] There has been a sizeable portion of work done by the international legal community on material transfer agreements and this has made its way into both the agreements.[65] The ITPGRFA lays out some of the basic conditions. Article 12.4 of the ITPGRFA states that facilitated access to the MS should be done through an MTA which shall include the conditions for use, restriction on intellectual property rights and continued access to the resources after the transfer and benefit-sharing.[66] The ITPGRFA also stipulates that the MTA should include the opportunity to seek recourse in an appropriate jurisdiction according to the party's legal system or a mutually agreed upon jurisdiction. This is an important condition for the MTA as it clarifies the means by which disputes in the context of the ITPGRFA will be enforced and resolved.

63. See CBD COP 6 Decision VI/24 Section C.
64. See *A Quick Guide to Material Transfer Agreements at University of California, Berkeley* at http://www.spo.berkeley.edu/guide/mtaquick.html.
65. See for example Lyle Glowka (1998) *A Guide to Designing Legal Frameworks to Determine Access to Genetic Resources*, Gland, Switzerland: World Conservation Union, June; Fernando Latorre Garcia, China Williams, Kerry ten Kate and Phillida Cheyne (2001) "Principles on Access to Genetic Resources and Benefit-Sharing, Common Policy Guidelines to Assist with their Implementations and Text", London: Kew Gardens, March.
66. See ITPGRFA Articles 12.4 and 12.3 (a), (d) and (g).

The exact details of the standard MTA were decided on at the First Governing Body in 2006 and followed these fundamental provisions as described in Article 12. The ITPGRFA's final MTA is very specific. It addresses details such as the applicable law and sets the FAO as the third-party beneficiary in the MTA. It also fixes the percentage (1.1 per cent) that a recipient of the genetic material in the MS shall pay when a product is commercialized using this material and does not make these products available without restriction to others for further research and breeding.[67]

So far, the CBD Guidelines were able to agree on the basic elements that should be included in a standard MTA and these are set out in its Appendix I. There is one distinction to note with respect to the Guidelines, that is the difference between MTA and MAT (Mutually Agreed Terms). The CBD uses this terminology for access to be granted "on mutually agreed terms".[68] This means that users and providers of genetic resources must agree on certain terms for sharing the utilization and commercial use of genetic resources but this does not necessarily have to be done using an MTA. According to the CBD, the critical elements that a standard MTA should include are: preambular reference to the CBD objectives; legal status of the provider and user; ABS arrangements including the terms of IPR; use of derivatives and use by third parties; and legal provisions that set out the choice of law, dispute settlement and any confidentiality arrangements.

Prior Informed Consent (PIC)

The right to know, or prior informed consent, is most commonly understood internationally as a legal principle embodied in the 1998 Convention on the Prior Informed Consent Procedure for Certain Hazardous Chemicals and Pesticides in International Trade. The PIC procedure, which is closely related to international environmental law principles such as the duty to prevent harm and to inform other countries of potential risks, has a slightly different application in the context of genetic resources. Instead of conferring information of a potential risk or threat, PIC, under both the ITPGRFA and CBD, require that users and intermediaries who acquire genetic resources must obtain consent from the original owners. In the case of the ITPGRFA, the owners of the resources are relatively easy to determine. At the outset of the ITPGRFA negotiations, countries agreed on the difficulty of determining the country of origin due to the fact that the genetic material in the MS is

---

67. Supra, *ITPGRFA Report First Governing Body Meeting.*
68. CBD Articles 15.4 and 15.7.

widely found in *ex situ* in a wide array of countries. Consequently, the ITPGRFA recognizes that the genetic resources contained in the MS are the sovereign resources of countries but that these countries give up their right of PIC and entrust this responsibility to the ITPGRFA. Of course, it is understood that the ITPGRFA will, in turn, ensure their protection and use, including benefit-sharing, for the common good of all parties, especially farmers in developing and least developing countries.[69]

The CBD also recognizes the sovereign rights of states over natural resources.[70] However, access is to be granted by prior informed consent from the contracting party that is providing the resource rather than a central authority as with the ITPGRFA. The CBD acknowledges the difficulties associated with obtaining access because of the "diversity of stakeholders and their diverging interests" and problems with determining "their appropriate involvement", meaning that a set system cannot work for all cases.[71] Nevertheless, as described above, the CBD sees an overall strategy, with PIC as a primary component, as the best approach.

The PIC component of the CBD ABS strategy extends responsibilities to both the users and the providers of genetic resources. At the national level, providers are to ensure that stakeholders, from the community to government level, are informed and that legal rights associated with genetic resources are respected when dealing with indigenous and local communities. In the same way, when traditional knowledge has been used, it should be obtained with their approval and in accordance with their traditional practices and domestic laws and policies.[72] A national responsibility also includes the need to make available a written and transparent document on whether PIC is granted or denied. Such a document could be in the form of an application, permit system or "appropriate procedures".[73] In the event that PIC is required from a different level of government, the provider must duly specify this requirement to the user.

The responsibilities on the part of the users primarily revolve around the imperative of obtaining PIC. The CBD Guidelines stipulate that if the genetic resources are used for a different purpose than otherwise indicated, then new prior informed consent must be obtained. Similarly, if the resources are provided to a third party, a new PIC must also be obtained. A noteworthy provision in the Guidelines is that for genetic resources held *ex situ*, in botanical gardens, gene banks and the like,

---

69. ITPGRFA, Preamble and Articles 10 and 10.2.
70. CBD, Article 15.
71. Bonn Guidelines, para. 17.
72. Bonn Guidelines, para. 3.1.
73. Bonn Guidelines, para. 38 and 39.

consent to use these resources or pass them on to third parties is also required from the competent authority that owns the resources. Overall, the PIC procedure contained in the CBD and through its Bonn Guidelines should ensure legal clarity, cost-effectiveness, transparency, timeliness and informed consent to all relevant stakeholders.

Applying the framework to the ITPGRFA and the CBD

The Treaty and the CBD offer a very powerful case of how two treaties, which have overlapping interests in the form of plant genetic resources, have cooperated and closely worked together. The interlinkage has spurred several key benefits that have improved the effectiveness of both treaties and which would not have occurred alone. This section of the chapter analyses the two treaties and their activities under the five categories set out in chapter 3 by which a treaty's effectiveness can be measured. These measurements include meeting the treaty's objectives, meeting its supporting provisions, robustness, improving compliance and monitoring, and finance.

Meeting the objectives of the treaty

Echoing the Nairobi Act in 1992, CBD Decision III/11 sets out the idea for the FAO to consider, under its Commission for Genetic Resources, the possibility of undertaking the negotiation of a protocol to the CBD or another type of legal instrument. This could be either binding or nonbinding, depending on appropriateness and would be in harmony with the CBD or fulfil its objectives in the area of plant genetic resources.[74] This type of international coordination is quite unprecedented. Rarely would one international legal regime request another to essentially negotiate a new legal instrument on its behalf. However, this rarity is understandable in two respects. Firstly, the CBD COP recognized the competency that the FAO had in the field of agriculture and, as such, decided to prepare for the FAO a first draft programme of work on agricultural biodiversity.[75] Secondly, it was well aware of the vested interest the FAO had in this area of plant genetic resources; the FAO has already spent seven years solely on the development of a non-binding instrument along the lines of the International Undertaking. Therefore, cognisant of the difficulties of negotiating a new instrument and the competency of the FAO, the CBD COP agreed to Decision III/11. Moreover, the CBD,

74. UNEP (1997) *Decision III/11*, para. 18.
75. Ibid.

as a relatively young treaty with a large mandate, also made the COP recognize the need to collaborate, from the beginning, with many different organizations and treaties in order to achieve its objectives.[76] The FAO, for its part, also realized early on in its work the potential scope of the CBD and the need to closely collaborate with it through its Commission for Genetic Resources.[77]

It therefore comes as no surprise that the resulting ITPGRFA has several provisions that overlap with the CBD and are mutually supportive towards achieving common objectives. Under Article 1 of the ITPGRFA, its objectives are "the conservation and sustainable use" of plant genetic resources for food and agriculture. Under the CBD, agricultural biodiversity is also now seen as an important category of biodiversity. Historically, humans have become increasingly dependent on fewer plant species, "about 7,000 plant species have been cultivated and collected for food by humans since agriculture began about 12,000 years ago. Today, only about 15 plant species and 8 animal species supply 90 per cent of our food."[78] So, despite the potential threats that agriculture poses for biodiversity loss, the preamble of the CBD takes a progressive view that biodiversity is not only critical for its intrinsic value but also "is of critical importance for meeting the food, health and other needs of the growing world population".[79] In 1995, after heavy discussion, the CBD COP clearly confirmed that agricultural biodiversity was interpreted as being within the CBD objectives.[80] This included genetic resources for food and agriculture which fall under this broader remit. Thus, maintaining the diversity through gene banks, or in their *in situ*, contributes directly to the core elements of the CBD objective of "conservation and sustainable use".[81]

Article 1 of the ITPGRFA also stresses another critical area of the CBD: "the fair and equitable sharing of benefits derived from the use of genetic resources for food and agriculture for sustainable agriculture and food security and in harmony with the CBD".[82] This article reinforces the CBD's primary objective of the "fair and equitable sharing of benefits",[83] derived from a narrower category of genetic resources for food

76. See UNEP, *Decision II/13* (1994), para. 4, Decision III/21 (1996), para. 3; Decision IV/15 (1998), para. 5.
77. FAO, *Statutes of the Commission on Genetic Resources for Food and Agriculture*, CGRFA-10/04/inf.1.
78. CBD (2006) available at http://www.biodiv.org/programmes/areas/agro/default.asp.
79. CBD, Preamble.
80. UNEP (1995) *Decision I/9*, Annex, points 5.9 and 6.3.
81. According to the CBD *in situ* and *ex situ* conservation includes domesticated and cultivated plants and genetic resources. See CBD, Article 2.
82. ITPGRFA, Article 1.
83. CBD, Article 1.

and agriculture but, nevertheless, an important contribution to CBD objectives.

Article 1.1 of the ITPGRFA explicitly confirms that its objectives and those of the CBD are connected and that they "will be attained by closely linking this Treaty to the Food and Agriculture Organization of the United Nations (which hosts the Treaty) and to the Convention on Biological Diversity". In Article 19.3, specific provision is made for the Governing Body of the ITPGRFA to cooperate with the Conference of the Parties to the CBD. The Governing Body shall:

(1) take note of relevant decisions of the Conference of the Parties to the CBD and other relevant international organizations and treaty bodies;
(2) inform, as appropriate, the Conference of the Parties to the CBD and other relevant international organizations and treaty bodies of matters regarding the implementation of this Treaty.

At COP 5 of the CBD the contracting parties themselves recognized the important role the ITPGRFA plays in fulfilling the objectives of the CBD:[84]

Recognise[d] the important role that the International Treaty on Plant Genetic Resources for Food and Agriculture will have, in harmony with the Convention on Biological Diversity, for the conservation and sustainable utilisation of this important component of agricultural biological diversity, for facilitated access to plant genetic resources for food and agriculture, and for the fair and equitable sharing of the benefits arising out of their utilisation.[85]

The ITPGRFA also addresses farmers' rights and *ex situ* conservation, which were identified as "outstanding issues" at the conclusion of the INC negotiations in 1991 but which could not be resolved and were consequently left to the future work of the CBD.[86] This work was important to the core objectives of the CBD but was never taken up until the adoption of the ITPGRFA.[87] As a result, the final text has made substantial progress in these two areas.

In the final day of the negotiations of the CBD, *ex situ*[88] conservation was a major issue that had to be politically solved by the negotiators in

---

84. Ibid.
85. CBD, *Decision VI/6*, (2001).
86. UNEP (1992) *Nairobi Final Act of the Conference for the Adoption of the Agreed Text of the Convention on Biological Diversity*, (22 May), Resolution 3, para. 4.
87. Regine Anderson (2002) *The Time Dimension in International Regime Interplay*, 2 Glob. Envtl. Pol. 3, 105.
88. *Ex situ* genetic resources refer to "the conservation of components of biological diversity outside their natural habitats", where "habitat" means "the place or type of site where an organism or population naturally occurs" (Article 2). Generally *ex situ* conservation is done via gene bank storage.

order to clear a major impasse in the negotiations. Many of the *ex situ* resources that had been taken from their countries of origin had already been further developed through plant varieties or genetic engineering and it would be very difficult to trace the original traits of these resources that were being used by farmers around the world. Even more complex, many of the genes were stored as germplasm in gene banks or in botanical gardens and these were not always obtained with the express permission of the country of origin, particularly during periods when these countries were colonial territories. It thus became impossible to establish the country of origin for each and every genetic resource. A compromise was therefore struck in the INC negotiations which recognized the principle that natural resources were the sovereign right of states[89] but that access to *ex situ* resources, as far as the CBD would be concerned, only applied to those resources acquired after the CBD had entered into force. The INC then agreed to bypass the issue and explicitly left access to *ex situ* resources prior to the adoption of the CBD to be resolved in the future by the FAO and the further negotiations of the International Undertaking, which later became the ITPGRFA.[90]

As the section on robustness below will further discuss, the issue of *ex situ* genetic resources and the strategic move by INC to unblock the final negotiations of the CBD stalled the subsequent International Undertaking negotiations for several years. But perhaps, in the end, it was worth it. The eventual ITPGRFA learned a valuable lesson from the CBD experience; it learned that bilateral access is too difficult to manage under an international instrument, whereas a multilateral system is much more efficient. So, even though the access to the genetic resources system that ITPGRFA eventually set up did not meet the expectations of the Nairobi Final Act, in the end, this was a preferable solution. The ITPGRFA, under Article 11, makes no distinction between *ex situ* resources before or after the entry into force of the CBD but, as explained above, creates a multilateral system to manage the most essential crops and staples for food and agriculture and creates a kind of custodianship of these to be managed by the treaty. At the same time, it facilitates access to these resources for non-commercial use, while recognizing the sovereignty of genetic resources.

As David Cooper observes, the negotiators of the ITPGRFA were very careful not to undermine the provisions of Article 15 of the CBD which states that the authority to grant access rests with the national government and that access must take place under mutually agreed terms with prior informed consent. These provisions are reiterated in the CBD Guidelines. The ITPGRFA further states that these are essential terms

---

89. CBD Article 15.1.
90. Supra, Nairobi Final Act.

and, in many cases, even strengthens them. For example, under Article 10 of the ITPGRFA the sovereignty of countries over their plant genetic resources for food and agriculture and the authority to grant access rests with national governments. However, in what is viewed as a nice balancing act and a political compromise, albeit one that took nearly 10 years to negotiate, Article 10 and the preamble of the ITPGRFA state that the Multilateral System was created in exercise of their sovereign rights to protect and access these resources.[91]

Farmers' rights were also an important area that was not adequately dealt with under the CBD but in which the ITPGRFA has made substantial progress. Farmers are a critical sub-group of local and indigenous communities who have historically played an important role in the conservation, sustainable use and exchange of plant genetic resources as well as their improvement and availability. The role of farmers goes to the heart of the CBD objectives to conserve and make sustainable use of biodiversity. The ITPGRFA developed what are regarded as collective rights that are contained in Article 9 of the ITPGRFA. The ITPGRFA provisions are very much linked to Article 8 (j) of the CBD and either echo or strengthen the CBD provisions.[92]

CBD Article 8 (j) encourages parties to "respect, preserve and maintain knowledge innovations and practices of indigenous and local communities embodying traditional lifestyles relevant for the conservation and sustainable use of biological diversity".[93] The Article goes on to require that parties should promote the wider development and use of this knowledge based on the equitable sharing of benefits arising from the use of such knowledge. The ITPGRFA, however, goes much further in its requirements. Similar to Article 8 (j), Article 9 of the ITPGRFA firstly states the need to protect local and traditional knowledge but the ITPGRFA uses stronger language and embodies the equitable sharing of benefits arising from the use of local knowledge as a right for farmers. Even further, still under Article 9.2 (c), the ITPGRFA states that, even though decision-making for the use of this knowledge remains in the hands of national governments,[94] farmers have a right to participate in such decision-making.[95]

Meeting the treaty's supporting provisions

The CBD and ITPGRFA can be viewed as being particularly close when looked at through the lens of their respective supporting provi-

91. ITPGRFA, Article 10.
92. Op. cit. Cooper, 3.
93. CBD, Article 8 (j).
94. ITPGRFA, Article 10.
95. ITPGRFA, Article 9.2 (c).

sions.[96] Though the ITPGRFA is still a relatively young international legal regime, there is already a strong work programme between the ITPGRFA secretariat of the Commission for Genetic Resources for Food and Agriculture (CGRFA) and the CBD. Much of this takes place in the mutual support for the Global Plan of Action for the Conservation and Sustainable Utilization of Plant Genetic Resources.[97]

The Global Plan of Action is a rolling programme that brings around a common table members of the FAO as well as a number of other international organizations and actors. The programme is built as a framework which sponsors cooperation on four priority areas of *in situ* conservation and development, *ex situ* conservation, utilization of plant genetic resources and institutions and capacity-building. It was adopted in 1996 at the Leipzig International Conference by 150 countries as a means of prioritizing needs, consolidating a growing mix of activities in the area of plant genetic resources and to direct dwindling finances towards a focused effort.[98] The concept behind the Global Plan was for the new Undertaking (then under negotiation and which later became the ITPGRFA) "to provide the overall rules of the game with respect to the exchange of agricultural genetic resources and to the rights to those resources, while the Plan should become the operational arm for practical action".[99]

As a result of the early bridging of the International Undertaking with the Global Plan in 1996, the subsequent ITPGRFA, which was agreed in 2001, reflects in its text the implementation of the Plan. By doing so, the ITPGRFA recognizes the common goals that the Plan had set out for plant genetic resources for food and agriculture and reinforces them.[100] Specifically, the ITPGRFA calls on parties to take effective action at the national level in the areas of capacity-building, technology transfer and exchange of information. Most importantly, from a perspective of realizing these objectives, it directs financial resources through benefits including those derived from the commercialization arising from accessing the Multilateral System of the ITPGRFA.[101] Under Article 18.3 of the ITPGRFA, the contracting parties are further obligated to create a

96. The main supporting components of the IT can be found in part V Articles 14–17. The supporting provisions for the CBD are not as clearly identified as compared to the IT because the CBD is a much broader agreement but its main supporting areas are in Articles 5, 6, 10, 12 and 13.
97. [hereinafter the Global Plan of Action or Global Plan], available at http://www.fao.org/ag/AGP/AGPS/GpaEN/gpatoc.htm.
98. See FAO (1996) *The Final Report of the Technical Conference on Plant Genetic Resources*, Leipzig, Germany, ITCPGR/96/REP, Annex 2.
99. GRAIN (1996) *The Global Plan of Action for Sustainable Use and Conservation of Plant Genetic Resources for Food and Agriculture* (May), available at http://www.grain.org/briefings/?id=10.
100. ITPGRFA, Article 14.
101. ITPGRFA, Articles 13.2, 13.4.

strategy that would in part mobilize funding directed to the Global Plan of Action.[102]

The CBD also directly supports the Global Plan of Action and has endorsed it as working towards the implementation of the Convention.[103] It has also directed its parties to create national strategies to implement key elements of the Plan, which many parties have done very effectively.[104] According to the Second National Reports (set up under Article 26 to provide information on measures taken for the implementation of the Convention and the effectiveness of these measures),[105] 75 countries have adopted activities at the national level that have helped implement the Global Plan of Action.[106] The CBD has also incorporated elements of the Plan into its own Multi-Year Plan of Work on Agriculture Biodiversity, which further strengthens its contribution to the supporting provisions of the ITPGRFA and the Global Plan.[107]

Another area where there is potential for cooperation concerning these treaties' supporting provisions is under Article 17.1 of the ITPGRFA. This envisages the development of a "Global Information System" and explicitly directs parties to seek cooperation with the CBD's Clearing House Mechanism. The expectation is that a global information system will facilitate the exchange of information and contribute to the sharing of benefits by making information available on plant genetic resources to all contracting parties. The information system will have to be based on existing systems, including those established by the Commission on Genetic Resources for Food and Agriculture, but the Clearing House Mechanism would already provide important information on scientific cooperation, promoting technology transfer, education and training and on potential funding at the national level.[108] It is expected that construction of the information system will get under way in 2008 at the Second Meeting of the ITPGRFA Governing Body Meeting.

Robustness

Much has been made of the fact that the ITPGRFA interlinkages with the CBD greatly benefited the ITPGRFA in its development and negoti-

---

102. ITPGRFA, Articles 18, 18.3.
103. See CBD (1998) *Decision III/11*, para. 19.
104. Ibid., para. 16 (a).
105. CBD, Article 26.
106. Based on the National Report Analyser of the CBD Secretariat (data compiled 20 June 2006).
107. See general work on agriculture biodiversity in the CBD (2002) *Multiyear Plan of Work Up Until 2010*, UNEP/CBD/MYOP/3 and UNEP/CBD/MYPOW/4.
108. See Web site of the *Clearing House Mechanism*, available at http://www.biodiv.org/chm/default.aspx.

ation phase. Stokke has argued that international regimes in the early stages of development will have a greater potential to learn from each other when they are functionally linked, have similar memberships, have common interests and similar levels of power.[109] This was certainly the case with the ITPGRFA and CBD. The experience of the CBD provided a breeding ground for the ITPGRFA to learn what would work and what would not. Its most valuable lessons have already been touched upon and concerned the multilateral approach to access and benefit-sharing and avoiding the pitfalls of establishing the country of origin.[110] However, what is not yet well documented in the literature is the learning experience that the CBD is now undergoing as it forges ahead to develop stronger provisions on access and benefit-sharing of genetic resources and negotiates a new "international regime".

Conscious of the close links between the potential international regime on access and benefit-sharing and the ITPGRFA, the parties of the CBD are looking for lessons that can be applied in the negotiation on the international regime.[111] This was evident from CBD Decision VII/19 which invited the FAO *inter alia* to cooperate with the CBD in the elaboration of the international regime.[112] The CBD is looking for experience in several areas, particularly in the potential development of a model material transfer agreement, which the ITPGRFA has been intensely developing in the last several years and which was adopted at its first Governing Body meeting in Madrid, Spain in 2006. The MTA adopted by the ITPGRFA is the first under an international treaty for genetic resources

109. See Olav Schram Stokke (2000) *Managing Straddling Stocks: The Interplay of Global and Regional Regimes*, 43 Ocean and Coastal Management, 205–234; Olav Schram Stokke (2001) *The Interplay of International Regimes: Putting Effectiveness Theory to Work*, FNI Report 14/2001, Oslo: The Fridtjof Nansen Institute.

110. For arguments on this see FAO, *Identifying Genetic Resources and their Origin: The Capabilities of Modern Biochemical and Legal Systems*, Background Study Paper No. 4, prepared by J. J. Hardon, B. Vosman and Th. J. L. van Hintum for the Commission for Plant Genetic Resources, First Extraordinary Session; also Cary Fowler (2004) 33 *Regime Change: Plant Genetic Resources in International Law, Outlook for Agriculture* 1, 9.

111. See CBD Decision IV/8 (2000) which calls upon the Access and Benefit-Sharing Working Group "to draw upon all relevant sources, including legislative, policy and administrative measures, best practices and case studies on access to genetic resources and benefit-sharing arising from the use of those genetic resources, including the whole range of biotechnology, in the development of a common understanding of basic concepts and to explore all options for access and benefit-sharing on mutually agreed terms including guiding principles, guidelines, and codes of best practice for access and benefit-sharing arrangements". Also see, for example, Co-Chair's Summary Expert International Workshop on Access and Benefit-Sharing co-sponsored by the Governments of Norway and South Africa in Cape Town 20 to 23 September 2005.

112. CBD, *Decision VII/19* (2004), Section D, para. 5.

and, though based on a multilateral access system rather than a bilateral access system, which the CBD is currently heading for, many believe there are certain insights to be gained. This would include the necessity to reflect in the MTA commercial practices, appraisal/valuation systems of the resource and systems to distinguish which part or percentage of the genetic resource has been used in the final commercial product. Here, the CGPFA conducted very detailed studies on the potential commercialization of plant genetic resources for food and agriculture which the CBD will surely have to undertake if they are going to create a useful MTA.[113] Still further, the FAO, before establishing the Multilateral System, also pondered the problem of jurisdiction as often the genetic resources are accessed in one jurisdiction but commercialized in another. It thus looked into this potential problem from the perspective of setting up an arbitrational system which could be useful for the CBD.[114]

Furthermore, there are some countries of the view that, instead of negotiating a completely stand-alone agreement under the CBD, given the cross-cutting nature of genetic resources, the "harmony" the ITPGRFA has with the CBD and the multiple forums in which it is dealt with and regulated, an umbrella-type agreement might be more practical. Proponents of such an approach argue that this would integrate the various components of ABS under a coherent structure.[115] For the time being, however, the Conference of Parties has not taken such an approach but they remain very aware of the link with the ITPGRFA and, as such, the current negotiating text as adopted at COP 8 has clearly distinguished the frontiers between the potential international regime and the ITPGRFA in two optional draft clauses:

> The international regime will not apply to the plant genetic resources [of those plant species] that are considered by [under annex 1 of] the International Treaty on Plant Genetic Resources for Food and Agriculture [or by the Commission on Genetic Resources for Food and Agriculture], [when those resources are used for the purposes of that Treaty].

---

113. See Clive Stannard (2005) *Aspects of Multilateral Access Arrangements*, Paper presented at the International Workshop on Access and Benefit-Sharing (15 September), available at http://www.norsafworkshop.com/Media/Uploads/432969b5dc205.pdf.

114. Gerald Moore (2005) *International Arbitration*, FAO Commission on Plant Genetic Resources Background Study Paper No. 25, available at ftp://ext-ftp.fao.org/ag/cgrfa/BSP/bsp25e.pdf.

115. François Pythoud (2005) *The International Treaty on Plant Genetic Resources for Food and Agriculture and Key Component of an International Regime on Access and Benefit-Sharing*, Paper presented at the International Workshop on Access and Benefit-Sharing (15 September), available at http://www.norsafworkshop.com/Media/Uploads/432969b5dc205.pdf.

The international regime is without prejudice to the FAO International Treaty on Plant Genetic Resources for Food and Agriculture and will take into account the work of the WIPO/IGC on the intellectual property aspects of *sui generis* systems for the protection of traditional knowledge and folklore against misappropriation and misuse.[116]

This type of explicit cross-referencing gives more predictability and certainty to the regime as has proven to be the case in other instances where this technique has been employed, such as between the UNFCCC and Ozone Convention concerning the coverage of common greenhouse gases and ozone-depleting substances.[117] It also shows that the regimes have distinguished themselves through a learning process.

Compliance and monitoring

Clear examples where interlinkages between MEAs have directly assisted a party that is in non-compliance to return to good standing are difficult to find. Primarily, this is due to the fact that neither of these treaties have had instances where the compliance systems have been triggered or employed. This is a common phenomenon with MEAs that have very general obligations and that rely more heavily on non-judicial approaches to compliance such as reporting, regular meetings and technical assistance. However, in "the fulfilment by the contracting parties of their obligations",[118] which is the broadly accepted definition of compliance, and in monitoring the obligations of the parties, there are some examples where the ITPGRFA and CBD cooperation has already borne fruit.

First, the ITPGRFA obligations contained in Articles 4, 5 and 6 are generally complementary to the CBD Articles and in many areas the ITPGRFA takes very general provisions contained in the CBD and

---

116. CBD (2006) *Decision VIII/4*, Annex paras 3 and 4.
117. In the case of the Ozone Convention and UNFCCC the cross-referencing adds value to agreements. As Werksman observes: "Carving out these substances from the coverage of the new regime avoids conflict, but also prevents negotiators from eroding what may be pre-existing higher internationally agreed standard. Were two regimes simultaneously to govern the same substances, States could choose to join the regime with the lower standard and still claim to be supporting global efforts to protect the environment." Op. cit. Werksman, 3.
118. UNEP, which was well aware of the common confusion between the terms of "compliance" and "implementation", as this book also highlights in chapter 1, extensively consulted MEA Secretariats to set this standard definition of compliance. Implementation is defined *inter alia* as "all relevant laws, regulations, policies, and other measures and initiatives, that contracting parties adopt and/or take to meet their implementation under MEAs and its amendments". See UNEP (2006) *Manual on Compliance with and Enforcement of Multilateral Environmental Agreements*", 49.

provides greater focus and coherence which the CBD lacks.[119] Article 5 of the ITPGRFA calls for the contracting party to "promote an integrated approach to the exploration, conservation and sustainable use of plant genetic resources for food and agriculture".[120] Here, the ITPGRFA fleshes out an important qualification on *in situ* genetic resources that the CBD has left ambiguous. Articles 8 (a) and (c) of the CBD calls for the protection of *in situ* resources primarily through the creation of protected areas and the regulation and management of those resources outside protected areas with a view to sustainable use and conservation but it does not describe the means by which this should take place.[121] The ITPGRFA, on the other hand, does provide a clear means for taking this important step forward and in doing so it defines a critical area left open by the CBD, which is *in situ* resources on farms. By requesting the parties to promote the management and conservation of on-farm plant genetic resources for food and agriculture, the ITPGRFA closes an important obligation left open by the generality of the CBD.

Another example is Article 6 of the ITPGRFA, which obliges parties to create policies and measures to promote the sustainable use of plant genetic resources for food and agriculture. The CBD has been implementing programmes to promote this primary ITPGRFA obligation. According to an analysis of the CBD Third National Reports, of the 66 countries that have submitted their Third National Reports, 50 have reported "activities for the conservation, on farm, *In-situ* and *Ex-situ*, of the variability of genetic resources for food and agriculture" (see Figure 6.1).

Moreover, a further example of complementarity is under Article 7 of ITPGRFA, which, *inter alia*, requests parties to integrate policies and measures to promote the sustainable use of plant genetic resources for food and agriculture into national agricultural and rural development policies. This Article complements the approach that the CBD takes in Article 6 (b), which calls for the creation of National Biodiversity Strategies and Action Plans and the integration of these into national "relevant sectoral or cross-sectoral plans, programmes and policies".[122] As a result of the complementarity of these Articles, many of the CBD National Biodiversity Strategies have already created national legislation that fulfils some of the obligations of ITPGRFA's Article 7.[123] This complementarity also holds true for the CPGRFA's Multi-Year Programme

119. H. David Cooper (2002) *The International Treaty on Plant Genetic Resources for Food and Agriculture*, RECIEL, (11)1 2.
120. ITPGRFA, Article 5.
121. CBD Articles 8 (a) and 8 (c).
122. CBD, Article 6 (b).
123. See, for example, the National Biodiversity Strategy for Canada whereby Agriculture and Agri-Food Canada has developed a national action plan for conservation and sustainable use of agriculture biodiversity.

CBD Parties

173. In the case of centers of origin in your country, is your country promoting activities for the conservation, on farm, In-situ, and Ex-situ, of the variability of genetic resources for food and agriculture, including their wild relatives?

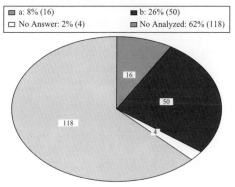

Figure 6.1 Promotion of conservation of plant genetic resources for food and agriculture CBD

Source: Generated from the CBD National Report Analyser, available at http://www.biodiv.org/reports/analyzer.aspx (created 20 June 2006).

of Work which was developed to facilitate the integration of biodiversity considerations within the national and international agendas for food and agriculture and "strengthen mutual cooperation with other international forums, including, in particular, the Convention on Biological Diversity".[124]

Another way that interlinkages between these two conventions have contributed to improving compliance is by mutual recognition of terms and definitions, thus reducing any ambiguity between the respective treaties. Peter Sand has argued that one of the main contributors to noncompliance is the uncertainty of terms used by treaties.[125] Through the close interaction between the ITPGRFA and CBD, the terms have remained consistent and in some instances, such as in the case of the definition "*in situ*" or "genetic material", the terms are identical. Other terms, such as "sustainable use" which appears throughout the ITPGRFA, remain undefined in the treaty text and will rely heavily on the CBD interpretation to identify the mostly widely accepted definition.[126]

124. See UNEP (2006) *Thematic Programmes of Work, Progress Report of the Food and Agricultural Organization*, UNEP/CBD/COP/8/INF/24, para. 9.
125. Peter Sand (1996) *Institution-Building to Assist Compliance with International Environmental Law: Perspectives*, Heidelberg Journal of International Law, 774.
126. CBD Article 2 defines "sustainable use" as the use of components of biological diversity in a way and at a rate that does not lead to the long-term decline of biological diversity, thereby maintaining its potential to meet the needs and aspirations of present and future generations.

A major contribution of the ITPGRFA to the compliance and monitoring of the CBD is through the State of the World's Genetic Resources Report (SWGRR).[127] This report is published periodically by the CGRFA,[128] the Secretariat of the ITPGRFA and parties of the ITPGRFA who are obliged to cooperate to ensure its reassessments and updating under Article 17.3. It is, without question, the most comprehensive report on country-by-country genetic resources. It monitors the conservation of *in situ* and *ex situ* genetic resources, monitors national strategies, provides surveys on sustainable agricultural practices and threats to genetic resources for food and agriculture and gives an overview of institutions working in the areas and their efforts towards capacity-building, education, training and awareness-raising. The information provided in the report is perhaps the best source available for monitoring the state of genetic resources worldwide. In particular, it is extremely useful for countries analysing information and monitoring the effectiveness of the implementation of conserving and sustaining plant genetic resources for food and agriculture. This report also complements the national report required under Article 26 of the CBD. Additionally, the SWGRR can assist the preparation of CBD compliance reporting by reducing procedural burdens, as it provides baseline data that can be easily built upon.

The CBD has recognized the importance of the work carried out in this report and the contribution to the report remains an element of the CBD work plan on agriculture biodiversity.[129] One major contribution this report will make in the future will be to the 2010 reduction of the biodiversity loss target. The next edition of the SWGRR is expected to be the key source for assessing and monitoring whether the CBD has met this target and in doing so it will make a "significant reduction of the current rate of biodiversity loss at the global, regional and national level as a contribution to poverty alleviation and to the benefit of all life on earth".[130]

Finance

The ITPGRFA itself has a unique built-in funding system which was designed to make the treaty more – or less self-financing through funds con-

---

127. FAO (1997) *State of the World's Genetic Resources for Food and Agriculture*, Rome, available at http://www.fao.org/ag/AGP/AGPS/Pgrfa/overview/ova2m.htm.
128. On the relationship between the FAO Commission on Genetic Resources for Food and Agriculture and the ITGRFA Governing Body see FAO, IT/GB-1/06/15 (2006).
129. CBD, Decision 5/V, Annex Agriculture for Biodiversity, para. 1.1.
130. CBD, Decision VI/26. The CBD has invited the Governing Body of the ITGRFA to assist it in achieving the 2010 target; see (2004) *Report of the Second Meeting of the CGRFA, meeting as the interim Governing Body*, CGRFA/MIC-2/04/REP, Italy, para. 29.

tributed to the Governing Body from accesses to the genetic resources in the Multilateral System. However, it would be unwise to depend on a single source of funding and there remains some uncertainty as to the level of funding the MS would eventually provide. Taken in this light, Article 18.2 of the ITPGRFA provides that "the Contracting Parties undertake to implement a funding strategy for the implementation" of the treaty.[131] The Article requests the contracting parties to take the "necessary and appropriate measures" with other international funds or funding mechanisms "to ensure due priority and attention" to the effective allocation of predictable and agreed resources for the implementation" of the treaty.[132]

In 2004, in order to meet this obligation, the parties set up a working group that evaluated *inter alia* the potential avenues for funding outside the scope of the Convention and, in 2006, it reported its findings to the First Meeting of the Governing Body.[133] The draft Funding Strategy that is expected to be eventually adopted makes reference to the potential links with the CBD but this will need to be further explored before the draft is finalized. One area that will be potentially important for the ITPGRFA is its direct links to CBD Articles 21 and 39 which outline the CBD's funding mechanisms, including the Global Environment Facility. Sam Johnston identifies the GEF as a prominent source of funding for the ITPGRFA that could be utilized through the links the ITPGRFA has with the CBD and their common objectives of conservation and sustainable use.[134] Johnson suggests several ways this relationship could be developed, including for the ITPGRFA Governing Body to invite the Conference of the Parties of the Convention on Biological Diversity to review their guidance to the Financial Mechanism in light of the entry into force of the ITPGRFA or the development of a memorandum of understanding between the Governing Body and the Global Environment Facility Council.[135] Already, the GEF has recognized its role in funding in sustainable agriculture and benefit-sharing of genetic resources, including those for food and agriculture, but these operational mandates

---

131. ITPGRFA, Article 18.1.
132. ITPGRFA, Article 18.2.
133. See the *Report of the Open-ended Working Group on the Rules of Procedure and Financial Rules of the Governing Body, Compliance, and the Funding Strategy*, Rome, Italy (December 2005), CGRFA/IC/OWG-1/05/REP, 14–17.
134. Sam Johnson (2006) *Report on the Types of Funding and Assistance and Institutions with Relevant Mandates to the Funding Strategy of the International Treaty on Plant Genetic Resources for Food and Agriculture*, Background Paper No. 29, prepared for the Commission of Plant Genetic Resources for Food and Agriculture acting as the Interim Governing Body of the International Treaty on Plant Genetic Resources for Food and Agriculture.
135. Ibid., 17.

are carried out through the CBD. Thus, for the ITPGRFA, the best avenue for finding outside funding through the GEF is through project collaborations with the CBD.

The CBD itself has already received a great deal of in-kind financial support from its close elaboration with the FAO and ITPGRFA. Included in this support has been the placement of a senior officer at the CBD secretariat for a number of years during the development of the ITPGRFA, which the FAO is planning to continue under the recently signed MOU.[136] The CBD also benefited from the FAO development of its Thematic Work Programme on agriculture biodiversity which has been prepared twice by the FAO.[137]

Conclusion

Chapter 6 provided a detailed analysis of the ITPGRFA and the CBD, both from the perspective of their negotiating history and from a comparative analysis of their overlapping provisions. This analysis provided the context to apply the analytical framework set out in chapters 4 and 5 and to determine whether the interlinkages between these treaties has led to improving their effectiveness. Under each of the categories applied, the results showed the same outcome; the cooperation between these treaties has improved the meeting of their primary objectives, the compliance and monitoring of their obligations, and the supporting provisions. The treaties have also learned from each other at consecutive intervals. Early negotiations of the International Undertaking led to the separate negotiations of the CBD. The CBD's difficulties with unilateral ownership of genetic resources became a lesson for the International Treaty negotiations to take a multilateral approach and vest the rights and benefits of the resources with a third party (the treaty secretariat). Now, as the CBD goes through the stage of negotiating an "international regime" on access and benefit-sharing, the lessons learned from the International Treaty in the area of material transfer agreements, property rights and definitions of benefits are contributing to the development of the CBD international regime. Lastly, the financing of the CBD and the International Treaty has benefited from collaboration and the treaties have managed to share resources and reduce redundancy; there is also scope for joint funding though the GEF.

This case study provides an excellent example of how two treaties, though fundamentally conflicting, have carved out a space where they

136. UNEP (2006) *Decision VIII/16*.
137. Supra, *UNEP Thematic Work Programme Info.*, 13.

can cooperate and they have enthusiastically and diligently pursued this cooperation. In the end, the benefits have outshone the potential conflicts and these treaties have profited by improving their overall effectiveness. This case study demonstrates the validity of my principal query that conflicting treaties, under the general branch of international environmental law and under a single pillar of sustainable development, can improve their effectiveness through interlinkages. The question that the next case study will address is whether this query is valid for conflicting MEAs and treaties outside the branch of international environmental law and under other pillars of sustainable development.

Part VI

Case study two: Understanding interlinkages as a factor of effectiveness of sustainable development law

7

The interlinkages of plant genetic resources: The CBD and ITPGRFA and their relationship with the TRIPS Agreement

Introduction

Whereas the story of the ITPGRFA and the CBD is one of positive and productive collaboration, the relationship between the TRIPS with the CBD and ITPGRFA, on the other hand, can be characterized as one of non-cooperation and continual conflict. One might easily dismiss this as evident given the fact that the TRIPS Agreement is firmly rooted within the sector of economic development rather than environmental protection. These Agreements would therefore have self-evident competing interests that would make them, by their very nature, incompatible. Rhetorically, such arguments are widely viewed and disseminated and act as a basis for the continuing trade and environment rift that has dominated the environmental and trade communities relationship ever since the GATT Dolphin-Tuna Dispute in 1993.[1] However, the underlying notion that fuels this debate need not necessarily be the case. Treaties with competing interests can cooperate and have a mutually supportive relationship so long as the legal and institutional set-ups have been worked out cooperatively through an interlinkages approach.

The case study in chapter 6 between the CBD and the ITPGRFA has clearly shown that, by these two treaties working closely together, the outcome can increase each treaty's effectiveness. The CBD and the ITPGRFA are no less compatible than the combination of the TRIPS

1. GATT (1992) *Dolphin-Tuna* Panel 1, BISD 29S/9.

Interlinkages and the effectiveness of multilateral environmental agreements,
W. Bradnee Chambers, United Nations University Press, 2008, ISBN 978-92-808-1149-0

and the CBD (or the TRIPS and ITPGRFA for that matter). In point of fact, and when closely examined from the subject of this analysis, in others words, from the perspective of plant genetic resources themselves, the CBD and the ITPGRFA are arguably potentially less compatible than the CBD and TRIPS.

By far the greatest threat to biodiversity loss is not trade liberalization or the current intellectual property regime; it is the conversion of ecosystems such as forests, marine and wetlands to agriculture.[2] However, as the last case study shows, and this case will reinforce, it is the very fact that the CBD and the FAO have collaborated and created greater positive interlinkages that has led to increased effectiveness and a constructive example. Conversely, as we will see from this case study, despite the potential for interlinkages between the TRIPS and the CBD and ITPGRFA, these interlinkages have not always been developed or adequately promoted and this has led to either a missed opportunity to strengthen the effectiveness of these instruments or, in some cases, even led to instances of ineffectiveness between these instruments.

As in the last case study in the preceding chapter, before embarking on an analysis of how the TRIPS Agreement fits in with the CBD and ITPGRFA and studying the impacts on effectiveness in each of the respective indicators, the first part of this chapter will give an overview of the history and the legal framework of the TRIPS Agreement. It is assumed that the other half of this comparison, the earlier legal history and analysis of the CBD and the ITPGRFA, will serve here also so will not be repeated since discussed in chapter 6; I will instead only focus on the TRIPS Agreement, the next topic in this comparative study on legal instruments concerning the regulation and management of plant genetic resources.

Brief legal history of TRIPS[3]

Originally, the negotiation of the TRIPS Agreement began back in the 1970s during the Tokyo Round but the scope of the issues that the parties

---

2. Millennium Ecosystem Assessment (MA) (2005) *Ecosystems and Human Well-being: Synthesis*, Washington, D.C.: World Resources Institute. Also see supra, chapter 3.
3. See WTO for all the negotiating documents of the TRIPS Agreement in the Uruguay Round 1986–1994 at http://www.wto.org/english/tratop_e/trips_e/trips_e.htm#NegHist (accessed 23 August 2006). The posting of these derestricted documents by the WTO secretariat, while not posting certain other records, has led to accusations by NGOs of the WTO attempting to skew the historical records. In defence of such accusations, see Peter Ungphakorn (2001) WTO Letter, *South-North Development Monitor* 4887, 29 May. For a multi-perspective version of the TRIPS history see Peter K. Yu (2006) *The First*

were seeking to undertake mainly concerned counterfeiting and piracy and their impact on trade. By the 1980s, American industry was becoming more concerned with losses over what they perceived as inadequate global rules for the protection of intellectual property in countries where their companies were now beginning to invest more heavily, particularly in the emerging areas of electronics, chemicals and pharmaceuticals.[4] Consequently, this led the US, in the early 1980s, to press for reform of the Paris Convention[5] and other intellectual property agreements under the World Intellectual Property Organization (WIPO). This move, however, produced few results and, after several failed WIPO conferences in 1980 and 1984, the growing dissatisfaction of the US soon turned into greater resolve and a wider strategy of trying once again to place intellectual property rights in the context of the international trade agenda.

With this strategy in mind, the US proposed the inclusion of intellectual property rights as an issue for the agenda of the Uruguay Round which was about to be launched in Punta del Este in September 1986. During the Punta del Este Conference the US pushed hard and, after some arm-twisting and tough negotiating, the conference yielded them success but it came with a concession that would delay serious negotiations of IPR in the round for nearly three years.[6] The concession was to include in the Punta del Este Ministerial Declaration a provision that the "inclusion of IPR on the new trade round's agenda would be without prejudice to other complementary initiatives that may be taken in the World Intellectual Property Organization and elsewhere to deal with these matters".[7] At the time, negotiations were already occurring in WIPO and developing countries, in particular, preferred this negotiation forum, not only because it was more democratic and there were no

---

Ten Years of the TRIPS Agreement: TRIPS and its Discontents, 10 Marq. Intell. Prop. L. Rev. Also see Robert J. Pechman (1994) Multilateral Protection for Intellectual Property: The United States "TRIPS" over Special 301, 7 Minn. J. Global Trade, 179.

4. See Thomas Cottier (1991) The Prospects for Intellectual Property in the GATT, 28 Common Market Law Review, 383, 385. See Report to the United States Trade Representative (1988) Foreign Protection of Intellectual Property Rights and the Effect on U.S. Industry and Trade, United States International Trade Commission Publication 2065, Washington, D.C.: USITC (studying the economic effects of inadequate international protection of intellectual property and concluding that the sales of infringing goods may represent an average profit of 10 per cent).

5. Adopted 20 March 1883, as revised at Stockholm 14 July 1967, in 828 UNTS, 305 [hereinafter referred to as the Paris Convention].

6. See GATT (1986) Ministerial Declaration on the Uruguay Round: Declaration of 20 September 1986 (Min. Dec.), in GATT, Basic Instruments and Selected Documents [BISD], reprinted in 25 ILM, 1623, 1626.

7. Ibid.

so-called "green rooms" where they could be pressured to make un-wanted compromises but also because developing countries had targeted the WIPO negotiations to produce results on technology transfer, some-thing these countries had been pursuing for several years as a strategy for international IPR reform.

The Ministerial Declaration delayed the transfer of the major IPR ne-gotiations to the GATT up until 1989, but this soon changed for three main reasons. Firstly, in the late 1980s, the US introduced new regula-tions, which took unilateral trade retaliation against states that condoned unfair practices on IPRs and rewarded countries that initiated domestic legislation to protect foreign IPRs. Secondly, as O. Adede recounts, de-veloping countries began to view the US position on IPRs in the round as an opportunity to get concessions on key areas of their interests such as on issues of textiles and agriculture.[8] Finally, developing countries also began to realize that their proposals for the inclusion of technology transfer were going nowhere in the context of WIPO and, after the 1988 Mid-Term Review of GATT Round Progress in Montreal, they were able to convince the US to take this issue more seriously under the round.[9]

By 1990, negotiations on a TRIPS Agreement finally started to move. At the Eleventh Session of the Trade Negotiating Committee (TNC) of the Multilateral Trade Negotiation (MTN), the European Community tabled a proposal that made major headway in the negotiations. Up until this point, the EC had also only reluctantly engaged in the negotiations on IPR but eventually came to the viewpoint that IPR was not going to make any progress in WIPO with the US resistance and therefore it de-cided to take a positive approach to attempting to get agreement under the Uruguay Round.

The European proposal was a comprehensive draft of a full TRIPS Agreement text, including all areas of intellectual property that had been proposed at the time. The European submission proposed to make IPR nothing short of an integral area of the GATT.[10] Three other pro-posals by the US,[11] Switzerland[12] and Japan[13] all built on the basic

8. A. O. Adede (2001) *The Political Economy of the TRIPS Agreement: Origins and His-tory of Negotiations*, International Center for Trade and Sustainable Development, Multistakeholder Dialogue, Aberdare Country Club in Kenya, July 2001, available at http://www.ictsd.org/dlogue/2001-07-30/Adede.pdf#search=%22history%20of% 20TRIPS%20Agreement%20%22.
9. See GATT (1989) MTN/11 (21 April).
10. See GATT (1990) MTN, GNG/NG 11, W/68 (29 March).
11. See GATT (1990) MTN.GNG/NG. 11/W/ 70 (11 May).
12. See GATT (1990) MTN/GNG/NG. 11/W/73 (14 May).
13. See GATT (1990) MTN/GNG/NG 11/W/74 (15 May).

architecture of the EC proposal.[14] A fifth draft agreement was tabled by 12 developing countries (Argentina, Brazil, Chile, China, Colombia, Cuba, Egypt, India, Nigeria, Peru, Tanzania and Uruguay), later joined by Pakistan and Zimbabwe.[15] The developing country proposal was divided into two distinct sections, one on issues relating to IPR trade in counterfeit and pirated goods and the second dealing with standards and principles of IPR. The strategy behind the division was that the developing countries wished to demonstrate their support for measures concerning the trade of counterfeit and pirated goods, an area very sensitive to US industry, but, according to some commentators, these countries also wished to minimize the creation of standards that would be imposed on their burgeoning domestic industries and to ensure that there were safeguard measures for protecting their industry.[16]

The eleventh session of the TNC resulted in a chairman's text that combined all five proposals, with square brackets around the areas of disagreement, into a composite draft. This draft became the primary negotiating document and, after several rounds of hard negotiations, it finally led to a text that left only 20 issues (mostly on patents) still under disagreement as well as a decision on the institutional framework for the agreement.[17] This text was forwarded to the 1991 Brussels Ministerial Meeting where it was finalized in the last quarter of 1991 and led to the tabling of the text that formed part of the Draft Final Act in December 1991. As a result of these discussions and progress made at the Brussels meeting, the text adopted at Marrakech Final Act, which concluded the Uruguay Round in 1992 and established the WTO, contained only very small revisions compared to the Draft Final Act Agreement.[18]

Two areas of the TRIPS negotiating history that relate to genetic resources, and are important to highlight for the purpose of this analysis, concern the coverage of patentable subject matter under Article 27.3 and the inclusion of environment as an exception to patents under Article 27.2. According to the WTO Secretariat's account of the TRIPS Article 27, negotiating most of the general areas of what could be included as patentable was relatively easily agreed at the outset of the negotiations and thus was the subject of less controversial discussions.[19] In contrast,

14. J. Reinbothe and A. Howard (1991) *The State of Play in the Negotiations on TRIPS (GATT/Uruguay Round)*, 5 EIPR, 157.
15. See Annex 1 GATT. MTN/GNG/NG 11/W71 of 14 May 1990.
16. Op. cit. Adede, 13.
17. WTO (1991) MTN.TNC/W/35/Rev.1 (December 1991).
18. WTO, *TRIPS and Environment*, WT/CTE/W/8, para. 81.
19. Ibid., para. 82.

the exceptions to the general rules on areas concerning public order and morality and the issue on patenting of plants and animals were points of contention. According to the Secretariat, three proposals were made concerning the coverage of patents in this area:

- The first was that there should be no permissible exception in this regard;
- The second was along the lines of the language found in Article 53 (b) of the European Patent Convention, namely that plant and animal varieties and essentially biological processes for the production of plants or animals, other than microbiological processes or the products thereof, could be excluded from patentability. Plant varieties, however, would have to be protected either by patents and/or by an effective *sui generis* system;
- The third was a broader exception which would cover any plant or animal-processes for the production of plants or animals and would also allow further limitations as regards biotechnological inventions.[20]

A comprise was eventually struck that combined these issues with other outstanding issues under the negotiations. The compromise was called the "patent complex package" and agreed on language based on the second proposal with some slight modifications but with the understanding that the provisions, which became the famous Article 27.3 (b), would be reviewed five years after TRIPS had come into force. This of course has now occurred and has been reinforced by a mandate under the negotiations of the Doha Round. The implications of this clause for the CBD and International Treaty will be closely examined below.

Article 27.2 in the provisions relates to exceptions to TRIPS that allow a contracting member of TRIPS to ban or reject a patent on the grounds of "ordre public". The proposal to include an environmental exception under this article did not actually occur until very late in the negotiations. According to the WTO Secretariat's historical account of the formulation of this clause, there were two options that were seriously proposed. One, referring to the need "to protect the environment" and "to avoid serious prejudice to the environment" and a second proposal that "provided that such exclusion [referring to the environment] is not made merely because the exploitation is prohibited by their law".[21] Apparently, the reason for this additional proposal was to ensure that the use of the environmental exception could not be interpreted as grounds to ban a patent "pending the completion of the normal testing procedures necessary to establish their effectiveness and safety prior to the grant of marketing approval".[22] More importantly, there was a concern

20. Ibid., para. 83.
21. Ibid., para. 88.
22. Ibid.

to ensure consistency with language contained under Article 4 *quater* of the Paris Convention.[23] In this regard, the final formulation contained under Article 27.2 reflects this compromise.

General comparison and overview of TRIPS provisions relating to genetic resources[24]

The TRIPS Agreement was created to ensure global standards on IPR and grants private rights on inventions in all areas of technology with a few exceptions. The purpose of TRIPS is to reduce distortions and impediments to international trade, promote adequate protection of intellectual property rights and ensure that measures and procedures to enforce intellectual property rights do not themselves become barriers to legitimate trade.[25] These goals should be read in conjunction with the provisions contained in Article 7, which are supporting provisions and contribute to the aforementioned objectives. Article 7 states that the TRIPS Agreement should contribute to technological innovation, transfer and dissemination of technology for the benefit of both users and producers in a manner which is conducive to social and economic welfare.[26] TRIPS is an agreement designed to make private rights time-bound and does not recognize collective rights or indefinite rights as normally needed for the protection of traditional knowledge.[27] The TRIPS Agreement has no requirements on benefit-sharing or on prior informed consent.

The TRIPS Agreement is the most comprehensive multilateral agreement on intellectual property. This claim is true mainly because it does not replace existing rules but rather subsumes them – in many cases well-practised rules that have been around since the turn of the last century. For example, the Paris Convention (adopted in 1883), which has gone through a number of revisions and has around 160 members, is considered the basic international system on patenting and industrial property and provides rights such as:

23. Article 4 *quater* of the Paris Convention reads as follows: "The grant of a patent shall not be refused and a patent shall not be invalidated on the ground that the sale of the patented product or of a product obtained by means of a patented process is subject to restrictions or limitations resulting from the domestic law."
24. For an early study on the impact of TRIPS on the CBD, see CBD (1996) *Impact of Intellectual Property Rights on the Sustainable Use and Equitable Benefit-Sharing of Genetic Resources*, UNEP/CBD/COP/3/22 (22 September).
25. TRIPS, Article 1.
26. TRIPS, Article 7.
27. TRIPS, Article 12 (life of the person or no less than 50 years for copyright protection).

- National treatment; each party to the Paris Convention must treat foreign patents as its does its national patents;
- Right of priority; when a patent is filed in a member state the patentee has 6 to 12 months to apply for protection in another member state and it will still be considered as if the filing date was the first date the patent was registered in the original country;
- Common rules on prohibiting the registration of well-known trademarks, including imitations, translations etc.
- Creation of administrative bodies under the Paris Convention.

TRIPS uses these existing treaties under the World Intellectual Property Organization not only on industrial property but other large accepted conventions like the Berne Convention, which protects Literary and Artistic Works, the Rome Convention, which protects the Performers, Producers of Phonograms and Broadcasting Organizations, and the IPIC (Treaty on Intellectual Property in Respect of Integrated Circuits), which protects integrated circuits.

The added-value of TRIPS is that it enhances these existing treaties by filling in some of the gaps where these treaties did not adequately address issues concerning compulsory licensing, details on the subject matter that are patentable, enforcement and remedies. It also supplements these treaties with basic GATT principles such as National Treatment (NT) and Most Favoured Nations (MFN) and exceptions, apart from the case of morality in the Berne Convention where the GATT members negotiating the TRIPS Agreement could not agree on what should and should not be included for copyright.

In GATT Article XX are the general rules of exceptions, including for the environment,[28] and they also apply to TRIPS as well as to all WTO Agreements.[29] However, these exceptions must be read in conjunction with TRIPS' own exceptions for patents, *ordre public* or morality, which, as was discussed earlier, explicitly determine the right to exclude inventions dangerous to human, animal or plant life or health, or which seriously prejudice the environment. Excluded from patents are also di-

---

28. GATT Article XX (d) and (g) cover the exceptions concerning environment. These exceptions must be "provisionally justified" before turning to determine if the measure were necessary in accordance with the with the Article XX's chapeau. See *United States – Standards for Reformulated and Conventional Gasoline*, WT/DS2/9 (20 May 1996). This interpretation has continued in subsequent panels and WTO appellate reports. See *United States – Import Prohibition of Certain Shrimp and Shrimp Products*, WT/DS58/AB/R (12 October 1998).
29. See WTO Agreement, Article 2, in *Brazil – Desiccated Coconut*; the Appellate Body referred to Articles II:2 and II:4 and Annex 1A of the WTO Agreement, as well as the DSU, to illustrate the "single undertaking" coverage of the WTO Agreement. See *Brazil Measures Affecting Desiccated Coconut*, WT/DS22/AB/R (1997), 12.

agnostic, therapeutic and surgical methods for the treatment of humans and animals, and patents on plants other than micro-organisms or non-biological and microbiological processes for the production of plants and animals.[30]

Specific principles of TRIPS (Article 8) recognize the rights of members to adopt their own measures to protect public health and public interests and to prevent the abuse of intellectual property rights so long as these measures are consistent with the provisions of the TRIPS Agreement.

The TRIPS Agreement sets out detailed rules on enforcing IPRs. These include civil and administrative procedures and remedies, provisional measures, special requirements related to border measures and even criminal procedures. The WTO, of course, does not directly enforce these rules as it is not a private international law treaty but it can take another WTO member to a binding dispute settlement system for not enforcing these rules. All TRIPS provisions are in fact subject to WTO dispute settlement, so, if TRIPS is not adhered to, and this affects a WTO member and the member takes the dispute to a panel and/or appellate body and loses, the member will have to rectify the situation or be subject to trade retaliation.[31]

Lastly, the TRIPS Agreement has created a monitoring body within the WTO to look after the Agreement and the parties. This is the so-called TRIPS Council.[32] Its job is: (1) to review national legislation by the parties implementing the TRIPS Agreement (and the implementation procedures were staggered so that the poorest countries of the world were given more time to develop their IPR law and TRIPS requirements); (2) to provide a forum for any problems related to TRIPS between countries; (3) to clarify rules and interpretations; (4) to provide technical cooperation and assistance to developing countries; and (5) to provide a negotiating forum built into the TRIPS Agreement as in the review of 27.3 (b), geographical indications for wines and any new developments. It also serves as the negotiating forum for areas handed down from the Ministerial Conference or General Council. For example, under the Doha Declaration there is an important decision on TRIPS and access to essential medicines taken by the Council.[33]

---

30. TRIPS, Article 27.3 (b).
31. See Dispute Settlement Understanding in Annex 2 of Marrakech Agreement Establishing the World Trade Organization [hereinafter WTO Agreement], Annex 1C, Legal Instruments-Results of the Uruguay Round, Vol. 31, 33 I.L.M. (1994), 81.
32. TRIPS Article 68.
33. See WTO (2003) *Implementation of paragraph 6 of the Doha Declaration on the TRIPS Agreement and Public Health*, WT/L/540 and Corr.1.

When TRIPS is compared with the CBD and the ITPGRFA, the relationship can be viewed as one of tension and intense debate, as will be seen in the subsequent analysis. This has been mainly due to political factors from the US Senate's reluctance so far to ratify the CBD.[34] In 1992, at the end of the CBD negotiations, the US publicly announced its dissatisfaction with the outcome of the Agreement, stating that it viewed the outcome of the CBD negotiations as hurried and it did not adequately take into account areas it believed conflicted with issues pertaining to IPR. The signing of the CBD carries the following declaration to this effect made by the US:

> It is deeply regrettable to us that ... whether because of the haste with which we have completed our work or the result of substantive disagreement ... a number of issues of serious concern in the United States have not been adequately addressed in the course of this negotiation. As a result, in our view, the text is seriously flawed in a number of important respects.[35]

The US non-ratification of the CBD and subsequently the ITPGRFA has led to concerns over the compatibility of these treaties. Moreover, the US has repeatedly blocked the CBD Secretariat from attaining observership on the TRIPS Council. Despite these reservations, the three treaties have provisions for guiding their overlapping relationship. Both the CBD and its Bonn Guidelines, as well as the ITPGRFA, recognize the possible interlinkages in specific sections and attempt to balance their jurisdiction with that of the WTO's. The ITPGRFA is the most explicit and recognizes the possible overlap through its preamble, taking a very similar approach to that used in the Cartagena Protocol. It states that nothing in the ITPGRFA changes the rights and obligations in other relevant treaties. However, the preceding paragraph of the preamble asserts that the aforementioned clause in no way creates a hierarchy between itself and other international agreements. It also clarifies that the ITPGRFA and other international agreements must be mutually supportive. The CBD Bonn Guidelines also have similar provisions.

The approach used in the CBD and the ITPGRFA is a political compromise between those countries that would like new agreements to avoid interference with the WTO and those that believe that the WTO should be ancillary to new treaties. However, as seen in chapter 3 in the case of the Cartagena Protocol, this compromise solves very little. Overlap does exist and the two Agreements will not be mutually compatible

---

34. Concerning why the US Senate rejected ratifying the CBD Treaty see the testimony of Senator Hutchinson in Congressional Record S13790, Friday, 30 September 1994, available at http://www.sovereignty.net/p/land/crhutchison.htm.
35. As cited in WTO (1995) *Environment and TRIPS*, WT/CTE/W/8, 60.

until there is stronger recognition of potential and actual overlap. The language now used in the ITPGRFA and CBD only serves to create uncertainty and risks future conflict between the two treaties. In the event of conflict, it is probable that the treaty with the strongest dispute settlement system will end up having preferential consideration, which, in the current circumstance, will be the WTO under its DSU.

On the side of the WTO there have been some reassurances as to the compatibility of its provisions with those of the multilateral actions such as MEAs, though there has yet to be a WTO case that has used an MEA as grounds to justify an exception under GATT Article XX. In *Dolphin-Tuna*, the GATT recognized that the US action against Mexico was unjustified because it had not exhausted other efforts under international law to protect dolphins: "The United States had not demonstrated to the panel ... that it had exhausted all options reasonably available ... in particular through the negotiation of international cooperative agreements". This early ruling implied that internationally adopted standards such as those pursuant to MEAs could be grounds for justifying an exception.[36]

These grounds have continued to appear occasionally under WTO jurisprudence. In *US-Gasoline* the WTO Appellate Body found that "WTO Members are free to adopt their own policies aimed at protecting the environment as long as in so doing they fulfil their obligations and respect the rights of other Members under the WTO Agreement."[37]

In 2001, *Shrimp-Turtle* came the closest to implying that the exception pursuant to an MEA would be justifiable under WTO rules:

> We [referring to the Appellate Body] have not decided that sovereign states should not act together bilaterally, plurilaterally or multilaterally, either within the WTO or in other international fora, to protect endangered species or to otherwise protect the environment. Clearly, they should and do.[38]

This has led many to believe that, in the event of a dispute, so long as the measure was applied equally to the national and foreign product and deemed to be necessary[39] in that it was "the least trade-restrictive

---

36. *Dolphin-Tuna* (1991).
37. See *United States – Gasoline* WTO Appellate Body Report, WT/DS2/AB/R, (20 May 1996), 30.
38. See *US – Shrimp* WTO Appellate Body Report, WT/DS58/AB/R (12 October 1998), para. 185.
39. See *EC – Asbestos* WTO Appellate Body Report, WT/DS135/AB/R (12 March 2001). The Appellate Body confirmed that a measure is "necessary" within the meaning of *GATT* Article XX (b) "if an alternative measure which [a Member] could reasonably be expected to employ and which is not inconsistent with other GATT provisions is [not] available to it". This was also found in US-Gasoline panel, see Panel Report on *US-Gasoline*, WT/DS2/R, 29 January 1996, paras. 6.26 and 6.28.

measure" at the disposal of the policy-maker, then, if pursuant to an MEA, this could represent legitimate grounds under GATT Articles XX (b) and (g), the two general exception articles under the WTO for the environment.

Applying the framework to these cases[40]

Meeting the treaty's objectives

At first glance, the objectives of the CBD and the International Treaty would seem to have nothing in common with the TRIPS Agreement. The objective of TRIPS is to put in place standards for intellectual property rights in national legislation in order to reduce barriers to international trade, while the CBD and the ITPGRFA were created to promote conservation and sustainable use of biodiversity and food security. A closer examination of the Agreements, however, shows that there is an overarching goal that binds all three instruments and makes their respective objectives broadly compatible, and that is the goal of sustainable development. Sustainable development appears prominently in the objectives of CBD and ITPGRFA and also in TRIPS Agreement's overarching preamble as contained in its umbrella framework under the 1994 Agreement Establishing the WTO. Here the TRIPS preamble states that:

> ... while allowing for the optimal use of the world's resources in accordance with the objective of sustainable development, seeking both to protect and preserve the environment and to enhance the means for doing so in a manner consistent with their respective needs and concerns at different levels of economic development ...

Article 2.2 of the WTO Agreement clearly establishes that its preamble applies *inter alia* to TRIPS.[41]

The goal of sustainable development appears in both the CBD and ITPGRFA's overall objectives and preamble. Article 1 of the CBD states that "sustainable use" of components of biological diversity is a core objective of the treaty. The CBD preamble states that parties should use their resources in a "sustainable manner" though they remain the sover-

---

40. For an early paper on the synergies between TRIPS and CBD see CBD (1996) *CBD and TRIPS: Relationship and Synergies*, UNEP/CBD/COP/3/23 (5 October).
41. Article 2.2 makes reference to the Agreement establishing that the WTO is "binding" and an integral part of the agreements listed in Annex One including TRIPS. Also see *Brazil – Desiccated Coconut* (1997).

eign property of the party; Article 8 (e) also makes reference to promoting sustainable development in areas adjacent to protected areas as a way of further protecting them. Like TRIPS and the CBD, the ITPGRFA makes reference to sustainable development in its preamble but it also makes numerous other references to the principle throughout its text. The primary provisions are found in Article 1, which states that the objective of the treaty is sustainable use of plant genetic resources for food and agriculture. These provisions are operationalized through the treaty text. In all, there are 24 references to sustainable development or sustainable use but the strongest operational reference is in Article 6 which states that parties must create appropriate polices and measures at the national level which will promote the sustainable use of agricultural plant resources.[42]

However, what does all this mean when it comes to actually implementing the individual objectives of each specific instrument? Unfortunately, the goal of sustainable development itself is broad and multidimensional and thus it is hard to realize how the three instruments could collaborate to work together for the same cause. Most of the literature which draws together the CBD and TRIPS and, to a lesser extent, the ITPGRFA (as the treaty is relatively new), speaks very little of the positive compatibility and much more of the potential incongruence, which makes comparisons rather difficult so the tendency to see the TRIPS Agreement in a critical way predominates.[43] This is mainly because of the cross-sectoral dimension between the Agreements – the fact that TRIPS, on the one hand, promotes the economic dimension of sustainable development while the CBD and the ITPGRFA, on the other, deal more firmly with the environmental dimension.

The lack of understanding of the cross-sector dimension is one of the greatest shortcomings of the concept of sustainable development. The concept, to a large degree, has been captured by the environmental community and is often taken as a catchword synonymous simply with

---

42. ITPGRFA, Article 6.1.
43. There is a vast literature on incompatibilities between CBD and TRIPS. See for example: Cynthia M. Ho (2006) *Biopiracy and Beyond: A Consideration of the Socio-Cultural Conflicts with Global Patent Polices*, 39 University of Michigan Journal of Law Reform, 433; Charles Lawson and Susan Downing (2002), *It's Patently Absurd – Benefit-Sharing Genetic Resources from the Sea Under UNCLOS, the CBD and TRIPS*, 5 Journal of International Wildlife Law and Policy 3, 211; Noah Zerbe (2002) *Contested Ownership: TRIPS, CBD, and Implications for Southern African Biodiversity*, 1 Perspectives on Global Development and Technology, 294: Muria Kruger (2001) *Harmonizing TRIPS and the CBD: A Proposal from India*, 10 Minn. J. Global Trade, 1, 169; Valentina Tejera (1999) *Tripping over Property Rights: Is It Possible to Reconcile the Convention on Biological Diversity with Article 27 of the TRIPS Agreement?*, 33 New England Law Review, 967.

environment, instead of considered in its original meaning of supporting a balance of the three pillars of social equity, economic development and environmental protection.[44] It is only now, through the lens of initiatives such as the Millennium Development Goals and processes such as the World Summit of Sustainable Development and the Monterrey Process, that there has been a gradual understanding of the links and feedback loops of sustainable development to public health, economic growth and poverty reduction as well as sustainable use of the environment.[45]

When taken in this broader light of sustainable development, the compatibility between instruments such as CBD and TRIPS is much closer than what the literature has portrayed (a clash between the industrialists and the environmentalists) and, if seen in this light, the links can be argued as being a sound basis for comparison of how these instruments could collaborate and could further strengthen the synergies that exist between the Agreements.[46]

Thus, looking at the TRIPS Agreement through the lens of sustainable development shows TRIPS in a particular light: it is seen to be promoting economic growth by stabilizing investment rules, to be encouraging innovation and development of new technology through intellectual property right protection and to be ensuring that services developed locally are afforded adequate protection from piracy and unlawful use[47] – for sustainable development, greater investment and economic growth can mean (under the right circumstances) poverty reduction, greater freedom of choice and higher standards of protection from unlawfully produced products, and innovation in new technologies could benefit sectors such as health care and welfare. In *US – Shrimp*, the Appellate Body discussed the meaning of the preamble stating that:

44. See the Brundtland Report, *Our Common Future*, in General Assembly A/42/427 (1987). Sustainable Development is defined as "development that meets the needs of the present without compromising the ability of future generations to meet their own needs".
45. See UNEP (2005) *Concept Note: Mainstreaming Environment beyond MDG 7, A High-Level Brainstorming Workshop* (July) available at http://www.unep.org/dec/docs/ Mainstreaming_environment_concept_paper.doc.
46. See Gary Sampson (2005) *The WTO and Sustainable Development*, Tokyo: UNU Press, 3.
47. The view has been expressed by some countries that the objectives of the CBD and TRIPS are entirely compatible arguing that patents can ensure the sharing of benefits and the conservation of biological diversity by granting licensing arrangements through material transfer agreements or "based on voluntary contracts; the requirements of the patent system material to patentability and inventorship can help prevent bad patents; the control over production and distribution given to patent owners and their licensees can facilitate the sharing of technology; and the protection of undisclosed information could help the implementation of biosafety and benefit-sharing rules". See WTO IP/C/ W/434, IP/C/W/257, IP/C/M/30, United States Communication on Relationship TRIPS to CBD, para. 154.

We note once more that this language [referring to the preamble] demonstrates a recognition by WTO negotiators that optimal use of the world's resources should be made in accordance with the objective of sustainable development. As this preambular language reflects the intentions of negotiators of the WTO Agreement, we believe it must add colour, texture and shading to our interpretation of the agreements annexed to the WTO Agreement, in this case, the GATT 1994.[48]

These goals, as set out in the WTO Agreement preamble and the interpretation of the WTO Appellate Body in *Shrimp-Turtle*, are certainly compatible with the CBD and ITPGRFA. Creating a stable investment environment and intellectual property standards are important to the CBD and ITPGRFA's broad objectives of sustainable use. In the context of the sustainable use of plant genetic resources, there are development opportunities for countries in pharmaceuticals, cosmetics and health-care products. Estimates have put the existing market in millions of dollars and the potential market in billions of dollars.[49] Companies wishing to make investments in these countries will want to ensure that their investments are protected by regulations and minimum intellectual property rights as basic entry prerequisites. The TRIPS Agreement provides this basic environment for stable investment and investor confidence. Unfortunately, the focus in the literature on sustainable use of genetic resources has not concentrated largely on the positive side of TRIPS, in other words the very fact that TRIPS provides the ground rules for stable investment. Instead, the focus has been on the failures of TRIPS (in some instances) to provide adequate protection to the genetic resource providers or on its not having adequately taken into account the special nature and requirements set out in the objectives of the CBD or the ITPGRFA.[50]

These objectives generally fall into the context of the protection of traditional knowledge or conditionalities that the CBD and ITPGRFA require, such as prior informed consent and benefit-sharing. Objectives, if looked at realistically, would not be well served or easily solved through the CBD or the ITPGRFA alone but would require a coordinated effort with TRIPS and WIPO if effective compliance of these objectives were to be achieved. The implication of monitoring and complying with these objectives will be explored later under the compliance and monitoring part of the framework that has been set out in chapter 3 for the case studies.

48. *Shrimp-Turtle* (1999), para. 152.
49. See Kerry ten Kate and Susan Laird (2003) *Commercial Use of Biodiversity*, London: Earthscan; also see Kelly Day Rubenstein et al. (2005) *Estimated Value of Crop Genetic Resources*, available at http://www.ers.usda.gov/publications/eib2/eib2b.pdf.
50. Supra.

Nevertheless, objectives of TRIPS could be argued not only to work towards the broad objectives of sustainable development but directly to the environment pillar too. The protection that the TRIPS Agreement effectuates includes that of the protection and development of new technologies in the field of environmental goods and services. This would include new technologies that can promote greater environmental conservation, such as environmental remediation, biotechnologies producing greater crop yields, resistance to pests or weeds, reduced water usage or faster growth for carbon sequestration. The CBD has recognized this potential link but has not determined whether TRIPS, as a general instrument to promote the development of these technologies, has a more positive effect in terms of promoting such new environmental goods and services and benefits for development or a more negative effect, such as through the promotion of terminator seed (Genetic Use Restriction Technologies or GURTS) technology or reducing biodiversity by promoting biotechnologies that lead to monocultures and the dependence on fewer seed varieties.[51]

One area where the broad objectives of the CBD and ITPGRFA together could run counter to the TRIP Agreement's basic objectives concerns the patenting of life forms. This issue not only has implications for the effective compliance of the CBD and ITPGRFA, which will be explored below, but also touches on the fundamental nature of the core objectives of these Agreements and demands an answer as to whether these treaties are in fact compatible.

The conflict arises over Article 15 of the CBD and Article 12 of the ITPGRFA which clearly state that the sovereignty over genetic resources rests with the country. Conversely, TRIPS was created to provide standards for the granting of private property rights and Article 27.3 (b) of TRIPS clearly opens the possibility of patent protection of genetic resources in the form of micro-organisms. Varying views have been expressed by countries over this debate and whether these objectives of the Agreement are indeed diametrically opposed.

On one side of the debate there are those countries, such as the United States, who have argued that the discovery of an isolated gene in the natural state and which has been identified through a biochemical process does not constitute ownership by the patentee but rather a prohibition of commercialization, the use of the same process to arrive at the gene or using the gene without a licence. The EU and Japan see the patenting of life forms more directly. If a significant innovative step has led to the discovery of a new gene in its natural state and this had involved "suffi-

---

51. Supra, IP/C/W/368/Rev.1 (2006).

cient human intervention" and the gene or new micro-organism is not of a previously recognized existence", then this is capable of satisfying the requirements for patentability.[52] Many developing countries, particularly a negotiating coalition of African countries called the "African Group" and several South American countries of the Andean Community, are opposed to this and see the patenting of a gene or the process to arrive at a new gene in its natural state as constituting ownership over genetic resources and life which are the sovereign resources of the state.

The question of whether the TRIPS Agreement and the CBD objectives are compatible or opposed, which will also have implications for the ITPGRFA given its closeness to the CBD, will not just rest with the analysis of academics and speculation by civil society. In 2001, the Doha Development Agenda (DDA) put this question squarely on the negotiation table and broadened the review of TRIPS that was already under way as a requirement under Article 71.1.[53] Paragraph 19 requests the WTO members to look at the "relationship between the TRIPS Agreement and the Convention on Biological Diversity, the protection of traditional knowledge and folklore".[54]

During the interim of the review of the TRIPS Agreement and the outcome of the Doha Round and despite the reservations that have already been expressed by various commentators concerning the compatibility of the CBD and TRIPS objectives, both decision-making bodies of the respective Conventions have recognized the potential mutual supportiveness that the treaties could share if greater cooperation were better cultivated.[55] If the good nature expressed by the CBD COPs and the TRIPS Council were developed and greater exploitation of the interlinkages between the TRIPS and the CBD/ITPGRFA were materialized, there would be a higher likelihood for greater effectiveness for all three Agreements under the broad umbrella of sustainable development than any could achieve alone. It is also plausible that, although these instruments are broadly compatible, the perverse incompatibility concerning the patenting of life forms could be worked on, as seems to be the approach now under way in the TRIPS review and the Doha Development Agenda. Similar conclusions will be seen as this analysis works its way through the other areas of examination under the analytical framework.

52. Infra, IP/C/W/368/Rev.1.
53. WTO (2001) Doha Declaration, WT/MIN(01)/DEC/W/1 (14 November), para. 19.
54. Ibid.
55. See CBD Decision III/17 or WTO WT/CTE/W/44, which states: "the potential mutual benefits of exchanging information related to Article 16 of the Convention on Biological Diversity and the laws and regulations received by the Council on Trade-Related Aspects of Intellectual Property Rights pursuant to notification requirement of Article 63 of the Agreement on Trade-Related Aspects of Intellectual Property Rights".

Meeting the treaty's supporting provisions

The issue of technology transfer as set out in the CBD, International Treaty and TRIPS is the only common area within each of these respective instruments' supporting provisions. The CBD contains several paragraphs that refer to the role of technology transfer and how the promotion of it can lead to the achievement of the CBD's overall objectives. Article 16.1 states that parties should "undertake to provide and/or facilitate access for and transfer to other contracting parties of technologies that are relevant to the conservation and sustainable use of biological diversity or make use of genetic resources and which do not cause significant damage to the environment".[56] The clause was based on the consensus that was reached at the 1992 UNCED, both under Agenda 21[57] and the Rio Declaration.[58] Since this time, it has also been reinforced in important documents such as the Johannesburg Plan of Implementation.[59] The premise behind these provisions is that technological know-how, not necessarily so-called "hard technology" such as infrastructure or new innovative goods but rather information and knowledge, can assist developing countries to achieve the CBD objectives of conservation and sustainable use of biodiversity. This could include management practices, monitoring systems or pest control methods.[60] Article 16.2 goes on to state that access and transfer of technology to developing countries "shall be provided and/or facilitated under fair and most favourable terms, including on concessional and preferential terms where mutually agreed, and, where necessary, in accordance with the financial mechanism established by Articles 20 and 21".[61] Paragraph 2, however, states that such access and transfer "shall be provided on terms that recognize and are consistent with the adequate and effective protection of intellectual property rights".[62] Article 16.3 requires that parties take legislative, administrative or policy measures "with the aim that Parties which pro-

---

56. CBD Article 16.1.
57. See UN (1992) Agenda 21, UN A.CONF/151/26, chapter 34.
58. See Principle 9 of *Rio de Janeiro Declaration on Environment and Development*, UN A/CONF.151.5 [hereinafter Rio Declaration] (16 June 1992).
59. See Johannesburg Plan of Implementation [hereinafter JPOI], *Report of the World Summit on Sustainable Development*, A/CONF.199/20, 4 September 2002.
60. The CBD Subsidiary Body on Technical and Technological Advice [hereinafter SBSTTA] has drawn up an indicative list of the types of technologies that this could include. See CBD (2003) *Technology Transfer and Cooperation, Indicative List of Technologies for Conservation and Sustainable use of Biological Diversity*, UNEP/CBD/SBSTTA/9/INF/13.
61. CBD, Article 16.2.
62. Ibid.

vide genetic resources, in particular those that are developing countries, are provided access to and transfer of technology which makes use
of those resources, on mutually agreed terms, including technology protected by patents and other intellectual property rights, where necessary,
through the provisions of Articles 20 and 21 and in accordance with international law".[63] Paragraph 4 requires parties "to take legislative, administrative or policy measures with the aim that the private sector facilitates
access to joint development and transfer of technology for the benefit
of both governmental institutions and the private sector of developing
countries".[64]

The provisions under the ITPGRFA are similar to the CBD's. However, they are viewed as a benefit derived from accesses to the Multilateral System rather than on bilateral terms as under the CBD. Article 13
states that "Contracting Parties agree that benefits arising from the
use, including commercial, of plant genetic resources for food and agriculture under the Multilateral System shall be shared fairly and equitably
through" *inter alia* the transfer of technology.[65] Article 13.2 (b) states
what types of technologies developing countries might benefit from and
reconfirms, as in the CBD, that these are unlikely to be "hard technologies" but rather the transfer of knowledge and technical know-how.
Under Article 13.2 (b) the ITPGRFA affirms that the transfer of technology should respect intellectual property rights but, even for those technologies that are protected by such rights, access should be "provided/
facilitated" to developing and least developing countries and countries
with economies in transition "under fair and most favourable terms", in
particular in the case of technologies for use in "conservation as well as
technologies for the benefit of farmers" in these countries.[66]

The TRIPS Agreement makes two indirect references to technology
transfer in its preamble and stipulates two positive obligations concerning
how this should be achieved in the body of the Agreement. The TRIPS
preamble notes the importance of intellectual property rights (IPR) to
technological development and the need of least developing countries to
have flexibility in implementing their domestic laws in order to achieve a
technological base.[67] The preamble thus sets up the link between IPR
and technological development but conditions this with a certain degree
of flexibility for least developing and developing countries when implementing the obligations of the TRIPS Agreement.

63. CBD, Article 16.3.
64. CBD, Article 16.4.
65. ITPGFA, Article 13.2.
66. ITPGRFA, Article 13.2 (b) iii.
67. TRIPS, Preamble.

Article 7 of TRIPS states that:

The protection and enforcement of intellectual property rights should contribute to the promotion of technological innovation and to the transfer and dissemination of technology, to the mutual advantage of producers and users of technological knowledge and in a manner conducive to social and economic welfare, and to a balance of rights and obligations.[68]

Article 7 reinforces the link between IPR and technological transfer found in the preambular language and further states outright that the protection and enforcement of IPR as required under the TRIPS Agreement should lead to the transfer of technology. It is worth noting here that Article 7 does not set up any specific programmes or mechanisms that would positively ensure that the transfer of technology takes place, but it merely states that one should reasonably follow the other. In other words, this means that, if TRIPS is put in place nationally and enforced effectively, then the benefit of the TRIPS regime should create the right conditions for technology transfer to flow. The TRIPS Agreement therefore predicates that technology transfer is a spin-off of its successful implementation through private transactions.

This link between IPR and technological transfer is quite controversial and many economists have admittedly commented that the evidence for technology transfer occurring as a result of IPR is imprecise.[69] The proponents that argue in favour of TRIPS resulting in technology transfer follow the logic that companies with new technologies will be more apt to invest in economies that have created minimum protection for their products, including against piracy and other unlawful uses. Opponents of this viewpoint have argued that the presence of the technology in an economy does not necessarily ensure the benefit of offshoots, such as local adaptation and derivatives, or that learning or training of locals will indeed take place. For example, some studies have shown that 80 per cent of transfers by US corporations and 95 per cent by German corporations in 1995 were made on an internal basis, compared to 69 per cent and 92 per cent respectively in 1985. This shows a rather declining trend and demonstrates perhaps that with the advent of more globalization and international deregulation through new global rules such as the General Agreement on the Trade of Services[70] that countries are no longer depending on local firms for selling their technology. Instead, they are set-

---

68. TRIPS, Article 7.
69. See David M. Gould and William C. Gruben (1996) *The Role of Intellectual Property Rights in Economic Growth*, 48 J. Dev. Econ., 323.
70. See WTO Agreement, Annex 2 (General Agreement on the Trade in Services) [hereinafter GATS].

ting up their own firms and franchises and transferring the technology to these firms instead of local indigenous ones.[71]

The WTO Agreement, however, tries in a way to compensate for this gap in Article 66.2 which obliges developed countries to "provide incentives to enterprises and institutions in their territories for the purpose of promoting and encouraging technology transfer to least-developed country Members in order to enable them to create a sound and viable technological base".[72] This clause requires positive action to take place to ensure that the transfer of technology does indeed occur. For a number of years this clause was a source of contention for least developing countries, which were promised the benefits of adhering to TRIPS but observed that they were receiving very little in technology transfer. Thus, in 2001, during the Doha Ministerial meeting, the least developing countries successfully tabled a requirement to make Article 66.2 more effective by requiring that each developed country should report the actions and incentives that it has undertaken for ensuring transfer and for monitoring the implementation of the obligations under 66.2.[73]

Coming back to our comparison with CBD and the ITPGRFA, the TRIP provisions on technical transfer are generally compatible in two ways. Firstly, the CBD and ITPGRFA request developed countries to provide the transfer of technology on the fairest and most favourable terms, including on "concessional and preferential" terms, where mutually agreed, while also remaining consistent with international regimes for IPR such as the TRIPS Agreement. While TRIPS does not use this direct language it is possible to interpret the TRIPS provisions concerning technology transfer to be entirely consistent with these goals.

The preambular language on technology transfer of the WTO Agreement states that its objectives should be met in a manner consistent with the respective needs and concerns of members at different levels of development.[74] Developed countries are charged with the obligation of providing incentives for the flow of technology to occur and not just to rely on the effects of the implementation of the TRIPS Agreement. Article 67 further states that developed country members should provide, on request and on mutually agreed terms and conditions, technical and financial cooperation in their favour.[75] Thus, it could be argued that, through these articles, there is a general obligation requiring developed

---

71. See non-paper submitted to the WTO by India (February 1999), available at http://www.indianembassy.org/policy/WTO/wto_india/ipt_india_02_99.htm.
72. TRIPS, Article 66.2.
73. WTO (2003) *Decision to Implement Article 66.2 of the TRIPS Agreement*, IP/C/28 (20 February).
74. Ibid., WTO Preamble.
75. TRIPS, Article 67.

country members of the WTO to bring about easy access to, and wide dissemination of, technology relevant to developing members and that this could include those members wishing to have technologies to improve their achievement in areas including sustainable development.[76]

A parallel between the TRIPS and CBD Article 16 can also be drawn in respect of the prevention of technologies that may threaten sustainable development. CBD Article 16.5 mandates contracting parties to the Convention to cooperate in order to ensure that patents and other intellectual property rights are supportive and do not run counter to the objectives of the Convention. This provision stipulates that CBD parties should prevent the abusive use of intellectual property rights which might impair the attainment of the Convention's objectives. Again, a parallel might be argued between 16.5 of the CBD and Articles 8 and 40 of the TRIPS Agreement, which contain principles and rules under which WTO members should control abusive practices by intellectual property rights holders. There is no reason why abusive practices could not be viewed from the scope of the environment, such as the CBD objectives, instead of just from the perspective of economic development.[77]

Broadly speaking, it is not entirely inconsistent, given the overlap in membership,[78] with the global mandate for technology transfer of sound environmental technologies coming from the global summits I have referred to above[79] and the WTO preambular mandate for sustainable development, that these three Agreements create joint programmes that could better facilitate transfer technologies. Hypothetically, these programmes could be on preferred terms to developing countries and could work towards sustainable development, including the conservation and sustainable use of plant genetic resources.[80] Such cooperation is not unfathomable and there is already a good example shown in the context of

---

76. On the parallel between Articles 16 of the CBD and Article 66.2 of the TRIPS Agreement see *Document Prepared by the International Bureau of WIPO for the Meeting on Intellectual Property and Genetic Resources 17–18 April 2000*, WTO IP/C/W/218 (2000), para. 19.

77. Ibid.

78. There is significant overlap in membership of the CBD ITPGRFA and TRIPS. As of 2005, 143 WTO members are also members of the CBD. See WTO (2005) *Membership in WTO and MEA: A Comparative Table*, available at http://www.wto.org/english/tratop_e/envir_e/membershipwtomeas_e.doc.

79. See Gaetan Verhoosel (1998) *Beyond the Unsustainable Rhetoric of Sustainable Development: Transferring Environmentally Sound Technologies*, 11 Geo. Int'l Envtl. L. Rev., 49.

80. In 1999, India proposed such a programme on the broad area of Environmentally Sound Technologies to the WTO Committee on Trade and Environment. It proposed that the owners of environmentally sound technology and products should sell such technologies and products at fair and most favourable terms and conditions upon demand to any interested party, which has an obligation to adopt these under the national law of another country or under international law. Available at http://www.indianembassy.org/policy/WTO/wto_india/ipt_india_02_99.htm.

public health where the WTO members were able to agree on a permanent arrangement under TRIPS that would promote access to pharmaceuticals for treating maladies such as HIV/AIDS.[81] Would this be so absurd for promoting other types of sustainable development goals?

There is a further argument that may justify this type of cooperation between the CBD and the TRIPS Agreement. Article 16.3 of the CBD puts technology transfer in the context of access to benefit-sharing by requiring that countries that have made their resources available should benefit from the new technologies derived from the genetic material.[82] This encourages countries to establish guidelines, legislation, administrative or policy measures, as appropriate, to ensure access from the provider countries of genetic resources. In effect, this is a dimension of ensuring that technology transfer becomes a standardized quid pro quo for access to genetic resources. However, an inherent limitation to national action, which is not foreseen under Article 16.3, is that most commercialization of genetic resources takes place through patents outside the country where the genetic resources were accessed. This would imply that most national legislation or policy measures would be outside the jurisdiction of the provider country and thus rendered ineffective in ensuring the occurrence of the type of technology transfer envisaged under Article 16.3.

As will be explored in the next section under compliance, this may call for cooperation with the TRIPS Agreements in order to ensure that CBD requirements are followed within the international patent regime. CBD Article 16.3 must be read in conjunction with its Article 16.5 which foresees the possible influence of intellectual property rights on the implementation of Article 16.3, as well as other parts of the Convention, and, therefore, states that the CBD parties should work under national and international law to ensure that IPRs do not run counter to the objectives of the Convention. I would argue that this means that contracting members of the TRIPS Agreement who also have membership in the CBD (by far the majority of members) have an obligation to ensure the harmony of the TRIPS with the CBD. In this context, it would also potentially mean ensuring some kind of conditionality of benefit-sharing under the TRIPS Agreement.

Compliance and monitoring

This section will continue to argue, as the preceding two sections have done, that there are positive interlinkages between the CBD and

---

81. See WTO (2003) *Implementation of Paragraph 6 of the Doha Declaration on the TRIPS Agreement and Public Health*, WT/L/540 and Corr.1 (1 September).
82. CBD, Article 16.3.

ITPGRFA and also the TRIPS but that these interlinkages have not always been exploited to improve the effectiveness of the three Agreements. With respect to the section on compliance and monitoring, however, the interlinkages are of a more serious nature and do not merely represent untapped potential but rather a serious threat to the compliance of these Agreements, albeit unnecessarily so if addressed positively through an interlinkages approach.

As we have seen earlier, there are a number of issues that touch on the compliance interrelationship between these Agreements; none are new, and they have been the focus of debate for some years between the CBD and TRIPS and now increasingly with respect to the ITPGRFA. As previously seen, the TRIPS Agreement, in the context of the raging trade and environment debates, is generally viewed negatively as a barrier to the compliance of CBD and ITPGRFA provisions on the protection of traditional knowledge, the principle of prior informed consent, access and benefit-sharing and the patenting of life forms. The misappropriation and application of genetic resources through the use of the global intellectual property rights regime, of which the TRIPS Agreement is the cornerstone, is also a key concern. With the launch of the Doha Development Round and a review under way on TRIPS, these issues have continued to resurface and have attained a much higher political plane.[83]

The issues of benefit-sharing, PIC and traditional knowledge[84] can be viewed as sharing a similar problem under compliance when viewed in the context of the TRIPS Agreement. All three issues have substantive obligations under the CBD and ITPGRFA but all three can be seriously undermined if an interlinkages approach with the TRIPS Agreement is not met. The reason for the commonality of the three issues is that they share a strong link with the enactment of an intellectual property right. PIC and benefit-sharing of genetic resources or associated traditional knowledge requirements can be promulgated through national regula-

---

83. TRIPS Article 71 requires the review of the implementation of the TRIPS two years after the expiration of the transitional period, which was 1999. Also see the Doha Declaration supra.
84. Access to genetic resources and intellectual property rights have a strong link with traditional knowledge as it is often this kind of local information that bioprospectors use to find leads to genetic materials that will have a practical industrial application which is eventually patented. Under the CBD, access and benefit-sharing and traditional knowledge fall under two different parts of the Convention and have had separate consultation processes; access and benefit-sharing fall under CBD Article 15 while traditional knowledge falls under Article 8 (j) and each have separate working groups deliberating on them. The International Treaty deals with traditional knowledge principally under Article 9 concerning farmers' rights.

tion, such as a permit system or licence for *in situ* plant genetic resources. This will allow a user, such as a bioprospector or drug research company, to search for an undiscovered resource or traditional knowledge but, at the moment of the access, before any discovery, the value of the potential genetic resources or associated traditional knowledge is unknown and normally remains so until the commercialization process.[85] This normally takes place after the granting of an IPR. Furthermore, access to *ex situ* plant genetic resources takes place outside the country, generally through third parties such as gene banks or botanical gardens well outside the jurisdiction of the provider country. In these cases, again the PIC and benefit-sharing generally become an issue only when a user attempts to exercise ownership over the resource through a patent or other form of IPR. From this perspective then, the PIC and benefit-sharing of a genetic resource or the associated traditional knowledge requirements are often triggered by the IPR process which, for the most part, with the exception of a few countries, has no criteria or obligation under the CBD or ITPGRFA provisions in their IPR application processes.[86]

This has led to the proposal that TRIPS should ensure the compliance of PIC and benefit-sharing and and oblige that the lawful use of traditional knowledge should have been granted by its owners to the patent applicant. Proponents of this view believe such requirements could be implemented through the use of a TRIPS standard for patent applications. This proposal is sometimes referred to as the "TRIPS disclosure proposal" and would require a patent relating to a biological material, such as a genetic resource or the use of traditional knowledge, to disclose at the time of the patent: the source and country of origin of the biological resource; the traditional knowledge used in the invention; evidence of

85. For a definition of "user" and providers of genetic resources see UNU-IAS (2003) *User Measures: Options for Developing Measures in User Countries to Implement the Access and Benefit-Sharing of the Convention of Biological Diversity*, UNU-IAS Policy Report (March).

86. Several countries do have PIC and benefit-sharing requirements for IPR on genetic resources but this practice remains relatively small in comparison to countries without these provisions. As two examples of national regulations see the Philippines Executive Order 247 titled *Prescribing Guidelines and Establishing a Regulatory Framework for the Prospecting of Biological and Genetic Resources, Their By-Products and Derivatives, for Scientific and Commercial Purposes, and for Other Purposes* passed in May 1995. Later on, this EO 247 was partially superseded by the Republic Act No. 9147 of 2001 [hereinafter Wildlife Act 2001]. The Brazilian government enacted a law called provisional measure (*Medida Provisória*) No. 2.186-16, on 23 August 2001, to implement the Articles 225, II, § 1° and § 4° of the Constitution of Brazil, and Articles 8 (j), 10 (c), 15, and 16 (3) and (4) of the Convention on Biological Diversity with regard to access to genetic resources and benefit-sharing, protection and access to traditional knowledge, and access to technology and technology transfer.

prior informed consent from the national authorities; and evidence of fair and equitable benefit-sharing under the relevant national regime.[87]

This proposal under TRIPS would require each contracting party to have disclosure requirements for patent applications in their national laws and regulations whenever a patent covered a genetic resource and/or associated traditional knowledge in their inventions.[88] The burden of proof in the case of non-compliance with disclosure requirements would be placed on the patent holder who would have to demonstrate that the genetic resources and/or traditional knowledge have been legally and legitimately accessed and that benefit-sharing had taken place. The patent applicant would be required to demonstrate that "all reasonable measures" to determine the country of origin and source of material used were taken but the onus on them would be limited to disclosure of evidence that is known or should have been known to them.[89] The disclosure standard would be enforceable through the WTO DSU against countries that failed to promulgate the standard or enforce its requirements nationally.

This type of proposal takes an interlinkages approach to the compliance of the CBD and the ITPGRFA. If a reporting procedure was also included, as has been envisaged by some countries such as Brazil and Columbia, it would increase the transparency and help provider countries to monitor and track the compliance with access and benefit-sharing rules in a cost-effective way.[90] Given that the use of genetic resources and traditional knowledge associated with them frequently takes place through the patent system, the reporting mechanism would allow provider countries to ensure that, even though the genetic material and associated traditional knowledge were patented in another country outside its own

87. WTO (2006) *The Relationship between the TRIPS Agreement and the Convention on Biological Diversity: Summary of Issues Raised and Points Made, A Revision*, IP/C/W/368/Rev.1, (8 February), para. 70.

88. Discussions have gone on for a number of years in the TRIPS Council and under the Doha Agenda on the appropriateness of such an amendment. Several developing countries in the African Group and Andean Community as well as India and Brazil have made proposals. The type of amendment being proposed might look like an addition to Article 29.

89. WTO (2004) *Elements of the Obligation to Disclose the Source and Country of Origin of the Biological Resources and/or Traditional Knowledge in Inventions: Submission from Brazil, Cuba, Ecuador, India, Pakistan, Peru, Thailand, and Venezuela*, IP/C/W/429/Rev.1 (27 September); see also WTO (2004) *Council for Trade-Related Aspects of Intellectual Property Rights, Minutes of Meeting Held in the Centre William Rappard on 1–2 December 2004*, IP/C/M/46 (2 December), para. 57.

90. See the following WTO submissions: Brazil, IP/C/M/48, para. 38; Brazil and India, IP/C/W/443; Brazil et al., IP/C/W/403, IP/C/W/356; EC, IP/C/M/46, para. 46, IP/C/M/44, para. 30, IP/C/M/37/Add.1, para. 228, IP/C/M/33, para. 121, IP/C/M/32, para. 128; India, IP/C/W/195, IP/C/M/48, para. 52, IP/C/M/40, para. 82; Peru, IP/C/W/447, IP/C/M/48, para. 18; Switzerland, IP/C/W/423, IP/C/M/42, para. 98.

jurisdiction, PIC and benefit-sharing arrangements had been addressed and adequately met.[91]

The disclosure proposal would definitely facilitate the enforcement of obligations under the CBD by providing incentives on patent applicants for meeting the CBD and ITPGRFA requirements. Otherwise, the right would be revocable for not meeting the requirements of the disclosure. It would also ensure that contracts such as material transfer agreements were consistent with the disclosure requirements under jurisdictions adhering to the TRIPS Agreement.[92] This would, in effect, ensure the patent was appropriate and, if not so, would create the legal recourse of revocation of the patent. Many countries have complained that the misappropriation of patent rights is difficult and burdensome to revoke and, if this revocation takes place outside the provider country's jurisdiction, then the costs can be very high.[93] In this way, the disclosure requirement would help improve the operation of access and benefit-sharing systems and make it difficult for those involved in acts of misappropriation to succeed.[94] Most importantly for contracting members of all three regimes, it would effectively enable measures to be in conformity with all international obligations under the TRIPS Agreement, the CBD and the ITPGRFA and contribute towards their implementation by members in a mutually supportive way, achieving the goals contained in the CBD and the ITPGRFA and mandated in the Doha Declaration.

In opposition to this approach, there is a viewpoint that the best way to ensure effective compliance with TK, ABS and PIC provisions are through national regulations and that TRIPS is not aimed at ensuring the compliance of CBD or ITPGRFA provisions. Moreover, the TRIPS Agreement in no way infringes or prohibits the creation of such a national system under either the CBD or the ITPGRFA.[95] Though a valid argument, proponents of this approach are taking a narrow view of treaty-making. International law is meant to be a consistent single body of law, not pockets of laws that run contradictory to each other. Even when the subject matter is not identical, treaties still have the possibility to overlap and the contracting parties have a duty to ensure the entirety and holism of international law.[96]

91. Brazil et al., IP/C/W/459.
92. WTO (2002) Minutes TRIPS Council, IP/C/M/37/Add.18 (November), para. 223.
93. Infra.
94. WTO (2004) Minutes TRIPS Council, IP/C/M/46, (2 December), para. 51.
95. WTO Secretariat (2002) *The Relationship between the TRIPS and the CBD: Summary of Issues Raised and Points Made*, JOB(02)/58C, (18 June), 5.
96. See *US – Gasoline*. The Appellate Body stated, "... there is specific acknowledgement to be found about the importance of coordinating policies on trade and the environment". WTO rules like any other rules are part of the greater corpus of international law; see Donald McRae (2000) *The WTO in International Law: Tradition Continued or New Frontier?*, 3 J. Int'l Econ. L., 27.

The conditionality of benefit-sharing could also be a source of conflict between TRIPS and so provides an additional argument for the TRIPS to cooperate more readily with CBD and ITPGRFA. Like most agreements of the WTO, TRIPS has a requirement to follow the principle of national treatment. This stipulates that the same patent protection[97] should be afforded to foreign patents as national patents. A situation of non-compliance of national treatment has not been observed but, justified under the CBD and ITPGRFA, it can easily be envisaged. For example, a foreign patent on a genetic component listed in the Multilateral System, such as breadfruit, a crop listed in Annex One of the ITPGRFA, would be obliged to pay a percentage of its commercial proceeds into the Trust Fund according to Article 19.3 (f). The patentee might argue that other types of patents not involving genetic resources or traditional knowledge are not required to make such payments and, therefore, there is unfair discrimination. This problem of compatibility could be rectified by requiring all national patents on resources in the Multilateral System to make payments to the Trust Fund, or other forms of benefit-sharing under CBD requirements, through an amendment to TRIPS. Thus, the issue of discrimination is eliminated.

Perhaps the strongest argument for greater interlinkages to be sought between these Agreements is the issue touched upon in the first section of this analysis concerning the patenting of life forms. Here, a perverse conflict of the highest order exists and could easily affect compliance of any three of these Agreements if the conflict is not resolved. Article 12.3 (d) of the International Treaty restricts the patenting of materials under the Multilateral System, including its components. The CBD also states the "sovereign rights of States over their natural resources" and "to determine access to genetic resources rests with the national governments and is subject to national legislation".[98] Yet, under the WTO TRIPS Agreement, members are allowed to ban patents on plants, animals and "essentially biological processes for the protection of plants and animals", but certain life forms are still open for patenting.[99] Plant varieties are one area that is still open for intellectual property protection under the WTO but members are requested to put in place effective *sui generis* systems. This provision on plant varieties would mean the ITPGRFA restriction on IPR for plants in the Multilateral System and Article 15 of the CBD is consistent with TRIPS as long as the country has its own *sui generis* system in place. For parties to the ITPGRFA this could also pro-

97. The WTO considers patent protections to entail "matters affecting the availability, acquisition, scope, maintenance and enforcement of intellectual property rights".
98. CBD, Article 15.1.
99. TRIPS, Article 27.4 (b).

vide the opportunity to create a new system to account for species within the Multilateral System.

However, while there is potential to harmonize provisions for intellectual property protection of plant varieties, the possibility of TRIPS creating non-compliance of CBD and ITPGRFA provisions remains perverse. The most serious potential inconsistency arises over the restriction of patenting of "parts and components". As Article 12.3 (d) of the ITPGRFA now stands, there is a potential conflict with TRIPS Article 27.3 (b), which allows WTO members to protect non-biological and microbiological processes for the production of plants and animals. In other words, the international standard which has been set by TRIPS and should be legally implemented in national legislation allows components or parts of plants or animals which are microbes to be protected by intellectual property rights – a direct contradiction to Article 12.3 (d) of the ITPGRFA.

With regard to compliance, how might this play out? The non-compliance would depend on which treaty is followed nationally. If an applicant was denied a patent wishing to privatize an application of a micro-organism or associated traditional knowledge application using the micro-organism because that genetic resource was a component or part of Annex One of the ITPGRFA or the sovereign resource according to the CBD, or, if the patent was denied because PIC and benefit-sharing had not been exercised, then this would be a violation of the TRIPS Agreement, which states that countries should allow patents on micro-organisms. If, on the other hand, the patent was granted on the grounds that Article 27.3 (b) allows patents of genetic material in the form of micro-organisms and the micro-organism happened to be a component or part of a genetic resource in the ITPGRFA Annex One or the sovereign resource of a CBD party, then, in fact, TRIPS would be the justification for non-compliance with the CBD and ITPGRFA.

In any dispute settlement over this perverse conflict between the CBD and ITPGRFA and the TRIPS Agreement one would have take into account the language in the CBD and ITPGRFA on "mutual supportiveness" with respect to other international agreements.[100] Nevertheless, how would these clauses be interpreted in practice given such outright conflicts? I would argue that, at a minimum, there is a requirement for greater dialogue than presently exists between the treaties, as the FAO

---

100. Infra. Also a factor, though non-binding, is the intent of the WTO members expressed in the Doha Declaration provisions calling for mutual supportiveness between the WTO and MEAs. See WTO (2001) *Doha Development Agenda*, WT/MIN(01)/DEC/ 1, (20 November), para. 31.

and CBD secretariats are still unable to attain observership in the TRIPS Council.

Contracting parties to these Agreements, however, should not allow these uncertainties to persist. Uncertainty could undermine their strength and could jeopardize compliance and implementation of both Agreements. Nor should parties wait for a dispute to arise and for a trade panel or appellate body or some form of judicial solution, as this may not be consistent with what parties originally intended in the Agreements. The governing councils of both Agreements should recognize the potential problems discussed here and either provide side-agreements on mutual recognition of interpretation or textual amendments, or direct recognition of the exceptions in the case of the other treaty. This is the approach used in TRIPS for Agreements such as the Paris Convention (1967), Berne Convention (1971)[101] or in the WTO SPS and TBT Agreements for Codex and ISO standards. The explicit inclusion is an approach that creates a positive certainty, which is productive for the effectiveness of international law. The potential for TRIPS to promote compliance of the CBD and ITPGRFA is certainly high but, as in the case of other areas of analysis above this, remains untapped and continues to require the political will and concrete programmes to make the potential a reality.

For the purposes of applying the analytical framework of this book, however, it is not necessary to engage in lengthy debates over the rights and appropriateness of the ABS, protection of traditional knowledge and PIC in the WTO. My purpose is to show that compliance of the CBD and ITPGRFA is affected by the TRIPS Agreement, and vice versa, and to show how an interlinkages approach could remedy this and in fact strengthen the effectiveness of all three Agreements in so doing. Under these circumstances, the arguments for cooperation through proposals such as an amendment to TRIPS make a great deal of sense and greater compliance would be achieved than if CBD, the ITPGRFA and TRIPS operated in isolation. Whilst creating national-level requirements of ABS and PIC is possible through the CBD and ITPGRFA, this would not guarantee that all countries would have such requirements. Patents using genetic resources could also be made in places without PIC and ABS, which is currently the trend in a globalized world where patents involving genetic resources are usually taken out in numerous countries and outside the country where the resource originated. In addition, the sector where a violation is likely to occur in a patent application is logically outside the realm of the ITPGRFA and CBD environment but one

101. TRIPS, Article 1.3 and Article 2.

very much within the scope of TRIPS. This suggests that the compliance for the requirements of ABS, PIC and traditional knowledge would be best served if carried out through TRIPS.[102]

Robustness

In the previous case study's section on robustness in chapter 6 we learned that the positive relationship between the CBD and ITPGRFA spurred an environment of learning that led to the Agreements having a robust and progressive approach to the regulations and management of genetic resources. Learning, however, does not only take place through cooperation, as this section will show; it also takes place through conflict. One of the most tangible outcomes of the turbulent years of the TRIPS and CBD debate has been the fact that the issues between these two Agreements, and now those that are also shared with the ITPGRFA, have graduated to the highest level of discussion with their relative decision-making bodies. In 2001, the Doha Declaration, adopted in paragraph 19, recognizes compatibility problems between the CBD and the TRIPS Agreement and it calls on the WTO members in the review of Article 27.3 (b) and the general review under Article 71:

> ... to examine, *inter alia*, the relationship between the TRIPS Agreement and the Convention on Biological Diversity, the protection of traditional knowledge and folklore, and other relevant new developments raised by members pursuant to Article 71.1. In undertaking this work, the TRIPS Council shall be guided by the objectives and principles set out in Articles 7 and 8 of the TRIPS Agreement and shall take fully into account the development dimension.[103]

The mere fact that this item is on the agenda of a WTO trade round and that it is being discussed at ministerial level was no easy feat and is the result of years of intense lobbying and analysis alerting trade policy-makers to the interlinkages between these Agreements. The agenda item has now forced an intense self-examination of the TRIPS provisions and the CBD as well as other instruments, such as the ITPGRFA, on issues of benefit-sharing, prior informed consent and TK. To this end, there have been multiple proposals and communications on the relationship between the CBD, TRIPS and, to a lesser extent, the ITPGRFA.[104]

---

102. For further discussion on the tensions between the on-access benefit sharing between the CBD and TRIPS, see G. Kristin Rosendal (2006) "The Convention on Biological Diversity: Tensions with the WTO TRIPS Agreement over Access to Genetic Resources and the Sharing of Benefits", in supra, Oberthür and Gehring, 79–102.
103. WTO, *Doha Development Agenda*, para. 19.
104. See infra.

The Doha Declaration also makes reference to MEAs in general and adopts language already contained in MEAs such as the CBD, which is no coincidence. Paragraph 31 of the Doha Declaration talks of enhancing "mutual supportiveness" of trade and environment, the same language used in Article 16 and Article 5 of the CBD[105] and the preamble of the ITPGRFA.[106] Paragraph 32 discusses the need for clarifying WTO rules with MEAs; paragraph 32 (i) singles out the TRIPS Agreement in this case. These negotiations are taking place under the WTO Committee on Trade and Environment and the Report to the Fifth Ministerial Conference recommends future actions including the desirability to engage in negotiations on this topic and showing how to create better information exchange between the MEAs and the WTO.[107] So far, in working towards these goals, there have been several consultations with UNEP and a number of MEAs and there have been several suggestions of how the MEAs and the WTO could better cooperate. Some of the suggestions contained in the Chairman's Report to the Fifth Ministerial Session include:

- Formalizing MEA Information Sessions in the CTE, and organizing them on a regular basis;
- Holding MEA Information Sessions on specific themes by grouping the MEAs that share a common interest;
- Organizing meetings with MEAs in other WTO bodies, either together with the CTE or separately;
- Organizing WTO-parallel events at the COPs of MEAs more systematically;
- Organizing joint WTO, UNEP and MEA technical assistance and capacity-building projects;
- Promoting the exchange of documents, while respecting confidential information;
- Creating avenues for information exchange between government representatives from the trade and environment sides;
- Establishing an electronic database on trade and environment.[108]

The result of the CTE's work under the Doha Round is likely to bear fruit and lead to a more conducive environment for the MEAs, such as the CBD and ITPGRFA, with the TRIPS and other Agreements under

---

105. Bonn Guidelines make reference as well to the need for mutual supportiveness. Section D, para. 10 states: "The guidelines should be applied in a manner that is coherent and mutually supportive of the work of relevant international agreements and institutions."
106. WTO, *Doha Declaration*, para. 31.
107. Ibid. para. 32.
108. WTO (2003) *Report of the Chairperson of the CTE Special Session to the Trade Negotiations Committee*, TN/TE/7 and Suppl.1, (15 July), para. 12.

the WTO. It will surely lead to better coordination of their activities and shared experiences that will undoubtedly result in greater robustness and learning between these Agreements. In the end, the most desired result is that the potential MEAs like the CBD and ITPGRFA and WTO Agreements like TRIPS increase their interaction and for this to have a positive impact on their effectiveness.

The final Doha Declaration's provisions on TRIPS and on MEAs in general will, however, be linked to the outcome of the overall Doha Development Trade Round itself, which, for the moment, has been suspended over issues of greater scope and implication for WTO members. Pascal Lamy, the Director-General of WTO, has, however, reminded WTO members, in a speech in May 2006 to the European Commission, of the significance of the WTO and MEA experience and that the Doha Round represents "a once-in-a-lifetime opportunity ... to confirm the need for mutual supportiveness between the WTO and MEAs".

Pascal Lamy himself has recognized the learning experience that has gone on on both sides of the trade and environment debate. In his speech to the Commission, he quoted the concrete examples that WTO and the environment community have learned from each other. He cited the 1991 Dolphin-Tuna Case, which at the time affirmed the need to address the "tension over sovereignty over natural resources", and stated that this led to the adoption of Principle 12 of the Rio Declaration that called on importing countries "to avoid taking unilateral environmental action outside their jurisdiction" and to work multilaterally though international consensus such as MEAs. He also reminded the Commission members that the results of the Rio Summit influenced the preambular language of sustainable development in the WTO Agreement, language which he states "is the ultimate aim of the WTO" and must guide any dispute between trade and environment. He also talked of the importance of the WTO dispute settlement and the effect it has had in cases such as the Shrimp-Turtle dispute which urged the disputants to reach cooperative environmental solutions and that "a little-known outcome of this dispute is that it gave birth to a new MEA, entitled: Memorandum of Understanding on the Conservation and Management of Marine Turtles and their Habitats of the Indian Ocean and South-East Asia". Lamy states forthrightly that he believes this is a concrete example of the "types of synergies that can exist between different legal regimes, and the very explicit kind of support that one regime can give to the other".[109]

---

109. See WTO (2006) *Speech by Pascal Lamy to the European Commission* (30 May), available at http://www.wto.org/english/news_e/sppl_e/sppl28_e.htm.

Finance

In this last section on finance and effectiveness we again approach the problem that there has been little cooperation between the TRIPS Agreement and either the CBD or the ITPGRFA. As a consequence, and in contrast to the last case study's section on finance, I can only show the potential that exists if an interlinkages approach were taken and show the consequences of the ineffectiveness that has resulted because it has not been taken.

Contrary to what some might easily speculate, the looming conflict that exists with the TRIPS Agreement has not had a chilling effect on the financing of the CBD or the ITPGRFA. The US, though not a party to either, has not played a destructive role in the financial support which it easily could have played given its power and influence. Its contribution to the CBD via the GEF and to the FAO financing still remains relatively constant compared to other MEAs, and neither the CBD nor the ITPGRFA have been singled out in any way.

It therefore makes the arguments under this section all the more difficult and nearly impossible to find any hard-core data on the financial implications the relationships of the treaties might have. It would be difficult to begin to estimate the financial costs that the conflict between the CBD and TRIPS Agreement has inflicted on countries in terms of time and resources for coordinating the problem, the communications and proposals prepared, the specialists required on delegations, the legal fees and consultations required to harmonize these Agreements under national legislations and so forth.[110] It is also difficult to estimate some of the costs that might have been saved if such proposals as the disclosure requirement, which has been suggested as an amendment to the TRIPS Agreement, had been created. Several countries, such as India,[111] have argued that this would be economically efficient compared to setting up a national system under the CBD. Moreover, there is very little data on

110. In the WTO TRIPS Council over the period December 1998 to November 2005 and concerning agenda items on the relationship between the CBD and TRIPS Agreement, provisions of Article 27.3 (b) and the protection of traditional knowledge and folklore, there have been the following number of submissions: 51 papers by members or groups of members; 27 papers on national practices concerning the relationship; 25 submissions on the review of Article 27.3 (b) and its relationship to CBD; 6 submissions by international organizations; and 11 information notes prepared by the secretariat. A table of all reports during this period for the TRIPS Council on this agenda item can be found in WTO (2006) IP/C/W/369/Rev.1 (9 March), 26.

111. See WTO (2006) *Doha Work Programme – The Outstanding Implementation Issue on the Relationship between the TRIPS Agreement and the Convention on Biological Diversity, Communication from Brazil, China, Colombia, Cuba, India, Pakistan, Peru, Thailand and Tanzania*, WT/GC/W/564/Rev.2, TN/C/W/41/Rev.2, IP/C/W/474 (5 July).

the real costs that have been incurred from the wrongful patents that have been filed, such as in the Turmeric,[112] Neem[113] and Basmati rice cases,[114] each of which took considerable time and resources to overturn in courts outside where the traditional knowledge originated.

I will therefore have to concede in this section that, logically, although collaboration between these Agreements could save time and costs which could be channelled to other more important aspects of the implementation of these respective Agreements, there is a lack of data to corroborate this aspect of my hypothesis.

Conclusion

The results of this case study clearly show that the CBD and ITPGRFA do not have to be inherently conflictive. Under each of the measurements for effectiveness (except in the indicator of finance), I demonstrated that these treaties working together can solve much more than working apart. Under their primary objectives, the TRIPS Agreement provisions on sustainable development can be viewed as a promoter of the sustainable use of genetic resources – national resources sometimes even referred to as "green gold"[115] which countries are seeking to develop but, for those countries who are members of the CBD and ITPGRFA, in a sustainable way. Through interlinkages, such as potential joint programmes, the

112. The 2002 Report by the UK Commission on Intellectual Property cites that overturning the US patent (no. 5,401,504) on turmeric (*Curcuma longa*) given to the University of Mississippi Medical Center cost the Indian Government about $10,000 in 1995. See *Integrating Intellectual Property Rights and Development Policy: Report of the Commission on Intellectual Property Rights*, 84, available at http://www.iprcommission.org/graphic/documents/final_report.htm.

113. An estimate of 20,000 Euros and 10 years to overturn (EU Patent No. 0436257) to the US Corporation W. R. Grace. However, most of the costs came from volunteers and incremental funding that was supplied by a Dutch development foundation (HIVOS). See *Submission of the International Federation of Organic Agriculture Movements (IFOAM), Research Foundation for Science, Technology and Ecology and The Greens/European Free Alliance in the European Parliament to the CBD Ad Hoc Working Group on Access and Benefit-Sharing* (12 April 2005), available at http://www.patentinglives.org/Revised%20ABS%20Submissionsept%2026%2005.doc (accessed 30 August 2006).

114. On 14 August 2001, the US Patent and Trademark Office struck down large sections of the Basmati patent held by RiceTec, patent No. 5663484. This took considerable time and resources. The action began by a petition to the Supreme Court of India for the Government of India to take action in the US courts. This led to the Indian Government challenging and eventually overturning the patent in the USPTO.

115. A. H. Zakri and W. Bradnee Chambers (2004) "Waiting for the Rush", *The Star* (Malaysia), 20 (February).

TRIPS could be used as a promoter to attract investment for the development of new technologies for the environment. These could be for environmental remediation, end-pipe technologies or even cleaner production technologies. In the context of genetic resources and biodiversity, the development of the technologies could be in the field of biotechnology or environmental services, such as methods for gene storage, identification or exploration.

The supporting provisions of the three Agreements share a powerful area of collaboration in technology transfer. When their provisions are read together arguments can be made for the three Agreements to work together in a mutually supportive way for the development and promotion of environmentally sound technologies. For countries that have participated in major summits and adopted Agreements such as Agenda 21 and the Johannesburg Plan of Implementation, which accounts for by far the majority of the WTO, CBD and ITPGRFA member states, these Agreements urged the transfer of environmental technologies to developing countries. If the three Agreements work closely together, programmes supporting such transfer in the area of genetic resources and other areas mutually covered by the Agreements could be more easily facilitated.

Under compliance, the argument for cooperation perhaps makes the most sense. The ITPGRFA and the CBD are directly implicated by intellectual property right protection. The most effective means of compliance of the provisions concerning the protection of traditional knowledge, PIC and benefit-sharing would be through a TRIPS standard, not through the CBD or ITPGRFA, which are neither equipped nor mandated to work in the area of intellectual property. Thus, an interlinkages approach whereby the TRIPS could be amended to support these goals would have a positive effect on the compliance.

Concerning robustness, there has been a great deal learned from the overlap of the TRIPS with the CBD and ITPGRFA and the issues that pertain to this overlap are now at the highest level of decision-making. If indeed, the outcome of the Doha Development Round creates an agenda for mutual supportiveness this will serve to demonstrate that, even through conflict, these treaties have learned from each other and in the end adapt to become even stronger and more robust Agreements.

Overall, as we saw in chapter 6, the case study clearly reinforces my proposition that by cooperating these three Agreements could create an improvement in the effectiveness either of one or, in some cases, of all three Agreements. Additionally, the case discussed demonstrates that treaties both outside their branches of international law and across sectors of sustainable development can improve their performance through an interlinkages approach even when the agreements are seen as fundamentally conflicting.

Part VII
Conclusions

8

Conclusions for public international law and treaty management

In recent years there has been growing awareness that a major reason for the worsening global environment is the failure to create adequate institutional responses to fully address the scope, magnitude and complexity of environmental problems. Much of the criticism directed at the global institutions has focused on the necessity for greater coordination and synergism among environmental institutions, policies and legal instruments, and the need for approaches that take better account of the interrelationships between ecological and societal systems. Part of the criticism has arisen from the notion that international environmental law has developed unsystematically and is based on issues that have attracted political agendas at one given time or another and that this has therefore led to fragmentation, lack of coordination and ultimately reduced institutional performance. This criticism is where this book opens.

After many years of environmental treaty-making, by the mid-1990s, there was increasing focus on the conflicts and the potential synergism that existed between multilateral environmental agreements. These agreements were viewed as the foundation of the international environmental regime and the only binding instruments in a system that was viewed as weak and non-legalistic compared to other regimes for global trade, international security or human rights. This has led to the introduction of a new emerging concept called interlinkages, a concept that represented the need to address the connections between MEAs and to formulate policies to enhance the cooperation between these agreements. This is a policy that still struggles to this very day and that has seen many

Interlinkages and the effectiveness of multilateral environmental agreements,
W. Bradnee Chambers, United Nations University Press, 2008, ISBN 978-92-808-1149-0

approaches and ideas including proposals to create a new world environmental organization.

However, as can sometimes be the case, new concepts and approaches to international decision-making are not always based on sound scientific advice or expert studies. There is sometimes a trend for bandwagon approaches to occur, especially in the midst of times of change and discontertedness, which this period of the mid-1990s was undergoing. New ideas attract the attention of politicians and finance, which the MEAs badly needed. The interlinkages concept conveniently fitted this bill.

Broadly speaking, the idea of interlinkages was a rational one and, on the surface it, made a lot of sense, both logically and from the point of view of straightforward cost-effectiveness. The international community had just come through an intense period of international environmental treaty-making. It had gone from a period in the 1970s where environmental treaties were barely even existent to a period where there were hundreds of agreements, many of which were large multilateral treaties of a board nature and some of which were even making front-page headlines, such as the Climate Change Convention. All of this occurred within a mere two decades.

This period was nothing short of extraordinary for the environment movement. But, with most of the major treaties now negotiated, policymakers began asking themselves, what was to negotiate next? The most obvious answer to this question was implementation. The negotiating part was easy compared to implementing the treaties on the ground nationally. It would take innovative approaches and large sums of financing in a period of declining ODA and renewed unilateralism.[1]

This is where the concept of interlinkages was seen as having added-value compared to standard approaches to MEA implementation. Moreover, if the MEAs had been created haphazardly and adopted with no systematic design, then they could now be retroactively linked together. As a result, ideas of how interlinkages could improve the implementation of MEAs became ripe within the UN and international organizations. There were suggestions to hold COP/MOPs back to back, which could save time and money. Some recommendations sought to link MEAs according to function and create common programmes for training or education, or to share scientific mechanisms. More ambitious proposals pushed the idea to create new international organizations. However, in almost all the proposals, it was assumed, and still is today, that only treaties that are linked by similar subject matter or closely related by scale could best cooperate. Also, it was believed that MEAs had the best

---

1. W. Bradnee Chambers (2001) "Kyoto a Triumph for Multilateralism", *Japan Times*, (29 July).

chance for cooperation compared to treaties that fell across the sustainable development divide, for example, MEAs working cooperatively with economic treaties such as those under the WTO.

Some of these views may well turn out to be right but very few of these proposals had anything more than desktop studies behind them; certainly no in-depth research or expert assessments were conducted. There exist, to my knowledge, no studies that have created an analytical framework to systematically examine the interlinkages effect and its relationship with the effectiveness of MEAs or to understand if treaties that come from different economic pillars of sustainable development can work with treaties of the environmental pillar. In effect, the broad policies of interlinkages were made, especially within the annals of the UN, without understanding if interlinkages would actually improve MEA performance.

It is in this context that this book is situated. It was written to fill the gap in knowledge and policy-making that exists and push our understanding on how we approach international environmental law. The book has studied the essence of the assumptions made about interlinkages and MEAs, it has provided a framework for measuring the effectiveness of MEAs and it has shown how the effectiveness of MEAs can be improved by interlinkages. It has also shown how MEAs that cooperate with treaties outside the environment in other sectors of sustainable development can improve their effectiveness. To the policy-makers and technocrats – both national and international – interlinkages can work; we simply have to be creative and think outside the traditional box on international law. The book comes to these conclusions through the following analysis:

Parts I and II (chapters 1 and 2) provide the essential background and context of the book. The introduction provides an overview of the major trends and thinking that have led to the development of the concept of interlinkages. It then introduces various definitions of interlinkages and provides a definition that could be applied to the study of international law and multilateral environmental agreements. Chapter 1 introduces the principal query of the book: "Can interlinkages improve the legal effectiveness of multilateral agreements?" A secondary but related question asks whether it can improve the effectiveness of international treaties outside the sector of environment and across sectors of sustainable development. The remaining sections of the introduction then describe briefly the overview of each chapter and its contribution to the book as a whole.

Chapter 2 sets the historical context of the book. It traces the development of international environmental law and the initiatives and attempts to coordinate and improve interlinkages from the Stockholm Conference on the Human Environment up until the aftermath of the World Summit on Sustainable Development. The chapter provides an important understanding of the motivation behind policy-makers' attempts to introduce better coordination between environmental institutions and why, in most cases, these attempts have failed.

Part III (chapter 3) follows on from the historical chapter but its focus is a detailed analysis of the legalities between treaties, an area that is intangible, poorly understood and not sufficiently written about in international law. Based on the little literature that does exist and the analysis given in the chapter, I conclude that the legal milieu for interlinkages of MEAs can be defined on three levels. One, the most obvious, is the Vienna Convention on the Law of Treaties and customary international rules such as *lex specialis*, which defines how successive MEAs, as international treaties, avoid conflict and are coordinated. These rules, though important, are not reflective of the time and are residuary to the needs of modern MEAs, which, in a world of treaty congestion and pressure to cooperate, require rules more appropriate to cooperation than conflict or succession.

The other international rules that do exist occur at both the external and internal levels, such as those governing international institutions. In many ways, these rules are unnecessarily complex and ill-defined; often they are at odds with each other and, as a result, they are ineffective in dealing with the current needs of modern MEA cooperation. The chapter establishes that the legal milieu for external interlinkages depends on the judicial personality of the MEA in question. Today's MEAs are showing increasing independence from their parent or supervisory organizations, so much so that many are regarded as autonomous institutional arrangements with legal personality equated to fully fledged international organizations. The legal personality provides the scope and flexibility for MEA secretariats and their bodies to formally cooperate externally with other MEAs through MOUs, liaison groups or formal agreements.

The internal legal milieu for interlinkages between MEAs is perhaps the least well-defined and requires substantial structural redress. Coordination problems exist between parent/supervisory organizations and their quasi-independent MEAs. Legally the MEA bodies and the international functionaries and officers that serve them are bound by the rules and regulations of the parent, as is demonstrated in the case of the UN. Nevertheless, in governance matters, the MEA secretariats remain independent to take instructions from the COPs or their subsidiary bodies. Internal coordination can have another dimension, not always well understood or legally defined, as is the case in the UN system, which administers many of the MEAs. Under the UN Economic and Social Council, the UN has created myriad internal mechanisms, such as the Chief Executive Board and the Environment Management Group, that are supposed to encourage cooperation. However, to date they have not lived up to their mandates and at the end of the day they have not created the kind of effective cooperation that might be possible if a more structurally well-defined MEA governance system was in place.

The analysis in chapter 3 is important to the central theme of the book because it shows how treaties are theoretically supposed to work together according to international law, but what becomes readily apparent from the analysis is that the international system is flawed and badly lets down the burgeoning potential that does exist for cooperation. The concluding part of chapter 3 offers some of the potential models for creating a more coherent structure for international governance, including the development of a World Environment Organization which would provide closer integration and thus would promote interlinkages which the book has shown increases the effectiveness of MEAs.

Part IV (chapters 4 and 5) is the core analytical framework of the book. In itself a progressive contribution to the study of international law, it begins with an analysis of the concept of effectiveness, a term that is randomly used in legal discussions but rarely defined consistently in the world of public international law. Chapter 4 challenges Hans Kelsen's positivist notion of international law[2] and argues that design of international treaties is a crucial part of international law that is badly neglected by legal study. The chapter conducts an in-depth review of the literature on effectiveness starting from its original concept in international law as it was used for the recognition of statehood or the establishment of an international right. The analysis in chapter 4 moves on to trace how the concept of effectiveness has developed in the legal world, from the point of view of rule-based positivist schools, and then moves on to more progressive schools of thought, which this book categorizes as social legal models. Given the fading lines between the disciplines of international law and international relations, and the increasing trend for international relations to become involved in the analysis and methods of international law, the chapter also draws on theories of effectiveness from international relations and political science.

This analysis itself has rarely been conducted from the legal perspective and adds value to the sparse literature that does exist in international law on this subject. The analysis, in the end, concludes that there are several ways to measure the effectiveness of international treaties. These factors include the objectives of the treaty; here an important distinction between this factor and that of compliance is made. The objectives of a treaty are what the contracting parties of the treaty have decided they desire it to ultimately achieve. This, however, does not necessarily mean that the treaty parties could agree on the binding measures that will, in

2. Hans Kelsen (1970) *Pure Theory of Law*, Los Angeles: University of California Press.

fact, achieve these objectives. The good intentions of some parties are not always attainable in multilateral treaties. As an example, the chapter cites the objective of the Kyoto Protocol to reduce greenhouse gas emissions below their 1990 levels, but the target the contracting parties set for the protocol falls very short of this and only obligates Annex-One countries to a decrease of 5.2 per cent of their 1990 levels.[3] Compliance, on the other hand, tracks whether the positive obligations in the treaty – in the case of this example the binding targets in the Kyoto Protocol – are in fact being met. Thus, both the objectives and compliance are important measurements but they are distinguishable and this must be kept in mind when thinking of treaty effectiveness.

Equally important, but again playing a separate role in the treaty, are its supporting provisions. These provisions often lack the binding nature of the main obligations; nevertheless they play an important role in complementing the primary obligations, and, indirectly, in contributing to the treaty objectives through training, creation of databases or clearing house mechanisms and other types of capacity and enabling programmes. It is these supporting measures that sometimes encourage greater treaty membership because poorer developing countries can find benefits from financial and other types of incentives under these provisions. Some developed countries take these non-binding commitments more seriously than others and contribute resources to their achievement and, in this regard, the other factors discussed in chapter 4 are also an important part of the treaty.

Robustness is an area that is poorly understood in treaty-making. Robustness mechanisms include systems of amendments, research and development clauses, scientific mechanisms and even the ability to create protocols and link themselves with other treaties through cooperative systems. Creating robustness provisions in treaties was an important lesson learned from early environmental treaty-making. If a treaty is too rigid and cannot adapt and change its approach, then it risks becoming stagnant over time and ultimately ineffective to the contracting parties. Many of the sleeping treaties of the early treating-making days are a result of not having robustness provisions that can permit them to learn and change.[4]

The last component that the chapter discusses, and which is critical for effectiveness, is a treaty's financing. A treaty needs stable and predictable

3. Kyoto Protocol, Annex One.
4. On "Sleeping Treaties" see Donald A. Brown (1996) *Thinking Globally and Acting Locally: The Emergence of Global Environment Problems and the Critical Need to Develop Sustainable Development Programs at State and Local Levels in the United States*, 5 Dickinson Journal of Environmental Law and Policy, 175.

financing in order to support its critical elements, such as meetings of the parties and subsidiary bodies; engaging a secretariat; monitoring compliance; producing programmes to support the implementation of the treaty and create a permanent seat for its headquarters. Finance is thus a logical variable that can measure the effectiveness of treaties.

Whereas chapter 4 provides an in-depth analysis of what effectiveness means and the components for measuring it, chapter 5 brings these measurement parameters to bear on the central theme of the book. In order to do this the chapter first reviews the theoretical literature on treaty interplay and shows that, though existing theories are useful for studying the behaviour of treaty relations, they add very little to the understanding of the consequences of such relations. The chapter therefore makes an important distinction between these theories, called "institutional interplay", and the concept of interlinkages, which is a normative theory whereby treaties working together can improve their performance. Chapter 4, having shown that no existing framework or theory would be adequate for the purpose of the book, then proceeds to add the additional components to complete an alternative framework, which is later applied to the case studies.

In Parts V and VI (chapters 6 and 7), the case studies provide the core evidence of the book. Concerning the principal query, "Can interlinkages between MEAs improve their legal effectiveness?", the evidence presented in the first case study clearly shows a direct relationship between the cooperation of the CBD and the ITPGRFA in the subject area of genetic resources. A spirit of cooperation between the CBD and the ITPGRFA has led to numerous complementarities in the treaty text. These provisions have been further enhanced through decisions of the COP/MOPs of both processes. In the end, this cooperation has greatly improved the effectiveness of both treaties under each of the measurements that I applied. The treaties have also demonstrated an ability to adapt and learn from each other, which has led to further enhancement of their cooperation and contributed to improving their overall performance.

What is interesting about the results of this case study is that they refute the notion that conflicting treaties cannot cooperate and resolve their differences in a way that leads to improving the performance of both. This presumption is often presented in the context of the trade and environment debate. Proponents of this view assume that the root of the debate ultimately lies in the irresolvable conflicts of trade liberalization leading to the overexploitation of resources that environmentalists are wishing to conserve and protect. Therefore, treaties under the WTO, or others in the field of economic law, are viewed as inherently conflictive with international environmental treaties.[5] Contrary to this argument, this case study clearly shows that this assumption is not necessarily true. The CBD and the ITPGRFA are in fact very much at odds, much more fundamentally than the MEAs and WTO Agreements. One of the most imminent threats to biodiversity loss and the depletion of diversity of genetic resources is, in fact, land use change from agricultural production.[6] The ITPGRFA furthers the goals of the UN Food and Agricultural Organization set up to promote agriculture production and provide food security.[7] Nevertheless, the ITPGRFA has learned to cooperate with the CBD even though their respective goals could be read to be competing ones.[8] These treaties have been able to overcome their underlying differences and create a relationship that is mutually supportive and which leads to the effectiveness of both treaties.

This conclusion raises a question that the second case addresses more concretely. Is the reason for the CBD and ITPGRFA being able to overcome their conflict the fact that they are in sectors that are roughly similar in scope? In other words, are they able to cooperate more easily because they are in the domain of environment and not within another sector of sustainable development such as economy? This is where the second case study adds clarity to this potential conclusion which the first case study starts to unravel.

The second case study examines conflicting treaties but this time across sectors of sustainable development. It takes the same subject of genetic resources so that the case studies are comparable but looks at the relationship of the CBD and the ITPGRFA with that of the TRIPS Agreement. The first case study differs slightly from the second inasmuch as the interlinkages between the treaties have already occurred, while in the second case study the interactions are limited and thus the analysis has had fewer concrete examples. Nonetheless, the analysis looks at the potential interlinkages and argues, with evidence, that the cooperation could indeed improve the effectiveness of the treaties under examination. The results of this case study reconfirm that cooperation between the treaties can improve the effectiveness of one or, in some instances, all three of the treaties. It thus reinforces the conclusion of the first case study and confirms the principal query of this book.

Additionally, the second case study suggests an important secondary proposition that was revealed in the first case study. Given that the second case study looked at interlinkages across sectors of sustainable devel-

5. Supra, chapter 7.
6. Supra, chapter 6.
7. Supra, chapter 6.
8. Supra, chapter 6.

opment, and in fact across branches of public international law, the results show that interlinkages do in fact improve the effectiveness of the treaties both within a single branch of public international law and within a single sector of sustainable development and, in addition, across branches of public international law and across sectors of sustainable development.

The results also demonstrate that treaty conflicts do not have to remain a barrier to treaty performance. On the contrary, these conflicts can be overcome and turned into synergies and lead to positive outcomes that would not have been achieved if the treaties had only worked in isolation or if they had let the conflicts persist. Furthermore, the results show a strong link with the conclusions in chapters 2 and 3 that the architecture, both from a historical point of view and from that of the existing legal system for treaty cooperation, is grossly inadequate. This implies that, if treaties have the potential to cooperate and create improved effectiveness but the means of cooperation is lacking, then the failure in the system is not with the treaties themselves but the environment in which they operate. This conclusion and the evidence proving my propositions leads me to draw some implications for the future of public international law. My conclusions have two dimensions. First, I will present conclusions under a status quo scenario that assumes the political barriers to deep structural reform are insurmountable to an environmental community with divergent views. This scenario is based on increasing the effectiveness of the current governance structure through greater interlinkages, but by only operating within the parameters of the existing international environmental governance structure. Second, I will present a deeper structural reform based on the assumption that the current political barriers and institutional barriers could be overcome if the political will existed.

A first implication under the status quo scenario is that the results of the book show that the internal rules for treaty interaction are woefully lacking. When Churchill and Ulfstein identified autonomous institutional entities of MEAs they remarked, in the title of this important article, that this was a "Little-Noticed Phenomenon in International Law", and it still remains unnoticed over six years later.[9] There has been little confirmation that MEA secretariats are indeed quasi-autonomous and, if they are, under which circumstances and legal parameters. There has been no ruling in higher courts or codification by the International Law Commission. The boundaries of legal personality for treaty secretariats are extremely important and I believe the most important power for

---

9. Robin Churchill and Geir Ulfstein (2000) *Autonomous Institutional Arrangements in Multilateral Environmental Agreements: A Little-Noticed Phenomenon in International Law*, 94 AJIL, 649.

secretariats to have is the flexibility to cooperate and the certainty to do so. In the same light, establishing the boundaries of the treaties' bodies with their parent organizations (which still retain certain powers and can exercise this power politically)[10] is also essential in the context of co-operation and flexibility. However, such clarifications are not likely to take place through international disputes given the nature of diplomacy in international environmental relations. Moreover, the UN Legal Office is not known for taking a law-making role. On the other hand, the International Law Commission should play a more active role in the progressive development and codification of this area of law.[11]

Secondly, and again under the status quo scenario, the rules and international principles in place for the management of interrelated treaties are two-dimensional, either according to the time they were consented to by the state or by the degree of their specificity, *lex specialis*. The reality of this view, however, is very different. Today, many treaties exist in parallel and function on multiple levels and interact neither in a static space in time nor are they successively displaced once a new treaty comes along. Ironically, public international law is a single corpus of law but the laws of treaties, both internally and externally, act as pressures to divide treaties into separate categories. According to international law there is no a priori hierarchy of laws[12] (except *jus cogens*[13]), yet international rules are negotiated and decided under separate processes and bodies

---

10. See chapter 3.
11. The General Assembly supported the International Law Commission's (ILC) recommendation for a broad study dealing with treaty conflicts, and that such a study should be oriented along the guidelines provided by the Vienna Convention on the Law of Treaties. UNGA (2003) *International Law Commission Report of the Study Group on Fragmentation of International Law: Difficulties Arising from the Diversification and Expansion of International Law*, UNGA Fifty-Fifth Session, at 6, UN A/CN.4/L.644.
12. Michael Akehurst (1974/75) *The Hierarchy of the Sources of International Law*, Brit. Y.B. Int'l L., 273, 274.
13. According to Article 53 of the 1969 VCLT *jus cogens* are "peremptory norms of general international law"; for legal scholarship on *jus cogens* see Ian Brownlie (1990) *Principles of Public International Law*, 4th ed., Oxford: Oxford University Press, 513; Gordon A. Christenson (1998) *Jus Cogens: Guarding Interests Fundamental to International Society*, 28 Va J. Int'l L., 585, 592; Egon Schwelb (1967) *Some Aspects of International Jus Cogens as Formulated by the International Law Commission*, 61 AJIL, 946, 949; Alfred Verdross (1966) *Jus Dispositivum and Jus Cogens in International Law*, 60 AJIL, 55, 58. Concerning the ambiguity of what laws are considered *jus cogens*, see George Schwarzenberger (1964) *International Jus Cogens?*, 43 Tex. L. Rev., 455. Also it has been argued that no treaty provision can prevail over the UN Charter; see Libyan Arab Jamahiriya v. United Kingdom, *Concerning Questions of Interpretation and Application of the 1971 Montreal Convention Arising from the Aerial Incident at Lockerbie: Request for the Indication of Provisional Measures*, ICJ Reports 1992, 3; and Libyan Arab Jamahiriya v. United States of America, ICJ Reports 1992, 114.

and even by different national departments and agencies. This leads to variations on rules and little understanding of how new rules relate to one another.[14] Joost Pauwelyn is correct and I agree with him. Increasingly, there are fewer successive treaties in a world of conflicting rules that continue to be confirmed and reconfirmed and treaties are now often "continuing" or "simultaneous".[15]

Thus, an important implication for the future of international treaty-making and the law of treaties can be drawn from this observation, as is demonstrated in the book. There is a need to create a positive rule of cooperation, a "principle of interlinkages" as it were, which promotes treaty negotiators and treaty interpreters to maintain consistency between treaties. It could oblige treaty bodies and future treaty negotiators with overlapping subject matters, or in instances where treaties have the potential to conflict, to cooperate directly once they have entered into force so that their effectiveness can be maintained and even increased.

Such a principle makes a lot of sense in two additional ways. Firstly, it would restrain those states wishing to create new treaties to counter-balance or offset other contradicting regimes, as has been the trend in recent times on issues dealing with biotechnology, traditional knowledge or even climate change. Secondly, within the branch of international environmental law, which has become highly congested in the treaty-making sense and which widely employs non-compliance mechanisms rather than confrontational dispute settlement systems, there is a tendency to produce less case law. Case law plays an important role in the interpretation of treaties and maintaining the consistency of principles and rules. In the absence of case law under international environmental law there has been arguably greater uncertainty and inconsistency, creating an operating environment that stimulates conflict and thus

14. James Crawford also speculated on the problem of the Vienna Convention for states that ratified contradictory treaties with separate states. As Special Rapporteur to the International Law Commission on State Responsibility he conjectured that "the Vienna Convention on the Law of Treaties does not contemplate that a treaty will be void for inconsistency with another treaty. Instead, it seeks to resolve the difficulties of conflicting treaty obligations by expressly reserving .... Thus it is no excuse under international law for non-compliance with a subsisting treaty obligation to State A that the State was simultaneously complying with a treaty obligation to State B. So far as the law of responsibility is concerned, this raises questions about the possibility of cessation or restitution in cases where it is impossible for the State concerned to comply with both obligations". See Int'l Law Commission (1999) *Second Report of State Responsibility*, A/CN.4/498, 7. For further reading on International Environmental Treaty Conflict see Rüdiger Wolfrum and Nele Matz (2003) *Conflicts in International Environmental Law*, Berlin and Heidelberg: Springer.
15. Joost Pauwelyn (2001) *Role of Public International Law in the WTO: How Far Can We Go?* 95 AJIL, 535.

uncertainty.[16] A principle of interlinkages could work towards resolving this and it would promote treaty-makers and treaty implementers to ensure consistency, not leaving it to chance and academic speculation to try and determine how the treaties interrelate.

An interlinkages principle could, furthermore, open a window for promoting interlinkages that is already ajar. The opening that I am referring to is Article 31 which creates certain concrete legal avenues for connecting decisions in other MEA processes through evolutionary interpretation. In my view, this has not been used to its full potential because of a lack of operational systems to promote such evolutionary interpretation. The international environmental law facilitation and conflict avoidance approach necessitates regular meetings and monitoring through Conference of the Parties. With the advent of framework treaties, regular meetings have also been required for the development of new measures while strengthening existing measures which were not fully possible at the time of negotiating the original frameworks. All this activity creates rich pools of untapped decisions and materials for furthering Article 31.

Why must these rich sources of material only be reserved for interpretation when disputes occur, which they seldom do? Why could not this material be positively developed as a means of connecting the MEAs, interpreting unclear clauses and providing guidance on how they could be connected? The answer to the question is not rhetorical; this possibility could be a reality with the right institution in place. Such institutions certainly are not through superficial inter-MEAs liaison talk shops like the Environmental Management Group which lacks any authority and operational capacity.[17] On the other hand, success could be achieved through an MEA law review commission established between the MEAs that could examine the decisions and better establish the interconnections between them as well as help codify and strengthen their international consistency. The commission could serve as a catalyst, consolidator and connector for MEAs. It could be established jointly by the COPs (many of which have the legal ability to create new bodies, see chapter 3) and the commission could make recommendations on interpretation to the General Assembly. The GA could in turn make authoritative resolutions on the connections and consolidated understanding on areas where MEAs overlap.

Ecologically, such a commission also makes sense given the increasing awareness by scientists that environmental problems do not fit nicely into the categories of the MEAs that have been negotiated the last three

16. See for example the usage of the Precautionary Approach in the Cartagena Protocol versus the Precautionary Approach in Agenda 21.
17. Supra chapter 2.

decades and they are now aware that many of the problems are interconnected. A recent report by Global Environment Facility argues that there are five main categories of biophysical interlinkages, climate change-biodiversity, climate change-biodiversity-land degradation, climate change-water degradation, land degradation-biodiversity, water degradation-biodiversity.[18] Many of these problems fall outside the scope of a single MEA or the treaties addressing these problems but these cross-cutting areas could be jointly addressed if there were greater cooperation between the MEAs. However, such cooperation is not going to occur if there are no incentives for it to take place, either financial ones or, in the event of a suggested commission which could legally rationalize the necessity for cooperation through an overarching authority such as the GA – but based on well-thought-out recommendations made from an inter-MEA commission.

If, however, policy-makers are indeed ready for deeper structural changes (which I believe is the best solution for creating greater effectiveness) then, in closing this book, I would like to draw attention to a more profound reform. It is not a reform of particular originality but it remains worthy of constant reminding. For more effective treaties it is incumbent upon policy-makers to create an international governance structure that will act as a conduit to inter-treaty cooperation (governance matters). The current system is a barrier; it has systematically created layer upon layer of inefficient mechanisms for cooperation. The time has come to start afresh and build a simple and straightforward international architecture that will create the incentives and the hierarchy for cooperation to take place. After 30 years of intense treaty-making for the betterment of the environment, the time has finally come to step back and admire what has been done, ponder the accomplishment with appreciation, but then finally build a house that is fitting of its needs so that MEAs can accomplish even more. I believe such a house would be the creation of a WEO to host the principal MEAs. As argued in chapter 3, it would have a compulsory dispute settlement system, which is both facilitative and enforceable, common institutional laws governing their internal procedures, perform major functions such as assisting countries to synergistically implement MEAs, provide oversight and policy advice, and create a common integrated science assessment and monitoring platform. Such a house is the most effective response to capturing the types of interlinkages that the book has shown are beneficial to all MEAs and such a house could be build from the foundation of UNEP.

18. Habiba Gitay, ed. (2004) "A Conceptual Design Tool for Exploiting Interlinkages between the Focal Areas of GEF", *Global Environment Facility Scientific and Technical Advisory Panel* (November), 14–15.

Appendix

Selected legal materials concerning MEA coherence, interlinkages and synergies

1997 Nairobi Declaration

UNEP, *Nairobi Declaration on the Role and Mandate of UNEP*, UNEP/GC19/1/1997, 1997.

> The Nairobi Declaration was agreed by ministers of the environment and heads of delegation attending the nineteenth session of the Governing Council held during January & February, 1997. The declaration defining the future role and mandate of UNEP was endorsed by the special session of the United Nations General Assembly held in New York in June, 1997.

The Heads of Delegation declare:

1. That the United Nations Environment Programme has been and should continue to be the principal United Nations body in the field of the environment and that we, the ministers of the environment and heads of delegation attending the nineteenth session of the Governing Council, are determined to play a stronger role in the implementation of the goals and objectives of the United Nations Environment Programme;

2. That the role of the United Nations Environment Programme is to be the leading global environmental authority that sets the global envi-

ronmental agenda, that promotes the coherent implementation of the environmental dimension of sustainable development within the United Nations system and that serves as an authoritative advocate for the global environment;

3. That to this end, we reaffirm the continuing relevance of the mandate of the United Nations Environment Programme deriving from General Assembly resolution 2997 (XXVII) of 15 December 1972 and further elaborated by Agenda 21. The core elements of the focused mandate of the revitalized United Nations Environment Programme should be the following:

   a) To analyse the state of the global environment and assess global and regional environmental trends, provide policy advice, early warning information on environmental threats, and to catalyse and promote international cooperation and action, based on the best scientific and technical capabilities available;

   b) To further the development of its international environmental law aiming at sustainable development, including the development of coherent interlinkages among existing international environmental conventions;

   c) To advance the implementation of agreed international norms and policies, to monitor and foster compliance with environmental principles and international agreements and stimulate cooperative action to respond to emerging environmental challenges;

   d) To strengthen its role in the coordination of environmental activities in the United Nations system in the field of the environment, as well as its role as an Implementing Agency of the Global Environment Facility, based on its comparative advantage and scientific and technical expertise;

   e) To promote greater awareness and facilitate effective cooperation among all sectors of society and actors involved in the implementation of the international environmental agenda, and to serve as an effective link between the scientific community and policy makers at the national and international levels;

   f) To provide policy and advisory services in key areas of institution-building to Governments and other relevant institutions.

1997 Renewing the United Nations Report

UNGA, *Renewing the United Nations: A Programme for Reform*, A/51/950, July 14, 1997.

Excerpts paras. 85, 170–179, 248

85. Member States appear to have decided to retain the Trusteeship Council. The Secretary-General proposes, therefore, that it be reconstituted as the forum through which Member states exercise their collective trusteeship for the integrity of the global environment and common areas such as the oceans, atmosphere, and outer space. At the same time, it should serve to link the United Nations and civil society in addressing these areas of global concern, which require the active contribution of public, private, and voluntary sectors.

D. ENVIRONMENT, HABITAT AND SUSTAINABLE DEVELOPMENT

170. Of the challenges facing the world community in the next century, none will be more formidable or pervasive as the attainment of a sustainable equilibrium between economic growth, poverty reduction, social equity and the protection of the Earth's resources, commons and life-support systems.

171. The recently-completed nineteenth special session of the General Assembly reviewed programmes and prospects on the fifth anniversary of UNCED and the twenty-fifty anniversary of the Stockholm Conference and underscored the difficulties and divisions which continue to impede progress towards agreement on the cooperative measures required to deal with these issues and to ensure enforcement of existing agreements.

172. A particularly important product of the Earth Summit has been the proliferation of new actors in the field of environment and sustainable development and their expanding participation in United Nations deliberations, negotiations and actions. This has led to changes in the scope of the international and environmental agenda to focus on the environment as a critical component of sustainable development. In addition, it is clear that the world of the twenty-first century will be predominantly urban and the transition to global sustainability will largely depend on the success in ensuring the sustainable development of our cities and towns. Sustainable development is now understood to consist of a positive synthesis between the environmental, social and economic dimensions of development.

173. In the United Nations, the Commission on Sustainable Development (CSD) has become an important policy forum; environmental capacities within major United Nations bodies and specialized agencies

have been developed; and the number of international environmental conventions with autonomous governing bodies and secretariats has been growing.

174. Overall the response to the needs of developing countries for new and additional financial resources has been disappointing and Official Development Assistance has declined since Rio. The Global Environment Facility (GEF), established to finance the incremental costs of certain sustainable development projects, has functioned well and now needs to be replenished at higher levels and its scope expanded. UNDP, the World Bank and other multilateral and bilateral funding agencies are devoting a growing proportion of resources to sustainable development-related projects and programmes. And with the increased role of private investment, the recent initiative of the World Bank to develop, in cooperation with other interested parties, voluntary guidelines for private investment, is a welcome development. Little progress has been made in developing new and innovative sources of financing for the transition to sustainable development. However, some promising prospects are emerging as, for example, the development of a system of "offsets" to carbon dioxide emissions through joint implementation and emission trading which could produce significant new flows of resources to developing countries.

175. What has emerged clearly from the experience represented by these events is the need for a more integrated systemic approach to policies and programmes throughout the whole range of United Nations activities in the economic, social and development fields through mainstreaming the Organization's commitment to sustainable development. This requires closer cooperation and interaction between UNEP and Habitat and between both entities and other departments, funds and programmes in the economic, social and development areas. It is necessary to that end to strengthen the system of task managers under the ACC Inter-Agency Committee on Sustainable Development (IACSD) in which both UNEP and Habitat are actively involved. At the intergovernmental level, the fact that the Governing Council of UNEP and the Commission on Human Settlements report to the United Nations General Assembly should not preclude or inhibit this process as both report through the Economic and Social Council.

176. UNEP is the environmental voice of the United Nations and the principal source of the environmental input into the work of the CSD. High priority must be given to according to it the status, strength and access to resources it requires to function effectively as the environmental

agency of the world community. This has been confirmed by the Nairobi Declaration, adopted by the UNEP Governing Council, at its nineteenth session, in February 1997. UNEP's role as the focal point for harmonisation and coordination of environment-related activities must be strengthened, and the Secretary-General intends to lend his full support to this process.

177. The important experience and capacities that UNEP has developed in the areas of monitoring and assessment, through its GEMS and GRID programmes, constitute an invaluable resource which must be further developed and enhanced in the period ahead. So too its key functions as the forum for development of international policy, law and negotiation and implementation of cooperative arrangements to deal with environmental issues, as a bridge between science and policy-making as well as its inter-acting relationships with national environmental organisations and agencies. One of the most notable achievements of UNEP has been its contribution to the initiation, negotiation and support of some of the most important treaties that have been agreed in the international field. Many of these continue to depend on continued support by UNEP. The operational projects at the country level that have been financed by the Fund of UNEP can now be more appropriately funded by UNDP and other sources. Accordingly, UNEP will discontinue implementation of such projects.

178. The High-Level Advisory Board on Sustainable Development appointed by the Secretary-General in July 1993 [7] has made a valuable contribution to the work of the CSD during its initial five years in analysing and elaborating a number of key sustainable development issues. With the initiation by CSD of promising new arrangements for consultations with and participation in its work by various relevant civil society actors, the Secretary-General believes that the functions of the High-Level Advisory Board on Sustainable Development could now be effectively performed through these processes.

179. On this twenty-fifth anniversary of the establishment of UNEP, and in light of the recommendations of the Istanbul Conference on Human Settlements, it is most timely and necessary to take immediate steps to strengthen UNEP and Habitat, while considering the fundamental changes that may be required to clarify and focus their structures and functions within a reformed United Nations in the economic, social and development fields as well as to revitalise political and financial support for them. The nineteenth special session of the General Assembly has provided useful guidance in this respect.

Action 12:

The Secretary-General will, in consultation with governments, the Executive Director of UNEP and the Executive Director of the United Nations Centre for Human Settlements, develop new measures for strengthening and restructuring the two organizations, based on General Assembly resolutions 2997 (XXVII) and 32/162 and taking into account the decisions and recommendations of the Governing Council of UNEP and the United Nations Commission on Human Settlements, and will make recommendations to the General Assembly at its fifty-third session.

248. Many activities which the United Nations system is mandated by various governing bodies to undertake involve more than one organization, some of which have activities and interests in the subject area concerned. Coordination of these activities has largely been the responsibility of the Administrative Committee for Coordination (ACC) machinery. But with the growing need for a systemic and integrated approach to development, traditional processes of coordination need to be supplemented by a series of practical arrangements which provide for more active, cooperative management of those issues by each of the organizations concerned, both within the United Nations system and extending to other involved intergovernmental and non-governmental organizations. There is already some useful precedent for arrangements of this kind, as for example, in the working parties established by the Secretariat of UNCED in preparation for the Earth Summit. The approaches developed by ACC to promote coordinated follow-up to global conferences and to implement the System-Wide Special Initiative on Africa are also relevant in this area.

1998 Report of the United Nations Task Force on Environment and Human Settlements

UNGA, *Report of the United Nations Task Force on Environment and Human Settlements*, A/53/463, 1998.

Excerpts paras. 11–14

A. Inter-agency coordination

11. Recommendation 1 of the Task Force relates to improved inter-agency coordination. In response to the perceived need for effective coordination, the Task Force recommended that the Secretary-General

establish an environmental management group under the chairmanship of the Executive Director of UNEP. The group would adopt a problem-solving, results oriented approach that would enable United Nations bodies and their partners to share information, consult on proposed new initiatives and contribute to a planning framework and develop agreed priorities and their respective roles in the implementation of those priorities in order to achieve a more rational and cost-effective use of their resources. It would also provide a forum and a mechanism to enhance complementarity between the analytical and normative activities of UNEP with the operational role of the United Nations Development Programme (UNDP). As such, the group would follow the "issue management" approach outlined by the Secretary-General in his reform report. The group would be supported by Secretariat arrangements that would draw on the existing substantive capacity of UNEP and Habitat.

The reports of the group could be made available to relevant intergovernmental bodies to enhance intergovernmental policy coherence. The Task Force recommended that following the conclusion of the current General Assembly session, the Secretary-General consult with members of ACC and decide on the establishment of the group.

B. Linkages among and support to environmental and environment-related conventions

12. A series of actions are recommended under recommendation 2 of the Task Force that have implications both at the secretariat and intergovernmental levels for UNEP, and are consistent with the mandate of UNEP as contained in relevant General Assembly resolutions and UNEP Governing Council decisions.

13. In pursuance of these recommendations, the Executive Director of UNEP would take action to:

(a) Base UNEP support to global and regional conventions on its capacities for information, monitoring and assessment, which should also be strengthened (recommendation 2 (a));
(b) Continue to sponsor joint meetings of heads of convention secretariats to ensure that the work programmes established by conferences of parties to conventions and the substantive support provided by UNEP are complementary, fill gaps and take advantage of synergy (recommendation 2 (b)).

14. The Task Force also recommended that the Secretary-General, through the Executive Director of UNEP, invite Governments and conferences of parties to consider the implications of operational inefficiencies and costs arising from the geographical dispersion of convention sec-

retariats and ways of overcoming this. Further consultations among the relevant United Nations entities will be required to develop the modalities for the implementation of this recommendation, and should result in specific proposals being made to the relevant intergovernmental bodies for their consideration (recommendation 2 (d)).

Excerpt paras. 19–31 (including Recommendations 1 and 2)

A. Inter-agency linkages

19. The Task Force considers that the United Nations system needs a strong and respected UNEP as its leading environmental organization. For this purpose, UNEP needs to be given adequate financial, staff and information capacities. In particular, it should be the recognized centre of a network of information, monitoring, assessment and early warning, and should play to the full its role as an implementing agency of GEF.

20. The Task Force's review of existing United Nations structures and arrangements in the field of environment and human settlements, linked to different issues and including in-depth examination of the energy and water sectors, has revealed that current United Nations activities are characterized by substantial overlaps, unrecognized linkages and gaps. These flaws are basic and pervasive. They prevent the United Nations system from using its scarce resources to best advantage in addressing problems that are crucial to the human future; harm the credibility and weight of the United Nations in the environmental arena; and damage the United Nations working relationship with its partners in and outside of Government.

21. What is needed is a problem-solving, results-oriented approach that enables United Nations bodies and their partners to share information about their respective plans and activities; to inform and consult one another about proposed new initiatives; to contribute to a planning framework that permits the plans and activities of each participant to be reviewed within the framework of the whole range of activities being carried on by all participants; and to consult with each other with a view to developing an agreed set of priorities and on the measures through which each participating organization can best contribute to those priorities and achieve a more rational and cost-effective use of their respective capacities and resources.

22. These needs were recognized by the Secretary-General in his report on reform under the heading "Strategy 8: Institute an issue management system" (see A/51/950, paras. 248–250).

Recommendation 1

The Task Force recommends that in order to meet these needs with respect to the environment and human settlements, the Secretary-General should establish an environmental management group. It would replace the existing Inter-Agency Environment Coordination Group, which should be abolished:

23. The environmental management group would be chaired by the Executive Director of UNEP, supported by a secretariat. The Chair would report to the Secretary-General. The group would include as core members the main United Nations entities concerned with environment and human settlements. Particular meetings would involve additional United Nations entities, financial institutions, and organizations outside the United Nations system that have experience and expertise relevant to the issues on the agenda.

24. The environmental management group would be concerned with environment and human settlement issues in the context of the linkages between environment and development, as defined at UNCED and subsequently elaborated. Habitat should be a prominent participant in the group, which should structure its operations so as to achieve an integrated United Nations work programme that bridges the gaps that have existed between the two areas.

25. The most important goal of the environmental management group should be to achieve effective coordination and joint action in key areas of environmental and human settlements concern. Another important objective should be to assist intergovernmental bodies in the area of environment and human settlements, in particular the UNEP Governing Council and the commission on Human Settlements, in the preparation of coordinated inputs to intergovernmental forums, notably the Commission on Sustainable Development. The group should report on an informational basis to ACC, and should bring an environmental perspective into the work of IACSD. The group should establish time-bound task forces or working groups covering clusters of issues in which representatives of the main institutions involved in a particular issue can work together quickly to solve important problems (for example, the recently reconstituted Ecosystem Conservation Group).

26. The environmental management group should include convention secretariats among its participants, when needed. In addition to facilitating the kinds of linkages among conventions that are recommended in

section III.B below, the group should act to ensure that there are appropriate linkages among activities that occur under conventions and relevant activities elsewhere in the international system.

27. The Task Force considered the question whether the environmental management group should produce a single United Nations environmental programme, similar to the former system-wide, medium-term environment programme. The Task Force concluded that in view of fast-moving global trends, a static programme, no matter how frequently it is updated, is bound to lag behind real needs. Instead, the group should create a dynamic process for review of planned activities and modification of goals and activities in the light of new knowledge. However, subgroups of the environmental management group may agree on sharply focused action plans as a means of coordinating actions at the programme level and allocating resources in the most effective manner.

28. Regional action and regional coordination are essential in the field of environment and human settlements. At the level of field operations, the existing system of United Nations resident coordinators is responsible for effective coordination of activities related to environment and human settlements, and should be strengthened. The environmental management group should from time to time review the effectiveness of this coordination.

B. Linkages among and support to environmental and environment-related conventions

29. The creation of a large number of legally binding instruments in areas of environmental concern has been a major success of the international community. However, asa result of decisions by Governments, the secretariats of environmental and environment-related conventions have been located in diverse geographic locations, with little regard to the functional relationships among conventions. That dispersal has resulted in loss of efficiency because of inability to take advantage of synergies among conventions and substantial costs through loss of economies of scale and fragmentation of administrative, conference and infrastructure services. The period after UNCED led to a significant increase in activities related to environmental and environment-related conventions, and the number of international meetings of relevant treaty bodies has increased significantly. This has created additional burdens, especially for ministers.

30. Bearing in mind that the main policy decisions under conventions are taken by their respective conferences of parties, which are autonomous

bodies, strengthening of the linkages between conventions with a view to achieving synergies and multiple benefits and promoting coherence of policies and actions should be a long-term strategic goal of the international community. Intergovernmental bodies, including the General Assembly in paragraphs 119 and 123 of the Programme for the Further Implementation of Agenda 21 (see General Assembly resolution S/19-2 of 28 June 1997, annex), have identified the need for more effective linkages and support. Decisions of the General Assembly at its nineteenth special session, in 1997, and prior decisions by the General Assembly and the UNEP Governing Council have provided a clear basis for UNEP to foster such linkages. Pursuant to these mandates, UNEP has sponsored annual meetings of the secretariats of selected environmental conventions, which have addressed common issues, such as implementation at the national level, including development of relevant national legislation and institutions, capacity-building and technical assistance.

31. Further steps are needed to strengthen linkages and provide support that will ensure that the international community derives maximum benefit from the investments it has made in this system of international instruments.

Recommendation 2

The Task Force recommends that, in addition to integrating convention secretariats and convention-related issues in the work of the environmental management group, the following actions should be taken by UNEP in pursuance of the above-mentioned mandate from the General Assembly at its nineteenth special session:

(a) UNEP's substantive support to global and regional conventions should be founded on its capacities for information, monitoring and assessment, which need to be strengthened substantially and urgently for this purpose. UNEP should build its capacity and its networks of support in order to ensure the scientific underpinning of conventions, to respond to their requests for specialized analysis and technological assessments, and to facilitate their implementation;

(b) The Executive Director of UNEP should continue to sponsor joint meetings of heads of secretariats of global and regional conventions, and should use this forum to recommend actions to ensure that the work programmes established by the conferences of parties to the conventions, together with substantive support offered by UNEP, are complementary, fill gaps and take advantage of synergy, and avoid overlap and duplication. These meetings also should explore ways of fulfilling common substantive and administrative needs. Recommendations from these meetings should be presented to the conferences of parties by the respective secretariats;

(c) The Governing Council of UNEP should invite its President to consult the presidents of conferences of parties to selected conventions on arrangements for periodic meetings between representatives of those conventions in order to address cross-cutting issues arising from the work programmes of these bodies and policy approaches being followed by them. The Executive Director of UNEP and the heads of the respective convention secretariats would organize and participate in these meetings. The conclusions of these meetings would be brought to the attention of UNEP's Governing Council and the respective conferences of parties by the respective secretariats;

(d) Concerned about the operational inefficiencies and costs arising from the geographical dispersal of convention secretariats, the Task Force recommends that the Secretary-General, through the Executive Director of UNEP, invite Governments and Conferences of Parties to consider the implications of this trend and ways to overcome the resulting problems. Every effort should be made to co-locate new conventions with other conventions in the same functional cluster (for example, biological resources, chemicals/waste, marine pollution) and with institutions with which they have a particular affinity. With respect to existing conventions, approaches should include promoting cooperation among the secretariats within each cluster with a view to their eventual co-location and possible fusion into a single secretariat, and, in the longer term, should include the negotiation of umbrella conventions covering each cluster.

1999 United Nations University Interlinkages Report

Excerpt: Section defining the origin and scope of the challenge

Defining the origin and the scope of the challenge

In the environmental realm, treaty making has often been segregated on the basis of topic, sector, or territory. The result has been the negotiation of treaties that may overlap and conflict with each other. In some instances, the implementation of one treaty may undermine the very principles upon which another is based. It is also the case that the network of environmentally related treaties, that has expanded along with our understanding of our planet, is in danger of becoming unnecessarily complicated. This places additional burdens at the national level, as signatories struggle to meet their obligations under several different agreements. If

MEAs were better co-ordinated, this may help to alleviate some of these burdens and also:
- Promote the efficient use of international and national resources;
- Ensure that internationally agreed environmental laws and policies are mutually supportive, and;
- Balance the potentially competing international agendas for promoting environmental protection and the law, policy, and institutions designed to promote other objectives, such as enhancing international trade and investment.

Research and analysis recognises that the need for greater international cooperation is not unique to global environmental governance. The fundamental starting point for any international law and policy making is the sovereign and independent nation state. States have tended to consent to new laws and institutions, such as MEAs, in an ad hoc manner, and only when growing awareness, and political momentum, force a response to a new problem. This momentum can be channelled through a variety of existing institutions and may lead to the creation of new institutions. The result is fragmentation. There have been a number of proposals to create an overarching, unitary structure for global environmental governance. Yet states have not yet, nor are they likely to soon, consented to such an approach. The co-ordination efforts of overarching bodies such as the Commission on Sustainable Development and the Economic and Social Council (ECOSOC) have been difficult because their mandates have been too vague and too broad, particularly in relation to the powers states have been willing to grant them. Besides, shortcomings in the effectiveness of MEAs are, in part, attributable to weaknesses in the ability of international law and international institutions generally to create or enforce rules. No amount of co-ordination of MEAs will overcome these fundamental shortcomings.

Divergent views exist in terms of the scope and seriousness of the implications of this fragmented governance for the effectiveness of MEAs. Some analysts call for strong co-ordination between MEAs, while others suggest that the absence of centralised procedures and institutions is a strength of thestatus quo, as it promotes healthy competition and opportunities for learning. The ability of the international system to generate new MEAs is often cited as evidence of the success of the present system. It is also common, however, to express concern over the bewildering number of MEAs, and to invoke an image of overlap and confusion. Treaty secretariats have indeed been physically dispersed around the globe, and intergovernmental meetings tend to take place in whatever country is willing and able to host them. It is possible to calculate the real and growing costs to international institutions, governments, and organisations that participate in MEAs. These costs, when multiplied by a large and growing number of agreements and meetings, can appear overwhelming.

1. Introduction

Within a practical analysis, however, fewer than a dozen MEAs emerge as being sufficiently global in their membership and in their reach to merit serious concern regarding overlap or conflict. While there is a growing appreciation of environmental relationships across national boundaries and regions, a relatively narrow range of environmental threats are truly global in scale. The challenges of global environmental governance are neither unique, nor insurmountable, and progress has already been made to promote coherence and effectiveness.

Recommendations and conclusions

Research reveals that, despite the apparent incoherence in the process by which MEAs are designed, the international community has been remarkably adept at anticipating and avoiding conflict, both among MEAs and between MEAs and other, potentially competing, regimes.

This coherence has been achieved through:
- Formal mechanisms,
- Informal, pragmatic approaches to implementation, and
- The self-restraint of policy makers, who have chosen not to exploit gaps or conflicts that might otherwise have led to disputes.

Indeed, it is possible to catalogue an impressive number of mechanisms, both formal and informal, that have already been put in place to promote co-ordination of environmental policy at the international level. Formal co-ordination through the conscious design of treaty rules, and through the decisions of Conferences of the Parties, has proved useful in staking out the distinct jurisdictions of certain MEAs. These rules and decisions may help avoid potential conflicts. This co-ordination has, however, taken place without the intervention of an overarching institution or process. Indeed there is some evidence to suggest that an overarching regime might have led to harder bargaining between parties, detrimental trade-offs, and weaker rules.

Agreeing upon formal rules for accommodating potential conflicts between MEAs and, for example, the WTO, may prove more difficult. While a wide array of proposals has emerged as to how best to balance the potentially competing objectives of environmental protection and trade liberalisation, agreement has not yet been possible. Recent developments in WTO jurisprudence suggest that trade-related environmental measures, when backed by an MEA, would be more than likely to survive a WTO challenge. While some comfort can be taken from the fact that no MEA has yet been challenged directly under the WTO, if a dispute does arise, it will likely be the WTO's compulsory dispute settlement system that makes the final judgement as to which regime prevails. The physical dispersal of treaty secretariats has been cited, by some, as a major lost opportunity for synergy and co-ordination. As intergovernmental meetings often take place at the seat of the secretariat, this dispersal has also had an impact on the ability of governments to provide regular representation to these meetings. Specifically, opportunities to support the permanent representation of developing country government delegations working on international environmental issues in a single location were clearly lost. It has, however, been suggested that physical co-location would not, in itself, have guaranteed synergies, and that well-managed agencies located in different parts of the world have had long histories of close collaboration.

Some MEA secretariats have sought, with the support of their parties, to patch themselves together through the use of formal agreements. These have proved to be generally formalistic and empty documents, although they have encouraged a process of interaction and provided a mandate for information exchange and reciprocal representation between regimes that could prove useful. Similar techniques have also been employed to link MEAs with potential "competitors" such as the WTO. MEA Secretariats are regularly invited to brief the WTO Committee on Trade and Environment on MEA trade-related issues.

A kind of spontaneous and organic co-ordination has taken place through the efforts of individual participants in the MEA processes. The proliferation of regimes and the significant (though still limited) resources made available through MEAs, has led to the emergence of a new breed of "super-delegate", and to the growing number of specialist MEA-focused NGOs. These individuals and groups may spend their entire working year following the meetings of the various MEA institutions, drawing attention to potential conflicts and cross-pollinating ideas between agreements. Co-ordination between institutions appears to have developed more readily when a clear division of labour is made between policy-making functions, and the provision of scientific and technical expertise or capacity building. The scientific, technical and capacity building resources of the UN system, and other existing international and non-governmental organisations, have served the policy making needs of the treaty bodies well, particularly in the areas of climate change and biodiversity. Through the efforts of these institutions, international instruments have been gradually coming to terms with the ecological interconnectivity of the areas they seek to regulate, and a number of potential conflicts have been avoided. These observations do not imply that conflicts will never arise, or that greater efforts at co-ordination are unwarranted. Even the suggestion that the lack of co-ordination leads to healthy competition implicitly recognises that the MEAs are and must be sufficiently "linked", formally or informally, to be able to "compete" through exchange information and experience.

A fundamental starting point for environmental law and policy is science. The bio-/geo-physical relationships between the sectors, substances, and activities that MEAs seek to protect or regulate, provide an obvious organising principle for MEA co-ordination. From this starting point, researchers often call for closer co-ordination on the basis of ecosystems, target substances, or protected species. Broader organising principles, most notably the concept of "sustainable development", have provided a less concrete and, therefore, a less helpful basis for co-ordination.

A common denominator for such analyses is an emphasis on improving the individual and combined environmental effectiveness and cost effectiveness of MEAs. One methodology for assessing the effectiveness of each MEA is to analyse its ability to promote, as efficiently as possible:

- Output (decision making that leads to new rules and norms)
- Outcome (changes in behaviour in the target actors)
- Impacts (the desired improvements in the environment problem)

Co-ordination has the potential to improve each of these aspects of MEA effectiveness by promoting the coherence of rules and norms, sending mutually enforcing signals about behavioural change, and ensuring that the desired impacts on the environment of one regime do not undermine the desired impacts of another. Pragmatic approaches to designing effective institutions support the adage that "form should follow function." It is possible to identify a range of functions typically carried out by the procedures and institutions created by MEA. Among the functions identified are:

- Agenda setting
- Decision-making for rules and norms
- Information gathering and management
- Scientific, technological and economic assessments
- Capacity Building
- Technical and Financial Support
- Assessment of Country Performance
- Non-compliance Response/Dispute Settlement
- Review of Regime Performance

Different types of institutions have been built up either within, or external to, MEAs that have been designed or assigned to carry out these functions. These include:

- Conferences of Parties
- Secretariats

- Bodies for Scientific and Technological Advice
- Bodies for Technical Assessment of Information
- Bodies for Assessing Compliance and Responding to Non-Compliance
- Financial Institutions
- Capacity Building Institutions

The principle of subsidiarity, which calls for decisions to be taken at a level appropriate to the problem they address, is often emphasised. It has been noted that many of the ecosystems of concern are best defined, understood, and protected at the regional or local level rather than the global level.

A number of studies suggest that, within certain sectors, MEAs or other international agreements or institutions that have a broad mandate and offer general, unifying, principles could serve as umbrella agreements. These, or new umbrella agreements, could co-ordinate the narrower and more implementation-focused efforts of other MEAs, or help to provide a regular focal point for agenda setting and co-ordination. It has also been suggested, however, that global co-ordination could lead to unnecessary inflexibility, and in some circumstances should be restricted to dealing with conflict avoidance, the provision of financial assistance, and to facilitating information exchange for "lessons learned".

The related principle of comparative advantage recognises that international institutions are endowed with different mandates, legal personality and capacity, resources, and expertise. The most successful attempts at formal co-operation have been careful to recognise this principle in dividing labour among international institutions. Several studies have emphasised the difference between primarily administrative agencies (such as Secretariats) which are generally constrained to operating within the mandate given to them by governments; and intergovernmental bodies (such as the treaty COPs) which can by the volition of their member states change their own mandates and direction.

Finally, initiatives on inter-linkages must be sensitive to fact that efforts at co-ordination will arouse invested institutional interests or, what could be described as, the threat of "turf wars". Drives for efficiency, while often motivated by the scarcity of resources, do not necessary lead to the availability of additional resources. In other words, existing institutions are perfectly aware that efficiency gains, whether they are achieved through increased co-ordination or heightened competition, may lead to a bottom line of budget cuts and job losses. Better-resourced MEAs are likely to prove less willing to co-operate out of concern that they will end up with a smaller slice of the pie; less-efficient, or under-resourced, institutions may press for heightened levels of co-operation in an attempt to benefit from others' resources.

2000 Malmö Declaration

UNEP, Malmö Ministerial Declaration, UNEP/GC/21/21/2000, (31 May 2000).

Except paras. 3, 24–25

3. The evolving framework of international environmental law and the development of national law provide a sound basis for addressing the major environmental threats of the day. It must be underpinned by a more coherent and coordinated approach among international environmental instruments. We must also recognize the central importance of environmental compliance, enforcement and liability, and promote the observation of the precautionary approach as contained in the Rio Principles (2), and other important policy tools, as well as capacity-building.

24. The 2002 conference should review the requirements for a greatly strengthened institutional structure for international environmental governance based on an assessment of future needs for an institutional architecture that has the capacity to effectively address wide-ranging environmental threats in a globalizing world. UNEP's role in this regard should be strengthened and its financial base broadened and made more predictable.

25. At the dawn of this new century, we have at our disposal the human and material resources to achieve sustainable development, not as an abstract concept but as a concrete reality. The unprecedented developments in production and information technologies, the emergence of a younger generation with a clear sense of optimism, solidarity and values, women increasingly aware and with an enhanced and active role in society – all point to the emergence of a new consciousness. We can decrease poverty by half by 2015 without degrading the environment, we can ensure environmental security through early warning, we can better integrate environmental considerations in economic policy, we can better coordinate legal instruments and we can realize a vision of a world without slums. We commit ourselves to realizing this common vision.

2006 International Law Commission Study Group on Fragmentation

ILC, (finalized by Martti Koskenniemi), *Fragmentation of International Law Difficulties Arising from the Diversification and Expansion of*

International Law: International Law Commission Study Group on Fragmentation, A/CN.4/L.682, 2006.

Selected excerpt paras. 5–26

Fragmentation as a phenomenon

The background

5. The background of fragmentation was sketched already half a century ago by Wilfred Jenks, drawing attention in particular to two phenomena. On the one hand, the international world lacked a general legislative body. Thus:

... law-making treaties are tending to develop in a number of historical, functional and regional groups which are separate from each other and whose mutual relationships are in some respects analogous to those of separate systems of municipal law.[8]

6. Very presciently, Jenks envisaged the need for a close analogy with conflict of laws to deal with this type of fragmentation. This would be a law regulating not conflicts between territorial legal systems, but conflicts between treaty regimes. A second reason for the phenomenon he found within the law itself. One of the most serious sources of conflict between law-making treaties is the important development of the law governing the revision of multilateral instruments and defining the legal effects of revision.[9]

7. There is little to be added to that analysis today. Of course, the volume of multilateral – "legislative" – treaty activity has grown manifold in the past fifty years.[10] It has also been accompanied by various more or less formal regulatory regimes not all which share the public law orientation of multilateral diplomacy.[11] One of the features of late international modernity has been what sociologists have called "functional differentiation", the increasing specialization of parts of society and the related autonomization of those parts. This takes place nationally as well as internationally. It is a well-known paradox of globalization that while it has led to increasing uniformization of social life around the world, it has also lead to its increasing fragmentation – that is, to the emergence of specialized and relatively autonomous spheres of social action and structure.

8. The fragmentation of the international social world has attained legal significance especially as it has been accompanied by the emergence of specialized and (relatively) autonomous rules or rule-complexes, legal in-

stitutions and spheres of legal practice.[12] What once appeared to be governed by "general international law" has become the field of operation for such specialist systems as "trade law", "human rights law", "environmental law", "law of the sea", "European law" and even such exotic and highly specialized knowledges as "investment law" or "international refugee law" etc. – each possessing their own principles and institutions. The problem, as lawyers have seen it, is that such specialized law-making and institution-building tends to take place with relative ignorance of legislative and institutional activities in the adjoining fields and of the general principles and practices of international law. The result is conflicts between rules or rule-systems, deviating institutional practices and, possibly, the loss of an overall perspective on the law.[13]

9. While the reality and importance of fragmentation, both in its legislative and institutional form, cannot be doubted, international lawyers have been divided in their assessment of the phenomenon. Some commentators have been highly critical of what they have seen as the erosion of general international law, emergence of conflicting jurisprudence, forum-shopping and loss of legal security. Others have seen here a merely technical problem that has emerged naturally with the increase of international legal activity may be controlled by the use of technical streamlining and coordination.[14]

10. Without going into details of the sociological or political background that has led to the emergence of special or specialist rule-systems and institutions, the nature of the legal problem may perhaps best be illustrated by reference to a practical example. The question of the possible environmental effects of the operation of the "MOX Plant" nuclear facility at Sellafield, United Kingdom, has recently been raised at three different institutional procedures: an Arbitral Tribunal set up under Annex VII of the United Nations Convention on the Law of the Sea (UNCLOS), the compulsory dispute settlement procedure under the Convention on the Protection of the Marine Environment of the North-East Atlantic (OSPAR Convention) as well as under the European Community and Euratom Treaties within the European Court of Justice (ECJ). Three rule-complexes all appear to address the same facts: the (universal) rules of the UNCLOS, the (regional) rules of the OSPAR Convention, and the (regional) rules of EC/EURATOM. Which should be determinative? Is the problem principally about the law of the sea, about (possible) pollution of the North Sea, or about inter-EC relationships? Already to pose such questions points to the difficulty of providing an answer. How do such rule-complexes link to each other, if at all? What principles should be used in order to decide a potential conflict between them?

11. Yet the problem is even more difficult. Discussing the British objection to its jurisdiction on account of the same matter being also pending before an OSPAR arbitral tribunal and the ECJ, the Arbitral Tribunal set up under Annex VII UNCLOS observed: even if the OSPAR Convention, the EC Treaty and the Euratom treaty contain rights or obligations similar to or identical with the rights set out in [the UNCLOS], the rights and obligations under these agreements have a separate existence from those under [the UNCLOS].[15]

12. The Tribunal held that the application of even the same rules by different institutions might be different owing to the "differences in the respective context, object and purposed, subsequent practice of parties and *travaux preparatoires*".[16] The UNCLOS Arbitral tribunal recognized that the meaning of legal rules and principles is dependent on the context in which they are applied. If the context, including the normative environment, is different, then even identical provisions may appear differently. But what does this do to the objectives of legal certainty and the equality of legal subjects?

13. The previous paragraph raises both institutional and substantive problems. The former have to do with the competence of various institutions applying international legal rules and their hierarchical relations *inter se*. The Commission decided to leave this question aside. The issue of institutional competencies is best dealt with by the institutions themselves. The Commission has instead wished to focus on the substantive question – the splitting up of the law into highly specialized "boxes" that claim relative autonomy from each other and from the general law. What are the substantive effects of such specialization? How should the relationship between such "boxes" be conceived? In terms of the above example: what is the relationship between the UNCLOS, an environmental treaty, and a regional integration instrument?

14. The Commission has understood the subject to have both positive and negative sides, as attested to by its reformulation of the title of the topic: "Fragmentation of international law: Difficulties arising from the diversification and expansion of international law". On the one hand, fragmentation does create the danger of conflicting and incompatible rules, principles, rule-systems and institutional practices. On the other hand, it reflects the rapid expansion of international legal activity into various new fields and the diversification of its objects and techniques. The title seems to suggest that although there are "problems", they are neither altogether new nor of such nature that they could not be dealt with through techniques international lawyers have used to deal with the normative conflicts that may have arisen in the past.

15. The rationale for the Commission's treatment of fragmentation is that the emergence of new and special types of law, "self-contained regimes" and geographically or functionally limited treaty-systems creates problems of coherence in international law. New types of specialized law do not emerge accidentally but seek to respond to new technical and functional requirements. The emergence of "environmental law" is a response to growing concern over the state of the international environment. "Trade law" develops as an instrument to regulate international economic relations. "Human rights law" aims to protect the interests of individuals and "international criminal law" gives legal expression to the "fight against impunity". Each rule-complex or "regime" comes with its own principles, its own form of expertise and its own "ethos", not necessarily identical to the ethos of neighbouring specialization. "Trade law" and "environmental law", for example, have highly specific objectives and rely on principles that may often point in different directions. In order for the new law to be efficient, it often includes new types of treaty clauses or practices that may not be compatible with old general law or the law of some other specialized branch. Very often new rules or regimes develop precisely in order to deviate from what was earlier provided by the general law. When such deviations or become general and frequent, the unity of the law suffers.

16. Such deviations should not be understood as legal-technical "mistakes". They reflect the differing pursuits and preferences that actors in a pluralistic (global) society have. In conditions of social complexity, it is pointless to insist on formal unity. A law that would fail to articulate the experienced differences between fact-situations or between the interests or values that appear relevant in particular problem-areas would seem altogether unacceptable, utopian and authoritarian simultaneously.[17] But if fragmentation is in this regard a "natural" development (indeed, international law was always relatively "fragmented" due to the diversity of national legal systems that participated in it) then it is not obvious why the Commission should deal with it.

17. The starting-point of this report is that it is desirable to provide a conceptual frame within which what is perhaps inevitable can be grasped, assessed, and managed in a legal-professional way. That frame is provided by the Vienna Convention on the Law of Treaties of 1969 (VCLT). One aspect that does seem to unite most of the new regimes is that they claim binding force from and are understood by their practitioners to be covered by the law of treaties. As the organ that had once prepared the Vienna Convention, the Commission is in a good position to analyse international law's alleged fragmentation from that perspective. It is useful to note what is implicated here. This is that although, sociologically

speaking, present fragmentation contains many new features, and its intensity differs from analogous phenomena in the past, it is nevertheless an incident of the diversity of the international social world – a quality that has always marked the international system, contrasting it to the (relatively) more homogenous domestic context. The fragmentation of the international legal system into technical "regimes", when examined from the point of view of the law of treaties, is not too different from its traditional fragmentation into more or less autonomous territorial regimes called "national legal systems".

18. This is why it is useful to have regard to the wealth of techniques in the traditional law for dealing with tensions or conflicts between legal rules and principles. What is common to these techniques is that they seek to establish meaningful relationships between such rules and principles so as to determine how they should be used in any particular dispute or conflict. This Report discusses four types of relationships that lawyers have traditionally understood to be implicated in normative conflicts:

(a) Relations between special and general law (section C);
(b) Relations between prior and subsequent law (section D);
(c) Relations between laws at different hierarchical levels (section E); and
(d) Relations of law to its "normative environment" more generally (section F).

19. Such relations may be conceived in varying ways. At one end of the spectrum is the case where one law (norm, rule, principle, rule-complex) simply invalidates the other law. This takes place only in hierarchical relations involving *jus cogens*. Much more often, priority is "relative". The "other law" is set aside only temporarily and may often be allowed to influence "from the background" the interpretation and application of the prioritized law. Then there is the case where the two norms are held to act concurrently, mutually supporting each other. And at this end of the spectrum is the case where, finally, there appears to be no conflict or divergence at all. The laws are in harmony.

20. This Report will discuss such relations especially by reference to the practice of international courts and tribunals. The assumption is that international law's traditional "fragmentation" has already equipped practitioners with techniques to deal with rules and rule-systems that point in different directions. This does not mean to cancel out the importance of the recent push towards functional specialization of regulatory regimes. But it does suggest that these factual developments are of relatively

minor significance to the operation of legal reasoning. In an important sense, "fragmentation" and "coherence" are not aspects of the world but lie in the eye of the beholder. What is new and unfamiliar, will (by definition) challenge accustomed ways of thinking and organizing the world. Novelty presents itself as "fragmentation" of the old world. In such case, it is the task of reasoning to make the unfamiliar familiar by integrating it into received patterns of thought or by amending those patterns so that the new phenomenon can be accommodated. Of course, there will always remain some "cognitive dissonance" between the familiar conceptual system and the new information we receive from the world. The problems of coherence raised by the MOX plant case, for example, have not *already* been resolved in some juristic heaven so that the only task would be to try to find that pre-existing solution. But the fact that the potential overlap or conflict between the rules of the UNCLOS, the OSPAR Convention and EC law cannot be immediately resolved does not mean that it could not be brought under familiar patterns of legal reasoning. This report is about legal reasoning. Although it does not purport to give ready-made solutions to a problem such as the MOX plant it does provide a toolbox with the help of which lawyers dealing with that problem (or any other comparable issue) may be able to proceed to a reasoned decision.

What is a "conflict"?
21. This report examines techniques to deal with conflicts (or prima facie conflicts) in the substance of international law. This raises the question of what is a "conflict"? This question may be approached from two perspectives: the subject-matter of the relevant rules or the legal subjects bound by it. Article 30 VCLT, for example, appears to adopt the former perspective. It suggests techniques for dealing with successive treaties relating to the "same subject-matter". It is sometimes suggested that this removes the applicability of article 30 when a conflict emerges for example between a trade treaty and an environmental treaty because those deal with *different* subjects.[18] But this cannot be so inasmuch as the characterizations ("trade law", "environmental law") have no normative value per se. They are only informal labels that describe the instruments from the perspective of different interests or different policy objectives. Most international instruments may be described from various perspectives: a treaty dealing with trade may have significant human rights and environmental implications and vice versa. A treaty on, say, maritime transport of chemicals, relates at least to the law of the sea, environmental law, trade law, and the law of maritime transport. The characterizations have less to do with the "nature" of the instrument than the interest from which it is described.

22. If conflict were to exist only between rules that deal with the "same" subject-matter, then the way a treaty is applied would become crucially dependent on how it would classify under some (presumably) pre-existing classification scheme of different subjects. But there are no such classification schemes. Everything would be in fact dependent on argumentative success in pigeon-holing legal instruments as having to do with "trade", instead of "environment", "refugee law" instead of "human rights law", "investment law" instead of "law of development". Think again about the example of maritime carriage of chemical substances. If there are no definite rules on such classification, and any classification relates to the interest from which the instrument is described, then it might be possible to avoid the appearance of conflict by what seems like a wholly arbitrary choice between what interests are relevant and what are not: from the perspective of marine insurers, say, the case would be predominantly about carriage while, from the perspective of an environmental organization, the predominant aspect of it would be environmental. The criterion of "subject-matter" leads to a *reductio ad absurdum*. Therefore, it cannot be decisive in the determination of whether or not there is a conflict.[19] As pointed out by Vierdag in his discussion of this criterion in regard to subsequent agreements under article 30 VCLT:

the requirement that the instruments must relate to the same subject-matter seems to raise extremely difficult problems in theory, but may turn out not to be so very difficult in practice. If an attempted simultaneous application of two rules to one set of facts or actions leads to incompatible results it can safely be assumed that the test of sameness is satisfied.[20]

23. This seems right. The criterion of "same subject-matter" seems already fulfilled if two different rules or sets of rules are invoked in regard to the same matter, or if, in other words, as a result of interpretation, the relevant treaties seem to point to different directions in their application by a party.

24. This is not the end of the matter, however. What does "pointing in different direction" mean? A strict notion would presume that conflict exists if it is possible for a party to two treaties to comply with one rule only by thereby failing to comply with another rule. This is the basic situation of incompatibility. An obligation may be fulfilled only by thereby failing to fulfil another obligation. However, there are other, looser understandings of conflict as well.[21] A treaty may sometimes frustrate the goals of another treaty without there being any strict incompatibility

between their provisions. Two treaties or sets of rules may possess different background justifications or emerge from different legislative policies or aim at divergent ends. The law of State immunity and the law of human rights, for example, illustrate two sets of rules that have very different objectives. Trade law and environmental law, too, emerge from different types of policy and that fact may have an effect on how the relevant rules are interpreted or applied. While such "policy-conflicts" do not lead into logical incompatibilities between obligations upon a single party, they may nevertheless also be relevant for fragmentation.[22]

25. This Report adopts a wide notion of conflict as a situation where two rules or principles suggest different ways of dealing with a problem. Focusing on a mere logical incompatibility mischaracterizes legal reasoning as logical subsumption. In fact, any decision will involve interpretation and choice between alternative rule-formulations and meanings that cannot be pressed within the model of logical reasoning.

26. Conflicts between rules are a phenomenon in every legal order. Every legal order is also familiar with ways to deal with them. Maxims such as *lex specialis* or *lex posterior* are known to most legal systems, and, as will be explained in much more detail below, to international law. Domestic legal orders also have robust hierarchical relations between rules and rule-systems (in addition to hierarchical institutions to decide rule-conflicts). In international law, however, as will also be discussed in section E below, there are much fewer and much less robust hierarchies. And there are many types of interpretative principles that purport to help out in conflict-resolution. Nevertheless, it is useful to agree with Jenks:

Assuming, as it is submitted we must, that a coherent body of principles on the subject is not merely desirable but necessary, we shall be constrained to recognize that, useful and indeed essential as such principles may be to guide us to reasonable conclusions in particular cases, they have no absolute validity.[23]

Notes

8. C. Wilfried Jenks, "The Conflict of Law-Making Treaties", BYBIL vol. 30, (1953) p. 403.
9. Ibid.
10. Over 50,000 treaties are registered in the United Nations system. See Christopher J. Borgen, "Resolving Treaty Conflicts", George Washington International Law Review, vol. 37 (2005) pp. 57. In the twentieth century, about 6,000 multilateral treaties were

concluded of which around 30 per cent were general treaties, open for all States to participate. Charlotte Ku, *Global Governance and the Changing Face of International Law* (ACUNS Keynote Paper 2001/2) p. 45.

11. Out of the various collections that discuss the diversification of the sources of international regulation particularly useful are Eric Loquin & Catherine Kessedjian (eds.), *La mondialisation du droit* (Paris: Litec, 2000); and Paul Schiff Berman, *The Globalization of International Law* (Aldershot: Ashgate, 2005). The activity of traditional organizations is examined in José Alvarez, *International Organizations as Law-Makers* (Oxford: Oxford University Press, 2005). Different perspectives of non-treaty law-making today are also presented in Rüdiger Wolfrum & Volker Röben (eds.), *Developments of International Law in Treaty-making* (Berlin: Springer, 2005) pp. 417–586 and Ronnie Lipschutz & Cathleen Vogel, "Regulation for the Rest of Us? Global Civil Society and the Privatization of Transnational Regulation", in R.R. Hall & T.J. Bierstaker, *The Emergence of Private Authority in Global Governance* (Cambridge: Cambridge University Press, 2002) pp. 115–140.

12. See especially Andreas Fisher-Lescano & Günther Teubner, "Regime-Collisions: The Vain Search for Legal Unity in the Fragmentation of Global Law", Mich. J. Int'l L., vol. 25 (2004) pp. 999–1046. The matter was, however, discussed already in great detail in L.A.N.M. Barnhoorn & Karel Wellens (eds.), *Diversity in Secondary Rules and the Unity of International Law* (The Hague: Nijhoff, 1995).

13. It should not be forgotten that the tradition of legal pluralism seeks precisely to deal with such problems. So far, however, pluralism has concentrated on the study of the coexistence of indigenous and Western law in old colonial territories as well as the emergence of types of private law in domestic societies. For a famous statement, see Sally Engel Merry, "Legal Pluralism", Law & Soc. Rev., vol. 22 (1988) pp. 869–896 and more recently (and critically), Simon Roberts, "After Government? On Representing Law without the State", Modern Law Review, vol. 68 (2005) pp. 1–24.

14. "Fragmentation" is a very frequently treated topic of academic writings and conferences today. Apart from the sources in note 11 above, see also "Symposium: The Proliferation of International Tribunals: Piecing together the Puzzle", New York Journal of International Law and Politics, vol. 31 (1999) pp. 679–993; Andreas Zimmermann & Reiner Hoffmann, with assisting editor Hanna Goeters, *Unity and Diversity of International Law* (Berlin: Duncker & Humblot, 2006); Karel Wellens & Rosario Huesa Vinaixa (eds.), *L'influence des sources sur l'unité et la fragmentation du droit international* (Brussels: Bruylant, 2006 forthcoming). A strong plea for unity is contained in Pierre Marie Dupuy, "L'unité de l'ordre juridique internationale". Cours général de droit international public", *Recueil des Cours* ..., vol. 297 (2002). For more references, see Martti Koskenniemi & Päivi Leino, "Fragmentation of International Law. Postmodern Anxieties?". Leiden Journal of International Law, vol. 15 (2002) pp. 553–579.

15. *MOX Plant* case, *Request for Provisional Measures Order* (*Ireland* v. *the United Kingdom*) (3 December 2001) International Tribunal for the Law of the Sea, ILR vol. 126 (2005) p. 273, para. 50.

16. Ibid., pp. 273–274, para. 51.

17. The emergence of an international legal pluralism has been given an ambitious overview in Boaventura de Sousa Santos, *Toward a New Common Sense. Law, Science and Politics in the Age of the Paradigmatic Transition* (New York: Routledge, 1995) especially p. 114 et seq.

18. Borgen, "Resolving Treaty Conflicts", supra, note 10, pp. 603–604.

19. This is not to say that the fact that two treaties may or may not belong to the same "regime" is irrelevant for the way their relationship is conceived. See further specially section D.3.(a). below.

20. E.W. Vierdag, "The Time of the 'Conclusion' of a Multilateral Treaty: Article 30 of the Vienna Convention on the Law of Treaties and Related Provisions", BYBIL vol. 59 (1988) p. 100.
21. The most in-depth discussion is in Joost Pauwelyn, *Conflict of Norms in Public International Law. How WTO Law Relates to Other Rules of International Law*, Cambridge Studies in International and Comparative Law, (Cambridge: Cambridge University Press: 2003) pp. 164–200 (noting the way the WTO bodies have used a narrow understanding of "conflict" as incompatibility). See also the distinction made by Jenks between "conflicts" and "divergences", "The Conflict of Law-Making ...", supra note 8, pp. 425–427 and for a rather strict definition of "conflict", Jan B. Mus, "Conflicts between Treaties in International Law", Netherlands International Law Review, vol. XLV (1998) pp. 214–217; Seyed Ali Sadat-Akhavi, *Methods of Resolving Conflicts between Treaties* (Leiden: Nijhoff, 2003) pp. 5–7.
22. For a discussion, see Rüdiger Wolfrum & Nele Matz, *Conflicts in International Environmental Law* (Berlin: Springer, 2003) pp. 6–13 and Nele Matz, *Wege zur Koordinierung völkerrechtlicher Verträge. Völkervertragsrechtliche und institutionelle Ansätze* (Berlin: Springer, 2005) pp. 8–18 (a categorization of conflict-types from logical incompatibility to political conflicts and overlaps of regulatory scope).
23. Jenks, "The Conflict of Law-Making..." supra note 8, p. 407.

2001 Report of UNEP Executive Director: International Environmental Governance

UNEP, *Report of UNEP Executive Director: International Environmental Governance*, UNEP/IGM/1/2, 4 April 2001.

Excerpts paras. 45, 47–50, 63–87, 143–146, 149

45. It is estimated that there are more than 500 international treaties and other agreements related to the environment, of which 323 are regional. Nearly 60 per cent, or 302, date from the period between 1972, the year of the Stockholm Conference, and the present.

47. The period from 1972 to the present has witnessed an accelerated increase in multilateral environmental agreements. Of the 302 agreements negotiated, 197, or nearly 70 per cent are regional in scope, as compared to 60 per cent for the earlier period. The emergence of regional integration bodies concerned with the environment in regions such as Central America and Europe have contributed to this trend. In many cases, regional agreements are closely linked to global ones. Of greatest impact has been the emergence of the 17 multisectoral regional seas conventions and action plans embracing 46 conventions, protocols and related agreements. By far the largest cluster of multilateral environmental

agreements is related to the marine environment, accounting for over 40 per cent of the total, the most notable being the United Nations Convention on the Law of the Sea (1982), new IMO marine pollution conventions and protocols, the Global Programme of Action for the Protection of the Marine Environment from Land-based Activities (1995), and regional seas agreements and regional fisheries conventions and protocols. Biodiversity-related conventions form a second important but smaller cluster, including most of the key global conventions: the World Heritage Convention (1972), CITES (1973), CMS (1979) and CBD (1992). As in the earlier period, the cluster of nuclear-related agreements remains important, with the addition of nine global conventions and protocols and several regional agreements.

48. In contrast to the pre-1972 period, two new important clusters of agreements have emerged: the chemicals-related and hazardous-waste-related conventions, primarily of a global nature, and the atmosphere/energy-related conventions. The first include several ILO conventions that address occupational hazards in the workplace. Most recently, we have the adoption of the Rotterdam Convention (1998), and it is expected that the new convention on persistent organic pollutants will be adopted in Stockholm in May 2001. At the forefront of the atmosphere/energy-related conventions are the Vienna Convention for the Protection of the Ozone Layer (1985) and its Montreal Protocol (1987), and UNFCCC (1992).

49. From a combined global and regional perspective, the resultant proliferation of environmental agreements has placed an increasing burden on Parties to meet their collective obligations and responsibilities to implement environmental conventions and related international agreements. For example, according to the European Environment Agency, European Community countries are Party to as many as 65 global and regional environmental conventions and agreements.

50. Most of the growth in the importance of international environmental law in recent years has come from the increase in the number of binding and non-binding international environmental instruments. Although the number of agreements negotiated since 1972 is a remarkable achievement, they lack coherence with respect to a number of important new environmental policy issues, such as the precautionary principle and scientific uncertainty, intergenerational and intragenerational equity, the life-cycle economy, common but differentiated responsibilities, and sustainable development.

A. Strengths

63. In the three decades since the Stockholm Conference, the environment has increased in significance in public concern and action at the local, national and international levels. Governmental bodies, organizations and other institutional arrangements, within and outside of the United Nations system, have been established to address sectoral environmental issues or categories of such issues. Multilateral processes to consider environmental and environment-related subjects have grown significantly. Networks among various entities and major groups have been developed and are growing. Such trends in institutional development have accelerated since the Rio Summit in 1992.

64. At the national level, in many countries, both developing and developed, national environmental legislation and related institutional arrangements have been developed to provide a sound basis for addressing the major environmental threats, often on a sectoral basis and governed by various authorities responsible for specific issues.

65. Within the United Nations system, UNEP has continued to provide critical environmental assessment and information for decision makers and has served as a global policy-making forum on environmental issues. The institution of the Global Ministerial Environment Forum by the General Assembly as a principal international environmental policy forum was a response to the demands generated by proliferating environmental forums and the need to ensure policy coherence. Consultation and negotiation forums have taken place under the auspices of UNEP to develop global and regional environmental agreements for catalytic actions to support the activities of Governments and coordinate those of relevant organizations. UNEP has supported environmental actions at various levels with national and international partners, both governmental and non-governmental.

66. Many multilateral environmental conventions and other agreements have been developed to address sectoral environmental issues, providing an internationally agreed framework for environmental governance of such issues. UNEP's Montevideo Programme for the Development and Periodic Review of Environmental Law has provided the international community with a significant impetus to this end for the past two decades, contributing to the development of regional seas conventions and protocols and action plans around the world, as well as global treaties governing the protection of the ozone layer, the control of transboundary movements of hazardous wastes, biological diversity, information exchange on hazardous chemicals in trade and persistent organic pollutants.

In addition to legally binding instruments, numerous non-binding international instruments have been developed to provide norms, principles, procedures, guidelines and codes of conduct to address environmental issues.

67. One of the central mechanisms by which international cooperation can be fostered is through the negotiation and adoption of international laws aimed at fostering the sustainable management of shared resources.

68. Clearly, the various conventions and protocols on the environment represent one of the most outstanding achievements of the global community in the environmental field to date. After Rio, the development of a distinct international law on the environment has been nothing less than remarkable. The number of such agreements is rising, whilst the average time taken to negotiate each treaty is steadily decreasing. At the same time, the scale of problems to be addressed has widened – from the regional through the hemispheric to the global – while the total number of sovereign States that have to sit down to broker such deals has gradually burgeoned. New concerns and principles – precaution, intergenerational and intragenerational equity, scientific uncertainty, sustainable development – have also arisen in recent years and now are not applied coherently and consistently in further development of relevant regimes.

69. The views on existing arrangements according to the responses to the questionnaire provided by the secretariats, include the following:

(a) Clustering provides opportunities for synergies, particularly within each cluster, where agreements have much in common in terms of issues to be addressed;
(b) Issues of common interest also cut across clusters – for example, trade, capacity-building, and the development of national legislation that supports the implementation of conventions and protocols at the country level;
(c) Opportunities exist for closer cooperation among the scientific bodies of the agreements;
(d) An increase is occurring in arrangements which enable conventions to work together in a more integrated manner, leading to the development of joint programmes of work in areas of common interest.

B. Weaknesses

70. The Malmö Ministerial Declaration adopted by the first Global Ministerial Environment Forum in May 2000 noted with deep concern an

increasing rate of deterioration of the environment and the natural resource base, an alarming discrepancy between commitments and action, an inadequate level of integration of environmental considerations into the mainstream of decision-making in economic and social development, and challenges to the implementation of multilateral environmental agreements.

71. To date, a number of Governments as well as other bodies and experts have reviewed the state of international environmental governance (see the list of references presented at the end of this document). They have identified certain problems and institutional weaknesses in current international environmental governance, which are enumerated in the following summary.

72. Current approaches to global environmental management and sustainability are increasingly felt to be inadequate. To date, international action has focused primarily on the transboundary movement of pollution and sectoral issues. There is a need to move toward a coherent and integrated management framework that addresses individual challenges in the context of the global ecosystem. New scientific knowledge is illustrating the close interconnectedness of environmental issues, calling the traditional "issue-by-issue" problem-solving approach into question. Increasing globalization, both economic and social, is also complicating matters. The current structure of international environmental institutions belongs to a different age. As we enter a new century, our approach to managing the global environment must reflect what we have learned over the past decades, and whether new and stronger arrangements and approaches are required to deal with global environmental issues.

73. Given the expanding environmental agenda and the fragmented approach to international action, the international community needs to consider whether the existing international institutional machinery can confront the challenges of the twenty-first century. The existing machinery remains fragmented, often with vague mandates, inadequate resources and marginal political support. The basic premise for charting a new course for institutional strengthening is that existing institutions do not and can not adequately address current and future needs.

74. The development of a large number of multilateral agreements on the environment has resulted in a very diversified body of rules. The institutional structures that govern international environmental agreements are fragmented. Agreements are often managed independently, though steps are being taken to improve their coordination and coherence.

75. The growing number of environmental institutions, issues and agreements are placing stress on current systems and our ability to manage them. The continuous increase in the number of international bodies with environmental competence carries the risk of reduced participation by States due to limited capacity in the face of an increased workload, and makes it necessary to create or strengthen the synergies between all these bodies. Weak support and scattered direction have left institutions less effective than they could be, while demands on their resources continue to grow. The proliferation of international demands has placed a particularly heavy burden on developing countries, which are often not equipped to participate meaningfully in the development and implementation of international environmental policy.

76. Structures which govern how production, trade and investment occur often pay inadequate attention to the task of protecting the environment and human life. Current economic governance structures should make rules that actively enhance existing environmental and social safeguards and strengthen the ability of national governments to respond adequately to new environmental concerns.

77. There is reluctance on the part of some agreements to cooperate with others. Many conventions continue to be inward-looking and are reluctant to share or give away part of what they perceive as their "sovereignty". Inadequate attention is paid to the harmonization of national reporting, though there is an initiative among environmental agreements under UNEP for the streamlining of national reporting focusing on the global biodiversity-related conventions. Attention needs to be given to harmonizing reporting under trade-related agreements in areas of common interest, such as work linked to customs and port authorities. There is inadequate implementation, coordination, compliance and enforcement at the national level, and environmental and performance indicators for measuring the effectiveness of an agreement are lacking. Funding for some agreements is clearly insufficient to address mounting demands.

78. A failure to keep in view the linkages between "distinct phenomena" like climate change, ozone depletion and biodiversity loss can cause, at best, waste of effort and funds and, at worst, exacerbation of the problem that was meant to be solved in the first place. There is a need for enhanced coordination between different environmental organizations and structures and multilateral environmental agreements.

79. International dispute settlement mechanisms are weak. The potential conflict between environmental regulation and the trade regime is often cited as a concern.

80. Competing for scarce funds and political commitment, existing institutions are frequently torn between competing priorities which are driven by overlapping and unfocused demands. There is a lack of financial resources for international environmental cooperation. The sense of disillusionment many developing countries have concerning implementation of Agenda 21 commitments by the industrialized countries continues to be an impediment to further progress. The lack of financial and technical resources to enable developing countries to prepare for, participate in and implement international agreements is a matter of serious concern.

81. International governance structures, and the rules that flow from them, must have the capacity to shape national policy. While international trade policy is rather effective in this regard, the impact of international environmental agreements is often less evident.

82. International environmental governance can be effective only if it is integrated into local, national and regional governance structures which encompass governments as well as civil society and the business sector. If international rule-making is to change local and national policy, then the citizens of affected countries have the right and duty to participate, either directly or indirectly, in this international decision-making. Whereas governance was seen largely as the job of governments for much of the twentieth century, there is an increasing realization that good governance requires the participation of all sectors of society.

83. If international environmental agreements are to be effective in the face of ongoing economic liberalization, it is important that they, too, have mechanisms which encourage compliance at the national level, and that economic imperatives are not given automatic precedence over environmental and social exigencies without a clear assessment of costs and benefits.

84. Solutions need to be based on the understanding that human society and the environment are interconnected and that, without a productive and viable environment, society cannot function. This means that environmental agreements need to take into greater consideration the development needs of the poor, and also that economic decision-making mechanisms need to operate with a fuller understanding of the linkages

between the economy and the environment. An interlinked, holistic approach to international environmental governance which puts the environment and people's needs first is essential to confront the challenges posed by the new century.

85. An effective international environmental governance structure needs to enable, support and encourage policy-making and decision-making, leading to an effective response to environmental management needs which require such a response at the global level.

86. Despite the recent successes in the revitalization of UNEP, there continues to be a need to strengthen the existing international environmental institutional structure in relation to assessment and problem identification. There is a need to enhance existing capacity in this area, in particular through increased scientific capacity and additional financing. Among other things, there is a need to strengthen the capacity to address interlinkages in an operational context. It is not clear where and how in the existing structure integrated assessment functions can be followed by identification and assessment of response options, assessment of their costs and benefits and choice of appropriate response options, followed by action.

87. Despite some successes, national environmental ministries and agencies possess neither the political influence nor the resources necessary to implement sustainable development strategies across all areas of government activity; and the same problem is repeated amongst international institutions. Some aspects can be addressed through better coordination at the national level, leading to more coherent government engagements in international policy and decision-making processes. Policy integration at the national, regional and international levels has a poor record, and must be addressed as a fundamental requirement for effective environmental governance.

143. Concern has been raised about the conflicting goals of large multilateral and bilateral bodies whose negative impact on the environment can compromise efforts towards improving international environmental governance. The solutions put forward to date are:

(a) To strengthen processes for integrating environmental considerations into existing international financial, trade, technical and development organizations in an effort to enhance their operations in pursuit of sustainable development. This would include integrating environmental concerns in development cooperation, for example by means of the World Bank's Comprehensive Development Framework and the United Nations Development Assistance Framework;

(b) To develop common environmental guidelines for export credit agencies to encourage integration of environmental considerations in investment decisions;

(c) To establish a counterpart environmental body to WTO.

144. Ideas put forward to date reflect a need for a stronger agency for governing the global environment. Options put forward include:

(a) Upgrading UNEP from a United Nations programme to a fully fledged specialized agency equipped with suitable rules and its own budget funded from assessed contributions from member States, through an annual session of announcements of contributions (based on the UNDP model), or under multi-annual negotiated agreements;

(b) Utilization of the General Assembly or the Economic and Social Council in a more comprehensive institutional manner, for example by transforming the Economic and Social Council into a Council on Sustainable Development, requiring amendment of the United Nations Charter;

(c) Establishment of a new World Environment Organization. Issues that would need to be addressed are: what functions it would have; whether it would act as an umbrella for the various multilateral environmental agreements; what financial resources and legal authority it would be endowed with;

(d) Transformation of the Trusteeship Council, one of the six principal organs of the United Nations, into the chief forum for global environmental matters, including administration of multilateral environmental agreements, with the Commission on Sustainable Development reporting to an Economic Security Council, rather than Economic and Social Council;

(e) Some consolidation between UNDP and UNEP;

(f) Broadening of the mandate of GEF to make it the financial mechanism of all global environmental agreements and link it more closely with UNEP to ensure coherence between policy and financing;

(g) Raising the profile of the Commission on Sustainable Development to integrate the three "pillars" – environmental, social and economic – with greater involvement alongside GEF and other programmes and the United Nations Development Group, and involving ministries other than environment ministries alone;

(h) Establishment of a new environmental court.

145. In order to decide on the most effective manner of strengthening international environmental governance, the following questions would need to be addressed:

(a) How coordination and synergies on environment-related issues among various organizations would be improved;
(b) How consistency of environmental standards and agreements would be enhanced, particularly in the context of environmental and trade agreements, and how disputes that arise would be dealt with;
(c) What role civil society, particularly environmental non-governmental organizations, would have in strengthened governance of the global environment;
(d) What role could be accorded to the private sector;
(e) What level of financing would be available, and with what level of predictability and stability, to ensure that mandates are realized.

3. Coordination

146. Given the fragmented nature of organizations and structures dealing with environmental issues that have been referred to, ideas put forward have highlighted the need for improved coordination and synergies among the various entities involved. While a strengthened international environmental governance body as suggested above could be given the capacity to coordinate, it would nevertheless need tools or mechanisms for doing so. The ideas put forward to date for doing so are as follows:

(a) Agreement on a structure to provide direction and coherence among agreements within the same category;
(b) On coordination between trade and environment agreements, establishment of a dispute settlement scheme for trade-related environmental issues, with the dispute settlement process independent of the rule-making and negotiating functions of WTO. In addition, establishment of an agreement on trade-related environmental measures;
(c) Improvement of UNEP's coordinating role, one suggestion being to bring together under the aegis of UNEP all organizations with a largely environmental remit in order to harmonize schedules, assessments, actions and strategies on a thematic basis;
(d) Utilization of UNEP's recently established Global Ministerial Environment Forum for setting broad policy guidelines for international action on the environment;

149. At the international level, the inadequate level of coordination among multilateral environmental agreements makes itself felt in difficulties arising from the dispersal of the location of secretariats between

Montreal (for CBD and its Biosafety Protocol and the Multilateral Fund), Geneva (for CITES and the Basel Convention) and, Bonn (for UNFCCC, UNCCD and CMS), as well as the dispersal of venues of Conferences of Parties and their subsidiary bodies. In addition, inadequate coordination has been noted in the timings of these conferences: in December 2000, the Intergovernmental Negotiating Committee on the Convention on persistent organic pollutants met in Johannesburg, the CBD Intergovernmental Committee for the Cartagena Protocol in Montpellier, the Twelfth Meeting of the Parties to the Montreal Protocol in Ouagadougou and the Fourth Conference of the Parties to the UNCCD in Bonn. At the national level, the fact that the various conventions have different focal points also points to inadequate coordination. The focal points for CBD and CITES are in the ministries of agriculture, those for UNFCC are in the ministries of energy or meteorological services, those for UNCCD are in forest or land ministries, those for UNEP are in ministries of environment and those for the Commission on Sustainable Development are in ministries of foreign affairs. In the absence of adequate national coordination of global environmental issues, it is difficult to ensure adequate international coordination. Ideas put forward to deal with this situation include:

(a) Co-location of secretariats of agreements;
(b) Development of umbrella conventions;
(c) Utilization of one scientific body to address the scientific or thematic assessment needs of agreements functioning on a demand-driven basis, instead of dedicating distinct ones for each agreement;

2006 UN Reform: Implications for the Environmental Pillar

UNEP, *UN Reform: Implication for the Environmental Pillar*, UNEP/DED/040506, May 2006.

Excerpt: Executive summary

1. UNEP was established in 1972 to provide general policy guidance for the direction and coordination of environmental programmes within the UN system and to review their implementation. Its mandate represented the mix of intergovernmental, secretariat, financial and interagency coordination functions deemed necessary at that time to ensure the system-wide follow-up of the Stockholm Conference. Efforts to enhance system-wide coherence have been a recurrent feature of the governing processes

of the ever evolving UN. UNEP has been subject to several reforms and decadal reviews of environmental activities in the UN system.

2. The number of organizations, multilateral agreements, agencies, funds and programmes involved in environmental activities has increased significantly since 1972. Both the Governing Council and the programme operations of UNEP have found it increasingly challenging to perform the original system-wide environmental coordination role. Although the General Assembly reaffirmed UNEP's role as the principal UN body in the field of the environment in 1997, repeated calls for enhanced UN system-wide environmental coordination have been made from the late 1990s onwards.

3. Paragraph 169 of the outcome document of the 2005 World Summit responds to UNEP's own call for a greatly strengthened institutional structure for international environmental governance (IEG). Within its mandate, UNEP is well placed to address the needs for system-wide coherence and more effective environmental activities in the UN system. This is particularly true in areas of demonstrated comparative advantage and expertise, such as in environmental assessments and networking, environmental law and policy guidance, and capacity building. This issue paper provides perspectives and proposals on how to address each of the needs identified in paragraph 169 regarding more effective environmental activities in the UN system.

4. Paragraph 169 also agreed on the need to explore the possibility of a more coherent institutional framework to achieve more efficient UN environmental activities. Such an institutional framework could be based on a clarification and rationalization of the roles, responsibilities and reporting lines of intergovernmental, operative, financial and administrative environmental entities of the UN system, according particular attention for example to UNEP, CSD, FAO, GEF, UNDP, UNESCO, UN-Habitat, WMO, World Bank and the MEAs. In doing so it should take full account of UNEP's role and demonstrated comparative advantage and expertise as the principal environmental UN body.

5. The General Assembly may wish to further empower its subsidiary body, the UNEP Council/Forum, as the leading global environmental authority that sets the global environmental agenda and promotes the coherent implementation of the environmental dimension of sustainable development within the UN system. In this regard, the full implementation of the recommendation emanating from the IEG review would be of strategic importance.

6. There is a clear continuum from 1972 to 2006 regarding the importance of UN system-wide coherence in addressing environmental change. Such change may, if not halted or significantly reduced, seriously limit development options of member states and increase their vulnerability in terms of natural disasters and conflicts resulting in need for humanitarian assistance.

7. This contribution by the UNEP secretariat encompasses views and perspectives of relevance to the work of the Secretary-General's high-level panel on UN system wide coherence in the areas of development, humanitarian assistance and the environment (the Coherence Panel), as well as to the informal consultations by the General Assembly on system-wide coherence regarding environmental activities (the Informal Consultation), both in follow up to paragraph 169 of the 2005 World Summit Outcome.

2006 Delivering as One Report

UNSG, *Delivering as One: Report of Secretary General's High Level Panel on System-Wide Coherence*, (advanced unedited version), http://www.un.org/events/panel/resources/pdfs/HLP-SWC-FinalReport.pdf, 2006.

Excerpts paras. 34–37, and Recommendations concerning environment

34. The UN institutions for the environment must be optimally organized and tooled, drawing on expertise in different parts of the UN system. Unless the UN adopts more comprehensive approaches, it will continue to fall short of its goals. The Panel is cognizant of the ongoing General Assembly Informal Consultative Process on international environmental governance and has interacted with the process. Our recommendations should give it greater impetus.

35. Fragmented institutional structures do not offer an operational framework to address global issues, including water and energy. Water is an essential element in the lives of people and societies, and the lack of access to water for basic needs inflicts hardship on more than 1 billion people. Similarly, energy is a main driver of development, but current systems of energy supply and use are not sustainable (more than 2 billion people in developing countries do not have access to modern energy services). More than 20 UN organizations are engaged at some level in water and energy work, but there is little evidence of overall impact.

36. The inadequacy of the current system is the result of having out-grown its original design. Developing countries are unable to cope with the extensive reporting and participation requirements of the current multilateral environmental structure, which has depleted expertise and resources for implementation. A survey by the Panel revealed that the three Rio Conventions (biodiversity, climate, and desertification) have up to 230 meeting days annually. Add the figures for seven other major global environmental agreements (not including regional agreements) and that number rises to almost 400 days.

37. As environmental issues have become more clearly defined and in-terlinked, they have come to influence the work of practically every UN organizations, all competing for the same limited resources. The institu-tional complexity is further complicated by the substantial environment portfolios of the World Bank and regional development banks, which are not well coordinated with the rest of the UN system. In addition, the UN Environment Programme, the UN's principal environment organiza-tion – with its normative, scientific, analytical and coordinating mandate – is considered weak, under-funded and ineffective in its core functions.

Recommendation: International environmental governance should be strengthened and more coherent in order to improve effectiveness and targeted action of environmental activities in the UN system. It should be strengthened by upgrading UNEP with a renewed mandate and im-proved funding.

Recommendation: An upgraded UNEP should have real authority as the "environment policy pillar" of the UN system, backed by normative and analytical capacity and with broad responsibility to review progress to-wards improving the global environment. UNEP should provide substan-tive leadership and guidance on environmental issues.

- UNEP's technical and scientific capacity should be strengthened as the environmental early-warning mechanism of the international commu-nity and for monitoring, assessing and reporting on the state of the global environment. This can be achieved through a system of network-ing and drawing on the work of existing bodies, including academic institutions and centres of excellence and the scientific competence of relevant specialized agencies and scientific subsidiary bodies of multi-lateral environmental agreements.
- Capacity should be built to promote the implementation of interna-tional commitments. The Bali Strategic Plan for Technology Support and Capacity Building should be strategically implemented to provide

cutting-edge expertise and knowledge resources for the sustained expansion of capacity at the country level. Where necessary, UNEP should participate in UN country teams through the Resident Coordinator system, as part of the One UN at country level.

- UNEP should take the lead in assisting countries in the two-step process of quantifying environmental costs and benefits and incorporating them into mainstream policymaking, in cooperation with UNDP and the UN Department of Economic and Social Affairs.

Recommendation: UN agencies, programmes and funds with responsibilities in the area of the environment should cooperate more effectively on a thematic basis and through partnerships with a dedicated agency at the centre (such as air and water pollution, forests, water scarcity, access to energy, and renewable energy). This would be based on a combined effort towards agreed common activities and policy objectives to eliminate duplication and focus on results.

- Greater coordination at headquarters should promote coherence at country level, and greater coordination efforts at the country level should promote coherence at the international level. There is a need to strengthen UNEP's coordination of system-wide environmental policies in order to improve cohesion and consistency. In this regard, the Environmental Management Group should be given a clearer mandate and be better utilized. It should be linked with the broader framework of sustainable development coordination.

Recommendation: Efficiencies and substantive coordination should be pursued by diverse treaty bodies to support effective implementation of major multilateral environmental agreements. Such coordination is being pursued by the Basel, Rotterdam and Stockholm convention secretariats (pending decisions of their respective Conferences of the Parties).

- Stronger efforts should be made to reduce costs and reporting burdens and to streamline implementation. National reporting requirements for related multilateral environmental agreements should be consolidated into one comprehensive annual report, to ease the burden on countries and improve coherence.
- Countries should consider integrating implementation needs of multilateral environmental agreements into their national sustainable development strategies, as part of the One Country Programme.
- Governing bodies of multilateral environmental agreements should promote administrative efficiencies, reducing the frequency and duration of meetings, moving to joint administrative functions, convening

back-to-back or joint meetings of bureaux of related conventions, rationalising knowledge management and developing a consistent methodological approach to enable measurement of enforcement and compliance.

Recommendation: The Global Environment Facility should be strengthened as the major financial mechanism for the global environment. Its contribution in assisting developing countries in implementing the conventions and in building their capacities should be clarified, in conjunction with its implementing and executing agencies. A significant increase in resources will be required to address future challenges effectively.

Recommendation: The Secretary-General should commission an independent and authoritative assessment of the current UN system of international environmental governance. To be completed as soon as possible and taking previous work into account, the assessment would review global needs as well as the specific roles and mandates of UNEP and other UN agencies and multilateral environmental agreements. It would provide the basis for further reforms toward improving system-wide coherence, effectiveness and targeted action. It should be complementary to the General Assembly Informal Consultative Process on the Institutional Framework for the UN's Environmental Activities, which should continue its work and provide guidance on the subject. The assessment should include an analysis of proposals to upgrade UNEP from among a range of organizational models.

Selected bibliography

Books

Birnie, Patricia and Alan Boyle, *International Law and the Environment* (2nd ed.), Oxford: Oxford University Press, 2002.

Boyle, Alan and Christine Chinkin, *The Making of International Law*, Oxford: Oxford University Press, 2007.

Brown Weiss, Edith and Harold Jacobson (eds), *Engaging Countries: Strengthening Compliance with International Environmental Accords*, Cambridge, Mass.: MIT Press, 1998.

Cameron, James, J. Werksman and P. Roderick, *Improving Compliance with International Environmental Law*, London: Earthscan, 1996.

Commission on Global Governance, *Our Global Neighbourhood*, Oxford: Oxford University Press, 1995.

Chayes, Abram and Antonia Handler Chayes, *The New Sovereignty: Compliance with International Regulatory Agreements*, Cambridge, Mass.: Harvard University Press, 1995.

Dodds, Felix. (ed.), *Earth Summit 2002: A New Deal*, London: Earthscan, 2000.

Edward L. Miles et al., *Environmental Regime Effectiveness: Confronting Theory with Evidence*, Cambridge, Mass.: MIT Press, 2002.

Haas, Peter, Robert Keohane and Marc Levy (eds), *Institutions for Earth: Sources of Effectiveness International Environmental Protection*, Cambridge, Mass.: MIT Press, 1995.

Kelson, Hans, *The Pure Theory of Law*, Los Angeles: University of California Press, 1970.

Najam, Adil, Mihaela Papa and Nadaa Taiyab, *Global Environmental Governance: A Reform Agenda*, International Institute for Sustainable Development, http://www.iisd.org/pdf/2006/geg.pdf, 2006.

Oberthür, Sebastian and Thomas Gehring (eds), *Institutional Interaction in Global Environmental Governance: Synergy and Conflict among International and EU Policies*, Cambridge, Mass.: MIT Press, 2006.

Sand, Peter (ed.) *Effectiveness of International Environmental Agreements, A Survey of Existing Legal Instruments*, London: Grotius, 1992.

Victor, David, Kal Raustila and Eugene B. Skolnikoff, *Implementation and Effectiveness of International Environmental Commitments: Theory and Practice*, Cambridge: MIT Press 1998.

Wolfrum, Rüdiger and Nele Matz, *International Environmental Treaty Conflicts in International Environmental Law*, New York: Springer, 2003.

Young, Oran, *International Cooperation: Building Regimes Natural Resources and Environment*, Ithaca, N.Y.: Cornell University Press, 1989.

Articles

Abbott, Kenneth, "Modern International Relations Theory: A Prospectus for International Lawyers", 14 *Yale J. Int'l L*, 1989, 335–411.

Bharat H. Desai, "Revitalizing International Environmental Institutions: The UN Task Force Report and Beyond", *Indian Journal of International Law*, vol. 40, No. 3, July–September, 2000.

Biermann, Frank, "Piecing Together a Global Environment Organization", 42 *Environment*, November 2000, 23–31.

Biermann, Frank, "The Emerging Debate on the Need for a World Environment Organization: A Commentary", 1 *Global Environmental Politics*, February 2001, 45–55.

Bodansky, Daniel, "The Legitimacy of International Governance: A Coming Challenge for International Environmental Law", 93 *AJIL*, July 1999, 596–624.

Churchill, Robin and Geir Ulfstein, "Autonomous Institutional Arrangements in Multilateral Environmental Agreements: a Little-Noticed Phenomenon in International Law", 94 *AJIL*, (2000), 623–659.

Dodds, Felix, "The Context: Multistakeholder Processes in the Context of Global Governance", in Minu Hemmati, *One Step Beyond: Multi-Stakeholder Processes for Governance and Sustainability*, London, UNED Forum & Earthscan (forthcoming). Accessed online, 8 June 2007, http://www.earthsummit2002.org/msp/book/04chap4.pdf.

Domoto, Akiko, "International Environmental Governance: It's Impact on Social and Human Development", *IUCN*, April 2000.

Downs, George, David Rocke and Peter Barsoom, "Is the Good News about Compliance Good News about Cooperation?" 50 *Int'l Org.*, 1996, 379–406.

Hyvarinen, Joy and Duncan Brack, "Global Environmental Institutions: Analysis and Options for Change", *Report Prepared for the Department of the Environment, Transport and the Regions, (U.K.)*, Royal Institute of International Affairs, September 2000.

International Institute for Sustainable Development, *Summary of the UNEP Expert Consultations on International Environmental Governance*, Cambridge, U.K., http://www.iisd.ca/linkages/sd/ieg/sdvol53num1.html, 28–29 May 2001.

Jacobson, H. K. and E. B. Weisis, "Strengthening Compliance with International Environmental Accords: Preliminary Observations from a Collaborative Project", 1 *Global Governance: A Review of Multilateralism and International Organizations*, 1995.

Juma, Calestous, "The Perils of Centralizing Global Environmental Governance", 42 *Environment*, November 2000, 44–45.

Newell, Peter, "New Environmental Architectures and the Search for Effectiveness", *Global Environmental Politics*, 1 February, 2001, 35–44.

Pauwelyn, Joost, "A Typology of Multilateral Treaty Obligations: Are WTO Obligations Bilateral or Collective in Nature?" 14 *EJIL*, 2003, 907–951.

Pauwelyn, Joost, "Role of Public International Law in the WTO: How Far Can We Go?" 95 *AJIL*, 2001, 535–578.

Skolnikoff, Eugene et al., "Do We Need a World Environment Organization?" *Panel Debate*, Harvard Law School, 23 April 1999, http://www.law.harvard.edu/Admissions/Graduate_Programs/cwe/chayes/enviro.html, 8 June 2007.

Stewart, Frances and Sam Daws, "An Economic and Social Security Council at the United Nations", *QEH Working Paper Series*, 68, University of Oxford, Queen Elizabeth House, March 2001.

Tamiotti, Ludivine and Matthias Finger, "Environmental Organizations: Changing Roles and Functions in Global Politics", 1 *Global Environmental Politics*, February 2001, 56–76.

Von Moltke, Konrad, "The Organization of the Impossible", 1 *Global Environmental Politics*, February 2001, 23–28.

Whalley, John and Ben Zissimos, "What Could a World Environmental Organization Do?" 1 *Global Environmental Politics*, February 2001, 29–34.

Young, Oran, "The Effectiveness of International Environmental Regimes", 10 *International Environmental Affairs*, Fall 1998, 267–289.

Young, Oran, "Inference and Indices: Evaluating the Effectiveness of International Environmental Regimes", 1 *Global Environmental Politics*, February 2001, 99–121.

Documents

CBD, *Synergies between Biodiversity-related Conventions*, CBD/COP/III/21, November 1996.

ILC (finalized by Martti Koskenniemi), *Fragmentation of International Law Difficulties Arising from the Diversification and Expansion of International Law: International Law Commission Study Group on Fragmentation*, A/CN.4/L.682, 2006.

Gitay, Habiba, *Climate Change and Biodiversity*, Intergovernmental Panel on Climate Change (IPCC), http://www.ipcc.ch/pub/tpbiodiv.pdf, 2002.

UNCCD, Decision taken by the Conference of the Parties to the *UN Convention to Combat Desertification to Seek Synergies between it and Other Environmental Agreements*, ICCD/COP(2)/7, 17 November 1998.

UNDP, *Synergies in National Implementation between the Rio Agreements*, Expert meeting, UNDP, NY 1997.

UNEP, Expert Consultations on International Environmental Governance, Cambridge, U.K. 28–29 May 2001, Chairman's Summary.

UNEP, *Feasibility Study for Information Management Infrastructure*, World Conservation Monitoring Center, August 1998.

UNEP, Governing Council, Decision 21/21, *International Environmental Governance*, 9 February 2001.

UNEP, Malmö Ministerial Declaration, UNEP/GC/21/21/2000, 31 May 2000.

UNEP, Nairobi Declaration on the Role and Mandate of UNEP, UNEP/GC19/1/1997, 1997.

UNEP, Open-Ended Intergovernmental Group of Ministers or Their representatives on International Environmental Governance (All documents available at http://www.unep.org/IEG/WorkingDocuments.asp).

UNEP, *Report of UNEP Executive Director: International Environmental Governance*, UNEP/IGM/1/2, 4 April 2001.

UNEP, Summary of Selected Papers, Note by the Secretariat, First Meeting, New York, 18 April 2001. UNEP/IGM/1/INF/2, 5 April 2001.

UNEP, UN Reform: Implication for the Environmental Pillar, UNEP/DED/040506, May 2006.

UNGA, *Renewing the United Nations: A Programme for Reform*, A/51/950, July 14, 1997.

UNGA, *Report of the United Nations Task Force on Environment and Human Settlements*, A/53/463, 1998.

UNGA, *Report of the World Summit on Sustainable Development (*including the *Johannesburg Plan of Implementation)*, A/CONF.199/20, 4 September 2002.

UNGA, *Resolutions on the Institutional and Financial Arrangements for International Environmental Cooperation*, Resolution 2997 XXVII, 15 December 1972.

UNGA, *Rio+5 General Assembly Special Session*, A/S-19/29, 27 June 1997.

UNU, Interlinkages: Synergies and Coordination between Multilateral Agreements, UNU, 1999.

UNSG, Delivering as One: Report of Secretary General's High Level Panel on System-Wide Coherence, (advanced unedited version), http://www.un.org/events/panel/resources/pdfs/HLP-SWC-FinalReport.pdf, 2006.

World Bank, *Protecting Our Planet Securing Our Future*, Joint UNEP-NASA-World Bank Study, 1998.

World Commission on Environment and Development, Our Common Future, Oxford University Press, 1987.

Speeches and statements

Chirac, Jacques, "Speech of President of the Republic of France to the World Conservation Union", Fountainebleau, France, 3 November 1998.

Commission of European Communities, Communication from the Commission to the Council and European Parliament, "Ten Years after Rio: Preparing for the World Summit on Sustainable Development in 2002", Brussels, 6 February 2001.

European Union, Statement on the Informal Consultations on the Reform of Institutional Framework for the Environment, http://www.un.org/ga/president/61/follow-up/environment/statementsJan07/statement_EU.pdf, 18 January 2007.

Government of Canada, "International Environmental Institutions: Where from Here? A Discussion Paper", Bergen Informal Ministerial Meeting, http://www.earthsummit2002.org/es/2002/bergen/canada_paper.htm, 15–17 September 2000.

Jospin, Lionel, "Speech of Prime Minister of the Republic of France", Opening Session of the Annual Bank Conference on Development Economics, The World Bank Group. Paris, 21 June 2000.

Kohl, Helmut, "Speech of Chancellor of the Federal Republic of Germany to the Special Session of the General Assembly of the United Nations, New York, 23 June 1997.

Lamy, Pascale, Remarks on the WTO and Environment to the European Commission, http://www.wto.org/english/news_e/sppl_e/sppl28_e.htm, 30 May 2006.

Meacher, Michael, Environment Secretary, U.K., "Speech to UNED-U.K. Conference", UK Preparations for Earth Summit 2002, The National & Global Dimensions, The London School of Economics, 20 March 2001.

Ruggiero, Renato, "Opening Remarks to the High Level Symposium on Environment", World Trade Organization, Geneva, Switzerland, Conference homepage: http://www.wto.org/english/tratop_e/envir_e/hlmenv_e.htm, 15 March 1999.

Topfer, Klaus, "Statement to the High Level Symposium on Environment, World Trade Organization, Geneva, Switzerland, Conference homepage, http://www.wto.org/english/tratop_e/envir_e/hlmenv_e.htm, March 1999.

United Kingdom, Select Committee on Environment, Transport and Regional *Affairs*, Sixteenth Report, House of Commons Paras, 69–71, Questions 160–177, March 1999. Accessed online, 26 April 2007, http://www.parliament.the-stationery-office.co.uk/pa/cm199899/cmselect/cmenvtra/307r/30715.htm.

Index